LITTLE MOSIE FROM THE MARGAREE

A Biography of Moses Michael Coady

Little Mosie from the Margaree

A Biography of Moses Michael Coady

Michael R. Welton

Mount Saint Vincent University

THOMPSON EDUCATIONAL PUBLISHING, INC.
Toronto

Information on how to obtain copies of this book may be obtained from:

Web site: www.thompsonbooks.com
E-mail: publisher@thompsonbooks.com
Telephone: (416) 766-2763
Fax: (416) 766-0398

Canadian Cataloguing in Publication Data

Welton, Michael Robert, 1942-
   Little Mosie from the Margaree : a biography of Moses Michael Coady

Includes bibliographical references and index.
ISBN 1-55077-122-1

1. Coady, M.M. (Moses Michael), 1882-1959. 2. Antigonish movement.*
3. Catholic Church - Clergy - Biography. 4. Clergy - Nova Scotia - Biography.
I. Title.

HD3448.5.C62W44 2001   334'.092   C00-932446-1

Copy Editing: Elizabeth Phinney
Cover Design: Elan Designs

Every reasonable effort has been made to acquire permission for copyrighted materials used in this book and to acknowledge such permissions accurately. Any errors or omissions called to the publisher's attention will be corrected in future printings.

We acknowledge the support of the Government of Canada through the Book Publishing Industry Development Program for our publishing activities.

Printed in Canada.
1 2 3 4 5   06 05 04 03 02 01

Table of Contents

Acknowledgements

The author would like to acknowledge gratefully the Social Science and Humanities Research Council for supporting this research project through an internal grant from Mount St. Vincent University and funding from the New Approaches to Lifelong Learning national project. The author would like to thank Kathy MacKenzie, chief archivist at St. Francis Xavier University, for her expertise and encouragement as I plied her with endless requests. I would like to thank members of St. Francis Xavier University's Adult Education, Extension Department and Coady International Institute for their unfailing hospitality and cheerfulness. They had to put up with many sudden appearances and listen to the latest marvellous find from the archives. I would like to acknowledge the warm support of my colleagues in Mount St. Vincent's Adult Education graduate program, Drs. Donovan Plumb and Patti Gouthro, who never complained when I sneaked away to Antigonish for more historical sleuthing. I must also thank Keith Thompson for his wonderful encouragement, and his excellent editor, Elizabeth Phinney, for her attentive work. The final word goes to my partner, Carmen Philippe, for her love and care through the exciting final stage of seeing this into print.

Preface

When Coady died in 1959 at age seventy-seven, many newspapers noted that he had been a big man, in every way. The biographer of Moses Michael Coady must immediately confront his subject's largeness. Although Coady was selected as one of a hundred most influential Canadians by *MacLean's* magazine several years ago, he is scarcely a household name in Canada today. Certainly many Maritimers still know the name, and the Coady International Institute has ensured that his name is still revered in many countries of the world. Yet, in his own day, the name of "Coady" attained heroic proportions. Obscure until the late 1920s, Coady, if one were to believe the myths, emerged like a colossus from a small, beautiful place, the Margaree Valley, located in perpetually tormented Cape Breton, Nova Scotia. In the desperate cultural and economic conditions of Nova Scotia of the early twentieth century, many people actually believed that the "modern Moses" had appeared to lead them to the promised land of hope and plenty.

Human beings are incessant storytellers. Essentially, we tell stories to affirm our identities and justify our beliefs and actions in the world. We do this to avoid falling into a huge bog of meaninglessness and chaos. Our stories attempt to stave off despair and darkness by celebrating our joys and successes, our liberatory moments. To be human is to story our lives. But the danger here is that our desire to live in an orderly, predictable and meaningful world will lead us to deceive ourselves. Stories are containers of meaning, but they are selective and may sweep dirt under the carpet or into some dank corner of our consciousness. Our desire that things end well does not mean that they will.

The biographer of Moses Coady and historian of the Antigonish Movement must grapple with its deep mythologization. It is difficult to penetrate beneath the "something added" to the "reality beneath." The Antigonish Movement glows with a soft halo, and Canadian adult educators (professors and students alike) have spun the Movement's story to accentuate the importance of adult education to social and economic transformation. For many of us, the Movement is a narrative of emancipation. We tell the story to authenticate our beliefs and practices, to affirm the usefulness of our activity in the world. After awhile, it no longer really matters whether the Movement actually did emancipate the Maritimes in any deep and lasting way. The Movement's truth lies in the myth itself. And the mythic story teaches us that adult education is an instrument of great magical power, a kind of golden key that unlocks the blocked potential of human beings. We, as adult educators, have had a vested interest in believing and perpetuating this myth—a myth, if you like, of authenticity and identity.

Coady himself was a purveyor of an appealing myth. Like poets and ancient storytellers, Coady fabricated a mythic redemptive narrative for his audiences. In the unpublished version of *Masters of Their Own Destiny*, Coady spun the myth of the Maritimes' golden age of wood, wind and sail into an appealing prophetic story. Coady believed that the Maritimes had fallen into decline after the golden age of mercantilism. But he imagined that an age of grace could be bestowed on his beloved land of suffering. If the common people awakened to the latest possibilities in nature and society, they could exit from their fallen world. With the memory of a former time of self-reliance burning in their imaginations, they could make the world anew. One of Coady's powerful metaphors—"fields of lost opportunities"—captured his fundamental belief that the Maritimes was, in fact, a field of economic potentialities that could be revealed to the creative imagination. He also believed that the common people had to take responsibility for their fates. They had defaulted the economic realm to others who gradually stole it from them. But they had it within themselves and their communities to take control of their destinies. By becoming owners they could release creative genius and imagination. Adult education was the potent instrument for setting this transformative process in motion. The archetype—creation, fall and redemption—framed everything Moses Coady taught the people. All stories have rhetorical intentions, and Coady's story of the little people inheriting the earth through co-operative action was crafted as a symbolic instrument to mobilize the people for enlightenment and action.

But historians must probe beneath the myths and self-understandings of the actors themselves and question the way others have narrated the story of Coady and the Antigonish Movement. This biographical study of "Little Mosie from the Margaree" presents the reader with worlds behind the public representations. A more anguished portrait emerges from a considered reading of his personal correspondence and voluminous writings. Coady was at the epicentre of an audacious project of wresting economic power from the "vested interests." He was very tough and believed fiercely that he had the blueprint to lead the oppressed masses out of their misery. And he was not able to stomach the failure of his co-operative vision to emancipate the common people. The story that emerges in this biography, then, is chock full of lessons and insights for those who try to exert control over the massive economic and social forces that determine our destinies. But these illuminations do not provide us, at the dawn of the twenty-first century, with easy prescriptions for our time.

Every biographer attempts to place his subject in historical contexts. *Little Mosie from the Margaree,* no exception to this interpretive axiom, places Moses Michael Coady in the midst of the great cultural, political and economic transformations of the late nineteenth and twentieth centuries. Some of these great streams have their origins in the remote past. Coady's world outlook was Roman Catholic, and he used some of St. Thomas Aquinas's teachings to legitimate his program of reform for the Maritimes centuries after the "Common Doctor's" teachings. Coady's particular version of Catholic social action is incomprehensible outside the great economic transformations that were sweeping over the earth in the late nineteenth and early twentieth centuries. The youthful Coady felt their rumblings in his obscure location on the periphery of Canada. He literally spent his life responding to these deep transformations in economic organization and production. Thus, telling the story of one person ends up being a story of many people and many contexts. The origins of the Antigonish Movement cannot be understood apart from the way the Roman Catholic Church in the Diocese of Antigonish was shaken up as Nova Scotia was pulled into the industrial, urban worlds of mass industries, trade unions and global markets. Coady believed that the future of the Antigonish Movement hinged on its ability to emancipate the fishermen by organizing them into dynamic co-operatives. Coady's baby was the United Maritime Fishermen. Readers with special interest in the history of the Maritime fishery will find its story woven into the larger fabric.

The biographer of Moses Coady must process an enormous amount of material. Most of the sources on Coady's life and times are held in the archives at St. Francis Xavier University. The archive essentially is organized into Extension Department papers (the business of running the Department), Coady's personal correspondence, Coady's writings, the papers of the various players in the Movement and papers pertaining to different economic sectors and co-operative organizations. These papers are not organized chronologically, and the researcher must cross-reference to understand a particular period. Beginning in 1930, Movement activists created the "Scrapbooks" of the activities of the Movement as depicted by journalists and other commentators. These Scrapbooks are invaluable for historians because they provide an immediate chronological ordering of materials. They include materials from newspapers and obscure magazines that normally would take the historian years to track down. The *Extension Bulletin* (later *The Maritime Co-operator*) also contains useful accounts of the Movement. Information about specific study clubs, for instance, were recorded in the *Bulletin*.

The *Bulletin* and *Maritime Co-operator* provide historians with more than enough data to grasp the intellectual structures undergirding the co-operative movement. Coady wrote little think pieces for a column called "The Anvil" and some of these have been woven into the story. The uncut version of *Masters of Their Own Destiny* is held in the St. Francis Xavier University archives. The complete text (which includes expunged chapters on the economic and educational history of Nova Scotia) is the basis for my chapter exploring Coady's systematic thought. It has only recently been discovered that Coady was working on an autobiography in his latter years. He had many unfinished thoughts and reflections on democratic practice and the origins of his life's work. The manuscript, and many other important papers, had been in the possession of Ellen Arsenault, his former secretary, for almost forty years, Coady having willed some of his private papers to her upon death. This is a major find for Coady studies and will help shape our understanding of Coady's life and thought. The Arsenault Papers, now held in the St. Francis Xavier archives, contain previously unseen correspondence regarding the origins of the credit union movement in Nova Scotia as well as salient documents Movement activists presented to Coady to assist with the writing of *Masters*. The Arsenault Papers also add early photographs of Coady's family that, to my knowledge, are not duplicated elsewhere. The Beaton Institute at the University College of Cape Breton holds the papers of Father James Tompkins. I drew upon these for a previous book, written with Jim Lotz, *Father Jimmy: The Life and Times of Jimmy Tompkins* (1997). The Beaton holdings are invaluable sources of data pertaining to the first two decades of the twentiteh century, an archivally thin period for Coady researchers. The National Archives of Canada hold impressive documents pertaining to the Maritime fisheries. The papers relating to the Michaud period in the federal Department of Fisheries and the co-operatives in the fishery contain valuable materials on the origins of the Extension Department.

This biography has relied almost exclusively on original, primary documents. I wanted to stay close to the ground and move, as much as is humanly possible, inside Moses Coady's world outlook and actions. Much attention is paid to the theatres in which Coady acted out his grand project. He was a man of his times, full of great passions and contradictions.

CHAPTER 1

A New and Disturbing Presence

I

n late November of 1927, a professor of education from St. Francis Xavier University (St.FX) in Antigonish, Nova Scotia, walked into the board room of the MacLean Commission inquiry into the crisis in the Maritime fishery in Halifax and sat down to testify. He was not particularly well known outside of educational circles and the troubled Catholic parish life of the Diocese of Antigonish in eastern Nova Scotia, but this man, plainly, was not of ordinary presence. He stood 6'2" tall and weighed around 210 pounds. He had broad shoulders, a ruggedly handsome face, was broad of forehead and possessed piercing, coal-black eyes. He exuded toughness and self-confidence.

This man, Father Moses Michael Coady, an expert in rural life, was the first witness called to offer his views on the multiple problems of the Atlantic fishery. The inquiry had been travelling through the fishing villages in Prince Edward Island and Nova Scotia, places with such unlikely names as Malignant Cove, Monk Head and Moose Bay, for a month and a half. Having begun in Summerside, Prince Edward Island, on October 19, the commissioners had arrived in Halifax by the end of November. The stories they had been hearing were deeply disturbing.

Coady addressed the inquiry in a fiery manner. He told them that he was interested chiefly in the educational phase of the industry. He insisted that the people, and not just the fishing machinery, should receive attention. Fishermen of the old days were better adapted to the work than those of the present, but the times had changed, and the fishermen had been unable to adapt. Coady thought that those who were engaged in the industry should be happy and contented. Through scientific knowledge, he claimed, fishermen could take advantage of possibilities yet unimagined.

According to Coady, three things were essential in the Maritimes. First, all the residents should appreciate its natural resources and the process which transforms them into dollars and cents. Coady did not think that Maritimers currently appreciated these resources, but through education, they could be made to recognize their value. Second, Maritimers had never been taught to think critically, Coady told the commissioners, and overlooked the necessity of planning. Many small industries could be established in the small villages if plans were made in advance. Third,

9

co-operation, in its broadest usage, was the way to progress. Coady pointed to the success of the Nova Scotia creameries as an example.

Coady thought that while the common schools could contribute a little to the solution of practical problems, the way forward really lay with community civic education. Perhaps, Coady hinted sarcastically, a whiff of Mussolini would wake the Maritimes up. We are too free and easy, and adult education is to blame. In other countries, it has a significant place. In the Maritimes, it has none. Adult education, he continued, is nothing more than an injection of ideas. Coady recommended that short and group courses be provided for the fishermen. "There seems to me to be a philosophy of grand isolation among the universities in this country. They hand pick the country and do nothing for the other classes. Our universities have taken the best brains in the country and exported them. If this Commission would declare a closed season on brains I think it would assist materially," he said. Since the universities had neglected to do anything, he urged the Commission to have the government institutions do the work. He concluded by arguing that unionism among the fishermen could do much good and would keep them alive to all current questions.[1]

No one who heard Moses Coady's presentation before the MacLean Commission in late 1927 could have imagined what a thorn in Nova Scotia's side this forty-five-year-old priest would become over the next thirty years. Nor could they have imagined the extent to which they would hear this big man reiterate, tirelessly, the themes of his comments to the commissioners. The world was changing irrevocably. The educational institutions of the people had not prepared them to grapple with this changed world. People took precedence over money. People had the potential to think their way to new solutions. They had to co-operate to reach their full potential, as individuals, as communities, as a province. Who would show them the way? What direction should their economic action take?

II

Coady did not know the answer to this latter question when he left the inquiry room in Halifax and headed back to Antigonish, the seat of the Roman Catholic Diocese of eastern Nova Scotia. Throughout the 1920s, reform-minded priests in the diocese had agitated unceasingly for an Extension Department in St. Francis Xavier University. Indeed, Coady's caustic remark about the failure of Nova Scotia universities scarcely masks his bitterness about his university's failure to respond to the plight of the primary producer.[2] However, the political strategy of using the Scottish Catholic Society as a foil to pressure the St.FX hierarchy into establishing an Extension Department worked. With the MacLean Commission deliberating, the public media in an uproar over mounting evidence of hunger,

impoverishment and destitution of fisher families, the coal fields in industrial Cape Breton literally in flames and priests and parishioners
everywhere distressed and agitated, the board of governors officially
approved the formation of the St. Francis Xavier University Extension
Department in November 1928. They asked Moses Coady, then professor
of education, to become its first director.

Coady (and his brilliant assistant, Angus B. [A.B.] MacDonald), had few
financial resources and only sketchy ideas about how to proceed. They
therefore spent six months travelling throughout eastern and western Canada and the United States, visiting adult education programs and
advocates, scouring for ideas about how they might set in motion a program of reform in beleaguered Nova Scotia.

Coady and MacDonald had little time for the course-giving approach of
eastern Canadian universities such as Queen's and the University of
Toronto. They were more attracted to the universities of Alberta and Saskatchewan, who identified the fate of their new institutions with their
ability to carry useful knowledge to the people. These universities, from
their inception in 1905, responded to the need for cultural enlightenment,
scientific and technical insight and human solidarity. The University of
Alberta, under Dr. H.M. Tory's pioneering direction and the inspired leadership of men such as A.E. Ottewell and E.A. Corbett, focused on the
cultural enlightenment of the farming communities, drawing professors
into intellectual circuit riding. Dr. Walter Murray, the University of Saskatchewan's visionary president, believed that the university had to be in
close touch with people's needs, and infuse agriculture with a scientific
spirit. He also wanted to prevent the professions, literary and scientific,
from becoming self-centred and indifferent to the great practical interests
of the people. Like the famed University of Wisconsin, Saskatchewan had
to be a service-university. It had not only to produce new knowledge, but
disseminate it to the farmers who faced concrete problems in their everyday work and farm organization.[3]

Coady returned to Antigonish in late spring of 1929 with a sounder sense
and firmer basis for the shaping of the Extension Department's program of
adult education. Still, questions remained. What were the appropriate educational forms for Maritime adult learners, many of whom were scarcely
literate? Should one begin with farmers first? Or everywhere at once?
What were the methods of mobilizing the people to take action? Were there
differences of approach between rural and urban learners? Where did one
get the financial, and people, resources to do what one wants? Coady did
not have to answer the question of where to begin. In the fall of 1929,
Coady was asked by the Canadian Department of Fisheries–the Hon. Mr.
P.J.A. Cardin was the Minister of Marine and Fisheries–to organize the
fishermen of eastern Canada. This would be the defining moment of his

career. It would also become part of the basis for the myth of the "modern Moses" who sought to lead his people into the promised land of co-operation.

The MacLean Commission had recommended that the federal Department of Fisheries appoint an organizer to establish co-operative organizations among the fishermen and that an experienced organizer in co-operative methods be hired.[4] The Department of Fisheries had accepted this advice. This decision, which would link inexorably the federal Department of Fisheries to the St.FX Extension Department for decades to come, was taken in the midst of much controversy and behind-the-scenes lobbying. For a variety of reasons, not everyone thought that Moses Coady was the right man for the onerous and treacherous task of organizing the fishermen. He faced opposition from several quarters. He had had no previous experience with the fishery. He was a vulnerable target.

Shortly after the Commission was presented to Prime Minister MacKenzie King's government in the summer of 1928, lobbying began. The Acadian priest, the Rev. A. Briand, pastor at Main-a-Dieu, Cape Breton, wrote to Cardin on July 21. The Fishermen's Federation (the main organization of fishermen in the Maritimes at the time) had held its convention at St. Peter's, with delegates present from Guysboro, Richmond, Cape Breton, Victoria and Inverness counties. Admitting that organizing the fishermen was "extremely slow and difficult," Briand informed Cardin that the delegates' unanimous choice was the Rev. Alfred Boudreau of Petit de Gras. Boudreau was bilingual and had been "connected with the work since its inception." He was the man best suited for the job. Several days later, MacKenzie King received a letter from D.D. Boyd, a lawyer living in St. Peter's. "There is, perhaps, no other man in the whole Province of Nova Scotia so actively interested in, and thoroughly familiar with, the needs of the fishermen as is Father Boudreau. As a matter of fact it was most unfortunate that he was not named as a member of the Royal Commission." Boudreau was very much in the forefront, along with fellow priests Jimmy Tompkins (Canso), Amiable Briand (Main-a-Dieu), Charles Forest (Larry's River) and Leo Keats (St. Peter's), in voicing the suffering and concerns of the fishermen and their families in the difficult and trying years following World War I.

Another man, M.A. Nickerson, living in Massachusetts, informed W.A. Found, the Deputy Minister of Fisheries, that he had founded the Fishermen's Union of Nova Scotia, 1095, the "first society of sea-food producers in the Maritimes." He also had organized the Fishermen's Union of Tignish, Prince Edward Island, in 1920, and drawn up the bill for *The Fishermen's Federation Act* passed in the Nova Scotia Legislature in 1927. He claimed that he had "assisted materially" in organizing Canso and Cape Breton units (of the Fishermen's Union), instructed by Father Boudreau and Capt. Robert Meagher of Canso. Nickerson presented himself as the "proper person for carrying out, to the full, the work of organization." For several years following this offer of his services, the old veteran of early attempts to organize Fishermen's Unions in the opening years of the century (beginning around 1907) niggled away at the Department of Fisheries' (and later, the United Maritime Fishermen's) strategies. He remained suspicious of Coady and doubted that fishermen could actually organize a centralized marketing agency.

In late December 1929, just after Coady had been chosen as the organizer (seconded from St.FX Extension), J. Cowie, an Ottawa insider with sympathies for the fish merchants, wrote Found a memorandum. In no way did he think that the fishermen should be "encouraged to form themselves into associations for curing and marketing fish." Displacing the merchant fish curer or dealer was out of the question. The fishermen should stay out of handling, curing and marketing fish throughout the whole year. However, Cowie insisted, it did seem appropriate for fishermen to form associations to discuss their problems, purchase fishing supplies, form groups or crews for purchasing bigger and better crafts. These "fraternal associations" would enable the Department to discuss matters with them from time to time. Nor did Cowie think it was wise to send out men who were not in the industry to speak to the fishermen:

> Take for example, Dr. Coady, who I understand is to be one of such. He no doubt has a first-rate general knowledge of economics, but his knowledge of the practical points proposed to be covered would not impress the average fishermen, and might even lead to awkward embarrassing situations in the event of questions being asked, as they no doubt will be at the meetings, and end in the Department being ridiculed, at least amongst the non-Catholic fishermen.

Cowie, it seems, mainly feared militant, organized fishermen. He was comfortable with something akin to a fishermen's club, an association that would be there when, and if, the Department needed it.[5]

Cowie was not the only one who was sceptical about the fishermen's capacity to organize. A. Handfield Whitman, managing director of Robin, Jones and Whitman, told Found that his experience in the past "has been that merchants in dealing with Fishermen's Unions were dealing with entirely irresponsible bodies. They live up to a contract if it suits them, but otherwise the contract is not worth the paper it is written on, as there is apparently no responsibility behind it." The fisherman's problem, Whitman informed Found, was that "they think the merchant is making a lot of money out of the product."[6] In turn, Found informed Whitman that the Department wanted the fishermen to "form themselves into Associations … to enable them better to consider their own problems; to make it a simpler matter to carry on educational work by having concentrated points of attack and to encourage co-operative effort where such is feasible particularly in purchasing and production." Found believed that co-operative effort appeared to be a "hopeful solution of existing difficulties, but to be as effective as it should be it should comprehend the marketing as well as the producing end of the industry."[7]

The federal government had clearly thrown down the gauntlet to the fishing industry. The Department of Fisheries had received voluminous evidence in the process of the MacLean inquiry that many shore fishermen were in an acute state of crisis. The Fishermen's Union movement, initiated in 1907, had lost vitality, and most of the unions had passed out of existence. Few unions attempted any kind of co-operative work (the fishermen at Petit de Gras did, however, engage in some co-operative buying). Yet without organization, the fishermen could only articulate their needs in a haphazard and disjointed fashion. The Department thought that unorganized fishermen would be inclined to make "representations of a destructive character. Such agitations are not wholly futile, as agitation is necessarily the first step toward organization, and the initial stage of co-operative movement. The wisdom and utterance of an organization is much more effective than that of solitary individuals crying in the wilderness."

For decades the fishermen had being crying in the wilderness. Along large stretches of the eastern coast of Canada, most shore fishermen had been left behind in the wake of

> change and progress that has marked the development of the fisheries in the past fifteen years.... This is particularly true of the smaller fishing villages and hamlets, and among the more scattered fishing populations remote from centres of fellowship, markets and trade. The problems of the home and means of livelihood are much more acute than in former years. These people are very old and native for many generations, and well worth every effort to re-voyage them for the future.

Other sections of the coast were more favoured. Districts such as Cape Island, Shelburne County, Briar and Long Islands, Digby County, Grand Manan and adjacent islands in the district of the Bay of Fundy, in New Brunswick, places largely dependent on the fisheries, were flourishing. Still, "conditions of disquietude and misgiving with regard to fishing equipment, processing, transportation, and marketing facilities, are, however, general along the whole Coast." The Departmental "Memorandum" on the "Fishermen's Co-operative Movement" asserted that "adaptation of all agencies to the common good is imperative. New wine in old skins does not improve the quality of the product, nor will time-worn equipment and imperfect methods produce sea foods for the table at worth while prices." Co-operation had worked in agriculture; it surely could work in the fishery.[8]

III

On September 28, 1929, Moses Coady began what he would call his "trying ten months" of organizing the fishermen in the Maritime provinces at Canso. This was the appropriate place to begin. His cousin, Father J.J. Tompkins, the firebrand agitator and Coady's mentor for over twenty years, was pastor at the Star of the Sea church in Canso, exiled there from his former position as vice-president of St. Francis Xavier University in late 1922. Tompkins had initiated a series of adult education for local action initiatives in and around Canso. His agitation had sparked George Farquhar's series of seven articles under the caption "Save our Fishermen" in June and July of 1927, which helped press the government to create the epochal MacLean Commission. Ironically, perhaps, officials in the Department of Fisheries would be harbingers of a coming new day for fishermen in the Maritimes. Working with remnants of the old Fishermen's Unions (organized into stations), department officials aroused the countryside for Coady's visit. When Coady "blew into Canso," the fishermen had gathered, six hundred strong, in the Ideal Theatre. The crowd was neither tense nor belligerent. One might have expected that, after all these bitter years, the fishermen would have been ready for a good fight. This was not the case: they appeared receptive to Coady's message. Recalling this historic meeting, Coady declared that they "weren't looking for handouts ... all they asked for that day was a plan of action."

After Canso, Coady made his way to Port Bickerton, organizing that territory down to and including the mouth of the Halifax. Before Christmas, he had covered the territory from Big Island to Havre Boucher, and then along the coastline from Pictou to Baie Verte. Coady's message was straightforward. Speaking in Glace Bay, Cape Breton, in the Old Country Hall on October 23, Coady extolled the benefits of organization. The wheat pools had been a boon for struggling western farmers; fishermen too could organize. Coady felt that Canada was headed for great things and wanted to see Nova Scotia and its fishermen play a big part in its advancement. The fishing industry, in Coady's view, had a wonderful future. However, the fishermen had to become educated about many things in order to share in the prosperity to come. While the fishing waters of other parts of the world were being depleted, Nova Scotia waters still contained an abundance of fish. All that was necessary was to educate the fishermen in modern methods of catching and transporting the fish. Coady also spoke of a new brine-freezing process that had revolutionized the industry. L.D. Currie, a local Cape Breton politician, spoke following Coady. He contrasted the fortunes of a few and the meagre living of the many. He felt, like Coady, that conditions would soon be changed so that those who braved the elements would get their fair share of the profits. One of the first matters the Fishermen's Union should take up, he thought, was the establishing of a fish plant, which was the greatest drawback now to local industry.

Organizing along the "eastern shore" was extremely arduous. Setting out in early December, Coady's large Buick (he loved those big cars) navigated along rutted, high-crowned roads. In most places, these roads were veiled with ice, making every mile a hazard. At times, Coady's vehicle skidded out of control, coming near to plunging into the open water. Keeping to schedule, he moved through the communities of Sheet Harbour, Spry Bay, Spry Harbour and Tangier. Everywhere fishermen awaited, eager for some direction.

From Tangier, he set out for Halifax, entering several miles of wood near Ship Harbour where the road was particularly nasty. At one point, he tried to brake, but the brakes were frozen and the heavy car slid into a brook. The time was late afternoon. The big, strong man got out of his car. Standing knee-deep in water, he laboured until he broke the jack. His huge shoulders failed to lift the car. He gave up and walked two miles back to Ship Harbour where he obtained a pair of horses and a heavy wagon. With the owner and his son, he returned. Their efforts were useless.

The group returned to Ship Harbour, where Coady was served a hot supper and purchased a pair of lumberjack socks. He telephoned the nearest garage, eighteen miles away at Musquodoboit Harbour, but the garageman wasn't much help either. His wrecking truck was out of commission with a frozen block. However, he came to the rescue with a car and block and tackle. By attaching the block and tackle to the tree, Coady's beloved Buick was pulled out of the brook. Coady decided to follow the garageman to Musquodoboit Harbour rather than going on into Halifax, but when they arrived at 1:30 in the morning, with the temperature at 10 below F., not a room was available. So Coady knocked on the door of the home of A.C. Day, the local Fisheries officer, and asked, "Can you put me up for the night?" The answer was, "Not possible." Coady then said, "I'm Coady—the guy who is organizing the fishermen," and received a different response: "Oh, that's different—come right in," said Mr. Day.

One might suppose that Coady would simply collapse into bed after such an ordeal. The Day family remembers that it wasn't quite like that with Moses Coady. While his garments thawed, and standing over a hot radiator, Coady spoke for an hour on the subject of social justice to fishermen. Then one of the Day's children was moved from bed, and Coady fell into sleep. The next day he was underway again, determined to finish organizing Nova Scotia's eastern shore. At Port Bickerton, the fishermen waited for an hour or so for Coady to arrive, as he was delayed by the bad roads. When this driven and impassioned man finally arrived, the fishermen refused to have their meeting until Coady had eaten. As it would turn out,

Port Bickerton would emerge through the 1930s and 1940s as an exemplary co-operative and rejuvenated fishing community, a jewel in the Movement's iconography.

On December 10, Coady started his sweep from Ballantyne's Cove up the coast to Port Elgin, New Brunswick. Time after time the Buick had to turn back as the Atlantic winter got the better of man and machine. Coady then resorted to horse and sleigh. He must have presented a striking image, garbed in a medium-weight top coat and wrapped with blankets, being pulled along by several of the fabled Maritime work horses. On one occasion, as recounted by Alex Laidlaw, Coady's associate director in the 1940s, Coady left the community of Wallace to travel the nine miles to Pugwash. They covered the distance in three and a half hours. Coady arrived with three frozen fingers, but pressed ahead with three scheduled meetings. One of Laidlaw's classic accounts is of the trip from Grand Anse to Shippegan, on New Brunswick's north shore. Coady had changed horses en route, but the new animal would promptly lie down in the snow upon sighting every major snow drift. For part of this trip, the driver broke the trail for the delicate horse, while Coady pulled the light pong sleigh. Although caught up in a mission, Coady consented to return to his beloved home in the Margaree Valley of Cape Breton for Christmas festivities at the end of 1929, the marker year of the Great Depression.

After Christmas, resplendent in a new fur coat, Coady met with the Fisheries officers for the province of Nova Scotia where he presented his scheme for the "education and organization of the fishermen." In January 1930, Coady held meetings with the Associated Boards of Trade of Campobello and Manan Island while on his way to New York and Boston to study the trawler issue. Nothing symbolized the shore fishermen's fears and plight more than the trawler. The big fish companies, such as the Maritime Fish Corporation, had begun using trawlers in 1910 (they purchased the *Wren* from A.N. Whitman and Sons of Canso, A.G. Jones and Co., and Arthur N. Whitman of Halifax). The *Wren* was followed by innumerable others. The names of the trawlers–*Claudius* (formerly *Titania*), *General Gordon* and *Triumph*–captured the grand ambitions of these big companies to sweep the seas efficiently, with their capacity to store hundreds of thousands of pounds of fish, and the shore fishermen, with their schooners, out of business. It is not known with whom Coady talked, nor the conclusions he reached in New York or Boston. Through all of Coady's years as director of Extension, the Maritime fishermen would protest about the impact of trawlers on their livelihood and communities.

From Boston, Coady returned to New Brunswick. There, Col. A.L. Barry, supervisor of Fisheries, joined him in Moncton to begin the organization of the fishermen of that province. Working through mid-January storms, they managed to cover the territory from Campellton to

Shippegan, and then from Richibuctou to Shediac. At Shippegan, an incident occurred that would assist their organizational efforts immeasurably. Coady snapped a tendon in his foot while walking in the crusty snow, and went to bed in the home of Father J.L. Chiasson. For three days, the French Acadian priest listened and took notes in a black book. Chiasson would go on to become an energetic member of the St. Francis Xavier Extension Department. During the three days spent organizing in and around St. Thomas, the Rev. J.H. Hill, rector of St. Thomas College (later Bishop of Victoria), joined Coady in his New Brunswick work. These three men—Barry, Chiasson and Hill—would anchor the Movement in New Brunswick for decades. Wily, courageous and intelligent, Barry was a crucial presence within government circles. He was also a trusted mentor, ardent defender of the fishermen and Coady's advisor on the intricate matters of fishermen and their industry.

The winter weather forced Coady to forestall his whirlwind organizing tour. The unfinished sections of Nova Scotia had to be left until April 1930, when Coady resumed his organizational efforts at Digby Neck, where he spent eight days. Coady met with little success down the "Neck." He had better results in the Yarmouth section, from Port Maitland to Argyle. Coady met his most fierce resistance in Lunenburg, the centre of the deep-sea fishery and cultural home of the Lutheran Protestants, who had settled in Lunenburg in the late 1700s. In no way did the large fish dealers want to see the fishermen organized. Lunenburg would remain resistant to co-operative movement initiatives throughout Coady's regime.

After organizing the Blandford peninsula, Coady left for Prince Edward Island on board the Hochelaga steam ship. Travelling with George Earle from the local Fisheries Department, they worked the small places on the Island for ten days. Not everyone was thrilled that Coady was on the Island. C.P. McCarthy, president of the Fishermen's Union of Prince Edward Island, Tignish Council, wrote to Nickerson on May 27, 1930.

> Dr. Coady is on the Island now, and is coming to Tignish tomorrow night. If he has nothing more concrete to offer than his proposals outlined in the Halifax Chronicle, that is to say, the establishment of a sort of fraternal society for Maritime fishermen, then I don't think we shall bother sending delegates to the proposed convention at Halifax on June 25th.

McCarthy also told Nickerson that he was not really in favour of one Maritime federation: "Each Province has its own particular difficulties and problems to solve, and these problems are to be dealt with more promptly, intelligently and effectively—and certainly more sympathetically—by a Provincial executive than by all-Maritime board." These thoughts did not bode well for provincial relations among Maritime fishermen.

In an interview published in *The Charlottetown Guardian* on May 22, 1930, Coady outlined the structure of the proposed United Maritime

Fishermen (UMF). The aims of the new association, as set forth in its constitution, were, fundamentally, to promote the "principles of co-operation in all industrial activities" and to "further the interests of the fishermen and fishworkers in all branches of the fishing industry." The proposed constitution, Coady stated, did not outline any scheme of co-operative merchandising, but it would be

> the work of the central board to set up the machinery for financial undertakings whenever a sufficient number of local organizations are ready for it…. The economic betterment of the small producer cannot be brought about in a day or a year, but must be a gradual process. The vital steps in that process are organization, education, and co-operative marketing. When the fishermen of our provinces get together, and put the best brains of the industry on the problems confronting them we shall get results.

By the time of the convention, June 25, Chester McCarthy, the Tignish lawyer and manager of a co-operative lobster factory, would take his delegates to Halifax, convinced that something new was emerging for Maritime fishermen. McCarthy would be elected the first president of the United Maritime Fishermen.

Following his visit to Tignish, Coady returned to the large smelt and salmon fishing district of the famed Miramichi River, which had been missed during the past winter. After that, he left for four days of organizing in the Magdalen Islands. From the Magdalen Islands, Coady returned to Halifax, where he organized Terrance Bay and Prospect, small fishing communities located twenty or so miles outside the capital city. At each place, delegates were selected to attend the proposed convention of the UMF.

The United Maritime Fishermen held its first convention in the Masonic Hall in Halifax, on June 25 and 26, 1930. This was a triumphant moment for Moses Michael Coady. The ten trying months were now over, and this big, rough priest had demonstrated that he had the stamina and will to handle adversity, opposition, conflict, appalling travel conditions, the loneliness of hotel rooms. He had discovered that he could handle his own in the rough and tumble of the Maritime meeting hall, with its dubious traditions of disputation and heckling. Any doubts Coady may have had about his abilities as an organizer were dispelled when he ascended the podium to address the two hundred delegates. "The introduction of the co-operative movement in the fishing industry is imperatively demanded by the best interests of our civilization," Coady thundered to his audience.

He then brought in the constitution he had prepared, and the organization was formed on motion from Norman Ferguson of Port Morien and H. Olsen from Northport. The eastern fishery was to be divided into twenty-two zones. Each would choose a director for the central board. Within the zone, each local federation was to consist of at least fifteen members. Annual dues for each local were to be paid at the rate of $2 per capita. The delegates chose McCarthy as their first president, and Robert Meagher of Canso as first vice-president. A meeting of the board of directors was held later in August, when Dr. Richard Hamer of Acadia University was selected as secretary, a decision that would later be controversial.

New energy was flowing amongst the fishermen. Harry T. Boudreau of Petit de Gras addressed the delegates.

> Let us not be ashamed because we have educated men in our midst. We follow an honourable calling. Our fathers before us sailed the seven seas when it took brains to pilot a ship and they did not have education. Today with modern compasses and inventions anyone can sail a ship. Let us speak and speak loud. It is the only way we can get anything for ourselves.

Moses Coady and his growing network of reformers were helping the fishermen to find their voice. They also intended to teach them that they could not face the modern world as illiterate or semi-literate men and women with only bred-in-the-bone knowledge of their craft. Something new had appeared on the scene. Few men or women had ever linked organization and education in quite this way. Few fishermen, many of whom were suffering from curtailed markets and deflated prices, had ever experienced a prophet in their midst. Possibilities yet undreamed of? What could this mean?

Coady had emerged from his "trial by fire" ready to lead his people out of their own wilderness. The "vested interests" of business, state and church now had a foe to be reckoned with. This new and disturbing figure had burst into Maritime history.[9]

CHAPTER 2

On the Side of the Impossible

I

N o one knows exactly what precise factors shape a person's character and outlook on life. We do know that the way we see the world and the choices we make grow out of our family milieu and surrounding community networks and influences. Fortune, good and bad, plays a key role in history, too. Some men and women come of age when the times are good and a spirit of ease and hopefulness abounds in the streets, shops, educational institutions, factories and playing fields. Others come of age when times are dispirited, when too much despair has seeped into the bones and sinews of the community, when a vibrancy is lacking, and life's possibilities are narrowed down. Difficulty of economic or social or political circumstance does not inevitably lead men and women towards defeatism and down-heartedness. Tradition and culture may serve as resources of hope and meaning, steeling the person for a long fight against historical odds. And then there are those who have the imagination to dream beyond, to whom barriers appear surmountable and vanquishable, who skirt the obstacles and dream of worlds that could be. Moses Coady was just such a person.

Moses Michael Coady was born into a humble, pious, hard-working, large Irish Catholic farm family, the son of Michael J. ("Whistling Mick") Coady and Sarah J. Coady (née Tompkins) on January 3, 1882, in the Margaree Valley of Cape Breton. The second of eleven children (one, Teresa, died in infancy), Coady was baptized on January 6, with Father Laffin officiating. His parents named him after the progenitor of the Doyles of the Margaree, Moses Doyle, nicknamed "Mogue."

Mogue Doyle had been the leader of a company of the United Irishmen in the Irish Rebellion of 1798. Having been taken prisoner in that uprising, Mogue escaped and arrived in America in 1799. One of his descendants, Myles MacDaniel, the first Irishmen to settle in Margaree Forks, arrived there in 1815. Myles had been born in the city of Wexford, Ireland, in 1788; he had landed originally in St. John's, Newfoundland, in 1807. Myles had married Rebecca Smith on September 11, 1811. She was descended from Capt. David Smith, who had sailed his own vessel from Truro, Cape Cod, and settled with his wife and family on Port Hood Island in 1787. Smith was of good United Empire Loyalist stock. An only daughter, Rebecca was

Coady's mother's grandmother. She died at North East Margaree Forks on February 28, 1864, at age seventy-seven.

Sarah MacDaniel, Rebecca and Myle's daughter, had married Nicholas Tompkins, who, in the fashion of the day for the Anglo-Celtic Catholics, had produced nine children. Sarah Coady's brother "Jack Nick" was the father of the Rev. J.J. Tompkins. Father Jimmy's brother, Chris J. Tompkins, taught school at the Margaree Forks schools, and influenced Moses Coady immensely in his early days. Throughout his life, Coady would correspond with Chris, who moved out west to Calgary during Coady's Extension years. Three famous Cape Breton priests—J.J. Tompkins, Miles Tompkins (who was Father Jimmy's cousin) and Moses M. Coady—were born in "Jack Nick's" home in the Margaree, close to Coady's father's old farm. Mary Coady (née MacNeil), Leo's widow, lives today in the handsome old farm house, nestled in the hills, about half a mile up a gravel road from the Coady-Tompkins Memorial Library at Margaree Forks.

Coady's own father, Whistling Mick, was descended from the Margaree Coadys. In 1830 three Coady brothers, Martin, Peter and John, had settled on and near the farm owned in the mid-1950s by Francis P. Coady. Apparently unhappy with the land they occupied, the brothers had made their way by canoe to the Margaree Harbour late one fall before the ice jams formed in the harbour. They walked to Cheticamp, an Acadian fishing settlement on the west coast of Cape Breton, to purchase a large farm in the area. On the way back, all of them drowned in the Margaree Harbour. Foul play was suspected; the money to buy the farm was never recovered. Martin's untimely death left his widow, Julia (née McCarthy), born in Dublin, alone with her two children, Pierie and James. She moved to Sydney Mines, where Pierie found work with her cousin, Mr. Londrigon, who owned and operated one of the early, small coal mining outfits at Sydney Mines. Her son, James, married Sally Doyle, and they in turn had eleven children, one of whom was Michael J. Coady, Moses Coady's father. Whistling Mick's brother, Moses, became a priest; he died at Reserve Mines in 1920.

Like his son, Whistling Mick was tall, handsome, upright, strong and pious. Coady's cousin, Chris J. Tompkins, writing to Coady, described Coady's father as a great man shortly after Whistling Mick's death in 1940. "Will there ever be his like again? I doubt it," he would write.

> Think of the career of the man; farmer, fisherman, fighter, carpenter, contractor, lumberman (for over a quarter of a century he made all the coffins in Margaree and vicinity), and financier, but in this last profession he was not a huge success. He was too honest for this profession.... Think what a man your father would have been had he opportunities possessed by the men of Canada and the United States and of whom volumes have been written. Your father would have surpassed them all. Morally, physically and mentally, he was a giant, even with his limited opportunities.[1]

Moses Michael Coady was entwined in a vast web of kin who lived in and around the Margaree Valley on the west side of the isle of Cape Breton. He relished his multiple roles as senior son, loyal brother, attentive cousin, doting uncle and somewhat nosy advice-giver. He took a special interest in his brother Joe's family, particularly Leo Gerard Coady and his wife Mary (née McNeil). Coady lavished advice on Leo and his sisters, Mary Teresa and Carmel. Coady would choose Leo as his protégé, his own lieutenant of the Antigonish Movement for the Margaree. Coady's protégé would struggle throughout his lifetime with some of the burdens this entailed.

Coady was made of the stuff of Coadys, Tompkins, Doyles, O'Neils, O'Briens, McDaniels and Smiths. Coady saw his ancestors as "fighters who had lost their battles … because their strength and courage had drawn them to the side of the impossible. They came to Margaree to fight a different kind of battle—against the river, the forest and the mountains." His ancestors had been committed to lost causes. However, like other children of Irish parents, he was "born rememberin.'" Coady believed that he had been pushed into the work of adult education and organizing the people for economic action.

> All the forces that went into my being conspired to this end. Fighters for impossible causes—men of tremendous physique and courage—these were my ancestors. And while it would ill become me to claim a share of that courage, I cannot deny having inherited the size and strength. Neither can I deny their imagination, their wonder, and their impatience to get things done.

Coady thought that his temperament and physical make-up came down to him in the "blood of rebel Irishmen." The Margaree Irish—the Coadys, the Doyles and the Tompkins—were fighters against political injustice.[2]

Coady shared the feisty spirit of many of his contemporaries. His cause burst in "ready-made in those post-Industrial Revolution days when the economic plight of the people in and beyond my home valley began to dawn upon me." The flight from the land would be inscribed in Coady's being. Even the little Margaree Valley could not escape the tremors of the Industrial Revolution, the "social seismograph" recording the "first faint tremors as people began to leave the land for the great and everlasting trek to the urban centres."[3]

Coady also felt pulled to the "unseen, the unknown and the things that needed to be done" by the natural landscape of his home. "The spot where I was born, high up on the mountain overlooking the North-east Margaree Valley, and the Southwest Valley where I spent my youth until I was 23 years old are the two beauty spots of a community that for scenery, in the estimation of travellers, ranks among the best of the world.[4] Coady attributed any poetic imagination he had to the beauty of the Margaree.

Coady loved, passionately, the natural world. He knew it intimately and was endlessly curious about its workings and wonders. It was, in the words of one of the few poems he penned (helped by Zita O'Hearn), the "Divine Mosaic by a Master hand / Inlaid with stream and meadow, rugged hill." The Margaree Valley is, in any estimation, a very pleasing landscape. The Margaree River cuts through a valley, fed from the South West River that flows out of Lake Ainslie and the North East River, which originates in the rugged Cape Breton highlands. As John MacDougall, author of an early work on the history of Inverness County wrote, "the Forks will strike a stranger like an oasis in the desert. He does not expect it, but it holds him charmed."

The Margaree River, which empties into Margaree Harbour, has long been known as a great salmon river. It was well known for its runs of gaspereaux; the farmers around the area would set aside their tasks to scoop them out of traps set in the river. The area known simply as the "Margaree," roughly a hundred square miles, includes the small communities of Margaree Harbour, Margaree Valley, East Margaree, Margaree Centre, South West Margaree and North East Margaree. While winding through these places, each with their own histories and legends, one is struck by the "incomparable blend of field and forest, of mountain and stream, interspersed with gentle uplands and peaceful valleys."[5] Over the years Coady would return often to the Margaree for spiritual nourishment, fellowship and good food.

No one knows for certain the origin of the name "Margaree." One version suggests that it is of Mi'kmaq (Nova Scotia's indigenous people) origin, the name of an Indian women who drowned in its waters. Acadian fishermen, the story goes, upon hearing the Mi'kmaqs lamenting her death, named the river for her. MacLellan, author of *Coady Remembered*, thinks that the most likely version is that the name, originally Marguerite, was given to the first white woman to settle in the area. The fact that Lake Ainslie was once known as Lake Marguerite lends authority to this view.

The famed river also served economic functions. In the early days, the Margaree River transported people into the country. The river was not always gentle, at times cresting its banks, and stories were told of pioneer settlers carried off into watery graves. Coady spoke of this river as the

> glorious enemy, the beautiful flood that had taken the lives of so many of my ancestors. I listened as the old folks talked at the fireside, of the community, and told tales of the drownings—of the big and courageous men who had lost their lives battling the river that was the only highway in the early days.[6]

Fierce winds from the Atlantic also push the "big ice" drifts down the river. Their eerie jagged shapes fill up the harbour in the dead of the Nova Scotian winter.

Metaphor springs from the human imagination, and imagination is often fed by the natural environment. The natural world—trees, mountains, rivers—plainly inspired Coady. Natural metaphors inevitably found their

Perhaps the earliest photograph of the Coady family, father Michael 'Whistling Mick" Coady with his wife, Sarah, and five children.

The newly ordained priest with proud parents and two of his sisters.

Ordained in Rome on May 10, 1910, Coady
described himself as a "slim but proud Levite."

Coady and his fellow priests poised to change the world.

way into his speeches. He had an almost Darwinian sense that life was a great battle, with mighty natural forces arrayed against humankind. Human beings needed to be strong to wrestle with these forces. They had to be even stronger if they were to manipulate social forces to serve social justice. Coady believed strongly that mountains played a large role in making people what they become. "Take a mountain at its face value," Coady would say, "and it is a wall, a boundary separating those inside from those outside, making them different. The mountaineer of the old ballads, the hill-billy, is a prisoner of his native hills. Take a mountain plus imagination and wonder…. [I]t is a challenge, and an exciting bridge to the wonderful world beyond." The forest also captured Coady's sensibility.

> In the winds of March, in the annual August gales, and in the chill blasts of winter, the voice of the trees was always in my ears. Clean and strong and beautiful, the birch, the beech, and the rock maple that had never known the axe, covered the slopes from foothill to peak. And in those seasonal gales, their creaking cordage took on a voice, a personality. The trees, created for man's use and service, were crying to achieve their destiny (*My Story*, 1957).

Coady recalls tramping into the back hills and discovering that the trees were dead. Here was a "precious natural resource, neglected too long," as no one had taken the trouble to tend the forest. This lesson stayed with him throughout his life.

II

As Coady came of age, he began to sort the "world beyond into more logical patterns. There were people in that outside world too, people with difficulties similar to or greater than those known by the early settlers of Margaree. In fact, it was to escape some of these hardships that my ancestors had come to this snug valley."[7]

The world in which Moses Coady grew up was a pioneering, largely pre-industrial, world. Men from the Margaree worked the surrounding forests, hauling lumber and pulpwood to the mills. They worked the land, farming and raising herds of cattle and sheep. They also fished, trapping the gaspereaux in the Margaree River and catching lobsters as well as cod, hake and mackerel. This pattern of weaving a livelihood together from diverse economic activities was a common Nova Scotia practice. It was also incredibly hard work and didn't make you rich. As the oldest boy in his family, Coady participated in all the activities usually associated with a pioneering farm carved out of the forest. "We were carpenters, coopers, woodsmen, fishermen, farmers all in one," Coady wrote. These settlers were cash poor and self-reliant. One is tempted to locate Coady's two most fundamental ideas—that human beings could be masters of their own destiny and that working the land was the best way of life—in his early life experiences.

By the age of ten, in 1892, Coady was doing a "man's work" on a farm in the South West Margaree, which his father had purchased. Mick Coady and his wife, Sarah Jane, had been residing with Sarah's parents. As the family grew, Mick had had to find a suitable farm to care for his wife and children. Michael J. Coady was able to buy the 650-acre old Campbell farm, located at the southern extremity of the Margaree Forks school section.

Coady's father's farm would eventually pass over to Joseph Coady, Moses' brother, and then to Leo Coady, Joe's son. Coady's father was, in his words, a "lion of a man" who was known for his hard work, attempting to build house, farm and barn simultaneously. Mick's son gained a reputation as a youth of formidable strength. Coady thought that his "rugged life [had] developed for [him] a great physique and the ability to endure long and sustained hard effort." In later life Coady considered that the varied experience of the farm—in producing, processing and marketing primary products—had tempered his idealism, preparing him for "realism in the co-operative phase of the adult education movement." Coady's private letters often surprise the reader with their intimate acquaintance with the details of agricultural life, from raising chickens to keeping deer out of the gardens.

In his mature years Coady knew with great surety that his ancestors had come to the Maritimes "inspired by a spirit of freedom and an idea of liberty," finding in the new land homes where they could "express their minds freely and fearlessly." Coady thought his ancestors had cast off "economic considerations" in their pursuit of "political and religious liberty." This strong commitment had rendered them "oblivious to the fact that economic considerations would eventually play such a determining role. They little realized that political freedom can be rapidly nullified unless founded on economic independence." Yet his forbears, while bringing little material wealth to the new country, did bring their "love of learning." Coady believed that his ancestors were convinced that "education would redress their wrongs and unlock the treasures of the new found world." It was not surprising, then, that his Anglo-Celtic forbears made such heroic efforts to create institutions of learning. In most communities they created elementary schools and set up grammar schools at strategic points such as St. Andrew's in Sydney, Cape Breton. Nova Scotia created, by law, free public schools in 1864; Prince Edward Island predated Nova Scotia by twelve years, and New Brunswick followed in 1871. In the early twentieth century, Coady's truly formative intellectual years, Nova Scotia would experience a mini-cultural renaissance, creating the Agricultural College in 1905 and the Nova Scotia Technical College in 1908. These latter institutions, led by stalwart progressives Dr. M.M. Cumming and Dr. F. Sexton, respectively, would play key roles in the educational and economic awakening of Nova Scotia in the post-World War I years.[8]

Throughout his mature life, Moses Coady preached the gospel of the power of education to release energy and solve pressing human problems. Education, for Coady, carried a heavy burden. The demands of the family economy, however, would keep Coady out of regular school attendance until he was about fifteen years old. In the custom of the day, the young Moses would spend a few weeks after planting in the spring at the Margaree Forks school and a little longer after the fall's digging. His parents taught him at home and gave him a solid grounding in mathematics, one of Coady's great loves. Its logic fascinated him, and one of mathematics' axial words, the "formula," would constantly grace Coady's vocabulary in speech and letter. This farm lad, whom the "Old Rector" of St. Francis Xavier University, H.P. MacPherson, figured could have beaten Jack Dempsey, showed enough promise in scholastic matters that he was sent to the Margaree Forks school where Jimmy Tompkins's brother, Chris J., was the principal. The Forks school was founded in the mid-nineteenth century, and generations of Coadys had attended it. For three and a half years, Coady was taught by the man he called the "most inspiring teacher of his life," his older cousin Chris J. Tompkins.

The other influential Tompkins, Jimmy, was very unlike his cousin in physique and temperament. Jimmy was small, somewhat sickly, fiercely intellectual in outlook and did not quite fit the requirements of pioneer farming. But J.J. Tompkins, Coady's senior by twelve years, was bolder in spirit than his giant of a cousin. Both men had the blood of rebel Irishmen flowing through their veins. Jimmy was more willing to go out on a limb, more willing to challenge authority in Church, state and economy, if the truth demanded it.

Coady was present in the great internal struggles within the Roman Catholic Church of the Diocese of Nova Scotia in the early twentieth century. He was part of the reform cadre of remarkable priests who agitated for social reform in the period of the Maritimes' great suffering. He poured considerable energy into the reform of rural schooling and teacher education during a grim time for Nova Scotia teachers. However, he did not spearhead the reform movement through the 1910s and 1920s. Others, like Father Michael Gillis, whom Coady admired deeply, and his cousin, were in the forefront of the movement to gain an instrument, an Extension Department, to further their reform project. Coady came in from the wings and assumed centre stage when he was almost fifty years old. Once there, his rebel heritage fully flowered.

Jimmy Tompkins went to Rome in December 1897 to study at the Propaganda College for the priesthood. Many Nova Scotian men of modest origin travelled to the Propaganda for their training, where they studied with men from many different parts of the world. This training lent a cosmopolitan and worldly air to the Diocese of Antigonish. These men, trained in a formidably disciplined and hierarchical manner, rubbed shoulders with other men from worlds under colonial domination. Jimmy arrived in Rome just six years after Pope Leo XIII published *Rerum Novarum* in 1891. It is unlikely that this encyclical made its way into the Propaganda curriculum, but the old Roman Church was turning its attention towards the plight of the industrial worker. All of the reform-minded priests of the Antigonish diocese knew that they at least had in this encyclical legitimization for their own reform plotting over the next few decades.

Cousin Jimmy sent a constant stream of pamphlets, leaflets, rosaries and books back to his younger cousin. One can imagine Coady hurriedly opening all of those intriguing packages postmarked "Rome," giving him his first experience of the world beyond the mountains. Jimmy Tompkins had chosen his cousin Moses for special mentoring. He taught him Latin by correspondence, which served Coady well when he attended college. Coady also flourished under Chris Tompkins' tutelage, developing his mathematical skills and forming a love of Shakespeare. On August 15, 1898, now sixteen years of age, Coady was granted the Grade D high school certificate. He had successfully completed his provincial examinations, obtaining good grades in History and Geography, Science, Arithmetic, Bookkeeping, Algebra, Geometry, English Literature and Grammar.

Coady completed the next two years of high school, obtaining Grades C and B, the equivalents of our current Grades 10 and 11. Coady's next move was away from the farm and teaching presented itself as a vocational option. Teaching was usually a stepping stone for men to something more lucrative. Poorly paid, poorly organized and poorly equipped, Nova Scotian primary and secondary teachers and their schools were in sad shape. However, few avenues were open for young men such as Coady, and he could at least help put himself through college by teaching. In the fall of 1900, at the century's turn, Moses Coady, now eighteen years old, enrolled at the provincial Normal School, founded in 1855, located in Truro, a busy service centre for the surrounding farms and dairies located about sixty miles from Halifax. His father drove him by horse and buggy all the way to River Denys from the Margaree, where he embarked for Truro from the River Denys train station.

Coady was met in Truro by the principal, Dr. Soloan, depicted by MacLellan as a "tall and overpowering figure, severe and strict, looking every inch the traditional schoolmaster" with his "high white collar with a greyish necktie" and "Prince Albert coat with striped trousers and shining black shoes." Coady probably didn't know quite what to make of Soloan's late-Victorian pretentions, but he was greeted warmly enough by him and professors Benoit and Connoly, who taught the pedagogics of science, mathematics and physiology. The Normal School curriculum consisted of courses entirely related to teaching processes. The staff was under considerable pressure to get their youthful trainees out into the rural communities, now desperate for teachers. On June 27, 1901, Coady received his Normal School diploma. His teachers rated his performance as only "fair." He worked hard, but his academic work did not foreshadow his later classroom and platform brilliance and intellectual acuity.

Returning to the Margaree, Coady worked with his fathers and brothers on the farm. In the summer of 1901, this brash young man was supremely confident of his physical power and strength. An early black-and-white photograph captures the teenaged Coady, smiling slightly, pitchfork full of hay in hand, standing in the back of an old wooden cart.

The 1901 school year ended and Chris J. Tompkins resigned as principal of Margaree Forks school. He recommended that Coady take up the position. Coady's application was duly taken up by the trustees—Martin Cameron, Alex McDougall and Donald Chiasson—who accepted the young energetic teacher as their principal. Coady began teaching in early August 1901. His responsibilities included Grades IX, X and XI, as well as supervision of the elementary children. Coady's salary amounted to $140 for 216 teaching days, about 65 cents per diem.

The nineteen-year-old standing before his class of thirty-two, with students ranging in age from eleven to twenty-one years and all possessing names familiar to him (Doyle, Campbell, Tompkins, MacDonald, Cameron, Coady, McDaniel), must have been struck by the oddity of his teaching situation. Bright kids, educated in the early grades in one big classroom, could hopscotch through several grades. Older youth, some in early adulthood, took time out for farm work. Coady saw that the ratio of boys to girls was about equal, with higher drop-out rates for boys in the elementary grades. Somehow Coady managed to hold the interest of his students through winter storms, impassable roads and farm life's consuming demands on children.

In early April 1902, the school inspector, James MacKinnon, travelling by buggy from Baddeck, about thirty miles from the Margaree, visited Coady's school. His comments—"This Department is very efficiently taught" or "Good order and first class work"—were recorded in Coady's register. Coady's school drew attention, and visitors came to see some of the new methods of teaching then in vogue. Coady was very busy. He taught fifteen subjects in three grades, from drawing and botany to bookkeeping and geography. No French was taught, even though the Acadian population (the other names in his class, such as Aucoin, Chiasson) overlapped from Cheticamp into the Margaree area.

His cousin, now "Father" Jimmy, had arrived back in Nova Scotia and had taken up residence at St.FX as professor of Greek and higher algebra. Father Jimmy would single out the most promising students at St.FX and press them to achieve great things, often suggesting a possible career line. Throughout his tenure as academic vice-president of St.FX, Tompkins would encourage one to go on to study physics, another agriculture, another advanced mathematics. He was the master of the one-on-one pedagogical encounter. Father Jimmy continued to work on his intellectually raw cousin through Coady's second year of teaching at the Margaree Forks.

In 1903, at age twenty-one, Coady entered St.FX. Coady was permitted to enter into the junior year; he would qualify for his bachelor's degree in two years. He registered for English, Church History, Philosophy, Latin, Greek, Trigonometry, Algebra and Geometry.[9]

Coady's athletic ability was much evident during these years. The famous world champion hammer-thrower, Simon P. Gillis, a native of the Margaree, had coached Coady for this event. Coady threw the "56," as it was dubbed, within six inches of the world's record, then held by "Mighty Matt" McGraw of New York. (This sort of story would feed into the legend of the Mighty Moses from the Margaree.) Coady played on the Xavier football team, and one has some pity for his opponents who endured the pain of being tackled by this irrepressible young man.

Coady's mental development now began to catch up a little with his physical prowess. Not only could this young man throw the hammer and pitch hay non-stop for days, but the university also awarded him medals for his proficiency in Latin and Greek, Philosophy and History. Tompkins' tutoring had paid off; he achieved the highest aggregate for his class. In later years, it was not uncommon to hear Coady flattered as "companionable, scholarly, brilliant, and irrepressible, his intellect … like a beacon flashing forth rays to illumine the land." One could, perhaps, see flickerings of these characteristics in the Moses Coady who graduated from St.FX in 1905, her golden jubilee year.

Coady obtained his bachelor's degree, qualifying for a Grade A teaching licence, with a very high aggregate record. Now quite adept in the classics, Coady read the address of Aeschylus, founder of Greek tragic poetry, to the graduating class. In his affectionate memoir, MacLellan tells us that he admired poets such as Byron, Tennyson, Burns and Kipling. Coady particularly liked Byron's "The Oriental Tale," some stanzas from "Childe Harold," "Break, Break" and "Blow bugle, blow" from Tennyson, "Highland Mary" and "Road to the Isles" from Burns and Kipling's "If."[10] Poetry, he thought, had great potential to develop the imagination. *The Xaverian*, the student newspaper, eulogized Coady as "one of the most energetic and successful members of the Class of 1905 who devoted his time chiefly to the study of Philosophy and the classical works of Latin and Greek." In this same issue, Coady is described as an upright student, the foe of meanness, one who played it straight by the rules. He seemed highly esteemed by just about everyone.[11]

Little is known about Coady's love life in those early days. He had some girlfriends, but they have faded from people's memory. And like the Margaree Irish, whom he described as dancers, fiddlers, dreamers, tough workers and hard drinkers, Coady probably drank with the boys. Coady believed that alcohol plagued the Coadys and Tompkins. He would be no exception.

Commentators often remark on Coady's genial character. A long-time American associate in the struggle to build the co-operative movement, Benson Y. Landis of the National Council of Churches, lauded Coady upon his retirement in 1952 as a man of "genuine friendliness and sympathetic insights ... spreading confidence and plain good humor."[12] Writing many years after his death, his long-time friend and co-worker Kay Thompson contrasted Coady's rather stern public persona, with fists pounding lecterns, splinters sometimes flying, with the off-platform man who was "mild and gentle, with boundless, almost boyish enthusiasm for all sorts of things."[13] Off-stage and relaxed, Coady easily slipped into the self-effacing role of "Little Mosie from the Margaree." He once greeted Teresa with "salutations from the little boy from the country."[14] Yet Coady had a less than genial side to his nature. Like his forebears, Coady seemed almost hewn out of granite. He had an arrogant and hard streak in his personality. He always seemed to know what was right for others and had little compunction about hectoring people into the truth.

III

Those men and women who choose the religious life of celibacy and dedication to Church and service to its people often speak of an inner voice calling them to their special life. Coady was no different. As George Boyle, author of the first biography of Jimmy Tompkins, tells us, Coady was reading a cheap edition of the Gospel of St. Luke when he heard the ringing of the bell of St. Joseph's Church in Reserve Mines, Cape Breton. Coady would thereafter regard this as the moment of his call to the priesthood, yet spirituality was also a part of his culture and tradition. Irish Catholic families kept an eye out for men and women whom they could "give" to the Mother Church. The priesthood (and sisterhood) was the main avenue for talented and ambitious men and women to exercise influence (and gain status and recognition) in their communities and larger society.

The Diocese of Antigonish had an unusual network of men and women who had chosen the clerical life. Bound by blood, tradition and memory, they had been chosen by their own people to provide intellectual leadership, guidance and consolation through life's problems and circumstances. Father Jimmy Tompkins, born in 1870, and his second cousin, Father Moses Coady, born in 1882, were part of a fairly large network of reform-minded priests born in the last decades of the nineteenth century. Priests such as D.J. MacDonald (b. 1881), "Little Doc" Hugh MacPherson (b. 1872), Miles Tompkins (b. 1880), James Boyle (b. 1885), Leo Keats (b. 1891), Charles Forest (b. 1889), Michael Gillis (b. 1883), Amiable Briand (b. 1881) and Alfred Boudreau (b. 1893) were born into suffering communities and had parents who were fishers, farmers and miners. They were of the place, knew its people, had little material wealth, heard stories of the terrors of the coal fields, saw neighbours leaving the land and witnessed the dreaded beam-trawlers invading their waters—and felt the threat of losing their faith.

These priests formed their outlook on life, discerned its hopes and possibilities, in a time of tentative renewal within global Catholicism. Pope Leo XIII's epochal encyclical *Rerum Novarum* shook Catholicism out of its slumber in 1891, and the Roman Catholic Church began to respond to the plight of working people in Europe and North America. The reform-minded priests, many of whom had studied in Rome, were ordained from the turn of the century to 1921. They were world-wise and well educated. On January 24, 1915, Father Jimmy Tompkins wrote to Moses Coady, who was then studying Education at the Catholic University in Washington, D.C., that he was confident that the "young priests are getting together as never before in the history of the diocese. They are aggressive and their faces are turned toward the light. All we want now are the leaders and enthusiasts before us. The trench digging and the spade work are practically completed."[15]

Fathers Tompkins and "Little Doc" Hugh MacPherson, one visionary and impetuous, the other experimental and placid, embodied the new wind of progressivism beginning to blow in the Diocese of Antigonish in the opening decades of the twentieth century. One of the central tenets of progressivism was implacable commitment to achieving social efficiency through the application of science to the solution of social problems. Dr. Hugh MacPherson was the first Nova Scotian adult educator to take the new scientific approach to agriculture to the people. Agriculture was in a very depressed state when "Little Doc" began to do something about it just before World War I. Appointed as the first agricultural representative in Nova Scotia in 1916, MacPherson worked through the war years with the Department of Agriculture, teaching farmers how to break the stranglehold of the rural merchants who were doing everything they could to kill their co-operative efforts. "Little Doc's" early work in wool marketing led him to expand to the marketing of lambs. This "apostle of scientific agriculture," a distinguished renaissance man who was adept in linguistics, engineering, music, chemistry and sports, lived to the ripe old age of 88. Late in his own life, Coady would write that MacPherson had "dignified agriculture in the minds of our people" and given the "country a jolt that it long needed." All of the reformers were trying to jolt their people into new imaginings and life.

Moses Michael Coady had made the momentous decision to become a Roman Catholic priest. In October 1905, after the usual summer of helping Whistling Mick on the homestead with all of his tasks, Coady, along with his classmate Hugh John MacDonald, embarked on the journey to the eternal city of Rome after travelling to Boston. They were bound for the famous seminary known as the College Urbanun, or more simply as the Propaganda College. Coady and MacDonald would be away from their families for five years. Other priests, such as Father Jimmy or Coady's namesake, Father Moses Coady, would have undoubtedly alerted these young men as to just what was in store for them. Coady tells us that when he graduated from St.FX in 1905, there was a spot open at the Propaganda, and he was selected to fill it. "This was an unprecedented opportunity for a poor boy from the country to see the world, to enjoy the inspiration of a five-year sojourn in the Eternal City, and to get the best in theological and philosophical training of the time."[16]

Although St.FX was not, in any way, at the forefront of intellectual thought in the early twentieth century—Tompkins would rail against its scholarly failings—Coady was proficient enough in Latin and philosophy to be able to enrol at the Academy of St. Thomas for philosophical studies. During his reign, Pope Leo XIII tried to establish Thomism as the Church's philosophical base. The St. Thomas Academy was noted for its studies in St. Thomas Aquinas' philosophy, the Church's still-influential intellectual giant, the thirteenth-century Common Doctor of the Church. Thomas fused Aristotle and Christianity and fashioned volume after volume of painstaking reflections on everything under God's good sun. Thomism provided Coady with some of his conceptual architecture. Coady's humble audiences gathered in modest community halls would have been surprised to learn that they were hearing a kind of bare-to-the-bone Thomism, shaped for the people's consumption.

St. Thomas Aquinas' thought is complex. Reduced to essentials, the Common Doctor imagined that God, the end and meaning of all existence, is knowable. The world is an ordered whole, and all beings within it fulfil their potential by serving other beings, with the chain of being progressing from lower to higher. Thomas placed a high premium on human reason. Through the exercise of intelligence, human beings could know "scientific and philosophical truth." In knowing the laws of nature, humans know God. Eminent Thomist scholar Etienne Gilson observed that, "by reason, man knows the universe and naturally desires to know its cause; by faith, he assents supernaturally to God's revelation; so not merely to know something about that cause, but to see it, is for man a possibility. So nature makes sense in the light of grace, and rational knowledge in the light of faith."[17] Cognition had a strong place in Thomas' way of imagining God. To teach such a doctrine, Thomas had to "entertain an unqualified confidence in the aptitude of human reason to know scientific and philosophical truth; at the same time he had to entertain an equally absolute confidence in the truth of the divine revelation as received by faith. Last, but not least, he must have been a man who could do both at one and the same time."[18] Human beings can, then, ascend to God through a "scientific" apprehension of the world; and they can receive "grace" through God's descent into their world through sacred text. Coady was driven throughout his intellectual life to find the scientific way of understanding the workings of the social, economic and political worlds. Nature, society, religious longings—nothing was outside the ordering of God's world.

Coady received his doctorate after two years of study at the Academy. Doctoral work was followed by three more years of strictly disciplined study for the duties of the priesthood. Coady's Roman teachers assessed their Nova Scotian student as having only ordinary ability; once again Coady had failed to impress his teachers with his conceptual acumen. Coady's mind was not a cloistered intellect that poured patiently over texts, relating text to traditions, searching for fine distinctions with analytical precision. His mind was powerful but roughly hewn, less tuned to ambiguity and shades of meaning than to the essence of the matter. Coady's mind cleared away the subtleties; he was compelled to simplify the world, to order it and bring it under control. Unlike his impetuously brilliant cousin, Father Jimmy, this man from the farm wanted the formula, the blueprint, the technique to make things and society work. His was the mind of an engineer; the scholarly mind eschews formulaic thinking. Coady was also simply too restless to sit closeted away in his study. He wrote many speeches, reports and letters, but only one book, and that one was literally sweated out of him by loving assistants. Even this powerful little book, *Masters of Their Own Destiny*, was a simple, exhortatory text.

Coady appears to have loved Rome. He met young clerics from all parts of the world. He was swept up in the city's cosmopolitan sophistication. MacLellan informs us that Coady loved operas such as *Carmen* and *Il Travatore*. He became fluent in Italian, and could, apparently, sing some of the operatic tunes.

On May 10, 1910, Moses Coady was ordained a priest of the Roman Church in the St. John Lateran Basilica by His Eminence Cardinal Respighi. This was a luminous moment for the son of Whistling Mick and Sarah Jane Coady. He was a long way away from the starkly beautiful, white wooden Catholic churches that sit overlooking the sea in so many Nova Scotian communities. These two worlds, one full of urban pomp, elaborate architecture, vast libraries and paintings, ceremony and hierarchy, the other rural, simple, vernacular and egalitarian, were melded for the rural-born Canadian priests. During his stay in Rome, Coady made life-long friends. One was Gregory Peter Agaganian, later Gregory Peter XV, of Beyrouth, Liban. Recalling his days in Rome, Coady wrote to his old friend on December 10, 1957:

> I remember how sweet was the sound of the voices of the representatives of so many nations of the earth singing the praises of the Blessed Virgin on the eve of the Immaculate Conception. We were the living proof of the fulfilment of her prophecy: "Behold from henceforth all nations shall call me blessed." Do you remember how the candles flickered on the beautiful picture over the high altar in our chapel as the wise men presented their gifts to her? I count my sojourn in the Propaganda as the greatest piece of good luck of my life.[19]

Coady spent most of the summer of 1910 travelling around Europe and the British Isles. He managed to visit his ancestral home of Ireland before arriving in the Margaree in August. The ascetic regimen of the Roman seminary had slimmed him down. Thinking back on his time at the Propaganda, Coady confidently observed that he came out a "slim but powerful Levite."[20] This powerful young Levite was welcomed home by his parents and the community of the Margaree region. Monsignor Finlay Chisholm, a much loved local priest, and D.D. MacFarlane presented their greetings, followed by community food and festivities. The neophyte priest, according to MacLellan, tested his pastoral skills on a few of the parishioners, and plunged in to the work of the farm.

"Little Mosie" was now the Rev. Dr. Moses Michael Coady, twenty-eight years old, holding advanced degrees, experienced in school pedagogy, full of vigour and strength. And he would need all the strength he could muster for the fights that lay ahead of him. The venerable Bishop of Antigonish, John Cameron, would soon be replaced by John Morrison. Reigning from 1912 until his death in 1950, Bishop Morrison would preside over the diocese's most dramatic and contentious period of history. Cousin Jimmy would spearhead the reform movement, beginning around 1912, challenging Morrison's complacency regarding the economic and social problems of the eastern region of Nova Scotia. The 1920s would be a decade of intense struggle against the Church hierarchy for the reform cadre of priests that was gradually coalescing into a unified force during the war years. It would also be a decade of bitter conflict in the coal fields and fishing villages of Nova Scotia. Old Bishop Cameron recommended to St.FX's president, Dr. Alexander Thompson, that Dr. Coady be appointed to the staff of St. Francis Xavier University; Father Jimmy was now academic vice-president of the university. Coady was duly assigned to the staff of the

St.FX High School, also serving as the Antigonish County Academy. His duties included teaching Latin and mathematics and supervising students in the residential hall known as the "Alleys." Coady thought of himself at this time as a "kind of fachino—not too pleased with my functions, not realizing that I was being prepared for the future job of building the economy of Maritime Canada."[21] Coady was also drawn into his inimitable cousin's plottings and agitation for reform within and without the university.

By all accounts, Coady was an inspired teacher. Coady threw himself wholeheartedly into the unenviable task of ensuring that his students matriculated. Coady prided himself on his ability to teach anyone mathematics, but he wasn't successful with everyone. Alex Laidlaw recalls taking a course from Coady in the mid-1920s. Scrawling a

> long snake-like equation across several feet of blackboard, [Coady] would say; "Factor that, MacNeil, and solve it." MacNeil attempted, for fifteen minutes, returning to his seat, defeated. "Can't do, eh? What course are you taking, MacNeil?" "Pre-med, Doctor," was the reply. "Better drop it, MacNeil; you'll never make a good medical doctor—I can tell by the way you go at a problem in algebra. You'll be taking a man's appendix out when the trouble is with his gall bladder—I advise you to drop medicine."

It wasn't clear what the logical connection between algebra and medicine was, but MacNeil went on to be a reputable surgeon.[22] Others, such as Justice Keiller MacKay, who studied Latin with Coady, were grateful for the experience:

> I still remember and once again acknowledge with gratitude your real contribution to the development of my education, and especially for instilling in my youthful mind an urge and love for the classics. Your part in stimulating an appreciation of the beautiful in literature and poetry in the minds of all your students has been large and of great profit.[23]

The spirit of the good, old-fashioned romantic humanist pulsed through Coady.

Coady was a strict disciplinarian in carrying out his prefect duties. The students were expected to rise at 7:00 a.m. and show up for Mass. This compulsory ritual didn't catch every student's fancy. A few played tricks on Coady, trapping him into breaking down a door to see where they were upon his noticing that they weren't in the chapel. Coady ended up having to pay for the damages. MacLellan tells the story of a mischievous and smart student who wired his door, hoping to catch Coady out. Now wise to student tricks, Coady had a master key which he used to enter the student's room. He put the key in, and the shock he received jolted him back against the wall. Excited over what had happened, Coady left the key in the door, and the devilish student returned the key to the bursar. Coady's lips remained sealed about this incident.[24]

In the years preceding World War I, something new was breaking into diocesan life. Father Jimmy, ever a lightning rod for new thinking and

action, had caught a glimpse of the power of adult education while attending an international conference in England in 1912. From that point on, the
driven Tompkins would be a whirlwind advocate for the liberating potential of adult education. Tompkins' first attempt to awaken the sleepy town
of Antigonish, surrounded by increasingly abandoned farms, took the form
of the "Antigonish Forward Movement." During the years 1913 to 1915,
Tompkins tried to goad the town's business class and citizens into taking
responsibility for sprucing up the town and imagining practicable and
appropriate forms of civic renewal. He hooked Coady into his boosterish
activities, giving him his first real taste of community action, and he and
Tompkins spoke to meetings around Antigonish. Coady advocated
co-operation in the marketing of farm produce, and the development of
cold storage and canning plants. Like Tompkins, he thought that
Antigonish could become a vibrant community, a place to which those
from the Maritime diaspora would desire to return. However, most of
Coady's considerable energy was not yet channelled into economic
reform.

Coady also supported the Sisters of Martha religious order, helping
them gain autonomous status. They moved out from the rector's jurisdiction and into their current motherhouse on a hill overlooking the
countryside. Throughout his career, Coady supported the Marthas and the
orders of Charity and Notre Dame. "If I had fifty Sisters of Martha," he
once said, "I could change the world." He often spoke to the novices, challenging them to great achievements.[25] The Sisters had a significant place in
Coady's blueprint for social reconstruction. "One hesitates to tell religious
people, especially Sisters," he informed them in 1952, "dedicated as they
are to carrying on the corporal and spiritual works of mercy and the saving
of souls, that they must understand the problems of this rough and revolutionary world."[26] But Coady didn't hesitate. Sisters such as (Irene Doyle)
Anselm, Marie Michael and Frances Delores would play brilliant intellectual leadership roles in the Movement.

St.FX University had been considering opening up a School of Education for several years. In 1914, university officials chose to send Coady to
the Catholic University of America in Washington, D.C., for graduate work
in Education. In September Dr. Coady left to study the "psychological and
philosophical aspects of education, as well as its historical development."
He received his master's degree in education in April 1915, returning home
a little disappointed that he could not stay for a further year of study. During his time in Washington, Coady corresponded with his cousin Jimmy
Tompkins, who encouraged him to learn the art of speaking well. He
chided Coady with the fact that he, Tompkins, was much more concerned
with making a difference in the real world than with pondering abstract
educational issues. Shortly after returning home, Coady was appointed

principal of the St.FX University High School, and he began to teach at summer schools in Halifax. He was coming to the conclusion that his "destiny was to work with teachers and help to regenerate the country through the education of youth."[27]

Coady ran the high school and lectured in apologetics and education throughout the war years and into the early 1920s. He participated in diocesan meetings from 1918 to 1921, when the regeneration of rural life and the problems in the coal fields were altering the face of conventional parish life. Tompkins had extended his reform campaign to the diocesan newspaper, *The Casket*, in which he roused people to take social and economic action through his column, "For the People."

IV

Coady's opportunity to "regenerate the youth of the country" came in 1921, the same year the famous Bluenose schooner was launched, prohibition was declared and *Knowledge for the People* was published. In the fall of 1920, Nova Scotia teachers were very dissatisfied with their lot and the system of union organization. The Provincial Educational Association (PEA) was led by government officials, and they would occasionally call meetings of the "union" (today we would call this a "company union"). At a PEA meeting, chaired by R.W. Ford, principal of the Wolfville High School, government officials–superintendent of schools, principal of the Normal College, school inspectors–were excluded. Despite the good will of men such as David Soloan of the Normal School, the association had not made many gains for teachers, whose situation was deplorable. The time was ripe to break with paternalism.

The down-hearted executive called a meeting for Easter 1921, at Truro. Moses Coady, for several years the principal of the Antigonish County Academy and head of the school system of the town of Antigonish, arrived in Truro having just participated in the epochal "People's School," held in Antigonish from January through March. Unsure of what to expect, Coady was "not particularly interested in the teachers organization and in an organization that was called a 'union'. The word had a bad connotation in many quarters."[28]

However, the socially conservative Coady was knocked out of his anti-unionism late one night in the rooms of the St.FX president. Dr. Learned of the Carnegie Foundation for the Advancement of Teaching, and Dr. Sills, president of Bowdoin College, were visiting in Antigonish as part of their examination of higher education in eastern Canada. After dinner in the College, they shifted to the president's rooms for conversation, during which Coady revealed that he was taking the night train to Truro to discuss the future of teachers' unions. Reacting spontaneously, Dr. Learned responded, "That is the white hope of education."[29]

The next day Coady went to the Truro Academy and found a small gathering of five or six people, remnants of the old "Teachers' Union." He didn't know any of them, and sat silently listening to the discussion. But "with the confidence born of Dr. Sills' remark the night before," Coady recalled,

> I finally summoned up the courage to say that I considered that by discontinuing the Teachers' organization we would be setting the clock backward and that future Nova Scotians would justly have a cause against that generation of teachers for not having done its duty. Somebody asked what I proposed.[30]

Coady proposed three things. He suggested that a sub-committee appoint an organizer for the Teachers' Union, that he be paid a salary and that he should edit a magazine for teachers. To his amazement—"I was stunned when they unanimously gave me the job"—the chair chose Coady to spearhead the revitalization of the Teachers' Union and edit the bulletin.[31] Strong local unions still existed in several cities, such as Halifax, Amherst, Truro and New Glasgow. Leaders such as Jessie Campbell from Amherst and J.T. MacLeod from New Glasgow "swung in with enthusiasm to organize the whole province."[32] Coady took the job seriously, beginning his work first in eastern Nova Scotia "where such an idea had not received any consideration."[33]

The organizers had their work cut out for them. In 1922 the Carnegie Foundation for the Advancement of Teaching published its inquiry, *Education in the Maritime Provinces of Canada.* "The widespread apathy toward public education in Nova Scotia chills one like an east wind," the report concluded. The findings were devastating. Nova Scotia was one of the most backward provinces in the Dominion. Educational policy was a political product. The province paid less per pupil in average daily attendance than any other Canadian province, except Prince Edward Island. Forty-three per cent of all Nova Scotia teachers were Class D, receiving an annual salary of $431. The report also depicted higher education as underfunded and fragmented. Writing in the *Teachers' Bulletin* for December 1922, Coady lamented that "hundreds of our young men of brain and promise, every year seek jobs in our mining centres or lumber camps and our talented young women are recruited for office work or for common housework, because teaching offers them nothing." They receive a "small pittance of salary… and thus the exodus goes on and nothing is done to stop it. The man on the street sees this and mourns over it. All know that something is wrong, but a weird pessimism has so benumbed everybody that nothing has ever been attempted to break the spell." In subsequent editorials Coady would continue, like his cousin Father Jimmy, to rail against the "chilling pessimism which unfortunately is not confined to the common people alone [and] prevents our people from putting forth their best efforts for the progress of their country."[34] How could it be, Coady wondered, that "notwithstanding the fact that we have a province of wonderful natural resources and rare beauty and a good moral and social environment, it never seems to occur to our people that this is a good country to live in or at least could be easily made such."

Coady remained as editor of the *Teachers Bulletin* and secretary-treasurer of the Teachers' Union for four years. He did not think that organizing the teachers was such a hard task. Notices were sent out to all teachers, a small executive was elected, missing teachers were signed up by letter and a local secretary would then forward 50 percent of all fees to the provincial secretary-treasurer. By February 1923, Coady could report that "well nigh one half of our Nova Scotia teachers are now active members of our organization." But it was also "rather humiliating," Coady added, "to have to argue with teachers about the good of such an organization." Coady pressed for a "competent teacher for every classroom in Nova Scotia."[35]

In an editorial in the February 1923 *Bulletin*, Coady supported the $500 minimum salary. "At the present time many people, on account of the inefficiency of rural schools, are constrained to send their children to boarding schools. This costs them, at the very least, $500.00 for one term alone." However, the government wasn't hearing the teachers' message, and teachers' salaries were cut in 1924. The dismayed editorials of the *Bulletin* of June 1924 noted that the "air today is full of criticism of school conditions in our province." The cuts had "revealed a shocking and shameful lack of appreciation of the fundamental importance of the public school to the well-being of the community and the Province."

While Coady was organizing the teachers of the province, Tompkins was working to break the spell of pessimism that had settled upon Nova Scotian culture. Father Jimmy had spearheaded the movement to amalgamate Nova Scotia universities into a kind of University of Nova Scotia, with federated denominational colleges, in 1921 and 1922. Tompkins believed that this bold reorganization of the system of higher education was necessary if Nova Scotians were ever going to dispel the gloom of their "appalling apathy." The St.FX hierarchy rejected amalgamation, defending faith and culture, and Tompkins was exiled to Canso in late December 1922. Shortly after the defeat of the amalgamation, Father Jimmy mused that it was very difficult to tell what might happen at St. Francis Xavier University.

> There might be an uprising headed by the laymen at any time and a delegation to the Bishop. As far as [the Bishop] and the rector are concerned–they are hopeless. They are utterly ruining St FX, and putting it and themselves deeper in the mire by each progressive move. Their utter lack of sense and scruple and their manifestly unfair tactics are daily adding great strength to our cause.[36]

In one of the most fascinating letters ever written by Tompkins, he suggested that Bishop Morrison and the Old Rector were consciously moving to undermine the reformers. This year, Tompkins told Learned, we have lost "Smith, Gautherson, Connolly, Thibeau, Boyle, J.R. MacDonald and they were anxious to drop Dr. Hugh MacPherson.... Boyle was put out–as a warning I suppose to the temerous."[37]

The Diocese of Antigonish was wracked with serious internal dissension and the reform cadre appeared to be under siege. Father Jimmy loathed Bishop Morrison's backward thinking, castigating him and the "Old Rector" (Hugh MacPherson) as Bolsheviks of the worst sort. Morrison wanted to put a stop to the reform impulses in his troubled diocese. Coady didn't like Morrison much, either, but later in life would confess that Morrison at least knew enough to let the Movement activists do their work.

Coady resigned from his duties with the Nova Scotia Teachers' Union in 1924. He later recalled that, upon his leaving, he was "still dreaming of regenerating the country through teachers and the education of youth. Going to the people, in my thinking, was an indirect action and would have to wait for the next generation for progress."[38] Coady's comment is a bit of an overstatement. By the mid-1920s, Coady was aware that people like "Little Doc" Hugh MacPherson had carried scientific knowledge to the people for many years. Coady himself had participated in the People's School in 1921 as an instructor in mathematics. In a booklet published by the Nova Scotia Department of Agriculture, *The People's School: its purpose, its history, what the professors, the students, and the public say about it,* Coady observed that the

> time is ripe, it would seem, for a vigorous program of adult education in this country.... If we wait for the slow evolution of our educational institutions and spend all our time and energy on the rising generation alone we may be too late. We have at hand thousands of men and women who although they received little preliminary education have nevertheless much natural ability.... Helping them to realize their possibilities by giving them more knowledge and broader vision is the shortest and most direct route to the progress of the country.[39]

The *idea* of adult education was there; however, in 1921 Coady was unclear about just how one could go the people. The People's School, he wryly noted, "was, after all, the old idea of bringing the people to the campus for education. The great desideratum was an educational technique that would bring the university to the people."[40]

As Coady tells it, his "great awakening" to the power of adult education came when, after a brainstorm, he went to the Margaree to establish a school that "would bring music and art to the people of that highly artistic and beautiful country." Coady imagined that this artistic "folk school" might produce some great musicians and artists. After he had conceived of the school, like Paul on the road to Damascus, Coady was "struck like a bolt

from the blue by an idea that turned out to be the turning point in my life."
It had dawned on Coady that the "short, quick, scientific way to progress in
the world, even in the field of the formal education of the youth, was
through the enlightenment and education of adults." Moving quickly into
action, Coady called a dozen or so members of the community to a meeting. Once there, he posed two questions to them: "What should people do
to get life in this community, and what should they think about and study to
enable them to get it?" By the end of the Christmas season of 1925, Coady
had held about twenty meetings with his small group. Here, Coady claims,
"emerged the technique of adult education known as the Antigonish Movement. It was the small study club, issuing in economic group action. We
had co-operation before in many parts of the country. We had academic
adult education, too. But this formula put the two of them together."[41]

The Sisters of Martha opened Coady's artistic school in September 1926.
Coady not only had his new school, but he also had a new appointment to
add to his professorship of education, that of professor of philosophy at
St.FX. Coady succeeded Dr. Dougald Gillis in this appointment. Always
relishing the classroom, Coady taught philosophy using a dialectical pedagogy of thesis and counter-proposition. Gesticulating with his large hands,
Coady taught his students to associate philosophic terms with geometric
figures. Coady, as MacLellan describes him, was a commanding, stimulat-
ing and alert presence in the classroom, but Coady's days of powerful and
dramatic university classroom teaching were numbered. The air, indeed,
was full of criticism, and it wasn't just of the school system.

V

During the early 1920s Moses Coady, as one of the leading members of
the reform cadre of priests, participated in the momentous struggle that created the St. Francis Xavier University Extension Department. During
1923, the reform cadre, one might suppose, nursed its wounds and considered how to proceed with its social agenda. The merger battle had been
lost, and the continuing struggle (ideology and action) for economic and
educational reform had to be in harmony with the Church's traditional
defence of Catholic rurality. Beginning in 1924 with the first "Rural" Conference, and spearheaded by Fathers Michael Gillis and John R.
MacDonald, the reformers called for university extension to co-ordinate
and implement programs for enriching the rural environment. The reformers chose three channels to implement their program. In the first, the Rural
Conferences, the reform cadre persisted in articulating the belief that the
"rural problem" was really an economic problem. The second channel was
that of the Scottish Catholic Society, whose members had discussed rural
renewal at their annual conventions for many years, and the St. Francis

Alumni Association. The third channel, less direct but not less influential, was Tompkins' educational agitation work among the destitute fishermen of Canso and Little Dover. These three channels, flowing separately until 1927, would converge in 1928, and the Church hierarchy would succumb to pressure to create a university extension department in September 1929.

Vacant lands, rural degradation and despair, the Church and the rural problem, rural education–these were the themes of the 1924 Rural Conference, and none were new. However, the plight of the rural farmer was ascendant, as is reflected in the resolution moved by Drs. T. O'Reilly Boyle and Moses Coady.

> Whereas the keeping of our people on the farm depends to a large extent on the education in agriculture which they receive; and whereas People's Schools and Study Clubs are all excellent means of giving this education; "Be it resolved that this Conference requests the College authorities to form a department of extension work, which will organize People's Schools in the central points of the diocese, and direct Study Clubs in all sections; Be it further resolved that the priests here assembled aid the College in this work."[42]

Some who were present at the Rural Conference meetings in the mid-1920s, however, did not think that a university extension program was the only answer to the rural question. The reformers continued to castigate rural schools as inefficient, calling for specific reforms such as the appointment of rural supervisors for each county. They also wanted young men trained in the new principles of scientific agriculture. At the third Rural Conference held in December 1925, the Rev. Michael Gillis and the Rev. M. MacCormack moved that members of the Conference "ask the Bishop of the Diocese to make the appeal to the various parishes to raise the funds necessary to finance twenty-five young men each year at the Winter Farmers' course at the Agricultural College, Truro, for the next five years, and that a committee be appointed to direct all details."[43]

Nonetheless, the most persistent theme throughout the Rural Conference meetings was the call for the institutionalization of the reform agenda. At the second Conference (held in late 1924) Coady had argued for a program of adult education for the masses; in 1925, we hear of more talk about the university directing study clubs; at the fourth Conference, held in November 1926, the assembled conversed about the possible establishment of a school of Rural Education.[44]

These demands climaxed in the 1927 Rural Conference, held on September 28 and 29. At this Conference, the reformers were organized and politically prepared. Terrible events in the coal fields and agitation in the fishing villages prepared the ground for reformers to articulate the collective plight of the farmer, fishermen and industrial worker. Even the arch-conservative Church hierarchy admitted that something had to be done in the industrial and fishing communities. Pressing their beleaguered Church to respond to the new industrial order, reformers such as Father D.J. Mac-Donald insisted that the Church would "lose ground unless it does something to satisfy the aspirations of the workingmen." Not surprisingly, Tompkins, fresh from the uprising of fishermen on the Canso coast, argued that "too much stress was being placed on agriculture. Prosperity depends much more on industry, commerce and manufacturing."

The Royal Commission inquiring into the Atlantic fishery published its investigation in May 1928; this report provided curricular themes for discussion at the sixth Rural Conference, held on October 8-9, 1928. The educational propaganda of the reformers was evident in the Commission's recommendations. The Revs. Michael Gillis and L.J. Keats made this historic recommendation at the October Rural Conference:

> That whereas the economic well-being of a people depends to a large extent on their acquaintance with economic history and economic and sociological forces at work is exploited now, because of the lack of knowledge of these forces at work in a country; And whereas it is believed that the common worker is exploited now, because of the lack of knowledge of these forces and principles; And whereas the time would not appear opportune for the adoption of adult education for the whole of Canada and particularly for the Maritime Provinces; Therefore, be it resolved that we pledge our support to the organization that would in the opinion of a committee to be appointed by the conference, best formulate the policy of Adult education; And be it further resolved that his conference authorize the proper agencies in this problem.[45]

Pressure to create the St. Francis Xavier University Extension Department had reached the boiling point, and developments within the Scottish Catholic Society, it appears, added oil to the fire. At their ninth annual convention held at Judique on July 17, 1928, Colin MacKenzie, the national treasurer, recommended that one hundred thousand dollars be raised over a period of five years to support rural education. Three months later, at a meeting held in Sydney on October, 24, 1928, Bishop Morrison commended the proposition, and a decision was made to proceed with the project.[46] In an honours essay written in partial fulfillment of the requirements for a B.A. in April 1947, John Glasgow observed,

> the move by the Scottish Catholic Society to proceed independently had been inspired partly by desperation, partly by the psychological motive of hastening the decision of those in charge of the University at the time. Whether this had any influence is difficult to say, but once the university had decided to move, the campaign plans for funds by the Scottish Catholic Society were dropped and the decision was made to support the College authorities in their new venture.[47]

On November 27, 1928, the St. Francis Board of Governors adopted unanimously the resolution to establish an Extension Department. The reformers had travelled down a rocky road in order to get their institution.

Something was seriously wrong in Nova Scotia. This beautiful land was in the depths of terrible suffering and agony. Every major sector of the economy, from the feudal conditions prevailing in fishing and coal mining, to a languishing agriculture, was in trouble. The dominant cultural institutions were experiencing their own internal crises of meaning and purpose. Stories from the coal fields (starving men and women, death by influenza) and from the fisheries (men and women barely able to feed their families) were making their way through the communities and into elite circles. It was particularly galling for Nova Scotians of progressive outlook to hear the stories of one Cape Breton clergymen, who revealed that families in his district were living on 4 cents a day. He told of families where the children were clothed in discarded flour bags and where the only bedclothes were old feed bags.

Bishop Morrison travelled into the coal fields. He wrote to his priests in late December 1925 that he had "very direct evidence that there is a large number of people who are the verge of starvation from which for the time being they are being precariously saved from day to day by the heroic effort of the less unfavored few of the affected communities." He counselled his priests not to be "callous or indifferent to such a grave menace."[48]

CHAPTER 3

Fields of Lost Opportunity

I

n the fall of 1930, like explorers surveying the possibilities and dangers that lay before them, Moses Coady and A.B MacDonald were ready for a magnitudinous adventure and uncertain fortune. Through the St. Francis Xavier University Extension Department, these men, now cast in the role of the people's intellectuals, were poised to start tackling the economic problems of the Maritimes.

Faint tremors of the new industrialism had been felt in the peaceful Margaree Valley of Coady's boyhood in the 1890s. However, throughout the 1920s, the upheavals of economic, political and cultural change were large in scale. Nova Scotia was in extreme turmoil about its economic condition and perplexed regarding its future possibilities. Enlightening the people to become masters of their own economic destiny must have seemed to many Nova Scotians to be an impossible project of "excessive expectations."[1]

Moses Michael Coady believed that he had been born at the tail end of the "golden age of the Maritimes." His narrative of the fall into an age of decline framed the thinking and action of the Extension intellectuals. Coady brilliantly fashioned a narrative of economic history into an appealing prophetic story that resonated first in the culture of eastern Nova Scotia and later in other parts of the world. Like the prophets of old, Coady would proclaim that the end of one world, the age of mercantilism, opened the way for the reception of a new one. The grief of Nova Scotians would permit them a new venture, a new journey. Living in the exile of a fallen world, the people could become "holy" and move out into another reality. And their memory of a time of self-reliance and mastery, would keep alive the possibility of a rejuvenated world in new historical circumstances.[2]

From 1850 to 1880, Coady thought that the story of settlement had been reasonably bright. Nova Scotia's 21,428 square miles, lauded by poet and singer alike, had been settled primarily by English, French, Irish and Scots.[3] The Diocese of Antigonish covered seven counties, with a total population in 1931 of 197.115. Of these, 97,887 were Catholic, with 50 percent residing in the coal towns. Sixty thousand Scottish Highlanders were scattered in the small farm and fishing communities, and they would also migrate into the coal and steel towns in the early twentieth century.

Coady believed that the settlers were people of "calm sanity and sturdy dependability." Their character matched the ruggedness of the land. "Here," Coady exclaimed, "we have the vigorous nights of winter–the wild, strong dawns in which the fishing fleets put out to sea. Here is hardship that destroys the weak and strengthens the strong. This territory, then, provides an excellent social laboratory." In the fashion of the day, Coady thought that a rugged character could not develop in warmer, tropical climates and that the cold, hard north produced more dynamic cultures and peoples.

The myth of the age of wood, wind and sail, so celebrated in Maritime folklore and song, originated in the "great boon" that lumbering, farming and fishing provided to shipbuilding and commerce. Coady participated in the romance of wooden ships and men of steel. "Wooden ships," he observed, "sailed from Nova Scotia ports to every known land. Not only did these industries prosper, but Nova Scotians built up a sound financial structure. Here were established no less than eight banks." The economic dynamism of the pre-Confederation Maritime economy fed ships and timber into Great Britain's "expanding commercial network, giving rise to a significant indigenous group of commercial capitalists."[4]

In 1867, Nova Scotia and New Brunswick were pulled into Confederation, a fateful historic moment. In Coady's narration, the residents of Nova Scotia, who "had a satisfactory trade agreement with England, the West Indies, and other parts of the world, were opposed and were taken into Confederation by their legislature." The consequences were drastic: "Repeal agitation began almost immediately and in the election which followed, the people overwhelmingly sustained Joseph Howe in his Repeal platform. The question was carried to the British Parliament and Confederation was upheld. Prince Edward Island joined in 1873." Coady believed that the "fear of the people of eastern Canada, that Confederation would be detrimental to the Maritime Provinces, was well-founded."

"From about 1880," Coady tells us, the "story is one of decline and decay. Population dwindled and business fell away to such an extent that Maritime Canada, especially Nova Scotia, has been called the graveyard of industry." Coady laid the blame at the door of Sir John A. MacDonald's "National Policy," designed in 1879 to hold the country together. However, the National Policy had

> unquestionably worked to the disadvantage of the Maritime Provinces. They were forced to buy in a protected market and sell in an unprotected one. It had been originally contended that the improvement in transportation facilities effected by the opening of the Intercolonial railway and the disappearance of inter-provincial tariffs would prove advantageous to the Maritimes and Canada ("The Maritme Setting." *Masters of Their Own Destiny*, original manuscript).

It worked for a time, but Maritime vulnerability was exposed, and the Maritimes ended up being forced to buy "most of its manufactured articles from central Canada." Central Canadian manufacturing firms, protected by tariffs, of sufficient size to be cost effective and able to market to a growing population, swallowed up Maritime companies. The small manufacturing base, Coady laments, was "destroyed in Nova Scotia." The completion of the Transcontinental railway, the eventual disappearance of tariff protection and the increasing economies of scale pounded nails into the Maritimes manufacturing sector's coffin. The National Policy cast the Maritimes to the economic periphery, turning it into the eternal "land of the commissions." The Maritimes had now earned the dubious right to be called the problem child of Confederation.

From 1890 to 1914, the Maritime regional economy declined steadily, sector by sector, with the qualified exceptions of coal and steel. Manufacturing output in central Canada slowly outpaced that in eastern Canada, growing at the rate of 4.3 percent to the Maritimes' 2.3 percent. While the labour force in manufacturing declined in the Maritimes, central Canada's labour force was now five times greater. The Maritimes' export of end-products also declined, and the regional market experienced slow growth. People began to leave—the infamous diaspora—with the Maritimes retaining its largely rural character in comparison to the rest of Canada. Coady would return often to the theme of the "de-population of the land," troubled that Nova Scotia had lost the critical mass of people needed to harness resources and human potential. However, it would be significant for the Movement that the Maritimes was "overrepresented in the fishery and in logging/lumbering industries."[5]

Coady's social laboratory, however, seemed singularly well blessed in natural resources. At any rate, Nova Scotia seemed to possess "large deposits of minerals, especially coal." Writing in the late 1930s, Coady estimated that she had "nine billion tons of coal yet unmined." Nova Scotia also had significant deposits of gypsum, gold and other minerals. Rich farmlands were found on her north-west side, from Cape Sable in southern Nova Scotia to Cape North in Cape Breton. Large areas were "admirably suited" to mixed and dairy farming and the lush Annapolis Valley was Canada's largest apple-growing area. The forests of New Brunswick and Nova Scotia (71 percent of Nova Scotia was covered with forest) were another "great asset of Eastern Canada." Although Coady thought that the forests had "passed over to financial concerns that [were] exploiting them for private profit," the people of eastern Canada had in their forests a "natural resource of the highest import which, if scientifically handled, [could] be preserved forever." (In his extension years, Coady emerged as a passionate conservationist and advocate of organic farming.)

While the west may have had its expansive prairies, eastern Canada had its "own great and fertile prairie," the Atlantic sea, which Coady described as an "expanse of water–the broad Atlantic–now calmly glittering under the summer's sun, now raging under a low, stormy sky." All native-born Maritimers loved the sea; it was their "worthy adversary." It also had the "great fishing banks of the North Atlantic," "table lands rising from the ocean's floor, totalling 70,000 square miles in area."

The fishery plays a very important role in the story of Coady and the Antigonish Movement. Highly decentralized, the fishery was organized on a small producer basis. Fishermen and their families lived in rural communities and villages hugging the shore. For most of these "sharecroppers of the sea," as Coady called them, fishing was a part-time occupation. They cultivated gardens, ranging in size from small garden plots in unfavourable, rocky settings to larger, more productive farms along the Northumberland Strait. The in-shore fishermen worked in the woods and took miscellaneous jobs to supplement their very modest incomes. In places such as Canso, the women worked in the fish plants for a pittance. Their culture was profoundly shaped by their harsh environment (the widow walk atop some Nova Scotia houses is there for good reason).

The fishermen were fiercely individualistic. They were self-reliant and lived a "hand-to-mouth" existence. They had little capital for reinvestment in the fishery.[6] The fishermen and their families did not have much formal education, and illiteracy rates were particularly high in these communities. And, throughout the 1920s, many would be hungry, destitute and desperate.

From the mid-1880s until 1910, the Maritime fishery contributed enormously to the total output of the Maritimes; this growth would sharply decline between 1911 and 1939. Still, from 1921 to 1926, 37 percent of all the fish caught in Canada were from the Atlantic. The commercial products consisted of cod, haddock, hake, herring, halibut, pollock, mackerel, sardines, salmon, smelts, alewives, swordfish, tuna and shellfish, principally lobsters, scallops, oysters and clams. Approximately thirty thousand fishermen and their families, settled along the coastline of Nova Scotia and New Brunswick (17,335 in Nova Scotia), were employed in the Maritime fishery. The MacLean Commission concluded rightly that "the fishing industry may therefore be regarded not only as of vital importance to the Maritime Provinces but also as a most valuable asset to Canada."

After World War I, the fishery began to go into decline. In 1919, the value of the Maritime fishery was $15,145,066; two years later, in 1921, it had fallen to $9,778,623. From 1923 the fishery was in a state of depression. Throughout the 1930s, fishermen averaged an income of little more than $244 per year. Everything was working against them. International, subsidized competition from Norway and Iceland for the dry fish markets cut into the Maritime market. For Coady, one of the

> most striking contrasts in the modern fishing industry, as compared with that of the pre-confederation period [wa]s the very marked decrease in the relative importance of dried cod exports, one of the mainstays of the whole Nova Scotia economy. This product ha[d] fallen in recent years from its lofty and traditional preeminence to a position, in terms of value-product, far below that of lobster, a relative newcomer among Maritime exports.

From his vantage point at the end of the 1930s, the fishing industry had found "partial compensation for this major loss in the parallel increase in fresh and canned fish sale. Live lobsters are now," he claimed, "the leading contributors to the income of Maritime fishermen. They are shipped largely to Boston, New York, Montreal, and Toronto, markets which have become of first magnitude only since the opening of the present century."[7]

In many ways, the fishery was primarily a barter system with a wicked twist. The bargaining power of one of the parties, the fishermen, had been almost entirely eliminated. The notorious fish merchants squeezed profits out of the fishermen by keeping prices low, and fishermen were also bound to the merchants through unscrupulous credit practices. The merchants could easily maintain their cost-price differentials because the individual producers were, essentially, in competition with each other. As the United Maritime Fishermen (UMF) put it in a brief to the Royal Commission on Co-operatives in 1945, in depression circumstances, the fishermen were as "helpless as one of his own dories in a typhoon." In the rough waters of post-World War I, when fish buyers and processors began to curtail their marketing operations, fishing communities were left "without an established marketing agency of any kind, except perchance the local merchant who at times took fish in barter for groceries and supplies at his own high price."[8] By 1926, eleven trawlers were operating in Maritime waters. Their presence symbolized an emergent structural conflict between a capital-intensive and labour-intensive fishery.

The village of Grand Etang, one of the largest Acadian villages, is situated on the rugged north-west shore of Cape Breton, and its story well illustrates some of the troubles of Nova Scotian fishermen. A relatively large parish, it consisted of 160 families with a total population of about 800 in the 1920s. For generations, the people of Grand Etang had subsisted on the sea without neglecting farming and while retaining considerable skill in handicrafts. Of Norman ancestry, the Acadians had settled in the area in the early nineteenth century. Closely knit, attached to tradition and religion, the parents and grandparents of the generation of the twenties had lived simple, self-sufficient lives and had produced most of their own food and clothing.

In 1876 Robin, Jones and Whitman had opened a branch of their Cheticamp organization in Grand Etang. They bought fish and sold groceries, general merchandise and fishermen's supplies. Before 1915, Grand Etang had thirty-two sailing vessels with crews of four men. The fishermen who owned the boats eventually lost them, placing them at the mercy of the fish barons, who determined the prices. The fishermen of Grand Etang never knew what their returns would be. Even when markets were favourable, the higher prices paid for fish were matched by higher prices for equipment, food and clothing. At the end of the season, a Grand Etang fisherman received no itemized statement regarding his standing in the business organization. Not infrequently, fishermen were simply told that they had an outstanding account of $50. Their debts accumulated through the winter; by spring fishermen had received credit for food, clothing and other supplies. Fishermen received very low prices for their catches and their returns were seldom in cash. Nor were they free to market their fish elsewhere; the buyers held them tightly to the payment of their debts. (When Coady visited Grand Etang in the fall of 1929, a majority of the fishermen were open to organizing for study to co-operate. The ground had, however, been prepared by the work of Father Joseph A. DeCoste who had been stirring up his parishioners to advance their educational and economic standing.[9])

The old system of marketing was ludicrously haphazard. Each fishermen processed his own fish, which led to a lack of uniformity and indifferent quality. Dealers paid low prices so that fishermen had little incentive to process and display a high-quality, attractive product. Commenting on the "Problems of the Fishing Industry" at the Rural and Industrial Conference held at Antigonish in August 1939, R.J. MacSween complained that Nova Scotia's oldest industry, the source of livelihood for one-sixth of Nova Scotia's population, had "failed to gain her share of the increased markets" and had "lost a large portion of the markets she once held." MacSween believed that an "exceedingly high proportion" of the shore fishermen were ill equipped to do their work efficiently. Their boats, gear and shore facilities were "far below standard" and, in some cases, "hopelessly out of date." Under these conditions, fishing operations could only be conducted with an "appalling waste of time and energy."

MacSween lambasted the outmoded methods used for handling the fish upon landing. Fishermen, he said, still left their fish to the vagaries of the elements. "Surely," he lamented,

in this age of progress some means could be devised of drying and preparing fish more scientifically and economically than by sun drying with its attendant hazards and its guesswork. And surely an up-to-date central fish store, owned and operated co-operatively in each community, would be more business-like than the multiplicity of dilapidated shacks now being used on our shores.

Fish could not be sold on "sentiment rather than on merit; on tradition rather than on quality appeal." How had it come to this?

> Along the shores of this fair Province the system still prevails under which many of the fishermen barter their season's catch of fish in return for supplies and the necessities of life. The price to be paid for the fish and the amount to be charged for the supplies is entirely in the hands of the merchant, and in many cases the price is not divulged until many weeks after the transaction has taken place.[10]

The UMF thought of its work as liberating a "sorely depressed people from economic bondage."[11] They weren't wrong.

II

The Extension Department's intellectuals and organizers had a big challenge ahead of them. Oppressed peoples often slide into cultures of resignation and defeatism; their economically and socially induced condition, after awhile, seems part of the inexorable fatalities of life. Coady took particular interest in the fate of fishermen and their industry throughout his Extension years. He often thought of adult education as dynamite, exploding encrusted minds into new imaginings and beginnings, and the feudalistic fishing industry needed plenty of dynamite. Even after ten years of arduous fieldwork and organization, it was still evident that the fishermen were difficult to organize and educate. Submissions to the endless Commissions—MacLean (1927), Jones (1934), Stevens (1935)—deplored the "lack of organization among the fishermen ... urging the formation of cooperative societies in the fishing communities."[12]

Alexander Laidlaw, a co-operator of pragmatic temper who would be Coady's number-one assistant in the early 1940s, thought that the fishery suffered acutely from a "lack of scientific attitude on the part of most people engaged in it." He didn't think that the early fishermen in the Maritimes had been either conservation-minded or interested in a rational management of the resource. In 1885, for example, one hundred million pounds of lobster had been harvested; by 1918, the catch had dropped to twenty-seven million pounds. The MacLean Commission had documented the careless way female lobsters were harvested. The state paid little attention to the "industrial aspects of the industry and were quite unconcerned about educational programs for the development of the fishery."

Laidlaw and the Antigonish intellectuals thought that the Atlantic fishery was strangely anomalous. How could an industry with such "great potential wealth for the Atlantic provinces" be supporting the "poorest class of people and the most backward communities"? Lack of research, lack of improvement of fish products, means of inspection scoffed at by commercial interests, little attention paid to the educational side of the fishery. The agricultural representatives had played the role of friend and counsellor to the farmers; the Fisheries officers often acted as policemen to an anarchic industry. "For too long," Laidlaw lamented, "the fishery was permitted to languish in backwardness and unscientific attitude. Its future prosperity and vigor must be based on greater enlightenment and widespread education."[13]

Economic historian James Bickerton believes that the Maritimes failed to "capitalize on the obvious strengths of its 19th century economy, particularly the vitality of its shipping and shipbuilding sectors."[14] By the century's turn, the Maritimes' natural industrial sector, shipbuilding, had been seriously neglected. It lacked customers mainly because the Canadian state was not interested in defence issues, the fishery remained labour-intensive, generating little demand for "mechanized and motorized steel-hulled vessels,"[15] and trade was diverted from Canadian ports. Repeated Maritime protests about the central government's failure to route significant trade through the ports of St. John and Halifax fell on deaf ears.

Cold statistics about the decline of manufacturing bothered Coady because he believed they did "not reflect the loss of the craftsmen who once constituted an integral part of the rural economy of these provinces."[16] Unemployed manufacturing workers added to the exodus from a troubled land (between 1901 and 1911, 24,000 rural inhabitants left for the "Boston states," points west and elsewhere). The lumber industry declined as the opening of the Panama Canal and lower ocean freight rates enabled west coast products to gain the upper hand. The iron and steel industries lost locational advantages as the tariffs were removed from imported coal. Coady thought that the relatively rapid development of iron and steel manufacturing had benefited from the "construction of railways and the National Policy,"[17] but the decline became a "real crisis in the 1920s. The period from 1923 to [1939]," Coady claimed, "might appropriately be called the Age of Royal Commissions. Every major industry has been investigated in turn."[18]

For a few years after the National Policy, Coady noted, the coal industry had flourished, but the "steady decadence of the coal industry" had "contributed more than any other single factor to that general condition of business decline which precipitated the movement for Maritime rights."[19] Coady deplored the way depletion of reserves in certain areas, increasing costs associated with the ever-growing distance between coal-face and pit head in the older mines of Cape Breton and Pictou County, as well as the inability to meet the competition from low-cost Pennsylvania coal, which enjoyed a double advantage of mining more accessible coal with more advanced technology, plunged the coalfields into chaos.[20]

From the 1890s well into the 1930s, "King Coal" was without doubt the most ruthless laird Nova Scotians had ever known. From 1893 to 1913, huge numbers of Nova Scotians and European immigrants entered the coal fields. Glace Bay, the centre of labour militancy and communist organizing, grew from 6,945 to 16,562 between 1901 and 1910. Many rural families (primarily from Victoria and Inverness counties) dealt with their economic uncertainty by moving to burgeoning industrial areas. Eighty-two percent of Glace Bay residents were Canadian born, the majority of whom were Scots who carried their deep sense of community and culture into the coal fields. In this "great trek" from farm to mine, they transported their religion. The census for 1901-1931 reveals that 52 percent of the population was Catholic; 29 percent was Presbyterian and 11 percent, other Protestant denominations. In 1931, 19 percent joined the new United Church of Canada; around three hundred Jews resided in Glace Bay by the early 1930s.

These miners shared many things in common. Their Christian outlook and values had been formed in a largely pre-industrial world. The majority shared Anglo-Celtic ethnic heritage and memories of the clearances; European-born immigrants were likewise often fleeing execrable economic and social conditions. The underground experience bound the men and their families to the pit. The coal culture was masculinist, sexist, rough and militant. The absence of a dynamic middle-class in Glace Bay forged a strong craft consciousness. An "us" against "them" outlook prevailed, but the presence of a minority of Europeans, from places like the Ukraine, presented a challenge to the community. They would face accusations that they were the source of the dreaded "Bolshevism."

It takes little imagination to locate the source of "class consciousness" in the Nova Scotia coal fields. From the early 1880s, coal miners faced employers who could call upon the state to send in the troops when things became rough or threatening. The manager of the Drummond colliery, Westville, managed to get a detachment of militia to protect him in 1879. The miners and steelworkers would see a lot of the soldiers in ensuing years. During the late nineteenth century, rank and file members of the moderate Provincial Workingman's Association (PWA; founded in 1879) wanted fortnightly wages, benefit societies and the abolition of company stores. The PWA's main political tactic was to use the courts to win some benefits from the coal and steel barons. This tactic would later be scorned by communist militants such as J.B. MacLachlan and "Red" Dan Livingstone.

Under the old system of local mines and owners, the companies had some tie to the local community. One of Coady's ancestors, Pierie Coady, had worked in such a mine in Sydney Mines. With the shift to monopoly capitalism, however, first by the Dominion Coal Company, then its successors, the British Empire Steel and Coal Company (BESCO) and Dominion Steel and Coal Company (DOSCO), the old paternalism of the small companies was snapped like a dry twig. Workers would now confront the likes of Roy ("the Wolf") Wolvin, BESCO's president and perhaps the most hated man in Nova Scotian history, whose profit strategy was simple. He assaulted the workers, reducing their wages by from 20 to 40 percent and refused to countenance a steelworkers' union.[21]

The miners and steelworkers faced each other like brawling giants in the boxing ring. A turning point for militant unionism came in 1909. The United Mine Workers of America (UMWA), District 26, was formed in March. Almost immediately, the Dominion Coal Company resolved to smash the union. The owners feared that their advantage in the American market, gained by paying exceedingly low wages and extracting long hours of work, would be lost if the workers gained a strong and militant union. Workers identified with the UMWA were fired; spies and company police infiltrated meetings and recorded names; miners who had worked lucrative "rooms" found themselves condemned to work in poor, wet, less lucrative conditions. The UMWA applied for a Board of Conciliation to stop the intimidation and meet their demands. The Board's report came down: the men learned that the company had not discriminated against the workers or treated them harshly.

The Board's ruling appeared to licence the Dominion Coal Company to terrorize and intimidate the mining communities of Nova Scotia.[22] UMWA leaders, including J.B. MacLachlan and Dan MacDougall, were fired. So were hundreds of others. Dominion obtained permission from the Cape Breton County Council to obtain 625 constables, drawn from company ranks and "loyal" miners. Once the men were unemployed, the Company proceeded to evict them and their families, with the help of the constables, from their dreary company homes. The fired men were replaced with transients and waterfront alcoholics, dredged up from the grimy port cities of Halifax and Montreal. Recruiters even went as far as Bulgaria to obtain new miners, luring them with promises never fulfilled. The collieries became armed camps. High fences were built around the collieries, topped with electrified wire. Housing for scab labour was also protected by these imposing barricades.

On July 6, 1909, a fateful day in Nova Scotian and labour history, UMWA, District 26, called a strike. The miners and their families would suffer unbearably during the next ten bitter months, barely surviving the ghastly winter of 1909-10 as diseases such as cholera, typhoid, scarlet fever and diphtheria touched nearly every household. In the end, the union was defeated. J.B. MacLachlan and hundreds of other miners were blacklisted; J.B. would never work in the mines again. He and his wife, Kate, and their children moved to a farm to keep body and soul together, but MacLachlan, the Scottish-born labour leader, would continue to exercise his leadership through pen and persuasion from his new place.

From the great strike of 1909 until the mid-1920s, miners battled each other to create the kind of union capable of facing off with Dominion Coal. In 1920, BESCO reorganized the Cape Breton coal and steel industry. No one in the coal fields could have imagined what was in store for them over the next five or six years. In the spring of 1920, Roy Wolvin took charge of BESCO, then the third-largest employer in Canada. After 1920, inflation and the cost of living soared out of control, bringing long hours, low pay and decreased shifts. Even moderate commentators on the struggles within the Cape Breton coal fields such as Eugene Forsey thought that Wolvin was exceptionally ruthless and hard-hearted. He was willing, it seemed, to literally starve the workers into submission. Imbued with anti-union and anti-socialist beliefs, perhaps he thought he was fighting a kind of "holy war" against MacLachlan and the coal and steel workers. As C.E.O., he faced serious problems in marketing Cape Breton coal, but his only solution seemed to lie in massively cutting workers' wages. By the end of 1922, suffering in the mining communities was utterly horrendous.[23]

On March 17, 1922, a desperate J.B. MacLachlan saw no possibility of justice unless capitalism and its state servants were overthrown. He declared war on BESCO. His vision of secular redemption through class warfare propelled the workers into an ill-fated strike. On July 3, 1923, at a meeting in the Alexander Rink in Glace Bay, 10,000 workers laid down their tools. Shortly thereafter, MacLachlan and "Red" Dan Livingstone were arrested and taken off to jail in Halifax. The coal fields were at war. Wolvin closed the Inverness mine, introduced a 20 percent wage cut in November 1924 and cut off credit at the company stores. *The Maritime Labour Herald's* office was burned down.

In the horrific month of June 1925, the coal fields exploded in violence and rampage. The workers in the coal fields of Cape Breton were suffering from acute privation and spiritual exhaustion. Fuelled by despair, desperation and alcohol, workers burned down the two antiquated wash houses (which had been a focus of complaint for years). They burned down company stores, looting hundreds of thousands of dollars worth of goods. Colliery No. 10 was flooded. The New Waterford collieries were seriously damaged. As the flames engulfed the coal fields, the miners, steelworkers and their families must have thought hell had come to earth. Some clergy members tried to prevent the workers from murdering their enemies. To this day, grandchildren of the strikers recall stories of looting by the starving, of women running through the streets with garlands of sausage twisted around their necks.

By August 15, 1925, the troops had left the coal fields. The miners had lost seven million dollars in wages. Still, BESCO demanded wage cuts. After five long months, the men were forced to go back to work. They accepted a wage cut of from 6 to 8 percent. On October 29, 1925, a federal election precipitated an inquiry into the troubles in the Nova Scotia coal industry. The "Old Rector" of St.FX, Hugh MacPherson, served as one of the commissioners. The Commission found high infant mortality rates in all mining communities controlled by BESCO. Dr. A.S. Kendall, a medical friend of the workers, told of mass outbreaks of scarlet fever, diphtheria and other diseases. Readers were informed of poor sanitary conditions, deplorable housing, prolonged malnutrition. Many had succumbed. Still BESCO continued to refuse to "open their books," wanting more wage cuts. In the end, the workers were "exhausted, beaten and damaged."[24]

BESCO's campaign had used blacklisting, control over housing and food, control of the press and an expanded police force to control the mining population. The Dominion government had stood by, hands in pockets, claiming that the troubles were outside their jurisdiction. Provincial state elites had little trouble repressing the UMWA, of ridding itself of the "Bolsheviks in our midst." Anti-Bolshevism was politically saleable. The workers also had to face the intervention of American labour boss John L. Lewis, who co-operated openly with BESCO to restrict District 26's autonomy. District 26 ended up badly divided; in 1932 yet another breakaway union would be formed. For the communists, the defeat of 1925 marked the end of their hold on the soul of the coal fields. Their project went up with the smoke of the burning collieries and company stores. The communists would never recover their influence in industrial Cape Breton, though a lively residue continued to agitate throughout the 1930s.

How did Moses Coady, the Catholic priest, respond to the dispiriting events in the coal fields? Coady observed that industrial development in Cape Breton in the early part of the century had brought in a "large influx of coal and steel workers from Great Britain and Southern Europe." They were often the source of "advanced social ideas that [had] proved a great source of trouble during the past three decades." Coady thought that the violent strikes of 1909 and 1925 had been fostered to a "great extent by the agitation of radical leaders from the Old Country." He was a lifelong foe of the communists and communism; they were his nemesis. However, he had grudging respect for J.B. MacLachlan, the Protestant Scot who was "reputed to be one of the most energetic Communists of Canada," publishing a "paper called 'The Nova Scotia Miner' which is openly Communistic and enjoys a comparatively wide circulation among the miners." *The Miner* enjoyed taking potshots at the Antigonish Movement once it got rolling in the industrial sectors. In *The Miner*'s April 6, 1935, issue, Fred X wondered, if it were "true that cooperatives offer such virtues for the economic and social ills of the workers, wasn't it very strange that it has remained until this deplorable stage in our economic development before its wonderful merits were discovered." Fred X was opposed to the Antigonish

Movement's ideology, which "falsely led" the people "up a blind alley, unconscious of their destiny."

Coady identified two sources of communism in the coal fields. One source was a "group of Ukrainians, about sixty families of whom are reputed to be Communistic in their tendencies." They organized young communist schools, with 115 children in attendance; 80 children participated in the May Day parade of 1926. In Dominion, they held concerts on Sunday evenings. Coady was particularly troubled that Catholicism was allegedly ridiculed at some of these meetings. "Several Catholic foreigners," Coady noted, "left these societies when they found that if they followed the doctrine of Lenin their babies could not be baptized. It is known and has been reported to government authorities that secret meetings have been carried on at which the Red Flag was displayed and revolutionary songs sung." A second source, the "real centre" of "communist activity in the town of Glace Bay," was the "Rukasin Building where a flourishing Communist educational club is carried on by the principal leader of the movement." The members of the Rukasin Club were "gradually indoctrinating legitimate trade-unionists with the revolutionary philosophy."[25]

Like the communists, Coady believed that the industrial workers had suffered from the abuses of the capitalist class; they were "harassed workers." However, the presence of "large numbers of propertyless wage-earners" was a matter of grave concern for Church and society. Without a "stake in the ground," Coady thought, the workers would look to others for the "solution of all their problems. This offers fertile field for the radical agitator. The general remedy for this is to hasten the day when as many of them as possible will own their own homes, and become wedded to the community by taking a hand in their own economic affairs." Like other thoughtful Catholics of the time, Coady feared most that the "grave unemployment situation" and "evident abuses" prepared the way for the masses to defect from their faith. "Something must be done," he exclaimed in 1934, "and done quickly, to render this occasion remote if the people are to remain loyal to the Church." Coady wanted an "adequate substitute for the allurements of socialism and communism." He also knew that a merely "negative program which consists of blanket condemnations of communism or socialism" would not keep industrial workers in the Church. The "plight of the Church" was intertwined with the "plight of the people."

III

Anyone surveying the economic condition of the Maritimes at the end of the 1920s couldn't help grieving over its loss of control of its destiny. Maritime provincial governments now had less influence in Ottawa.

Manufacturing had slipped from the Maritimes' grasp. The traditional primary economy of fish, lumber and agriculture was languishing, unable to respond to new challenges. The coal fields were in a shambles. Labour historian Ian MacKay believes that the "fatal weaknesses" of the Maritime economy had been revealed in the 1910s: economic dependence, an unreconstructed state and an absence of a unified business class with a coherent strategy of development.[26] MacKay also thinks that the 1910s were the last decade when the burning question "How can we adjust to this dizzying pace of economic growth and social change?" was asked. Thereafter, he says, Maritimers would only wonder how they could attract capital, fated to a cap-in-hand existence. Coady and the Antigonish intellectuals would have disagreed with MacKay, the late twentieth-century ironist.

The new industrialism was reshaping the everyday lives of Nova Scotians and other Maritimers. It was also generating various kinds of protest movements in the different sectors of the economy and in civil society.[27] In Halifax, the capital city of Nova Scotia, progressives—animated largely by Protestant "social gospel" beliefs in the possibility of a more harmonious and just social order—fought for female suffrage, a more sober population, planned towns, public health and housing, technical education and domestic science. The Halifax Local Council of Women entered male political bastions through the skilful extension of "women's issues" into public debate. They fought for the protection of young, working-class women who were vulnerable to unscrupulous men in the rougher parts of the city. They fought for more playgrounds for children and sought female representation on local boards. They pressured the state from their civil society bases using the new languages of "efficiency" and "function." And the intrepid *Halifax Herald* carried the new language of reform into the public sphere. Indeed, the *Herald*'s coterie of journalists, women such as Evelyn Tufts and men such as Kingsley Brown, wrote unwaveringly in support of the Antigonish Movement's initiatives well into the 1930s.

In the sphere of education, higher and lower, a small awakening was occurring in the early twentieth century. The Agricultural College at Truro was firmly in the hands of the Dr. M.M. Cumming. Cumming had close links with Antigonish reformers such as Tompkins and "Little Doc" Hugh MacPherson and advocated progressive approaches to farming. Cumming pressed for a scientific approach to farming's many problems; he was one of Nova Scotia's great advocates for extension programs among the agricultural workers. In higher education, progressives such as J.J. Tompkins spearheaded a movement for the amalgamation of Nova Scotia's small sectarian universities into the University of Halifax around 1921 and 1922. This is an oft-told story, but Tompkins was not alone in criticizing Nova Scotian universities for their paralysis in the face of massive economic and social problems. *Knowledge for the People*, self-published in 1921, was an educational call to his own university to respond to the plight of its people—or else. By the mid-1920s, teachers were waking up from their slumber. With Coady's assistance, they had revitalized their union. In the mid-1920s, a dynamic visionary named Dr. Henry Munro, the new superintendent of Education, began to shake things up within the school system. He was a great friend of adult education, assuming the presidency of the Canadian Association for Adult Education in the late-1930s.

In July 1920, something new broke in to the dreary world of Nova Scotian party politics. Voicing "their protests against the contemporary preoccupation with urban and industrial development,"[28] farmers had shifted allegiance to a third party, the United Farmers, electing seven farm and four labour candidates in the provincial election. This was a wake-up call to the government and reflected the farmers' struggle to find alternative economic solutions, such as co-operatives. The Maritime United Farmers Cooperative was founded in 1920, publishing the *United Farmers Guide* that same year. And the Maritime Rights movement emerged as a form of political protest to restore the "conditions that had nurtured industrial development in the first place." Neither the third party nor the Rights movement could survive the "massively dislocating economic factors,"[29] nor could militant trade-unionism. Yet, despite the lack of success of varied protest movements, a tiny renaissance was beginning in Nova Scotia.

At the beginning of 1930, then, Father Moses Coady and the growing cadre of reform-minded priests of the Diocese of Antigonish faced huge, not to say overwhelming, problems. The first problem for Coady and the Antigonish reformers lay with his own Church. The Roman Catholic Church of the Diocese of Antigonish had been largely paralyzed by the troubles in industrial Cape Breton. Through the nineteenth century, the Church had fashioned a viable, rural, socially conservative Catholicism, a kind of fortress Catholicism that struggled to keep out new ideas and hold on to its constituents. Its celebration of hard work on the land and sea, parishioners meeting God in church and nature, its emphasis on charity for the unfortunate, had worked fairly well in the pre-industrial world, but with the coming of the new industrialism, the Roman Church was rocked to its core. Its very identity seemed threatened as rural parishioners migrated into the pits and steel mills. Here they either worked underground, manipulating machines in the blackness, or above ground, in the face of the fiery ovens. This new industrial world seemed far from God's green earth. At home, in the shabby coaltown bars or on the playing fields, men and women of rural origin learned to think of themselves as a class, as a group bound together through a new work culture against pitiless bosses. The harsh, simple rhetoric of "proletariat versus ruling class" resonated with the experience of many Cape Breton coal and steel workers, but the new languages of trade union militancy and socialism perturbed the Church deeply.

In the early twentieth century, many priests in the diocese were opposed to unions, almost as a matter of course. Coady himself thought of unions as a "bad thing" until his revelation and experiences of the early 1920s, when he helped to organize the teachers. The strike against Dominion Coal in 1909 was a poignant moment for the Catholic Church. The strikers marched into Bridgeport only to be met by the army and machine guns that had been placed on Father Charlie MacDonald's church at Bridgeport. Events such as this increased the distance between the Church and the industrial worker. By the late 1920s, however, some priests were comfortable with collective forms of organizing to create a more just world.

The Catholic intellectuals' primary task was to forge a new social Catholicism that would be faithful to sacral traditions and speak to the modern condition. The papal encyclicals *Rerum Novarum* (1891) and *Quadragesimo Anno* (1931) provided an ambivalent conceptual frame for addressing the social question. However, they provided few specifics. Coady and his reform band would have to create an indigenous social philosophy, one crafted for the particularities of the Nova Scotian and Maritime milieu. Moses Coady had to adopt a rhetoric that didn't offend his Church and tradition, while simultaneously resonating deeply with the agonizing reality of people's lives. Rhetoric alone, though, works no miracles. The Antigonish reformers had to develop a practical project that both captured the imagination and delivered the goods.

Moses Coady and A.B. MacDonald were setting out to become nothing less than architects of a new social order. But none of us, reformers included, can simply create whatever we desire. The historical conditions of our time and place rule out some options and push us towards others. The economic conditions of Nova Scotia presented the St.FX Extension Department with formidable learning and organizing challenges. Coady had begun to organize the fishermen for co-operative action at a historic moment when the fisheries had not yet been fully incorporated into capitalist relations of production and distribution. Coady was committed to defending the in-shore fishermen's way of life. One of the major challenges he faced was to maintain the traditions of Church and sea without allowing the bypass of modernizing impulses. How could that be done? There were other lesser challenges—provincial rivalries, rifts between Acadians and Celts, internal squabbles in the UMF, fickle international markets and opposition from fish merchants, big and small.

In the coal fields, Extension faced at least two problems: one, to win the allegiance of the workers, many of whom were suspicious of the Church, and two, to craft a project of social action that could meet the pressing needs of working people in the realm of consumption. Moses Coady did not think that workers could actually gain control of production in the 1930s. In 1934, he surmised that

> with the decentralization of power and the universal use of machinery it would seem that the day has come when groups of people could co-operate to produce many of the commodities they need for personal use. It is understood, of course, that heavy industry and luxury industry should continue in the great industrial centres as they are to-day.[30]

He did imagine, though, that light industry might be shifted back to the rural areas. The reconstruction process could tackle the perennial "debt problem" and undermine capitalist control of distribution and retail processes. The Movement would also address the urgent need for adequate diet, health care, housing and libraries.

In the agricultural sector, Extension faced numerous irksome problems. The farming industry's major problem in early twentieth-century Nova Scotia was marketing. When brilliant "Little Doc" Hugh MacPherson of St. Francis Xavier University began to work with the farmers around World War I, private dealers and traders completely controlled the marketing of livestock and livestock products. Farmers had no way of knowing about the requirements of the market or prices. They relied on what the buyers told them. Much business was actually conducted on a barter basis. Worse, farmers faced uncertain markets. Nova Scotia farming also lacked consistent grading procedures. In 1913, a Royal Commission had recommended a system of grading for Canadian wool. Under MacPherson's direction, 12,000 pounds of wool were graded at Antigonish (the only grading station for the Maritimes) and marketed co-operatively in 1915.[31]

The situation of farming in Cape Breton in the early 1930s illustrates the plight of the farmer and the challenge for the adult educator. Production per farm was very small and no organized system for marketing local farm products existed. The amount of food imported into the Sydney area was simply staggering, and Cape Breton farmers failed to supply the market. There were no marketing organizations between the people in the Sydney produce trade and country producers. Extension workers faced four specific problems. First, individual farmers relied on themselves, producing small amounts, which was unattractive to the distributors of foodstuffs in the urban centres. Second, in the main, Cape Breton farmers offered poor quality articles (stale eggs, mixed lots of diseased potatoes, unfinished poultry, poorly packed berries or coarse vegetables) for the market. Third, any successful marketing requires volume. Only the "combined production" of many farms could establish lasting connections with the urban centres. Extension workers confronted the "attitudinal problem" of the individualistic farmer who conducted his business privately. Fourth, small individual farmers only peddled their stuff in the Sydney market from August to

November. They then withdrew for the rest of the year, leaving the work of supplying consumers to someone else.

MacSween recognized that this method was going nowhere fast and "would even be more hopeless in the future."[32] St.FX took its lumps in the early days when they created the Cape Breton Producers Co-operative in September 1931 to bridge the gap between the market and the potential productive capacity of the farmers. This project was constantly hampered by irregular deliveries, poorly graded produce and consumer rejection. Incorporated without capital, this co-op died a natural death after existing for a little over two years.[33]

There were, however, a number of successful co-op ventures on the economic landscape that signalled hope. The British Canadian Co-operative Society store in Sydney Mines, founded by miners in the early twentieth century, exemplified the potential of co-operative retailing. The provincial government's Department of Agriculture, through its talented agricultural representatives, was committed to co-operative solutions to Nova Scotia's marketing problems. Even the cagey premier, Angus L. MacDonald, favoured co-operatives as a partial solution for his primary industries in the early 1930s. It remained to be seen whether a coherent economic project, fusing the interests of primary producers and industrial workers, could be forged in crisis-torn, politically fragmented and culturally dispirited Nova Scotia.

CHAPTER 4

Mobilizing the People for Enlightenment (1930-1935)

I

In the fall of 1930 the work of organizing the Extension Department of St. Francis Xavier University began in earnest. The director, Moses Coady, had to turn St.FX into a dynamic educational mobilizing centre, but the university had few financial resources for this task. The department would have to find the money elsewhere. An Extension office needed to be furnished in order to meet the demands of hundreds of people in the diocese. Secretaries had to be hired to run the office. Books and literature had to be purchased. The Extension Department had only two full-time employees with whom to launch its project, but Coady had an ace up his sleeve.

Coady's assistant director, Angus Bernard MacDonald, was one of the most talented organizers and spell-binding platform speakers Canada would ever see. Like Coady, A.B. MacDonald was an impressive, big, dashing man. Always attired in a well-cut suit, MacDonald appeared to have just emerged from a corporate boardroom. His appearance was very deceptive, as this elegant man was not on the side of business interests. He proclaimed that the only safe depository of the ultimate powers of society were the people themselves. The common people loved his wit, humour, style and passionate advocacy for a people's economy. He was also tough. One story tells of MacDonald arriving at a raucous meeting hall, filled with rough lads ready to make trouble. Without missing a step, he broke a beer bottle on the edge of the table and proceeded to the platform. There was no trouble that night.

A.B. MacDonald had been hewn from strong timber and imbued with democratic ideals. Handsome, with a sense of mischief, Coady's associate had a reputation as lady's man. He had enormous energy and panache, easily moving through four or five meetings a day. Moses Coady had enormous respect for his colleague. He saw MacDonald as a "brilliant leader in a new profession, the profession of adult education for democratic action." According to Coady, MacDonald had a "keen and penetrating mind, always ahead of the people yet practical enough to keep within the range of what was possible." Coady hailed MacDonald as Canada's greatest "long distance organizer" who was "able, in a most spectacular way, to organize people from Cape North to Cape Sable, from Louisburg to Edmundston, and to do it by some kind of sixth sense of telepathy."

A.B. MacDonald had grown up on a tough Nova Scotia farm near Heatherton. Prodded by Father Jimmy to spurn the lucrative professions for a career in agriculture, MacDonald dedicated himself to "trying to build an economic empire of the little people in Canada, and all over the world."[1] Colleagues who travelled with him into people's homes, modest school houses, cold and poorly lighted halls and rough fishing shanties heard his message of hope.

As much as Coady loved blueprints, he and MacDonald did not have a detailed one in hand in the fall of 1930. Alex Laidlaw explains:

> Initially, leaders did not have a predetermined formula for the ills of the country. Whatever formula there is in the program came later. They simply went about gathering facts and spreading ideas. They found farmers discouraged, industrial workers restless, fishermen utterly disheartened, and young men and women fresh from school convinced that only far away from the Maritimes could they hope to find a satisfying life. Scepticism, lack of enthusiasm, the defeatist outlook, despair—these were all encountered and had to be broken down.[2]

As a first gesture, Coady and MacDonald had sketched an outline of "Possible Activities of the Extension Department" (probably drafted in the early summer of 1930). The general purpose of the Extension Department was to improve the "economic, social, educational and religious conditions of the people of Eastern Nova Scotia." Their initial focus was on the eastern sub-region of Nova Scotia, the locus of the Diocese of Antigonish. They wanted to survey the "economic possibilities in farming, mining, fishing, lumbering, etc." towards the "possible social improvement in industrial and rural communities." They wanted to discover the "best educational practices for the development of Eastern Nova Scotia." They envisaged short courses, both cultural and vocational; leadership training courses; correspondence courses; study clubs in the rural and industrial areas; radio courses and the development of technical and folk schools. They saw Extension extending "information" through letters, circulating libraries, organization of debates and public speaking competitions.

They also wanted to discover what agencies were working in the field. Coady and MacDonald knew well that they would not be able to make any headway in mobilizing the people for enlightenment unless Extension was linked to a social web of organizations and associations in the local communities. They saw clergy, churches, government officials, particularly agriculture representatives, existent co-operatives, community associations and professionals as some of their possible allies in Extension work. They had to proceed astutely and respectfully in the communities of Nova Scotia, many of which were mixes of Protestants and Catholics, Celts and other ethnic groups.

The Extension Department was rooted in Catholicism and ecumenical in spirit, but it had to grapple with unpleasant Nova Scotian legacies of anti-Semitism, racist attitudes towards Blacks and Mi'kmaqs and endemic religious prejudice. Sadly, even the big-hearted Moses Coady did not target Black Nova Scotians and aboriginal peoples as a priority for organizing. He did not think highly of Mi'kmaq ambition. On January 21, 1935, Coady confided in a letter to Dr. Alex Johnson of Ottawa:

> I agree with your findings but I should be interested to know how much the lack of education and consequent inactivity and lethargy of the people themselves have to do with our present plight. May it not have been that during all these years the lack of ambition and the ability to act in the right way at the right moment have been a very important cause of Maritime decline? I agree that fundamentally economic causes are responsible for a lot of things, but forty million MicMacs [sic] in the British Isles, notwithstanding the Maritime position and the position of coal and steel, would not have resulted in much of a civilization. May it not be that the human factor is underestimated in our situation?[3]

Coady was Anglo-Celtic from stem to stern and old-fashioned in outlook on race and character.

Coady informed Helen Dingman of Berea College, Kentucky, on January 24, 1938, that the

> movement we have on here can be successfully carried on with any people and in any community, irrespective of the Church they belong to…. Our movement on the whole is going just about as well as among non-Catholics as it is among Catholics. It is true that the Catholic priest is a good local leader in many cases. It is also true that he is a stumbling block in many other places. Some of them have been definitely opposed to it. Some clergymen of other denominations have been whole-heartedly with us. The whole scheme rests to some extent on the possibility of finding local leaders, be they clergymen, schoolteachers, or any other kind of leaders.[4]

The task of finding local leaders to "open up new vistas and dynamite through the lethargy of the people"[5] was fundamental. The Extension Department needed a communication network; local leaders who would serve as starting points for the study clubs and emergent forms of community action. Several prominent clergy, men such as the self-effacing, Baddeck-based United Church minister J.D. Nelson MacDonald and Coady's priestly colleagues Michael Gillis, Charles Forest, J.J. Tompkins, Leo Keats, A. Boudreau and James Boyle, devoted extraordinary amounts of time to community organizing along with ordinary parish duties. Later, Father Boudreau would turn against the co-operative movement.

On August 16, 1930, Coady and MacDonald wrote to Dr. Hugh P. MacPherson, secretary of St. Francis Xavier University's board of governors, requesting $10,000 to run the Extension Department. In 1931, Coady requested funding from the Carnegie Corporation and received $10,000. Coady would take a salary of $1,000 per annum; MacDonald would receive $4,000. They needed periodicals for the preparation of packaged libraries and a clipping service; they needed an open-shelf library, since few communities had any facilities for organized reading; they needed stenographic work for the typing of study courses, reading guides and correspondence courses.

In 1931, Coady asked Katherine Desjardins (née Thompson), a graduate of Mount St. Bernard College, Antigonish, and the Nova Scotia Teachers College, to return from New York to act as his general assistant for the Extension Department. She was a superb choice–a dedicated social reformer, excellent journalist and skilful organizer. Other talented women, such as Zita O'Hearn (née Cameron) and Ida Gallant (née Delaney) would follow Kay Thompson into the cyclonic atmosphere of the Extension Department's early days. Coady and MacDonald would soon be men with suitcases, making their way from community to community, and meeting after meeting, to create study club nuclei as necessary preparation for social action.

Father Jimmy Tompkins had said that the place to begin was at the people's own doors. Start knocking. Help them learn to act with and for others while they do their own thinking. Coady and MacDonald had learned through trial and error that, first, one had to capture the interest of the adult learner, many of whom had minimal formal education. For Nova Scotians, the idea of studying together was a unique one, never before attempted among the primary producers and industrial workers. Would it work? What were the precise techniques to be used? Second, the learning process in these small clubs could not be academic or speculative. The primary producers had to see that their learning had a pay-off, that they were solving real problems. Coady thought that Extension had to "demonstrate that thinking pays."[6] The adult educator had to prepare study materials that struck the right note in accessible language. Father LeBlanc, an Acadian priest in Port Felix, wanted to receive co-operative literature for his parishioners that was "easy for them to understand as most of them have not had much schooling." This plea was typical.[7]

The study clubs were the vehicle to organize the enlightenment process. Studying must channel learning into action. In the early stages of study club development, the clubs functioned largely as locally based self-help initiatives. The *Extension Bulletin*, launched in November 1933 and edited by George Boyle, referred to the Extension Department's program as the "self-help plan."[8] People had to get their feet wet, try things out, experience the exhilaration of learning by doing and the joy of small beginnings. The Extension organizers had to nurture forms of action that were relatively easy to accomplish at the outset. By the late 1930s Coady figured that he knew the secret of working with poor people.

> We think now that the easiest beginning can be made in the field of money by establishing a credit union. This is non-controversial and teaches the technique of group action. Through this they move into the study of Rochdale principles, and when they are

ready, into the field of marketing and production and processing. The important thing is to find something that is safe and easy. This is very important in the case of very poor people.[9]

Start safely, proceed easily. Only gradually would a coherent project for building a new economic and social order take shape in practice and imagination. Extension had to grow into a movement, and nothing was guaranteed in the fragility of the early moments.

With messianic passion, Coady believed that adult education could mobilize

> the spiritual and intellectual forces of the people for the purpose of attacking the problems confronting them. The intellectual awakening is brought about through the medium of the small study club, educational rallies, special courses for leaders, and general and regional conferences. The interest of the common people in such a program can only be aroused and sustained through appealing and energizing study material. It has been found that literature exposing the social and financial maladjustments of our times strikes the most responsive chord in the minds and hearts of the disinherited eighty per cent of the people.[10]

The ultimate purpose of the educational process was to enable the primary producers and industrial workers to "get their hands on the throttle of their own destiny." They had to learn how to do for "themselves what they have been paying others so dearly to do for them in the past." If the "common" people achieved this "measure of economic freedom," they would have acquired a "potent instrument for their education and their intellectual and spiritual advancement."[11]

II

Coady's first organizational task was to organize study clubs in the fishing and farm communities. Extension organizers would not enter the coal fields until the spring of 1932. A communication network, imperfect but adequate, was in place in the fishing communities. They had been organized into units of the United Maritime Fishermen. Seasoned, committed and competent leadership existed in most of the Nova Scotian fishing villages, particularly on the north-west coast of Cape Breton and along the Guysborough coastline and north shore of New Brunswick. The ground had been prepared. In the agricultural communities, federal and provincial agricultural representatives ("ag reps") had been busy for over a decade, experimenting with buying clubs and other forms of co-operative activity. The "ag reps," astute fieldworkers such as J.F.C. MacDonnell, S.J. MacKinnon and R.J. MacSween, were committed co-operators and passionate defenders of the interests of the primary producers. They knew the people and had their respect. So did many of the priests in the farm communities. In the coal fields, the time was ripe for social action initiatives that might heal some wounds and solve some urgent problems, and Extension had a few radical priests such the taciturn M.J. MacKinnon and the pro-labour T. O'R. Boyle to help them.

The main organizing strategy of the Extension Department was to use, wherever possible, the existent parish structure, with its informal and formal communication system, to announce mass meetings as a means to organize the clubs. If they couldn't depend on the local clergy, they tried to find someone else in the community who could serve as a starting point. (The training of local leaders would emerge as one of Extension's most important educational challenges.) These mass meetings were calculated to inspire and arouse the community, a kind of intellectual bombing operation.

After the smoke settled, communities were organized into neighbourhood groups. Groups were composed of from five to ten members who met in homes, halls and schoolhouses. Most communities had several groups operating. The Extension Department organized general meetings in parishes or communities, encouraging debates and discussions on larger issues. Coady thought that "something new had happened in the country when common men who were never before known to speak in public were able to stand up before large audiences and discuss intelligently the problems of the day."[12] Occasional rallies brought the Extension intellectuals (usually annual meetings of different kinds of associations) into the communities to sustain people's hopes.

Coady's role in the initial mass meetings was to stir the people into believing that they could do marvellous things. Accounts of his performances at these meetings indicate that Coady often appeared, in the first two or three minutes, to be inarticulate. His hands would paw the air awkwardly as he searched for the right word. Then the flow would come, and the rhythm of his speech would glide effortlessly over homespun and powerful metaphors designed to stoke the people to action.

Coady's biggest challenge was to place the scattered local initiatives within a coherent, larger, interpretative framework. He had to show how the people's small actions contributed to the building of a better world for the primary producers and industrial workers. He had to show how little actions fit into the big picture. At the same time, he also had to attend to endless practical problems and the opposition that appeared quickly on the Nova Scotia scene. The prophet had to be both an organizer and a trouble-shooter. He had to be present at key decision-making rallies and meetings of people's organizations such as the UMF. He could not simply preach the beauty of the future kingdom; people had to see signposts, now, pointing the way. Between 1930 and 1935, the signposts began to appear, first among the lobster fishermen and the farmers, and slightly later in the industrial sector. This was the Extension Department's great utopian phase, a time when tremendous creative energy was released into community life.

On October 23, 1930, Coady sent out a letter to the farm and fish communities informing them that he and MacDonald had prepared a lesson, "Some Fundamental Considerations," on the general economic situation of farmers and fishermen. It was heady stuff; the Extension intellectuals believed that the primary producers, quite a few of whom were barely literate, had to understand the events of the Industrial Revolution to get a "proper understanding of the economic problems today."[13] They even bumbled by recommending a five-hundred-page text on farming for use in the agricultural clubs, which didn't work. They reminded the study club organizers that "from the very outset ... our studies should all tend to the solution of actual difficulties confronting us today."

In the earliest stages, the study clubs were quite free to determine their own problems and issues. However, the balance between local experiment and coherent plan, and grassroots local democracy and expert leadership, was delicate. Coady and MacDonald could not impose the form of self-help action on the local communities. They had to see what was working and where the emergent patterns were. The "co-operative blueprint" unfolded in interplay with the local experiments. They couldn't predict that, in one fishing village, the people would create a lobster cannery, which in turn would spark a similar initiative in another fishing village. Or that farmers and other vocational groups would say to themselves, "If study, organization and co-operation can produce these spectacular results for fishermen, why not for us?"[14]

Coady and MacDonald constructed a powerful and appealing meta-narrative for their actions. At one time, farm households had been self-sufficient, producing their own clothing, food, household equipment, implements and leather. They had little need for cash. Rural communities ceased to be self-sufficient when technologies and factories shifted into urban centres. Farmers were now dependent on produced goods, from boots to farm implements. And here was the rub. Production of farm products had not increased materially for thirty years. Farmers' income had not kept pace with the amount needed for articles of production, and they needed to become more efficient. Coady and MacDonald told the farmers that they now had to study the questions of how "to overcome distance, how to secure a steady supply of sufficient quantity, how to use standardized grades and how to let the rest of the world know what is offered for sale."

These questions had to be studied thoroughly in order to solve the rural problem, but efficiency wasn't enough. Farmers needed bargaining power. If marketing alone, farmers were at a "constantly increasing disadvantage. The corporations operated as organized groups; they fixed prices that the farmers had to accept. A farmer had "no voice in fixing the price at which he sells or at which he buys." For Coady and MacDonald, this is where the tragedy lay. Farm groups had to learn how to "organize group marketing. They had to determine their own prices. When that occurred, the Nova Scotia farmer would again be on an equal basis with organized industry. Big business on the farm will balance big business in the city ... and Nova Scotia agriculture will become again a wealth holding industry as well as a wealth producing one." Only through the "right ordering of the forces of marketing and production" could farming be profitable.[15] These two Extension intellectuals had to mobilize the people for enlightened co-operative action. They knew the direction they wanted to lead the people. They didn't know the details, or the twists and turns of the journey. At the end of the day, only the people themselves could change their circumstances.

Coady and MacDonald knew that the "old methods of the past" would not "suit modern conditions." Those who followed "the old ways of doing things whether it be in agriculture, fishing, teaching or lumbering" would "inevitably fall behind in the present keen struggle for existence." The people had to break away from the old ways of seeing and doing; the study club was the educational vehicle to help people gain a "sound knowledge of the new."[16] But there was no "easy way of securing knowledge on the business of farming. Considerable effort and study are necessary if the members are to derive any benefit from the work of the study club."[17]

The message that old methods would not suit new conditions fell like sparks on dry tinder. The people were ready to learn to think about new possibilities. By the end of 1931, 173 study clubs had been organized with 1,384 members. In 1933, the number doubled to 350 study clubs with 5,250 members; by 1935, 8,460 people in the communities would be participating in 940 clubs. In 1932, the first credit unions, co-op stores and buying clubs, lobster factories and fish plants took their place on the Nova Scotian landscape. The February 1933 issue of *The Casket* captured the sentiments emerging from the communities. Dan Murray from New Waterford exclaimed: "We are all beginning to feel that our problems are not insurmountable at all." Mrs. D. O'C. Doyle of Melford felt that she had "developed a sense of appreciation as never before of the many possibilities for the future welfare of the districts we represent."[18] Coady informed his cousin Chris J. Tompkins that "things are moving here at a great rate."[19] This elated phrase peppered Coady's correspondence in the early 1930s.

Coady's personal letters reveal how badly he wanted his own family and community to succeed. While this filial concern was genuine, Coady's own self-interest was also at play—he really wanted to showcase the co-operative movement in the Margaree Valley. Several letters written in late winter of 1932 reveal how Coady was often poking in dark corners, attempting to unearth economic opportunities for his family members. He advised James Coady, a tanner in Margaree Forks, to loan Francis Coady $200 so he could get into poultry: "He has no courage but I know he is a good sober man and both he and his wife know this business and could make a success of it."[20] A month later, Coady told Dr. A.C. Chisholm of Margaree Harbour that he had been getting some of the Margaree people interested in poultry

> but they don't seem to want to do anything like this.... If they (Francis and his wife) are successful it will be an eye-opener for others. The people of Inverness County don't produce more than the smallest percentage of eggs consumed in the town of Inverness. There is a good market for them and nobody is smart enough to take hold of it.

This advice was followed up by the obligatory must-read list of self-help books.[21] Coady followed these letters with further advice to Francis Coady to use some "cod liver oil and olive oil" to stop the flu bug then making its rounds.[22]

Coady was constantly scheming, hoping to stimulate small-scale local economic initiatives. Poultry farming was just one of the holes in the Nova Scotian economy. Over the years, Coady would attempt to fill many more, from encouraging an indigenous furniture industry to setting up a mink farm at the Margaree Forks.

III

The Extension Department planned to open up a branch office in Glace Bay, and sought to hire a point man for their work in the coal fields. Alex S. MacIntyre was a rather austere, former left-wing trade union militant. MacIntyre had gone into the pits in Cape Breton around the turn of the century. Over the years, he had risen to prominence in the labour movement, and he had been a member of the ill-fated left wing in the convulsive 1920s. Blacklisted after the riots of 1925-26, MacIntyre had spent some years as a salesman to make ends meet.

Converted to the co-operative way in the early 1930s without ever divesting himself of his commitment to trade union struggles, MacIntyre had shocked the diocese with his vehement criticisms of their outright neglect of the miners at a diocesan conference called by the Bishop to discuss whether the Extension Department should send its workers into the industrial towns of Cape Breton. For two hours, MacIntyre set the record straight in the blunt language of the working class. If the miners had left the Church, it was because the Church had turned its back on them in their time of distress. The miners had embraced communism because its followers were the only ones to offer help. Most of the men were not communists in their hearts, simply desperate workers fighting for a better life for themselves and their families. MacIntyre told the assembly of his own struggle, of his personal spiritual crisis when he had been fired by the union and was without work or prospects of it. In a study club, he had seen how he could remain faithful to his church and retain the confidence of the workers.

The leaders of the Antigonish Movement realized that they had found their man in Cape Breton. On August 19, 1932, the St.FX Extension Department opened an office in Glace Bay, in the very heart of industrial despair and discontent. Eight days earlier, the town's paper had carried the headline "Glace Bay Relief Situation reaches very acute stage." Coady travelled to the town, met with local leaders and addressed a meeting of the Stirling Athletic Club, telling his listeners that, with conditions so deplorable, there were many problems the Extension Department might take up. Alex S. MacIntyre's presence at the Movement's forefront served as a reminder, for those who knew, of the Catholic Church's laggard response to the miners' plight in the early twentieth century.

Antigonish-style co-operatives took hold in industrial Cape Breton in the early 1930s, and MacIntyre had much to do with this. The later myth of the Antigonish rout of the communists (The Antigonish Movement saved the Maritimes from communism), however, was simply untrue and self-serving. The communists had more or less run out of gas by the time the Catholic Church got around to organizing various co-ops in the disordered coal fields, and hard-core communist activists had little trouble deflating exaggerated claims emanating from poverty-stricken communities such as Little Dover.

Reports from the Sydney-Glace Bay area communities streamed into the Extension office. The first *Extension Bulletin* of November 7, 1933, told of thirty-seven self-help groups that had been organized. These groups, composed of unemployed men, exchanged their labour for goods and services. They farmed vacant lots of land, given to them by interested people. They set up small cottage industries, such as window screen manufacturing, in abandoned warehouses. Written in August 1933, MacIntyre's report informed readers that the associated study clubs in Reserve Mines and surrounding areas were putting their studies into practice. The clubs were functioning as buying societies. They contacted the co-operative study clubs in the farm communities and brought in large orders of meat, fish, poultry, hay, lime and so on. The Petit de Gras fish producers delivered five and a half tons of fish to the industrial study clubs. Coady and MacDonald wanted to ease people gradually into full-fledged consumer and producer co-ops by having them first test the waters in fairly safe ways.

A visionary in his own right, Alex S. MacIntyre believed that these small-scale co-operative actions would develop a "co-operative consciousness in the people." Co-operative stores would spread to every community in the mining districts. Once these were in place, co-operative wholesales and factories could emerge to supply the wholesale and retail stores. Then, "we could put our sons and daughters to work in those wholesales, stores and factories and burn our own coal in those co-operative enterprises. We could link up the co-operative producers, such as farmers and fishermen with the co-operative consumers and make this a land fit to live in." This buoyant and resilient dream of unified producers and industrial workers animated all of the Extension intellectuals.[23]

The members of the study clubs were learning about an amazing diversity of economic activity. At Big Pond Centre on Cape Breton Island, members of one study club co-operated in cutting their winter's supply of firewood. They then planned to dig a bog for a compost. The club members of the Glencoe District were learning about the tanning of leather, credit unions, ice storage and budgeting of farm earnings and expenditures. Veteran activist Ernest Pellerin of the largely Acadian community of Larry's River informed Extension that his group intended to open a co-operative store in the early spring of 1934. He wanted information as to where they could obtain stock. A correspondent from Grand Mira North wanted pamphlets on farm management and on how to bring in run-out soil. In Cheticamp, the men had studied co-operative canning and then proceeded to open a factory in 1934. They were now turning to the study of credit unions. Kay Thompson, the secretary who became a philosopher, fielded the study clubs' endless questions on topics ranging from farm management to the growing of turnips.

Credit unions easily captured the imagination of the debt-strapped communities. George Bennett of Dominion, a coal town that had seen many a battle, told Extension that their club had been named "Keen" (after the Canadian co-operator, George Keen, long-standing director of the Canadian Co-operative Union). It had a large membership and was progressing rapidly. Its aim was to form a credit union in the town of Dominion. Ten clubs were now functioning, and Alex S. MacIntyre had recently addressed their club on credit unions. Initial steps had been taken to form a co-operative credit society to serve New Waterford and the adjoining territory, known as district 20. Forty-six citizens had signed a petition addressed to the Registrar of Joint Stock Companies in Halifax to authorize "The New Waterford Credit Union."

Bennett went on to say that regular weekly classes were held in the Town Council Chamber on Saturday evenings for the officers of the study clubs, under the leadership of MacIntyre. These classes were to continue, taking up the study of co-operative buying and the operation of co-operative stores, and had been designed to enable the officers to conduct similar classes in their own study clubs.[24] MacIntyre was pleased that the miners could use the people's banks to replenish their houses, depleted of furnishings (bedding, stoves, kitchen utensils) during the "three years of terrible depression." The credit unions were eliminating the "usury installment buying plans that kept the miners' wives in perpetual debt."[25]

News from elsewhere confirmed this interest in people's banks. In Rear Port Hood, reported William Gillis, seven or eight clubs were chiefly interested in studying credit unions and co-operative store organization. Angus B. MacLellan of South West Margaree wrote that fourteen members were 100 percent in favour of organizing a credit union in the parish. They all realized, he observed, that "it will be the means of solving many of our economic problems."[26] J. Fougere, another stalwart activist from Larry's River, reported that, on January 17, the study clubs of New Harbour had invited Father Forest and the leaders of the Larry River's study clubs to meet together in the interest of the co-operative movement. Upon their arrival, forty members learned that they were anxious to organize a credit union. The people were taking the *Bulletin*'s advice—"Apply what is right and applicable in your communities"[27] to heart.

Father Jimmy Tompkins had begun considering the place of credit unions within a social reform movement soon after his exile to fog-bound Canso in 1923. Scouting the reform landscape in North America, Tompkins had found Roy Bergengren of the U.S. Credit Union National Association. He peppered Bergengren with questions and emerged from the ensuing dialogue with a bedrock belief in credit unions as one of adult education's primary schools.

Through the 1920s, the restless and determined Tompkins agitated for experimentation with credit unions at Little Dover. Correspondence between Bergengren and Tompkins in 1931 and 1932 indicates that Bergengren believed that they should "first get a law, and then organize a typical credit union at Little Dover, meantime making a careful survey to determine whether or not it is commercially possible for the relatively small number of fishermen at Little Dover to provide enough lobsters, for example, to make a canning factory commercially worthwhile."[28] Bergengren travelled to Nova Scotia in the fall of 1931 and spent a couple of hours with Coady. Bergengren informed Tompkins on November 18, 1931, that Coady planned to "take the credit union matter up with the Premier."[29] Bergengren firmly believed that if they could "get a credit union law enacted by the Nova Scotia Parliament during 1932" they should "be able to prove before the year is out that it will constitute a very valuable, even if a bit belated, Christmas present for the people of Nova Scotia."[30]

With the Depression breaking down ordinary credit agencies and the rapid increase in the extent and severity of usury as practised by private money lenders, the Extension activists pressed onward. Tompkins and Bergengren encouraged Coady to get the Bill through parliament. In mid-March 1932, Bergengren expressed his concern over the credit union situation in Nova Scotia. "It has been my legislative experience," he wrote Tompkins, "that to get a bill of this sort enacted, it must be drawn a long time before the session starts, and a great deal of hard political work must be put in in order to insure its enactment."[31] By early April the Premier had offered the Bill, and the Liberal leader of the opposition, Angus L. Mac-Donald, was not opposed. By May 10, the credit union Bill had "passed the Legislature without difficulty."[32] The Extension activists breathed a sigh of relief. In mid-June, 1932, while in Boston, Coady visited Bergengren, chatting about making some "experimental use fairly soon of the recently enacted Nova Scotia credit union law." He suggested to Dr. Coady that

> the most effective way to make progress with a credit union development in Nova Scotia would be by taking two or three typical groups; a group of fishermen, for example, a group of farmers, and possibly a typically more or less city parish in some such place like Halifax. This would give us three distinct types of credit union operation, and would afford a sufficient experimentation in order to enable you to try out the new machinery, and to determine just how it is going to work.[33]

On the cold, miserable evening of December 1, 1932, Coady, MacIntyre and Roy Bergengren bounced around in the car carrying them through the half-frozen mud and snow of the road to Little Dover. However, the storm was so bad when they reached Monastery that they feared they might not be able to get to Little Dover. Bergengren recalled that he

> found weather prophets everywhere I went, and they all seemed fearful lest some big storm might maroon us at some particularly desolate spot. As a matter of fact we went out to the first meeting at Broad Cove–a few miles out from Inverness in a very cold snow storm, and our final meeting at Reserve Mines was also held under pretty mean weather conditions.[34]

Bergengren described the meeting at Broad Cove, a few miles out of Inverness in Cape Breton, as very enthusiastic. They managed to establish the first credit union in Nova Scotia; Father Jimmy would not be able to add the first credit union to his list of brilliant initiatives. From Broad Cove, the three organizers travelled into the industrial part of Cape Breton.

At the meeting in the mining town of Reserve Mines, chaired by A.S. MacIntyre, the three visitors presented their case. To improve their lot, the first step was to start a credit union. Criticisms of this idea poured in from the floor. One miner summed up the dilemma of all present: "How can we save? Do these speakers know that we are getting only one day's work a week and that 60 per cent of the people in town are on relief? Surely it is folly to think that we can help ourselves by beginning to save money when we haven't enough to feed and clothe our children decently." The three visitors gave the assembled miners examples of poor communities in which residents had saved thousands of dollars in their credit unions by pooling their dimes and quarters. One miner shouted: "The people of the mining communities can get plenty credit now. Some of us can borrow from the banks. All of us can buy on the installment plan anything that we need, and most of us can get credit at the local store."

The guests pointed out the high cost of credit. Instalment buying cost purchasers 20 to 30 percent interest. Through credit unions, propertyless workers could control a fund large enough to enable them to buy goods and services for cash. They could secure the lowest possible prices for what they needed to make a better life for themselves and their families. The miners' objections continued: They were not smart enough to run a credit union; credit unions were untried; it was doubtful whether they could alleviate the poverty of the people of Reserve. The visitors pointed out that Frederick Raiffeisen had started credit unions among starving peasants in Germany eighty years earlier. They stated that the provincial government had passed a Credit Union Act earlier that year.

In his characteristic way, MacDonald turned the meeting from talk to action. Nineteen of those present pooled their spare cash, collected $4.75 and began to study how to start a credit union. Reserve Mines would go down in history as having begun the second credit union in Nova Scotia. Writing to Tompkins after his fateful trip, Roy Bergengren said that he believed that the

> credit union is going to have really important work to do in Nova Scotia. I have reached the conclusion that there isn't much hope for the world unless we can accomplish two or three very simple things. First, the nations of the world must sufficiently appreciate the common interest, so that they will work intelligently together for the common good. The time has come very definitely, it seems to me, to reject the extremes of nationalism. The rapid development of machinery has made it possible for every man, woman, and child in Inverness, Nova Scotia to share in the abundance of things designed to make life comfortable, interesting, and really worthwhile. The difficulty, of course is that our system of economics prevents this new machinery from spreading what might be its blessing by choking up the distribution of things.[35]

Ida Gallant's short history of the Coady Credit Union of New Aberdeen, a part of Glace Bay, depicts poignantly just how little miners and their families had in the early 1930s. Miners received on average about $3.25 a day, seldom worked regular shifts and had a long list of deductions paid to doctors, hospitals, the union, relief society and others. Families had no resources with which to supplement their small incomes. Without social legislation, communities did the best they could. Volunteers ran soup kitchens for kids at lunch time, tossing in boiled cabbage for extra vitamins. Many families kept a cow in the backyard, and even without pasteurized milk, lots of kids survived on cow's milk. It is touching to imagine the miners dressing up to go to town in the Depression days of 1933 to deposit 25 cents into their accounts without shame or embarrassment because many others were there too. And Michael McNeil, who would be voted a $15 per month salary as manager in 1939, had to come to the office very early on Saturday mornings to build a fire so that the office was comfortable when the time came for business. It was often so cold that the ink had frozen in the ink bottles. Even the blotting paper had to be thawed before it was fit for use. These experiences goaded the directors into obtaining a proper building.

Of the forty-seven men who applied for a charter in 1933, only one had even attended high school. Women were not usually members of credit unions in those early days. The main reason for this was that women didn't have independent incomes, and families doubted the value of having two members pay the 25-cent dues. Later, at Bergengren's insistence, women would be allowed to join. In 1937, the first "lady tellers" were hired at the Coady Credit Union. Many of the men in the charter group were in their teens or early twenties. They were aware of their fathers' experiences of the hard life in the mines. They knew about job insecurity, low wages and industrial strife. They saw some light, it seems, at the end of the co-operative tunnel.[36]

IV

Women, however, poured into the study club movement. Some participated in clubs with the men; many others formed groups for women only. One energetic women's club in Brook River wrote that its members were getting more "interested all the time." They found the Department's literature on the washing and preparing of wool, as well as the soap recipes, very helpful: "They all make some soap, but none was to compare with her soap made from goose oil and tallow, with lye, from one of the recipes. Two of our young ladies are learning to spin yarn, and are going to demonstrate at our next meeting."[37] Many of the women's clubs focused exclusively on handicrafts. In several districts, the art of weaving was revived, and the products of this would often be on sale (or displayed) at the co-op stores. Janet MacDonald, secretary of the women's study club at St. Andrew's, reported that twelve members of her group had been meeting at regular intervals from last October. They read books such as *Your Money's Worth* and *The Awakening Community*, and discussed how to choose textiles for quilting and crocheting. She also reported that one Miss Pepper from the Dairy Department in Ottawa had spoken at a special meeting on "Food and its relations to health."[38]

The women of Larry's River provide an excellent example of how the women's clubs worked. Maggie Richard wrote Extension:

> We have organized four groups of an average of from eight to ten members in each group. After pooling our five and ten cents we purchased raw wool and followed the old self-help method of carding, spinning and knitting it into mitts and socks which we sold through the efforts of some of our live wire members. We also made some lovely mats. We realized the sum of twenty five dollars with which we purchased material to improve and beautify the interior of our church.[39]

The world was opening up for people in the small communities. They were hungry for knowledge. Taft Cameron of River Denys Station listed the topics their clubs were considering studying: ways and means of improving our community, fertilizers, animal nutrition, the British marketing act, social reconstructionism, taxation and price spreads. *Bulletin* editor George Boyle figured that the "people of River Denys will probably know more about political and social problems than the white-collared gent who is going to tell them how to vote at the next election."[40] Mrs. A.S. Harris of Three Brooks, Pictou County, would have fit right in with the River Denys people. Among the subjects discussed by the members of her group were lime and fertilizer, the curing of meats, the making of rugs for sale from the wool of local sheep, increasing the consumption of milk and cream and credit unions.[41]

Study clubs for women had been started, so the *Extension Bulletin* explained, not in answer to the question of their usefulness, but as a result of "deciding which of a bewildering number of problems that press on us from all sides we are to study first." The Bulletin believed that problems related to the home would demand attention first.

> We boast with a great deal of pride and truth about our Nova Scotian homes and home life, but conditions in too many of them are far from satisfactory. In our rural homes especially there is too much drudgery and drabness. We are a proud and sensitive people and often those of us who are poor expend our energies in putting up a brave front to hide our poverty.

The *Bulletin* imagined that all Nova Scotian women would want to "study the question of proper food for the family, how to build up strong and health citizens," and "lessen the economic burden caused by sickness and mental disease."[42] Anne Chisholm thought that the Extension Department was not only helping her to "save dimes and dollars for her family by joining a consumer's co-operative, but also to play a vital part in the saving of Christian civilization."[43]

The *Extension Bulletin*'s "Woman's Page" constructed women's primary role as wife and mother. They had responsibility for care of the home, the spiritual aspects of home life, child rearing, the health and well-being of family members and education; all in all, a formidable, grinding task in poverty-stricken conditions. While acknowledging the busy role of women, *Bulletin* articles still encouraged them to get involved in the Movement in order to help maintain the unity of family life, serving as "man's helpmate."[44] The *Bulletin* also recognized that women were the chief household managers, controlling household budgets, such as they were. Extension thought that women's participation in the study club movement was vital in order that they learn more about economic benefits and the co-operative theory behind such things as the co-operative store. They particularly encouraged women to partake in arts and crafts activities. The *Bulletin* proclaimed: "It has been said that the way to get at the brain is through the hands. This is one of the fundamental reasons why we consider

One of Coady's beloved "sharecroppers of the sea."

The fish barons believed that "an educated fishermen is a dangerous man."

Larry's River was an exemplary co-operative community in the 1930s and 1940s, led by Father Forest (seated on Coady's left).

These small "people's banks" attempted to break the common folk from the stranglehold of debt.

handicrafts as an important phase of adult education."[45] By today's standards, the *Bulletin*'s vision of women's place in the movement failed as it did not progress beyond their role as wife, mother and socially responsible citizen. Their role was in the household and, sadly, their men would even block the way to leadership on boards of the very institutions (credit unions, co-op stores) they so clearly had a stake in.

Slowly, the people's confidence was boosted as a result of their participation in the study clubs. M.A. Kenedy of the Johnstown parish in Cape Breton thought that one couldn't really place a value on the ground they had covered in the last few years in dollars and cents: "People look to the future with confidence. Improvements are noticeable in many ways. Better system of farming through the study of farm management, study of soils, care of livestock are instances."[46] Even the youth caught the spirit, as communities organized junior study clubs. A.G. Buchanan of Baddeck Forks exuded excitement. "During the coming winter we expect to have two junior clubs, one of which is already started. We are eager to urge every move to stimulate community action among the juniors here, as it seems our only hope to encourage and promote action."[47] And it wasn't only the young who were excited. James J. Donovan, an older man from Ingonish, Cape Breton, had learned to read and write in the Clyburn Brook night school. "I am 67 years old and I could not read or write. I have learned to read and also to write and do sums in addition and division. I have up till now read four books on self-help that I received from Mr. [J.F.C.] MacDonell."[48]

Sometimes existing voluntary associations would initiate study clubs. The Catholic Men's Society of Westville, J.B. McAllister told Extension, thought they had good prospects for study clubs. Among the subjects they had studied over the past winter was Pope Pius XI's new encyclical, *Quadragesimo Anno*. They were also keen on learning and practising the art of public speaking.[49] At Little Dover, in Father Jimmy's territory, thirty-five young men had been organized into a Progressive Club. They were studying and attending to town improvement and sporting activities.[50] Typically, the peppery Tompkins saw great things happening in the Progressive Club's meetings.

An important feature of the study club movement was the rally, or special gathering. Coady and MacDonald encouraged the various clubs in nearby communities to federate into associated study clubs, as the Extension leaders wanted to build solidarity among them. This was crucial if the Movement was going to move from its fragile beginnings to something solid and rooted. In Canso, the clubs sponsored an oratorical contest. Participants spoke on topics such as *Rerum Novarum*, liberalism and socialism, and the place of the state in social recovery. In Larry's River, a predominantly Acadian fishing village, the study clubs organized an evening program of culture and talks. The organizers interspersed short talks, such as "The Capitalist System" by John Fougere and "The Aim and the need of study clubs" by Ernest Pellerin, with step-dancing and songs. In the coal fields, MacIntyre organized large picnics for hundreds of study club members, who gathered to play softball, watch wrestling competitions, listen to fiddling, sing and hear speeches. The miners easily transferred their organizing skills, hewn in many a bitter struggle, to co-operative forms of association.

George Boyle, the pugnacious editor of the *Extension Bulletin*, thought that the idea of study was a "most important phase of the self-help movement." Its primary meaning was "cultural and spiritual." He believed that the study club infused the term "neighbour" with new value. The concept of community, a "spiritual and economic reservoir," was being re-vitalized as men and women spoke and listened to each other in these face-to-face cells. Boyle thought that study club participation was breaking many communities out of the "old groove of sullen and oftimes jealous isolation." The people were intelligent enough to realize that, even though they might differ in "politics and what-not," they could still "work together as good citizens and partners in their community." Still, the "values of the re-awakened neighbourly spirit and the mental stimulation of study and discussion groups" were not easily measured.[51]

Despite the success of the study groups, the difficulty of interesting the masses in study could not be underestimated. A downtrodden people could easily lose heart, or spend all their time in study without following through with action. Boyle felt that many communities imagined that people's organizations just dropped from the sky. He pinned his hopes on the influence of the "strong individual" who could be a "force for good or evil." If public-spirited, he could "change the mentality and outlook for hundreds." He thought that the situation in Dover provided a good example of how enthusiastic individuals were keeping the co-operative cause alive.[52] Before long, Extension would begin to organize short courses in community leadership training.

V

The UMF had emerged triumphantly out of acute travail in late June 1930. Now the taxing work of building a viable organization and delivering the goods began. Public opinion predicted a short life for the organization, as it had few financial resources and lacked skilled fieldworkers. Coady didn't have long to wait to test his trouble-shooting skills. The querulous Charles MacCarthy resigned from the presidency in 1931. He was replaced by Alfred Hanlon of Canso, one of Tompkins' cadre of reformers; he was one of the study club leaders and had been active for years in the fishing struggles. On January 21-22, 1932, UMF auditors decided that Dr. Richard Hamer had not handled the finances properly. He was asked to resign, but refused, holding on to UMF records, despite pressure from Premier Angus L. MacDonald. The UMF was compelled to force his dismissal. Hanlon thought it "unfortunate and yet not without precedent, that the UMF [would] have trouble with its officers in the initial stages of the organization."[53] At this time Coady stepped in as acting secretary.

Coady supported the appointment of Burke McInerney, working behind the scenes to ensure he was hired. On February 19, 1932, the UMF executive appointed McInerney as the new central secretary. This was a fortuitous choice. A graduate of St.FX, and manager of O'Leary's General Store and Fish Business in Richibucto, New Brunswick, he was generally described as a man of the "highest degree of honesty and integrity, with a pleasing personality and excellent business training, and native ability."[54] McInerney had a flair for detail and exactness; his job (at a salary of $3,000 per annum) was to put the UMF on a solid business basis. On February 24, 1932, McInerney wrote Coady that he was indebted to him for his support. "I am prepared to give this new work constant application, honest effort, and the experience of 14 years of business life." Coady had another good man in place in the organizational social network.

The UMF's central task was to consolidate and unify the activities of the many isolated and scattered local groups.[55] In the early 1930s, organizational efforts were quite restricted. The UMF did not yet have the funds for fieldworkers, and bad economic conditions still prevailed in many communities. A great number of fishermen were entangled in the "meshes of the credit net." For the most part, Hanlon claimed, the fishermen were "unwilling victims of the vicious credit system and not in a position to grasp the opportunities which organization and co-operative activity will hold out to them."[56] From 1932 to 1935, however, some fishing communities were able to establish lobster factories and fish plants. These successful ventures enabled the UMF to navigate its way through the precarious early days.

On February 17, 1932, the Acting Minister of Fisheries commented on the UMF's demands to the government. The government was willing to continue the grant to the UMF, but would reduce it by 10 percent for 1932-23 (from $5,000 to $4500) and would continue to subsidize the transportation services for lobsters from eastern Nova Scotia. The UMF would not acquire the fieldworkers it urgently needed until the late 1930s. However, the fieldworkers they acquired at that time were very good—mostly young, unmarried idealists (such as Norman MacKenzie, Lloyd Matheson and Gus MacDonald) who worked for small salaries and were fired with enthusiasm by their encounters with Extension's "big guns," Coady, MacDonald and MacIntyre.

Norman MacKenzie worked with Extension from September 1938 to September 1939 with the fishermen of North Victoria County in Cape Breton Island. A Protestant seminarian, MacKenzie would go on to a prominent career with the United Church doing mission work in China. A.B. MacDonald lauded this exceptionally talented young man.

> He put into his work as adult educator and counsellor to the poor fishermen all the enthusiasm and good will that could be expected of any man. He travelled over his territory, a probable radius of 50 miles, on foot, by motorcycle, and by dog-team. The fishermen idolized him, and the good results of his work were everywhere apparent. He is zealous, an untiring worker, sincere and able.[57]

In early 1932, prior to the hiring of these exceptional fieldworkers, the Acting Minister thought that the Fisheries officers' annual courses for fishermen were adequate. He also thought that the Fisheries Experimental Stations were "designed to do for the fisheries all that experimental farms do for agriculture." He had no idea that the UMF needed idealistic fisheries fieldworkers to teach, cajole, persuade and organize community by community in order to fulfil its mandate. Not until the Hon. J.A. Michaud, an Acadian Liberal, became Minister of Fisheries would Extension and the UMF have a truly sympathetic ear in the Minister's chair. The Deputy, W.A. Found, was solid enough.

The UMF adopted a militant rhetoric in the early days. Its short-lived newspaper, *The UMF* (published from December 1932 to May 1934), hammered away relentlessly at the trawlers, the UMF's nemesis. Anti-capitalist language pervaded the organization. In a circular to officers and members of the UMF, penned in June 14, 1932, Hanlon declared:

> We are living in a world of great excitement. Hardly a day goes by which does not bring us news of the collapse of a great financial structure or the failure of some prominent economic expert. In our own Maritime Provinces some old established commercial institutions are failing whilst others are tottering on the brink of failure. It is a day when the survival of the fittest is the rule. Of all the solutions offered by those representing the Church, finance, education, professions and state, the one great remedy of all is that of co-operation.[58]

Hanlon informed UMF members that the organization was determined to "counteract and defeat all attempts at anything that savours of the exploitation of the great industry which it represents."[59] It didn't take long for the "exploiters" to react to co-operative initiatives in the fishing communities.

Father James Boyle, parish priest in Havre Boucher, a picture-perfect, ethnically mixed fishing community near Antigonish, had launched a lobster canning operation in 1932. In the autumn of 1931, the community had decided to build a lobster factory in the face of strong opposition. Though they had neither money nor lumber, they possessed idealism. On a Monday morning the men took their axes, cut down trees and had them sawn. At the end of the week, the necessary lumber and timber was ready for the builders at the factory site. Scottish, Irish and French joined hands in supplying the material and putting up the buildings. The women raised $400 to help pay for the necessary glass, nails and shingles. Though they used their own sweat and time in erecting the factory, the fishermen had to borrow money to purchase equipment in order to provide adequate facilities to handle the fish produced by the members.

The fish merchants' main strategy in undermining competition from the co-operators was to lure fishermen away from co-operative marketing by offering them higher prices. Boyle wrote to Coady on March 3, 1932, informing him that Roy Savage was willing to "pay a high price for lobsters in order to damage us. He is a protégé of Magee who could afford to lose a couple of thousand in order to demolish our menacing competition." Boyle wondered if the Extension Department, linked with the UMF, could become a selling agency for products from Grand Etang, Havre Boucher, Dover, Larry's River and Port Felix, as pooling would enhance their bargaining power. Isolated, Boyle figured that they would be "worsted in the fight." He also told Coady that Father Forest had tried to get cans for his Tor Bay Canning Company from Magee, who had given him the run-around. Boyle referred Forest to the Windsor Fisher Ltd. in Charlottetown, which was willing to sell the cans directly to him.

Boyle's main problem, though, was that of chartering a boat to ship their lobsters to Boston. A government-authorized boat charged $3.50 a crate; unsubsidized, they would pay $6. On April 11 Boyle told Coady that Savage was now threatening R.W. Hendry of the Nova Scotia Shipping Company regarding the transporting of their lobster to Boston. Savage had warned Hendry "not to come here and made a threat if he disregarded his warning." The people of Havre Boucher were having difficulties getting a boat. Consequently, they had written to the Deputy Minister of Fisheries, Found, asking him to co-operate with Hendry in order to finalize the plan. Apparently Hendry needed to have permission from the Department of Trade and Commerce to allow his boat to come to Havre Boucher. He concluded that the "enemy is working to head us off for he wants the profits himself."[60] On the same day, the eleventh, Coady informed Found of their problems with Savage. Two days later, Found promised to get the Department of Trade and Commerce to make some arrangements for the transportation of lobsters from Havre Boucher to Arichat.[61]

At the annual meeting of the UMF, held in Charlottetown, October 17-18, 1934, the delegates passed more than twenty resolutions addressing their many concerns. They wanted the beam trawlers abolished, a perennial demand. They wanted fish representatives on provincial marketing boards. They needed co-op legislation to facilitate the development of co-operative enterprise among the primary producers. They were troubled by high tariffs imposed by the United States government and the high cost of gasoline. They believed that provincial marketing boards could extend their markets for pickled and boneless cod, as well as extending markets into the West Indies. They complained about the lack of suitable transportation facilities for live lobster and advocated for the continuation of subsidized lobster collection. And they requested additional supervision of lobster fishing; apparently a few fishermen were prone to overhauling another's gear and stealing their catch.[62]

In the late spring of 1935, after being laid up for six weeks with a serious illness, Coady left for north-east New Brunswick with Father A.P. Poirier of Canso on June 3 for three weeks of organizing. Coady had not been able to accomplish much during his first organizing tour of this area where mostly poor, struggling Acadian fishermen resided. Developments there seemed to be lagging behind eastern Nova Scotia, and the Bishop of Chatham, F.P.A. Chiasson, felt that extension work needed to expand and develop among the French-speaking population. "We do not wish to segregate and separate from the now established organization," he wrote the Hon. Grote Sterling, Acting Minister of Fisheries, on July 25, 1935, "but simply to further the work along the same lines and in the language which the people will understand."[63] At this time, St.FX Extension had been publishing only in English. According to Alex J. Boudreau, Coady, unlike Tompkins, had little understanding of the need to run study clubs in Acadian communities in French. He had to be pressured, for instance, to send a French-speaking fieldworker into Mabou in the late 1930s.[64]

The Bishop wanted to create a Bureau for Adult Education and Social Welfare in his diocese. He appointed Father J.L. Chiasson, Coady's protégé, to look after the adult education interests of his people in the northern and eastern parts of New Brunswick. In 1936, with the support of Michaud, Minister of Fisheries, Coady hired Chiasson as an Extension fieldworker among the New Brunswick fishermen. Michaud informed Coady on June 19, 1936, that St.FX Extension ought to do the "educational work in preparing the people for group activities" and the UMF should organize locals and take such "steps as may be required to guide local groups in their activities to a successful outcome."[65] Five days later, Coady clarified the Extension Department's function within the network of Maritime organizations by stated strongly that no man was

> competent to organize the fishermen unless he has a clear-cut and complete program to hold out to them. Not that it is all going to be put into operation at once, but the man who does the organizing should be able to give them the blueprint of their future organized activities in every field. The function of the Fishermen's organization (UMF) would be to carry out the activities that the fishermen would initiate when they are ready.[66]

Father J.L. Chiasson believed that "with an extensive campaign of education through the formation of study clubs, where they could be taught the principles of co-op work and group activities, we could achieve as good a success as in Nova Scotia."[67] The Bishop didn't think that the federal Department of Fisheries was doing much to help the New Brunswick Acadian fishermen to assist themselves along co-operative lines. For his part, McInerney thought that fishermen in a number of communities in Kent, Northumberland and Gloucester counties were pretty well informed about what the UMF could do for them; they needed to seize the opportunities for co-operative work. Unless opportunity presented itself, there was "little possibility of a group surviving, even though in the first place it may have been well set up."[68] Skilled fieldworkers could aid in this transition from the organization of enlightenment to the organization of action.

The UMF struggled to establish a foothold in rugged and difficult terrain in its early days, but at the sixth annual convention, held in Sydney in late October, 1935, a new hopefulness was evident. D.H. Sutherland, the Chief Supervisor of Fisheries, told Found on November 1 that the meeting had been the best yet.

> One of the outstanding features was the progress that has been made during the past year by the Central Office in the way of marketing the products of local groups, such as canned lobsters, and in the purchase of rope and other supplies furnished to these groups. The local stations that have been organized are going steadily along, and their business is expanding each year. This is a stimulus for other groups not so well organized to develop along the same line.[69]

Coady thought that the UMF had "produced some spectacular results from the very beginning" in lobster canning.[70] This "ugly old crustacean" of the sea was a great source of inspiration for the fledgling Maritime co-operative movement. In late 1948, in a speech in Kansas City, Coady would tell his American audience, that "lobster, one of the homeliest of fishes, proved to be the economic liberator of our people, and it may be the cultural and spiritual liberator also."[71]

Judique, a small community of some 150 families on the west coast of Cape Breton, enjoyed a wealth of natural resources from land, forest and sea. Before 1932, they had been content to leave the processing, packing and marketing of their products, the financing of their industries and the supplying of consumer needs largely in the hands of private dealers. In 1932, the people of Judique formed twelve study clubs. They learned that their ignorance was being exploited. They learned that, through applying co-operative business to their activities, they could regain control of the services needed to produce wealth, finance their enterprises and supply consumer needs. In the spring of 1934, the fishermen of Judique organized and built a lobster factory. With thirty members, they were able to pay for the building and equipment of their factory (about $4,500) in two years. They organized a second lobster factory, worth $3,500; these two factories did a yearly business of $35,000 in the late 1930s. They improved the quality of the lobster pack and, with the UMF's help, began to regulate the marketing of canned lobsters. A credit union soon followed in 1935, and a co-operative store in 1936. The people of Judique informed Extension that they were "much richer than we were a decade ago, both economically and spiritually. We have gained much confidence in ourselves through directing and managing our own affairs."[72]

The Richmond Fishermen's Co-operative of Petit de Gras, animated by Father Boudreau's militant leadership, organized a fishermen's co-op open to all fishermen in Richmond County, in 1931. Before this plant was organized, there had been times when the fishermen couldn't even dispose of their fish, and, typically, they received a low return. Using a considerable amount of free labour (sweat equity), the plant had cost $8,000. By the late 1930s, the Co-operative had paid for its plant and distributed some $40,000 in cash for labour to its members. The community had a credit union, with a share capital of $2,000, and the local branch of the UMF carried on a bustling business in gas, oil, salt, barrels and rope, amounting to about $6,000 a year. A group of men had acquired property in order to start a co-operative store as soon as conditions were favourable.

The communities of Port Felix and Cole Harbour had the honour of starting the first consumers' co-op venture in the Maritimes under the sponsorship of the Extension Department. In the spring of 1930, fifteen men studied the principles, philosophy and history of the co-op movement. They then raised the princely sum of $85 and used the money to repair an old building in which they started a co-op store. Despite great opposition, the store conducted business in the sum of $5,600 in its first year, 1932; they had a share capital of $250. The same year, the co-op financed a lobster factory, which employed several persons. Shortly thereafter, a new 20' by 30' store was constructed, and a co-op fish store was started, where fish could be cured and processed. Thousands of pounds of boneless cod were processed, providing employment to a good number of fishermen from Port Felix and Cole Harbour. In 1934, the store did business in the sum of $10,384.53, had a share capital of $526.00 and assets of $7168.16. By 1937, merchandise sales had jumped to nearly $17,000. The group of co-operators from Port Felix and Cole Harbour thought that what was most interesting was "not the material progress achieved, but the change of attitude in the minds of the people towards solving their own economic problems." They had a "different mentality, so to speak, a new vision of the future."[73]

The fishermen of Grand Etang had sent Denis Cormier as their representative to the founding UMF convention in Halifax in 1930. When he returned, a mass meeting was called, where the fishermen decided unanimously to begin immediately to market their lobsters co-operatively. Forming a lobster cannery required little capital outlay. The technology was simple, sweat equity was readily available and the returns were high, relative to quantity caught. Many of the lobster fishermen felt that they had suffered great exploitation; they had much to gain from co-operatively organized marketing. And, fortunately, they were able to rent a local canning plant. During the first year of operation, twenty-three member-fishermen realized a profit of $900. From 1934 to 1936, the co-op marketed through the central organization, the UMF. From the beginning, the UMF paid better prices than the private buyers. In fact, the Grand Etang fishermen's early attempts to group bargain with private buyers such as Robin, Jones and Whitman earned extremely poor returns.[74]

When Coady had visited Grand Etang in 1929, he had not included credit unions in his program. It didn't take too long, however, for credit unions to appear as an integral component of the economic emancipation of the Acadians on the west side of Cape Breton, and their appearance on the Nova Scotia landscape was a godsend for the people of Grand Etang. The nearest bank was in Cheticamp, thirty miles away. Credit was nearly impossible for them to obtain, and the merchants became the people's creditors. From the fall of 1934 until late in 1935, the people of Grand Etang, with the assistance of scrappy Alex J. Boudreau (who had been appointed as "ag rep" for North Inverness county on January 1, 1934), studied the possibility of a credit union. In November 1935 they started the Lemoyne Credit Union with twenty members. Accumulating funds slowly, members purchased $5 shares on an instalment plan at 25 cents per share per week. At the end of the first month, they had $10.50 worth of share capital. Grand Etang had its small people's bank and its lobster cannery.[75] The little people were awakening from their long sleep.

It is easy to underestimate the significance of these tiny initiatives. Robin, Jones and Whitman dominated every aspect of the lives of fishermen and their families on the Gaspe coast and the west side of Cape Breton. Men and women had to get permission from the company just to get married. The company gave liberally to Roman Catholic churches, effectively silencing any rebellion from the clergy. Late in life, Alex J. Boudreau recalled that Robin, Jones and Whitman "didn't want their fishermen to know how to read. They were against education. And that was another of their principles. 'An educated fishermen is a dangerous man.' So, they must be kept in debt and they must be kept illiterate. That's the only way we can control them." The Acadian fishermen were "all deadly afraid of what would happen to them. All right, it's all right, we set up our own co-operatives—who's going to give me flour next winter? Who is going to provide me with molasses next winter? And that's the only argument the companies had." Gradually, tireless workers such as Boudreau succeeded in untying the knots that bound the fishermen to companies like Robin, Jones and Whitman. "If you want organizations, you've got to get rid of the merchants."[76]

CHAPTER 5

In the Eye of the World (1935-1939)

I

In his early struggles of building the Extension Department, Moses Coady could not have imagined how his emancipatory project in this obscure little Atlantic province would capture the imagination of so many who were searching for hope in desperate times. Coady had survived his trying ten months of organizing United Maritime Fishmen locals. He had set his opponents on their heels and established his power as a leader to be reckoned with. When Father Michael J. MacKinnon assumed directorship of the Extension Department in 1952, Coady confessed that "none of us had any particular training for the fisheries" and knew "very little about the problems of the fisheries."[1] Coady had also survived the early fumblings of the Extension Department. Many of the first study clubs had been "sickly things" and largely "inapplicable to the needs of the individuals."[2] In fact, for a spell in the second year, the "prospects of the educational movement looked as black as night. There were some brilliant beginnings but they flickered out, only to leave the scene through contrast all the blacker, as the darkness of night is intensified after a flash of lightning."[3]

By the mid-1930s light had begun to dawn. Local leadership had broken through first in the fishing villages, such as Larry's River, Petit de Gras, Little Dover and Havre Boucher. These success stories, told on numerous occasions, served as narratives of possibility. "We ... used the story of Havre Boucher on many occasions in the early days," Coady exclaimed, "not only with fishermen but with farmers and miners, to show the power of ideas. Ideas are more powerful than bullets. They will wreck or build great empires, economic and political, more effectively than the best war material yet invented."[4] Other fishing communities, such as Port Felix, Ingonish, Judique, Arisaig, and Whitehead, added their own stories of self-help co-operative action to these primary "stories of early community developments."[5] The Movement did not take hold as easily within the farming communities. However, buying clubs appeared all over the country, and gradually "co-operative stores replaced the buying clubs" and began to function "both in the producer and consumer field."[6]

Although it was not easy to gain a hearing in the industrial areas, miners responded to the idea of the co-op store. New Waterford was particularly enthusiastic, starting fifty-five study clubs in a population of 8,000. It was not until credit unions first appeared in Nova Scotia in January 1933, one in the rural community of Broad Cove, the other in the mining town of Reserve Mines, that Coady discovered that the simplest way to "capture the interest of the people" was to arm the "members with confidence and cooperative experience for the difficult business of establishing their stores."[7] For Coady, the credit union "marked not only a milestone in our economic development but it served as a stimulus in our adult education program. If a credit union could be studied, established, and serve the best interests of the group, what might not the study of other topics do?"[8]

Coady thought that the credit union provided the ideal educational form to help the workers develop techniques of group action to prepare them for co-operation in more difficult fields. It also supplied finances to make entry into general producer and consumer fields possible. Here Coady was echoing Roy Bergengren's remarks to the Diocesan Rural Conference in September 1-2, 1931, upon his first visit to Nova Scotia; namely, that credit unions were the big factor in securing economic independence for industrial labourers, farmers and fishermen. No matter how poor people were, a credit union could be started to the great advantage of its members. Coady thought that he could sequence the learning for enlightenment and action process: "study clubs–rallies–conferences; credit unions–retail stores–wholesales. Later, a tie-up with primary producers as farmers, fishermen, etc. milk–fish, etc. offer good illustrations where this procedure solves the problems connected with the delicate inter-relationships between primary producers and industrial consumers."[9] This was the blueprint.

Coady had hit his stride by the mid-1930s as the prophetic voice of the downtrodden primary producers and industrial workers. Though he had followed his radical cousin, Jimmy Tompkins, through much of the 1920s, he had now become his own man. He was no longer waiting in the wings, but was playing to the increasing numbers of people who were crowding in to the theatre to see and hear the "modern Moses." On May 7, 1932, Coady had written to Chris Tompkins, his old teacher: "Things are moving here at a great rate. I have a world revolution in my head and Dr. J.J. Tompkins has another. We have not met for a month and I don't know if our revolutions will synchronize or not."

This comment captures an element of edginess present in the relationship between the Thomist Coady, ever searching for the blueprint or the formula for "world revolution," and the anarchic Tompkins, who embraced the pragmatics of "local action." Coady imagined world revolution, and thought that it could be engineered by visionary leaders and a mobilized and disciplined working class. Tompkins' mind was more instinctively oriented towards what could be done, immediately, in the here and now. Tompkins' creativity tore apart pessimism and gloom, as his mind worked overtime imagining practical ways that people could be awakened to new possibilities. Little energy was left to soar into the heavens of world revolution or to consider the co-operative movement as the final solution to global suffering and problems.

In contrast with Tompkins, Coady never stopped thinking or writing about world revolution. Donning the prophetic mantle in the early 1930s, Coady crafted his message of redemption for Maritimers who were, yet again, living through hard times. In meeting hall after meeting hall, Coady told his Depression audiences that, although the Maritimes were "fields of lost opportunities," there were still opportunities that "were not being taken advantage of." But in order to take advantage, the "mind had to be educated." It was only "through study and education that a people could see and seize the opportunities that would be profitable." To illustrate this, Coady once informed his New Glasgow Rotary Club audience that, if the miners in Glace Bay had only established a co-operative savings bank twenty-five years prior, they "could now buy out the whole British Empire Corporation."[10] This bold message challenged people to imagine that they could exert control over their own economic destinies.

Coady refused to give in to the pessimism that enveloped the Maritimes in the decades following World War I in his address to the Union of Nova Scotia Municipalities in late August 1932. Coady reasoned that with "more intelligent effort, and carefully applied work there is no reason why the Maritime provinces cannot be one of the most prosperous sections of the North American continent." Maritimers had neglected to "develop the physical possibilities of their own country." Consequently, the "road was strewn with wreckage of lost opportunities." The Depression, it seemed, was teaching "many needed lessons." People were not going to "long stand to have natural resources remain undeveloped and government-owned water powers run to waste, while healthy, honest people remain idle and their homes lack the helps and comforts of life." Coady finished his address with a flourish:

> We certainly are our brother's keeper; yes, his condition is as important as our own. We have no more right to let his children suffer than we have to let our own children suffer. We are all brothers one of another and children of the same God. This does not mean that we should attempt legislation or any other artificial means to disrupt the laws of economics, but it does mean that we must have the Christ spirit of endeavouring to help the little fellow and must unloose the great natural resources of our countries for the greatest good of the greatest number.[11]

In one of his first speeches to an American audience, "Economic Education needed today," as reported in *The Casket* of March 30, 1933,[12] Coady argued that the self-sufficiency of the common man had been swept away by the Industrial Revolution, which had turned everyone into a consumer. As a result, the "creative genius" of the people had atrophied. However, "if they owned and operated industrial plants that would minister to their needs, courage and creative genius would come back to the countryside." As owners, the people would develop a "keener consciousness of their own dignity and importance, and the realization that they were at least masters of machines would go a long way to enable them to put their hands on the throttle of their own destiny." Coady firmly believed that the Western world had evolved into an "economic group age," and that the "betterment of mankind" lay in "group activity." The adult educators of America faced the challenge of educating the "masses to the point where they were made competent to co-operate in the great task ahead." And Coady thought he knew the remedy, the way forward: co-operative business, co-operative credit, co-operative marketing and co-operative industry.

"Merchandizing is one of the ways in which the so-called capitalist class has taken its toll from the common man... Common people can bring about their economic betterment by controlling their own credit... These two movements—co-operative business and co-operative credit—carried on simultaneously would be, in my estimation, sufficient to change the economic face of the earth... It is plain common sense that the good of the common people of this earth demands that the producer get as much of the consumer's dollar as it is humanly possible for him to get." The constituent elements of Coady's prophetic narrative were in place.

One of Coady's powerful metaphors—the Maritimes as "fields of lost opportunities"—captured his fundamental belief that the Maritimes held economic potentialities that could be revealed to the creative imagination. He believed that the common people had to take responsibility for their plight; they had defaulted the economic realm to others who had gradually stolen it from them. Still, they had it within themselves and their communities to take control of their destinies. By becoming owners, they could release their creative genius and imagination. And adult education was the potent instrument for setting this transformative process in motion. This was Coady's elemental rhetorical frame.

II

By 1934, sufficient activity was evident in eastern Nova Scotia to render Coady's message plausible. The Extension Department's fragile survival time had ended and new energy and enthusiasm flowed through the communities like an electrical current. *The Xaverian Weekly* of February 18, 1933, had exulted: "A new life is springing up in our province. People recognize the necessity of an awakening. Consequently, they are beginning to do their own thinking and, having the courage of their convictions, they act accordingly. Cooperative ideas are abroad."

From 1934 onward, rising to a peak at the outbreak of World War II, the modest accomplishments of Coady and the Extension Department began to catch the eye of the outside world. The modestly consequential work of the St. Francis Xavier Extension Department turned into the "Antigonish Movement" and caught the world's imagination. Journalists, liberal-minded religious leaders, papal authorities, theologians, professors, newspaper editors, foundation managers, politicians, social reformers, co-operators, poets and various intellectuals came to witness the miracle of Antigonish. Antigonish became, not just a movement worth attending to and learning from, but an imaginative space into which people with varying interests could project their own desires and longings. Many people in the 1930s desperately wanted to find a non-revolutionary alternative to fascism and communism. They wanted Antigonish to be the Promised Land and Father Coady to be their modern Moses.

This attention, not all of it wanted, forced the Extension workers and intellectuals into presenting the Movement to a widening audience. This process—laudatory attention and ambiguous response—contributed to a kind of "halo effect" that thereafter surrounded the Movement and Moses Coady. Movement publicists were under considerable pressure to present a good face, to underplay organizational weaknesses and conflict and to mask the weight of the negative forces that constantly punctuated their utopian dreams.

Gregory MacDonald, writing in the *G. K. Weekly* of July 12, 1933,[13] was rather taken aback that organizations such as the Cape Breton Island Producers' Co-operative (of five hundred farmers) was able to sell garden produce, fruits and poultry to towns in Cape Breton, that lobster factories had sprung up, that members of a study club at MacKinnon's Harbour had decided to improve the potato crop by purchasing better seed "during a period of economic collapse." MacDonald was amazed that these forms of community self-organization had appeared in a "poor and backward area, among a people of no great education, many of whom had already been affected by communist influences." MacDonald also thought it remarkable that "three single men" were expending such a "fund of energy" to maintain a "wide and straggling territory of 183 study clubs." These men were whole-heartedly and self-sacrificingly devoted to finding solutions to social issues.

The Halifax Herald soon showed an interest in what was happening in the small communities of eastern Nova Scotia. Journalist Michael Ryan drove over hard-packed snow from Antigonish to nearby St. Andrew's in mid-January 1934 to witness the Movement for himself. Ryan was evidently entranced. "Worked-out farms now offer," he wrote,

subsistence to happy families; fishing villages stagnated by lack of markets are bustling communities resounding to the shipwright's maul and the builder's hammer; dejected seasonally employed industrial workers have learned a measure of independence through the ability to help themselves.... In three years the old order of things has been replaced by the new outlook.

Happy families, bustling communities, independent workers: all of this was wrought in group action.

Ryan believed that St. Francis Xavier University, a "center of spiritual and educational leadership," had sent out sparks that had been fanned into flames. The "experimental stage" was past; the "future" was now "filled with hope." St.FX was "spreading adult education and encouragement direct into thousands of homes." It had become a "light toward which men and women are rapidly turning for guidance while new production and marketing methods are taking shape."

Ryan's imagination caught fire. These relatively modest, yet exciting self-help ventures appeared to be aiming a "death blow" at "laissez-faire." Co-operative industry was accomplishing amazing things. Ryan turned, as so many writers would, to the example of Dover:

> Look at Dover, a fishing hamlet embracing 35 or 40 families near Canso. Years of education work directed in an indefatigable manner by the Rev. Dr. J.J. Tompkins, parish priest and former vice-rector of St. Francis Xavier's University, preceded the experiment. A communally owned lobster canning factory was built two years ago. Not a horse or cow was owned in the village. Timber had to be carted by hand. Success was instantaneous! Two power lobster smacks were built last year, a third is on the stocks. Last year fishermen were paid a cent a pound bonus on their catches, factory workers got 10 per cent bonuses, all debts were paid off. Today the fishermen have a capital investment of $5,000 in their cannery and boats and there is a substantial cash balance in the bank. Lobsters are either canned or shipped alive. Soon they will open their own store and fish plant and begin cooperative marketing of fresh, cured and pickled fish. Stagnation has been wiped out.[14]

Many writers would follow in Ryan's footsteps, transporting Dover into mythic status. Coady would later grumble that such descriptions were "misleading and absurd."[15]

Kingsley Brown, a left-leaning, progressive Halifax journalist, covered the Extension Department's work for *The New York Times*. At this time, the United States was being swept up by President Roosevelt's "New Deal," and Brown cast Moses Coady, Premier Angus L. MacDonald and Prof. A.B. MacDonald as three leaders in Nova Scotia's "new deal" or "group plan." Brown saw great significance in Premier Angus L. MacDonald's epochal address before a conference of lumber operators on January 12, 1934, where he declared that "the time has come when every industry in the province must organize on a co-operative basis." Brown observed that Premier MacDonald had been so encouraged by the progress made by St.FX's Extension Department that he was planning a "broader application of the co-operative plan." Co-operative marketing of lumber under government guidance seemed to hold out great promise for the revitalization of this sagging industry.

Brown believed that the Extension work had become a movement that was undermining private enterprise. "There already exist in Eastern Nova Scotia," he informed his American readers,

> dozens of communities where the phrase "private enterprise" has been dropped from the vocabulary. One will find in those communities retail stores, fish plants, fruit and fish canning factories, textile mills, community banks and marketing agencies–all operated for the common benefit of the communal owners on co-operative lives. The ... big coal mine at Inverness [is] now the property of the 450 miners and engineers who operate it.

But Brown thought that the co-operative movement had been of "inestimable value in removing the burden of unemployment relief from the provincial and municipal governments, having made many communities virtually self-sustaining." In one small community, Brown continued, where sparse vegetation prohibited the raising of cows, community members formed a co-operative to raise goats to replace their milk shortage.

Brown was astounded by the study clubs in the small communities of Nova Scotia.

> One will find groups of fishermen, for instance gathered around a stove while one of their comrades reads an article about Soviet Russia by Walter Duranty in the New York Times.... A farmer in the highlands of Inverness may astonish you by his ready knowledge of collective farming in Soviet Russia; a fishermen in Richmond county will talk with fluent ease about the corporative state of Mussolini or the code system of Roosevelt. It has been study clubs and libraries such as these, and their wide influence, that has stirred the people of Eastern Nova Scotia–tens of thousands of them–into a determined enthusiasm of a sort which a recent visiting McGill University professor declared was paralleled only by the enthusiasm found amongst the shock brigade in Russia. A youth movement is rapidly crystallizing in many sections of Eastern Nova Scotia and is destined to play a major role in the future reconstruction of the province.

Brown probed the ideological connections of the Movement. The leaders denied that the Movement was either "communist" or "socialist."

> The entire movement, they claim, is something indigenous to Nova Scotia and evolved to meet the problems peculiar to this province. They will deny that it is "communism" or "socialism" and prefer to describe it formally as "group action". But whatever its name it is the antithesis of "laissez-faire, "rugged individualism" and "private enterprise," so one can draw one's own conclusions.

Brown thought that the "really radical" parties–the Co-operative Commonwealth Federation (CCF) and the Communist Party–had made "remarkably poor" progress in Nova Scotia. The "cooperative movement, having its leadership in the new premier and the directors of St.FX University and confining its activities to practical development on the economic plane while leaving politics alone, stands as the only substantial force offering a new economic order to Nova Scotia."[16]

Movement coverage was snowballing in 1935. More writers than ever were busily constructing the Movement as an epic story of mythical proportion. Gustav Beck, the debonair director of the Labor Temple School of

New York, wrote in the *Journal of Adult Education* of his "thrilling experience" while visiting scattered Nova Scotian communities where "all hope
had died." He had observed "many touching stories in this epic of the modern St. Gallen giving battle to both ruthless capitalism and embittered
communism, substituting class cooperation for class antagonism, multiply-
ing loaves and looms and, above all, restoring self-respect to a once
bewildered and drifting people." Like others, Beck couldn't resist the story
of Dover. These "poor and simple folk" were now "alert and interested in
public affairs…. The entire morale of the settlement has changed. Most of
the people have formed steady reading habits." Beck's imagination transformed unpretentious self-help efforts in an underdeveloped economy into
a movement of grand proportion.

> The economic foundation for the change has been laid; the superstructure is still in the
> early stages of building. The movement may, as one of its leaders told me, issue in a
> new civilization in which the rural and industrial elements of Nova Scotia will be
> wisely interrelated and in which an entire economic transformation shall have been
> achieved through education instead of dogmatic propaganda or bloodshed. Thus, the
> new St. Gallen like the old stands as the protector of its people against those forms of
> barbarism which the various dictatorships of Europe are now inflicting upon their
> unhappy countries.[17]

The fledgling people's movement of eastern Nova Scotia was viewed as
much more than the aspirations of the "poor and simple folks" who were,
after all, using rather simple technologies to create co-operative lobster
canning factories for a relatively small number of fishermen.

In just over five years, the activities of the St.FX Extension Department
had been transfigured into a modern miracle. J. King Gordon, one of Canada's outstanding social gospel theologians, toured Nova Scotia in early
1935. Arriving in Antigonish in that "utterly desolate hour that most trains
arrive there," Gordon was entertained by "Little Doc" Hugh MacPherson,
A.B. MacDonald and Coady. An astute social analyst, Gordon learned that
the economic conditions of Nova Scotia had kept the people "shackled by
poverty and ignorance." The Extension Department sought to "create in
the people a desire to learn, and a confidence in their ability to learn."
Gordon considered Coady and MacDonald to be "prophets of the new day
who incited the people to discontent in their present conditions and
opened up before their astonished eyes the possibilities of reorganized
social and economic life." He thought that Coady's rhetorical powers were
"unrivalled even in that land of orators." After speaking in a community,
there were "always a few who catch fire with Coady's dynamic enthusiasm.
Then come calls for volunteers to assume responsibility in study club organization. Then the careful follow-up work which is AB's speciality."

Gordon captured the spirit propelling the Extension office.

Here is Sister Marie Michael who is in charge of 250 women's study clubs. She is typing away, cutting stencils to prepare for the mimeograph. Her chief interest is health and diet. She tells you about the death rate from tuberculosis, the primitive concepts of diet, ignorance of first principles of sanitation and hygiene, the lack of economy practices by housewives in buying. She laments the decline of the native industries and tells how better weaving is being introduced. There is Kay Thompson at her typewriter, answering the morning's mail. Hundreds of inquiries, study club leaders writing in for information, wanting Dr. Coady to assist in organizing a new group, wanting AB to set up a credit union, wanting material for a debate on communism or on capitalism. An educator from a prominent teachers' college wishing information "on your interesting curriculum of adult education," the head of a workers' school in the southern states wanting advice on how to organize a canning co-operative. Father Sumner with the proofs of the new bulletin before him. Professor A.B. MacDonald rushing in from a lecture, dictating a letter or two, ransacking the files for every conceivable kind of information for the earnest searcher after truth from central Canada, finally inviting him out to see the organization of a credit union in the afternoon.

Gordon believed that this "astonishing experiment" precipitated important questions. He wondered if it threw light on how the church or the churches might contribute to social reconstruction. Was co-operation the best form of social reconstruction to be attempted in a country made up of essentially farmers and fishermen? What was the relationship between this kind of education and organization and the radical workers' movements in the mining areas? What was to be the political expression of this new people's movement? Gordon, too, couldn't help speculating that it was not "at all an impossibility that we shall see emerging in our most easterly district in Canada a gaelic Denmark, which will be on the highroad to co-operative reorganization while other sections allegedly more enlightened will be still in the bogs of a decaying capitalism."[18]

In late summer of 1935, the feisty journalist Evelyn Tufts was swept up by the Movement. Like Kingsley Brown, Tufts was sympathetic to progressive causes. A member of the whimsically named Song Fishermen (which included Charles G.D. Roberts, Bliss Carmen, Robert Norwood, Stewart MacAuley, Kenneth Leslie, Evelyn Butler), Tufts lived a little of the Roaring Twenties style of life. She was searching for something to give her hope and found it in the Antigonish Movement. Her first article, "Hundreds of Nova Scotians throw off their shackles and are co-operating," opens with a quotation from a Newfoundlander who had come to see Antigonish. "I came here," he said,

because there is something electrifying going on in this little town, something it may be, of vital importance not only to your dominion but to the whole of North America. I came to see for myself what is happening here and how a handful of theologians have worked a modern miracle in the lives of men and women, found a way to beat the depression, and managed—most difficult of all things—to make groups of people behave decently toward one another, to co-operate instead of keeping on cutting one another's throats in the good competitive fashion.

Tufts was incensed by the multiple forms of exploitation of the common people. "Racketeering politicians and greedy middlemen" had had free reign until the Antigonish warriors arrived. "The time came when they wouldn't even offer us 1/2 c a pound for our fish," William Feltmate, a kind of folk hero fishermen from the Protestant community of Whitehead, pointed out. "With our backs to the wall, there was only thing left to do, and that was turn and fight. We're still fighting, and we mean to keep on, English and French, Catholic and Protestant, every mother's son of us. With thy help, and my help, we will build a wall around this city of Jerusalem, whereby the enemy may not enter."

Tufts was bitterly critical of the Canadian university's failure to help the citizenry solve its problems. Despite being surrounded by suffering, it "still keeps grinding, and blandly dumping its product upon an already saturated market." How was it, she queried, that St. Francis Xavier University was

> the only university we have that seems to be aware of such things as hunger and cold and illiteracy among our people? How is that it is the only one which shows any resentment of the cruel social injustice which has made pitiful paupers of whole sections of our population, the only one which is determined, before God, to fight this thing to demand a decent living for our fishermen, our farmers and our industrial workers? Have the other universities no interest in these people, do they feel no responsibility for them whatever?

People living in the coves and fishing villages were "hapless victims of a system of exploitation which is a disgrace to mankind, a system which makes it possible for a few unprincipled men in Nova Scotia to have millions, while little children suffer and die for lack of milk and vegetables, and warm stockings and shoes." Tufts thought that she was witnessing a "complete breakdown in the morale of a whole people, the portent of a collapse of entire civilization." Musing, Tufts asked if Nova Scotians had fought World War I to

> perpetuate a system under which boys are driven to riding the rods and becoming homeless vagrants, because there is no work for them anywhere in the world. Did they fight for a chance to come back home and get two shifts a week in the coal mines, or two cents a piece for mackerel which the same afternoon will be sold for twenty five? It is all very well to call them bloody Bolsheviks now, just because they complain that they can't make a decent living. They are not Bolsheviks. Not yet.[19]

In her final article, "Thousands secure solid benefits in co-operative move," Tufts asked why Nova Scotians had "fallen so hard for co-operatives." The answer wasn't hard to find: it was because the co-operative system was the "only one to stop profiteering, and dishonest, unfair trade practices." Tufts dramatically portrayed the results of this system. In the co-ops, members were getting honest weight and measure and full value for their money. Through credit unions, the "stranglehold of rapacious banks" had been loosened from "round the fishermen's and farmer's necks." And the consumers co-operative movement was the "only one in existence that has as its sole object the protection of the consumer as such. Is it any wonder that the places that have tried it have taken on a new lease on life?" Tufts was convinced that wherever the Extension movement had taken root,

> reform of abuses and better returns for local products follow almost automatically; whereas in the unorganized districts such as some of those I visited in Halifax city a few weeks ago, exploitation and distress, as usual, are going hand in hand. The sheds are piled full of salt fish, and the fish companies are offering $3.50 for mackerel which cost the fishermen $4.40 or more to lay down.

Tufts didn't think that one needed to be a follower of Karl Marx to know that a "cultural revival almost inevitably follows an economic revival.... An economic upswing in Nova Scotia would be reflected almost immediately in the universities in the form of more students, better support and fatter subscriptions."

The hard-headed Tufts, pounding away at the exploitation of Maritimers with handfuls of statistics and baskets of anecdotes, also contributed to the mythologization of Antigonish. As she left Antigonish and looked back, it seemed to her "that a sort of radiance filled the sky, as if a hand had touched the east to light once more the star of which a great poet once wrote so movingly, 'the star that shone when Hope was born.'" Evelyn Tufts thought of

> another town, familiar to us all in a far-off, obscure, downtrodden, pastoral country not wholly unlike our own, in whose dark streets mankind had once found shining the Everlasting light. 'With thy help, and my help, we will build a wall around this city of Jerusalem, whereby the enemy may not enter.' Even yet, we might be able to do that very thing. Even yet, if we all combined, we might save this country from ruin.[20]

For Tufts, the little town of Antigonish had become the modern sacred city; the unadorned stable, the St. Francis Xavier University Extension Department; and Moses Coady, the new messiah.

III

In the late 1930s, the "modern miracle" of Antigonish broke free from its moorings in eastern Nova Scotia and spread west across Canada, down the eastern seaboard through Boston and New York, into the mid-west of the United States, across the Atlantic to the metropolis of London and down into the British West Indies, particularly Jamaica. The story of the "little people" of eastern Nova Scotia and their "heroic leaders" circulated through several pre-established social networks, in which Tompkins and Coady moved constantly, particularly in Boston, New York and Washington, D.C. One was the international Roman Catholic circuit. Two American Catholic organizations, the Catholic Rural Life Association and the National Catholic Welfare Conference, welcomed Coady's message.

Canadian Catholic organizations also opened their doors to the Antigonish intellectuals. The Federal Council of the Churches of Christ in America, led by stalwart Protestant proponents of the social gospel Dr. J. Henry Carpenter and Benson Y. Landis, became a loyal supporter of the Antigonish project. Carpenter and Landis became two of Coady's admiring colleagues and friends.

A second circuit was that of the emergent co-operative movement in the United States and Canada (later, elsewhere). In the U.S., the Antigonish intellectuals developed close ties with the Co-operative League of the USA, led by E.R. Bowen, Murray Lincoln and the Ohio Farm Bureau, and Roy Bergengren of the Credit Union National Association (CUNA). Ideas flowed both ways. To this day, the Roy Bergengren Credit Union in Antigonish serves as a historic reminder of Bergengren's pivotal role in fashioning appropriate legislation for the Nova Scotia credit union movement. In Canada, the Antigonish intellectuals linked with the national organization, the Co-operative Union of Canada (CUC), under the sure-footed, cautious direction of George Keen. Many other co-operative organizations, such as the Manitoba Pool Elevators, or associations with affinities to the co-operative movement (such as the University of Alberta Extension Department), would seek out Coady, A.B. MacDonald, A.S MacIntyre, and J.D. Nelson MacDonald (the United Church minister who was a part-time fieldworker) for advice and inspiration. Both British Columbia (through its Extension Division under Gordon Shrum) and Newfoundland (through its Commission of Government) would invite St.FX to help them organize their fishery. Numerous other civic and co operative organizations would call upon St.FX for aid and insight. A.B. MacDonald was even on the Board of the socialist League for Social Reconstruction in the early 1930s, though this was not exactly publicized.

A third circuit was the growing adult education networks in the United States and Canada. Father Tompkins was the only Canadian who had participated in the meetings that led to the formation of the American Association of Adult Education (AAAE) in 1926. He was well connected in the American scene and had friends in the Carnegie Corporation. In late May 1934, W.J. Dunlop, the conservative director of the University of Toronto Extension Division, had called for delegates from "adult education" organizations to convene to consider the formation of a national association of adult education. At that seminar, eighty-six delegates from forty-six organizations learned that Canada was "pulsating with adult education activity."[21] There, Canadian delegates heard publicly for the first time what was happening in Canada's periphery.

By the late spring of 1934, A.B. MacDonald's star had risen. Canada's greatest long-distance organizer had begun to carry the co-operative message outside the province of Nova Scotia. At the Toronto seminar,

MacDonald outlined St.FX's Extension program in clear, no nonsense, radical language. Nothing less than an economy controlled by the common people would suffice, he declared, no doubt perking up the ears of some of the Canadians present who hadn't really thought much about "adult education" as an instrument of "economic transformation." St.FX wanted its people to gain "spearhead knowledge": knowledge necessary to cut the cords that bound the working class to its exploiters, control of merchandising, control of credit, control of capital.

In 1935, partly as a result of pressure from Morse A. Cartwright, president of the AAAE, Canadians formed the Canadian Association for Adult Education (CAAE). Nova Scotia-born E.A. Corbett was chosen as its first director, amid some controversy. Something of a legend in his own right, Corbett left the directorship of the University of Alberta's dynamic Extension Department for this position. He would make many trips to Antigonish over the years; he, too, was hooked by the charisma of Coady and company.

Moses Coady was now caught up in a movement that had spilled over its circumscribed boundaries. The work of the Extension Department had been transformed into the "Antigonish Movement," but this nomenclature was no longer restricted to the specific geographic space of "eastern Nova Scotia." It referred to a plausible, coherent educational-co-operative process of achieving a new economic and social order. Coady no longer belonged exclusively to the incipient Atlantic Canadian co-operative movement. Larger than life, he was the giant who travelled ceaselessly, when not in the hospital, moving through the web of communication circuits to spread the co-operative revolution. For example, Coady attended the Carnegie Foundation centennial in New York City. He told them that "we are putting instruments in the hands of the people with which they can lift themselves to new planes.... Economic group action is the only way out for our people. It is not a question of co-operation or something else; co-operative action has become the only way." In the summer of 1935, Murray Lincoln and Carl Hutchinson of the Ohio Farm Bureau had both participated in the Rural and Industrial Conference. In March 1936, Coady returned the favour and addressed the Bureau in Columbus, Ohio. There he spoke to state employees, gatherings of adult and co-operative educators, went on a co-operative field trip, toured farm bureau offices and gave several talks to co-operative groups in Cincinnati.

The Carnegie Foundation recognized the "far-reaching importance and results of the University's co-operative project" and funded a National Catholic Welfare Conference-sponsored whirlwind tour of the United States. Coady's voice was assured and confident. He told the Dallas Civic Federation in early April 1936 that though "this movement of the common people to gain control of the fruits of their own labor has met opposition from big business it is so firmly entrenched and is spreading so rapidly in Nova Scotia that its success is assured." Coady also informed his Texas audience that Canada was "swinging to the left" more than the United States. While in Dallas, Coady met with staff members of the district resettlement administration (he was a member of the Land Settlement Commission in Nova Scotia from 1931 to 1933) and farm leaders of Dallas County and several other voluntary associations. From Texas, Coady travelled to California, where he spoke on "Consumer Co-operation" at the Berkeley High School auditorium on April 22. Both the California Cooperative Council and Catholic Rural Life sponsored Coady's lecture on adult education. He addressed convention groups of the Cooperative Council and the Catholic Rural Life conference. Coady also spoke at meetings held in Grafton, North Dakota; Albuquerque, New Mexico; and Atchison, Kansas. After arriving back in New York, he was one of the principal speakers at the AAAE meeting, held on May 20, 1936.[22] Coady understood that he and the other Movement leaders were really "new missionaries of applied economics" who were making themselves the "eloquent spokesmen for a people sorely beset and exploited by ruthless middlemen."[23]

The Rural and Industrial Conferences of the late 1930s, held at St.FX in Antigonish in late summer, became the place for social reformers to be seen and heard. These Conferences, which drew many leading Canadian and American intellectuals and activists of the day, were important public forums for the learning of and reflection on the salient issues of the day. Bertram Fowler, known for his unrestrained prose, got it right in his article of 1937, "Ownership returns to Nova Scotia," when he observed:

> Tucked away in that isolated corner of Nova Scotia living upon the fruits of almost incredible poverty, these tiny communities are today exerting a tremendous influence upon the thinking people of all over the U.S. and Canada.... The tremendous impact of this tiny renaissance has touched men and women thousands of miles away.[24]

Reportage from the thirteenth annual Rural and Industrial Conference, held on August 20-21, 1935, noted that the St.FX adult education movement was beginning to "attract attention all over the world." Although Roy Bergengren of the U.S. Credit Union National Association and George Keen of the Co-operative Union of Canada had previously visited Antigonish, this was the first major meeting attended by American co-operative leaders. Murray Lincoln, secretary of the Ohio Farm Bureau, Columbus, Ohio, E.R. Bowen, general secretary of the Co-operative League of the USA and Dr. Carl Hutchinson of the Recreation Co-operatives Inc. of Indiana were at this meeting. Speaking for the others, Bowen claimed that the visitors "found a unique program of world significance being carried through, for the University, as a university should do, was reaching out to the 'little man.'"[25]

The Rural and Industrial Conference was an important deliberative space for the politics of civil society. The participants at the 1935 meeting passed resolutions that had significant implication for government policy. The delegates recommended that unemployed men be organized for the production of garden crops and poultry to supplement the paltry income derived from their irregular occupations. They also urged the government to organize the present land settlement policy so that rural-minded young men could be encouraged to settle on suitable farms. These latter resolutions reflect the deep-rooted ambivalence of the Roman Catholic Church towards industrial forms of work in mine and mill; the mythology of mining as the devil's domain was woven into the Catholic spirituality of the early twentieth century. Father Michael Gillis, who had influence with Coady, was a committed agrarianist who pressed the Department throughout the 1930s and 1940s to wrench the miners from their underground worlds and settle them above ground on farms.

The Rural and Industrial Conference of 1936 convened amidst considerable panic about the global future of democracy and the world economy. *The Halifax Herald* of August 19, 1936, reported that "upwards of seven hundred working fishermen and farmers and miners from eastern Nova Scotia, leaders in the local schools of study-in-action movement were gathered ... for the 14th annual rural and industrial conference under the auspices of the now-famous extension department of St. Francis Xavier University." Those who gathered heard from American and Canadian intellectuals, librarians, editors, historians, intellectuals, co-operative organizers and local organizers. Dr. Charles Beard, president of the AAAE and a distinguished progressive historian, addressed the Conference, declaring that "democracy is dependent historically upon a wide distribution of property. When property is concentrated in the hands of the few, democracy dies."

Michael Williams, editor of the national Catholic weekly *The Commonweal,* spoke on "An Editor's View of the World Crisis." Williams, a former Cape Bretoner, asserted dramatically that the "black beast" of the immediate future was not communism, whose heroism was worth emulating, but "Big Business Fascism." Williams spoke to the religious dimension of the world crisis. The fundamental struggle, he thought, was between the "religious" and the "atheistical" conception of life. Convinced that the world was in the throes of its greatest crisis ever, Williams pleaded for a united religious front (Jews, Protestants and Catholics) to fight organized atheism. Williams was proud of the "constructive revolution" being effected by St. Francis Xavier University.

Other speakers included the Rev. James Byrne, executive secretary of the Catholic Rural Life Conference of St. Paul; Nora Bateson, director of the Carnegie Library Demonstration; Elmer Scott, executive secretary of the Civic Federation, Dallas, Texas; the Rev. J.M. Campbell, executive secretary of the National Co-operative Service Bureau of Ames, Iowa; and Dr. P.S. Campbell, Nova Scotia Deputy Minister of Health. The speaker's roster was filled out by locals from the grassroots communities as well as the Antigonish intellectuals. Coady himself hammered away on the theme of "What stands between the people and a better world."

Delegates at the 1936 Rural and Industrial Conference discussed the credit union movement, arts and crafts for women, electrification, public speaking, women and a better social order, reports from the grassroots communities, dramatic representation of study clubs in action, building a healthy people, adult education and democracy. These discussions seemed to confirm Dr. Gustav Beck's judgement, given in a Halifax address, that St.FX's initiatives were the "boldest and most constructive attempt to conquer this depression that is threatening to overcome the entire world. There is no solution which meets this territory so excellently."

The resolutions of the Conference, however, rode close to the ground. The delegates had learned that the British Canadian Co-operative Society was being taxed as a profit-making chain store. They proposed an amendment that would enable the famous Co-operative society to be taxed as a non-profit agency. They also resolved that the government be "urged to organize the present land settlement policy so as to be effective in encouraging rural-minded young men settling on farms." Two years later, Coady wrote candidly to Edmund des. Brunner of Columbia Teachers' College in New York that he had tried to

> put out hundreds of these people on vacant farms but, in the main, the scheme was a failure. For the last three years some of us have been pushing the Premier of Nova Scotia to inaugurate a land settlement scheme for young men who were brought up on Nova Scotia farms. Just recently the Premier has decided to start in a small way. He is going to take a few good men from each county, given them a short course at the Agricultural College, and then given them land almost free. In time is hoped that the scheme may develop to include larger numbers.[26]

Delegates from the coal fields stirred up interest in finding new uses for coal. They urged the Dominion government to have its fuel-testing staff at Ottawa investigate the most suitable method of low-temperature carbonization for Sydney coal, as they wanted the resulting semi-coke to displace the imported anthracite. The women at the Conference expressed their resentment at the "many forms of advertising displayed in both American and Canadian women's magazines. We find many of them both exaggerated and indecent."

The delegates left the 1936 meeting brimming with verve and enthusiasm. They expressed their thanks to the officers for the "wonderful conference which was so aptly described as 'The Most Rousing Thing in the World.'" The Extension leaders appeared to be successful in their goal of filling people with energy and creative ambition at these summer conferences, energy which would in turn flow back into their own communities.

IV

No matter how things actually were in the beleaguered communities of eastern Nova Scotia–"Dover today, is not, as many contemporaries write, a prosperous or a model community. Such descriptions are misleading and absurd,"[27] Coady complained–many observers constructed a redemptive narrative, the myth of the modern miracle. People desperately needed hope in their lives, communities needed economic liberation and the Movement intellectuals needed to deliver the goods. Despite his protestations, Moses Coady was psychically predisposed to find the answer to people's problems. He was a utopian thinker who believed that the co-operative millennium could be made manifest, and thousands of people now looked to him as their messiah. The myth of the Antigonish miracle served his purpose in awakening the Maritime imagination, yet this myth would also be his Achilles' heel.

The Extension Department added something new to its 1937 Rural and Industrial Conference: a co-operative movement tour co-sponsored with the Co-operative League of the USA. The brochure announcing the tour informed Americans that Father Coady had "developed and directed one of the most practical and interesting cooperative ventures in North America. The program as worked out has changed the lives and viewpoints of many thousands of the fishermen, miners and farmers of Nova Scotia." Participants of the tour were promised the opportunity to confer with Coady, Tompkins, A.B. MacDonald and other leaders of the Movement. They would visit stores, credit unions and canning factories in the fishing, mining and farm communities. They could then sit in on the annual Conference of these co-operative organizations. Tourists of the co-operative revolution would be able to "revel amid the historical settings and beauties of the 'Land of Evangeline', and to study and see this significant cooperative undertaking."

The Extension Department took this tour very seriously, drawing on the "big guns" of the Movement (Coady, Tompkins, Ida Gallant, Sister Marie Michael, A.B. MacDonald, M.J. MacKinnon, James Boyle, A.S. MacIntyre, R.J. MacSween and Peter Nearing). The tourists heard these leaders expound on the Antigonish philosophy in preliminary gatherings, interwoven with community singing, Scottish dancing and games. Then the tourists left Antigonish (from the local creamery of course), travelling through fishing communities such as Petit de Grat and D'Ecousse and arriving in Cape Breton the following day. The "little people" were now on display as the Movement struggled with how to present itself to the outside world. A.B. MacDonald informed Rev. A. Boudreau that the tour would

arrive in Petit de Gras at about 10:15 on the morning of August 13th. These visitors will want to chat with and question some of the people of the community and we think that if you had the directors of the cooperative and the credit union on hand at that hour it would help to give the people what they want as well as make it interesting for them. Again, some one person should be selected to give a ten-minute talk on what has been accomplished in P de G during the last two or three years. This perhaps could be done outdoors in front of the plant.[28]

In Cape Breton, groups visited some of the Movement's showcases: the Cape Breton Dairymen's Association, Dosco Credit Union, Sydney Co-operative Society, the British Canadian Co-operative Society and the Little Bras d'Or Lobster Factory. On Sunday, the tour went round the Cabot Trail, arriving in time for supper at Cheticamp. On Monday, after early morning deep-sea fishing, the group visited co-operatives in Grand Etang, had lunch in Margaree Forks and travelled through Mabou, Judique and Port Hawkesbury. On the final day of the tour, the group left for Canso and spent the day observing the vibrant co-op life on the Guysborough shore (Port Felix and Larry's River).

The 1937 Rural and Industrial Conference continued in the spirit of the previous year. Intellectuals and social reformers from the United States were very much in evidence. Participants in wide-ranging discussions of economic and political solutions to the world crisis included the Rev. Paul Furfey, head of the sociology department at the Catholic University, Washington, D.C., and author of the millenarian text, *Fire on the Earth*; Joseph Schenk from the Indiana Farm Bureau, Indianapolis; Bertram Fowler, a journalist from New York; Herbert Agar, associate-editor of *Free America* and the *Courier-Journal*, Louisville, Kentucky; and Wallace Campbell of the Co-operative League of the USA. E.A. Corbett, enthusiastic director of the CAAE, addressed the audience on "Some Aspects of Adult Education in the Nineteenth Century." The Nova Scotian leaders (such as J.D. Nelson MacDonald and A.S. MacIntyre) chaired the various sessions, as the audience heard addresses by both Americans and Canadians, listened to panel discussions (Coady led the one on "Is our Democratic Program Adequate?"; participants included John T. Croteau from P.E.I., the Rev. J.L. Chiasson from Shippegan, Bertram Fowler and Wallace Campbell) and heard stories from the grassroots of Atlantic Canada.

Bishop Morrison and St.FX president Dr. D.J. MacDonald (A.B.'s brother) welcomed the delegates at 2:30 on Wednesday afternoon. The session was opened by the Rev. Alex MacKenzie of Westville, who had only recently returned from Italy. MacKenzie's speech was extremely controversial, and illustrated the seduction of fascism for some Catholics. Father MacKenzie thought that Mussolini was the "man of the hour," who had turned Italy away from communism. He praised the "best features of the system" and Mussolini's support for co-operatives. Coady condemned both fascism and communism, and no doubt his back-room machinations led the Conference to pass this resolution:

> Whereas the philosophy and principles of the Co-operative movement are diametrically opposed to any order that would limit the freedom and therefore the activities and growth of all individuals, be it resolved that this conference place itself on record as opposed to Fascism, National Socialism, Communism, and all other such forms of dictatorship.[29]

Other priests in the diocese apparently agreed with Father Mackenzie. Coady wrote importunately to Father Jimmy on November 16, 1937: "I consulted some of the fellows here about the matter and they are all of the opinion that it would be a tremendous mistake for Catholics to align themselves in any way with the Fascistic idea.... I think the way to take [Father] Quinan is to be canny and non-committal." Father Quinan, one of Coady's priestly foes, had tried to stir up trouble by suggesting that the Protestants had been behind the anti-fascism resolution. Coady continued:

> I think the real trouble with Quinan is that he is sore over the little incident with Boyle last year. Quinan's reference to undue influence of the Protestant element is only a suspicion, probably floated by some of our own people who were sore. The resolution was passed in, as all resolutions are, by an individual. It was put before the Conference and unanimously passed. In other words, the Conference in Antigonish, which was overwhelmingly Catholic, did not believe in the Mussolini regime, notwithstanding the fact that Father MacKenzie gave a glowing account of its achievements. Our Conference probably expressed the opinion of Catholics generally in North America. Quinan should be asked what evidence he has for thinking that the great body of Catholics assembled at our Conference were forced to that conclusion by a Protestant influence.[30]

However, what Coady didn't tell his cousin was the extent to which, in the Toronto diocese, fascist and Catholic leaders had a "natural affinity for one another."[31]

The 1937 Conference saw the arrival of a quietly formidable force on the stormy Cape Breton scene. Michael J. MacKinnon ("Father Mike"), who as a young man had stood in a dark hall in Cape Breton and told his coal-miner father that he would follow Coady "wherever he goes," was twenty-three years younger than his mentor. He had a brilliantly incisive mind. Addressing the delegates on "A Program for Eastern Canada," MacKinnon argued that only group action that fostered the "fullest expansion of individual personality" and prevented "rugged individualism" would suffice. "To be effective," MacKinnon explained,

> these groups must be vocational groups of farmers, fishermen and industrial workers.... Through our program we hope that these various groups will become economically powerful to express themselves, and by doing the things against [which] there is

no law, human or divine, become realists in the political field and begin a crusade for social justice and social reconstruction.

In later years, Coady would credit Father Mike with routing the communists from the coal fields.

By the mid-1930s, the Movement's intellectuals had reached a consensus on the procedural phases of building a co-operative movement. Coady and the others had understood clearly that the credit union was the product of the Movement's toddler stage. As the Movement found its legs, it could venture into co-operative processing and marketing of products of the primary producer. "We have," MacKinnon said in his conference address, "already organized and established sound co-operative enterprises of this nature, as witness, our lobster factories, fish processing plants, livestock, poultry, and egg pools, as well as co-operative saw mills."

The third step was to set up consumer stores. MacKinnon addressed the fears expressed by retailers around Nova Scotia that the consumer co-operative movement had been "organized for the sole purpose of destroying the business of native retail merchants, and bringing ruin to them, and their families." Fundamentally, MacKinnon thought that most "retail merchants will concede that the greatest danger to their means of livelihood" lay in the "chain stores, big business combines." "The objective we have in view," Father MacKinnon continued,

> is the reconstruction of society on a Christian basis, and to bring about that we must have consumer retail stores. This concerns the common good, and the common good comes before the individual. If the consumer stores are to fill the purpose for which they were organized they must federate, and organize a co-operative wholesale society. From co-operative wholesalers it is necessary to go back into the fields of production, and manufacturing.

MacKinnon thought this could be done in eastern Canada. He concluded his provocative address by arguing that only free agencies such as St.FX could mobilize adults for the "purpose of scientifically studying their varied problems." And he insisted that religious conviction was the "vitalizing force" that would motivate both leaders and people. Real religion supplied the dynamics to start the program and keep it moving.

The mystical Rev. Paul Furfey, speaking on "The Christian Revolution," encouraged the assembly to follow the uncompromising dictates of Christ. Furfey believed that most Christians were selfish. If Christians were to practice true charity, a more equal distribution of this world's goods would result. Furfey's call to Christians for radical, social discipleship was in tune with Movement spirituality. Herbert Agar argued in a similar vein that the great need was "to get back to the spiritual foundation so necessary to democracy."

Though not well attended, the last day of the Conference was given over to resolutions. These resolutions signalled the delegates' desire to press the co-operative movement forward. Two resolutions, one focusing on the need for a special organization to formulate "progressive and protective policies for the movement" and the second emphasizing that the volume of co-operative business warranted it, argued that the movement needed a co-operative wholesale. Delegates also recognized that the "high hopes of the people" would not be realized "unless co-operative business is conducted efficiently." They resolved that a "special extension course for co-operative managers, prospective managers and bookkeepers" be given at St.FX that winter. During the previous winter, Movement leaders had waged a struggle to reorganize the People's Co-operative Society in Antigonish. In April 1937, A.S. MacIntyre had informed Coady that he was glad to hear of the reorganization of the People's Co-op. "An ideal co-operative set-up in the town of Antigonish would be an example for the rest of the county." Still he wondered how they would solve the "question of management." MacIntyre said it wouldn't surprise him if "it were to prove a greater problem than re-organizing the society."[32] In response to the continued presence of significant opposition to the co-operative movement, delegates resolved that a "co-operative periodical" was necessary to "counteract the insidious propaganda" coming from "attacks from private interests." Finally, delegates affirmed that a "complete program aiming at the reconstruction of our social order" necessitated the "development of youth," using an "adequate and balanced program" that integrated physical, intellectual, social and religious activities.

The year 1938 was another banner one for the Extension Department. Requests flooded into Extension offices for information about the Movement in such quantity that Extension produced an essay, "Millions of dollars turnover in Maritime Co-operative efforts," to distribute to readers. This document, published in *The Halifax Herald*, offered a fascinating window on how the Movement understood itself at the nadir of its utopian hopes and energy. No doubt reflecting Coady's touch, it stated that they had "at last found a common denominator in this Maritime country to which all can be reduced for the good of the whole." Above all, "through this movement the people of Maritime Canada are forging instruments which in one decade, if the work goes forward in vigor, can again establish industries in the Maritime provinces which no interest can buy or bankrupt." Extension imagined that when the people got a "clear vision of the blueprint that is involved in this whole movement they will have a new pride in their own ability and a new sense of realism that will have repercussions in every phase of the activities of Maritime life. This is a plan for tomorrow." It seemed that nothing could erode Coady's exuberant spirit of the late 1930s.

In 1938 Extension had a staff of eight full-time members, not including stenographers, and seven part-time field organizers. They were assisted by regular university professors from time to time and local leaders, particularly clergy from all denominations. From expenditures of $2,416.94 in 1929-30, the Extension Department now spent $25,069.73 for its operations. However, St.FX was in a poor situation financially and there was some danger of curtailed resources for Extension. The Department was also depending on Carnegie Corporation funds. Carnegie had provided $49,000 for general use since the early 1930s, as well as $10,000 for the purchase of books for the period from 1936 to 1941. They promised a further grant of $9,000 for the general needs of the Department. The federal Department of Fisheries also provided funding for fieldworkers among the fishermen.

Now that the Movement had helped people to find "new hope, sense of responsibility and initiative," its leaders were "aroused to take more interest in health, recreation, co-operative housing, and other fields."[33] This statement is significant, as the Antigonish Movement cannot be fully understood as an adult education movement oriented to strictly economic outcomes. By the late 1930s, communities had turned their attention to revitalizing civil society. Tompkins, who took up parish duties in the Reserve Mines in 1935, had sparked interest in co-operative housing, assisted by the amazing Mary Arnold. The miners who had cut their teeth on trade union politics and moved in droves into the credit union and co-operative consumer movement agitated for co-operative medicine in the face of much opposition from the Nova Scotia medical establishment. (In November 17, 1939, the first socialized health centre was established in Johnstown, Cape Breton, under the direction of Dr. Daniel MacDonald, a veteran medical practitioner from Sydney.)

On February 25, 1938, *The Halifax Chronicle* reported that A.B. MacDonald had threatened to resign from his position as assistant director of Extension. He wanted more money to support a growing family, and the Co-operative Union of Canada wanted him. The veteran battler of the coal fields, A.S. MacIntyre, wrote Coady that he was down in the dumps over A.B. MacDonald's threat to leave Extension and the apparent waning of interest in co-operative action. St.FX convinced MacDonald to stay on for five more years, and Coady told his downhearted co-worker MacIntyre that Tompkins had indicated to him

> that the possibilities of getting some outside money were fairly bright. If we do, we are on the crest of the biggest wave that ever broke. If we even get the money to put on more workers, the result in the next five years will be nothing short of a miracle. The housing proposition, if carried through successfully, will have the effect of winning back many people who have been alienated from the movement because they feel it cuts across their vested interests.... This has tremendous significance to our movement ... as important, probably, as the credit unions were in 1933. So keep your courage up. Things are going to break.[34]

News of the exploits of St.FX continued to spread, even to the inner sanctum of Rome. In 1938 Pope Pius XI bestowed papal benediction on the work of Extension. "Social life has a sacredness all its own when imbued with the spirit of the gospel and based on justice and charity," Cardinal Eugenio Pacelli (later the controversy-generating Pope Pius XII) wrote on the Pope's behalf. He praised the leaders who had "dedicated themselves and their all to the betterment of the Christian people." *The Halifax Herald* noted: "As the message from His Holiness to Bishop Morrison states, the leaders of the Antigonish Movement are striving to help the workers better their lot 'in such a way that the full teachings of the encyclicals Rerum Novarum and Quad. Anno may be put in practice'."[35] Official support from the Catholic Church continued into the fall when nineteen Bishops of eastern Canada, led by Cardinal Villeneuve of Quebec, published a joint pastoral urging immediate formation of co-operative unions among farmers "to serve as a bulwark against communism and to re-establish the rural economy on a more stable basis."[36] Everyone, it seemed, had their own "Antigonish Movement."

Journalists continued to praise the work of the Extension Department. "Something strikingly new in adult education comes from St.FX."[37] "Credit unions continue to spread in province; Halifax has active part."[38] The year 1938 would also see the first publication of a full-length book on the Movement, Bertram Fowler's *The Lord Helps Those ... How the People of Nova Scotia Are Solving Their Problems through Co-operation.*[39] It wasn't a great book; the style was too breezy and the familiar clichés were in evidence. The Movement was described as a "modest miracle ... worked out unpretentiously by humble people,"[40] and Coady, as the "burly, hard-hitting apostle of the new St.FX doctrine who had been found by Tompkins' teaching school in a little Cape Breton village."[41] Meant to be inspirational rather than analytical, Fowler's text nonetheless revealed an important American sub-text. Like many other progressives in the 1930s, Fowler longed to return to the idealized world of the old, small-property-owning "Golden Age" of early America. Fowler thought that the Golden Age was being reborn in eastern Nova Scotia. With abandoned farms and wasted acreage now transformed into a "genuinely balanced system for the rural economy, a resettlement of these lands with prosperous farms is now possible."[42] The *Extension Bulletin,* however, scolded Fowler for focusing too much on the leadership of one or two men. "The great characteristic of the movement is, that it is not the product of the thinking of one or two men.... If it were not for the loyalty and the collaboration of these men and women in the field, the adult education program of St.FX would have been able to accomplish only a small part of its amazing achievement."[43] Coady's *Masters of Their Own Destiny* would be dedicated to these men and women.

The Antigonish Movement insiders often poked fun at journalists who were worse even than Fowler.

> Ah, the journalists! The writing fraternity could be divided into two classes: the serious and the kooks. The latter, smelling a good yarn (National Enquirer style), had no patience with small success or gradual growth. Where they could not find shock and miracles they invented them. They did not let the facts get in their way.... One story in a reputable Canadian magazine began: "'The people can do ten times what they think they can do.' Thus spoke young M.M. Coady from Margaree, Cape Breton, when he stepped off the train at Antigonish to enrol as a third-year student at St.FX College."[44]

Zita O'Hearn commented acidly that this observation had been made some thirty years later, after decades of educating and dealing with the people. Extension staff had particular fun with an article from *Coronet* magazine. The journalist had come to Antigonish for a couple of days and wrote this gem: "The people of Antigonish are poor. They are starving. Their faces are pinched and chalky. They do not smile." O'Hearn thought that this

> irresponsible reporting did damage in two ways. It produced sneers from local people who were not sympathetic to the movement which they felt threatened their monopoly on commercial enterprise. They insinuated that these writers had been coached by Extension personnel and were only writing what they had been told. The other effect was that the stuff was taken for gospel by readers in distant places, with some amusing results.[45]

One young couple wrote Coady asking if they could honeymoon by first sitting at his feet before plunging in to help the poor in the slums.

Coady was heartened in mid-1938 by the continuing growth of the credit unions and the emergence of organizations such as the Sydney Co-operative Society in the "face of criticism, doubt and untold discouragement."[46] He also knew that the conditions in the fishery were still very poor. In Halifax to attend a Fisheries conference at Province House in early July 1938 with the Hon. J.E. Michaud, Minister of Fisheries, Premier MacDonald and Hon. J.L. Ilsley, Minister of National Revenue, and others in attendance, Coady informed the influential policymakers that, "first and foremost, the public representatives who called and participated in this conference should set out to determine, once and for all, the reasons for the wide and unjustifiable spread between what the primary producer receives for his fish and what the consumer pays in retail fish prices." The fishermen wanted to know why the government would not proceed to fix a minimum price for fish.[47]

From his first tour of the fishing communities in the Maritimes, Coady had known that transforming the fishery into a complex co-operative enterprise would be a formidable task. However, he didn't doubt that co-operatives could "bring industry back to eastern Nova Scotia—a graveyard of industry." Canada's first co-operative housing venture in Reserve Mines, Tompkinsville, had just celebrated its opening, and his redoubtable and unpredictable cousin, Father Jimmy, was scheduled to speak at the upcoming Rural and Industrial Conference. Even though Coady saw his cousin as being a bit of loose cannon, he wanted him to "put across the idea that unless the people have industry and energy enough in them to organize themselves for enlightenment, they get nowhere. The study club and conference techniques and the other things make up a practical, inexpensive and fruitful technique. We want the people to realize this great truth."[48] Tompkins would give his most famous speech, and stay on topic. His poetic words echo to this day.

> Our experience in the Antigonish Movement is that there is more real Adult Education at the pit heads, down in the mines, out among the fishermen's shacks, along the wharves, and wherever the farmers gather to sit and talk in the evenings, than you can get from one hundred thousand dollars' worth of fossilized formal courses. It springs from the heart and pains of the people.[49]

The Movement was at its most buoyant at the time of the 1938 Rural and Industrial Conference. The press described the Conference as "one of the major forces for progress at a time when giant forces are demanding much of little men and bringing forth scholars, saints, statesmen and reformers of unusual calibre."[50] Many leading American educationalists participated in its summer tours. The Co-operative League of the USA had organized two tours under the general direction of the Rev. J. Henry Carpenter. The Rev. James Myers, secretary of the Division of Industrial Relations, Federal Council of Churches (USA), and the young firebrand Wallace J. Campbell, secretary of the Co-operative League, were tour leaders.

Two hundred men and women came from points across Canada and the United States to participate in the pre-Conference, a tour and the Conference itself. At the main Conference, these participants were joined by the key Movement leaders from Atlantic Canada (Gerald Richardson, Newfoundland; Dr. J.T. Croteau, P.E.I.; Rev. J.L. Chiasson and Rev. J.W. Hill, New Brunswick, and Rev. J.D. Nelson MacDonald and Rev. A.W. Guild from Nova Scotia presented regional reports), all of Extension's male and female leaders (Tompkins, Coady, A.B. MacDonald, MacIntyre, Sister Marie Michael, Sister Anselm, Kay Thompson, Zita O'Hearn, Ida Gallant, and Mary MacMillan), luminaries such as the poet Ken Leslie (who would pen "O'Malley to the Reds," a poem about Coady), intellectuals such as Dr. Harold Innis of the University of Toronto and community activists such as Dorothy Day of the Catholic Workers in New York.

Two young Canadian adult educators, Guy Henson and Alex Sim, who would go on to accomplish great things in adult education on the national scene, were in attendance. Henson, who was already having some success organizing credit unions in and around Halifax, was elected vice-president of the Conference. Sim, who was doing community development work in the eastern townships of Quebec, was fast becoming a figure to be reckoned with in CAAE circles. Sim would also play a key role in the success of Canada's Farm Radio Forum.

The 1938 Conference convened with war clouds looming on the European horizon and world capitalism still in crisis. Shortly after the Conference, the Rev. J. Henry Carpenter wrote to Coady and several others that it

> hardly seems possible that this conflagration is going to be started in Europe.... All of these things certainly give us great pause, but on the other hand we can only go on in the feeling and assurance of the love of God, and that the only final solution to our most complicating social and economic problems, both nationally and internationally can be solved through brotherhood and lives. This is the time it seems, when we should work even harder with determination and not despair, to go on in the development of our principles of co-operation and love.[51]

The participants who assembled for this gathering were fiercely determined not to give in to despair. Fusing Christian ideas with their reading of the nature of the economic and political crisis, speaker after speaker argued that it was "impossible to have spiritual welfare without material welfare and economics and religion must go hand in hand, just as body and soul."[52] Dorothy Day, who had deep ties to the American left and would go on to be a legendary servant of New York's poor and lowly, proclaimed:

> We have to recognize the struggle of the workers is not for just wages and hours, but for ownership, because only with ownership can man be conscious of his dignity as a man. We must get back private property, ownership for the worker, and that can only be done through co-operative enterprise and communal land. We must emphasize the dignity of the person, and to combat the heresy that man is subject body and soul to the state. We must emphasize the communitarian movement to get away from rugged individualism.[53]

The Rev. James Myers agreed with Day. The "only practical economic system" that coincided with "fundamental ethics" was "one primarily for human service, like the co-op movement." This militant reconstructionist spirit pervaded the Conference.

Remarkably, the gathered had arrived at a consensus as to what the problem was (loss of ownership) and its solution (co-operative enterprise). Agrarianists (such as Michael Gillis and Liugi Ligutti) continued to find considerable support for their argument that the restoration of human dignity would come only if humans found their way back to the land and were not swallowed up in Blake's "satanic mills." The irrepressible Fowler, always riding the upsurge of the wave, insisted that "behind the need for all these organizations stands the implacable and soul destroying system of tenancy, of economic slavery, in which a system owns and controls the destinies of a people whose great longing is to be free: to be owners of their own economic structures, captains of their own economic fate." These Antigonish-inspired Christian militants hinged their fate to the future of the co-operative movement. Some Movement followers used the language of the "middle way" to capture the deep meaning of the "Antigonish project."

But the middle way rhetoric obscures the radical nature of the fundamental idea that the restoration of the person to full dignity requires that persons, together, own the basic economic instruments of production and distribution.

On the women's side, vivid intellectuals such as Ida Gallant understood profoundly that the restorative process involved the reparation of the lifeworld. The formation of woman's guilds opened up possibilities for women to plunge into the organization of regional libraries, community recreation, co-operative medicine and nursing. The forms of capitalism and governance Nova Scotians had experienced kept many of them ignorant, unhealthy, with few avenues for self-development.

In 1939, the Co-operative League of the USA published a remarkable little pamphlet, "A Tour of Nova Scotia Co-operatives: Report of Conference Tours Conducted under the Auspices of the Co-operative League of the USA and the Extension Department of St. Francis Xavier." Antigonish and Canso, places inhabited by several thousand souls, were circled on a crude blue and white map of Nova Scotia. Out in the deep blue sea, a large lobster icon was poised, ready to pounce on Cape Breton. The inside and back covers featured reproductions of old black-and-white photographs, one of the co-operative housing project in Reserve Mines and one of Mary Arnold holding a model of one of the homes that would be built in Tompkinsville. Other photographs captured the vernacular architecture of lobster factories, co-operative dairies, fish plants and co-op retail stores, the famous British Canadian resplendent with its striped awnings and stocked shelves. Other photos were of the smiling Tompkins, Coady and MacDonald, and several showed the study clubs in action.

For the men and women who travelled to Nova Scotia, many of whom were prominent American Christian social gospel proponents, the tour was wonderful and inspiring. With utopian fervour, Dr. J. Henry Carpenter claimed that

> one could never really complete the story of the joys, the dust, the cars stuck in the mud or in the ditch, the groups who lost the leaders, the hospitality of the people, going over the tortuous Cabot Trail by moonlight and arriving at twelve o'clock midnight for supper! All of this was a part of that wonderful and inspiring something which brought us closer together and impressed even more deeply upon us the reality of what we saw and heard—the advanced adult education through study groups, the unity of purpose between Catholic and Protestant, the changed lives with new hope and vision of men and women in whole communities, the development of Cooperative Democracy in place of extreme socialistic or communistic tendencies, the relationship of the church to the whole Cooperative Movement in Nova Scotia.[54]

Carpenter, a Protestant church leader, saw the Movement as a model of faith in action. "If our priests and ministers and rabbis could work early and late, and serve in reality as these men in Nova Scotia are doing, a new order would be quickly developed, based upon the very foundation principles which social thinkers and prophets down through the ages have said would bring into being that 'better world we are all striving to create.'"

Sprinkled among the selected essays by Movement thinkers are fascinating glimpses into how observers made sense of their experience. For Joseph Schwenk of Indianapolis, Indiana, co-op organization demonstrated vividly how "any people or country, no matter how bad their conditions are, can materially improve them if they will apply themselves to studying the reasons for their plight and then work together to remedy them." The Director for Rural Education, Julius Rosenwald Fund, J.C Dixon, imagined that co-operatives became a "spiritual movement, a renascence far transcending the mere making of a living ... the stimulus for developing a new set of values wherein the economics of life have, it is true, their rightful place, but only this, with no undue emphasis ... the urge driving men to develop hope in the face of despair, pride in the face of poverty." He thought that the program could be a godsend to the people of the South. Mabel Carney, Professor of Rural Education at Teachers College, Columbia University, had little doubt that Nova Scotia was "rapidly becoming a second Denmark and, indeed, the numerous study clubs, originated by Father Tompkins, which were our special interest seem to involve an advance over Denmark, and to offer tremendous possibilities for the varied millions of our own population in the United States."

Dr. Lee Brooks, with the assistance of several others, wrote a detailed account of the 1938 tour through the Movement's villages and small towns.

> Communities all along the line have been aroused from static plight to dynamic light; from unfair exploitation to reasonable expectation. This is the important heart of the movement. Imponderable social values are seen transcending ponderable money values. Here is social regeneration in process, thanks to educational leadership that knows when to take hold of a community and when to let it go under its own power.[55]

Brooks was impressed with the accomplishments of Nova Scotia's common folk. At Judique, the co-operative store, which was started in 1934 with $350, now grossed $25,000 in sales and had 76 members. Port Hood had 50 or 60 people in its study clubs, a fledgling credit union of 70 members and a young store that now had 91 members, up from 31 only three months prior. At Mabou, located five miles from the coast, Scottish, Irish and French farmers and fishermen had watched their credit union grow from 58 members in March 1934 to 250 members. The main co-operative store, which had been started with some difficulty, now had a manager, a full-time bookkeeper and a clerk. This community was now interested in producers co-operation; farmers wanted better market organization. A poultry pool had been started in 1936 through the store; fourteen tons of turkey were shipped to Sydney in the fall of 1937.

Brooks and his fellow travellers left the beauty of the Cheticamp shore and entered the mining region. There they discovered a thriving co-operative movement. At North Sydney and Sydney Mines, for instance, the British Canadian co-operative store, with its seven branches, was now doing over a million dollars in business and had 3,548 members. At New Waterford, in spite of a 42 percent drop in pay, July 1938 sales of $17,000 were $2,000 higher than the previous year. "Probably," Brooks observed, "no consumers' cooperative on the continent can show a better record of sales, service, and loyalty of its members. Now they are studying and working toward a community centre. Study, more study, still more study." In Sydney, the heart of steel country, the Co-operative Society showed rapid growth. Some 4,000 steelworkers (at least half of whom were enrolled in credit unions) and some 40 percent of the miners in the area had joined up since the store had opened in 1936 with 157 members. Now it had 547 members, and sales had jumped from $3,000 to $45,000 in two years. Brooks was also visibly impressed with the DOSCO Credit Union of the Dominion Steel Company. "Against the seemingly inevitable drabness of the steel plant is the brightness, the human aspect afforded by the credit union office itself, provided by the plant: small but regular deposits, character loans, check-up committees, 'decent' interest rates that follow customary standards of credit unions."

At Reserve Mines, tour participants learned that the Coady Credit Union, organized in 1933 with thirty-three miners, now had nine hundred members. It had loaned $196,000, without one bad loan. It had financed nineteen homes. Like so many others who visited Father Jimmy, Brooks found Tompkins' study stacked high with books. "Father Tompkins would rather talk to his visitors in his study-lending-library about the promises and prospects of books and adult education than heed the dinner bell. His books—and he wants attractive books in content and print—go far and wide to the shelves of credit unions and stores." When the tour arrived in Reserve Mines in early August 1938, Canada's first co-operative housing venture was in full construction. Houses cost $2,500, and financing was available through the credit unions. Miners had to put down only $100 since the housing commission considered the miner's labour in building his own home to be worth $900. The remaining $1,500 was cared for through twenty-five-year amortization, which involved monthly payments of $12.15. Dr. H.G. Lull of Emporia, Kansas, believed that "one would have to travel far to find a more promising development in industrial and economic democracy than that of Eastern Canada." Most of the tour members would have agreed with Lull. Here, it seemed, was a "self-help movement being built on a sure foundation through the development of discussion groups."[56]

The 1938 Rural and Industrial Conference was a personal triumph for Coady. Obviously the hub of the Antigonish Movement, his ideas were now circulating widely in progressive circles. Outside observers were

clearly enraptured with the co-operative activity in all of these unlikely little places. Coady assessed the situation several months after the
Conference. He informed S.O. Bland, chair of the Commission on Merchant Marine and Fisheries, Washington, D.C., that the "eastern shore of
Nova Scotia, especially in the fresh fish business, has been depressed for
years, and just this fall the first ray of hope was seen. But it took ten years of
study and organization to get them to the point where they could be helped
and we still have lots of headaches in connection with the whole thing."
Although the Movement was running into a "good deal of opposition from
private concerns and the vested interests," it was "getting so strong that
there is hope that in the near future we shall have plain sailing."[57]

But Coady was not pleased with the inflated claims and expectations of a
few of those whose eye had been caught by the Movement. He told J.J.
Harpell, the incendiary editor of the *Instructor* who had spent some time in
jail over a libel suit, that

> we are a little fearful here of the effects of over-publicizing the Antigonish Movement.
> The cause has already been hurt by many writers who over-stated the achievements of
> our movement and did not interpret it properly. Your "Instructor" gives the impres-
> sion that the credit union has already solved the problems of many communities down
> here. This is not true. We are on the road to the solution of the people's problems.
> Then, again, the credit union is only a part of our program and probably a minor part.
> That alone will not solve the problems of the people.

Coady also didn't agree with Harpell's method of attacking various people.

> Only on the positive side can we permanently find real motivation for the people....
> Apart altogether from the abuses and sins of our present system there is still need for
> readjustment of society which can only be done by an enlightened people who will
> create institutions in the economic and social field over which they alone have con-
> trol.[58]

Although Coady was a little fearful of excessive publicity, time and again
his impatient longing for the new world would push him to exaggerate the
Movement's power to usher in a people's economy.

IV

The successes of the Movement and the resultant media attention placed
considerable pressure on Moses Coady and the Extension staff. For some
time, Dr. Coady had been urged to produce a textbook for the guidance of
interested educators and community developers from outside the Maritime region. Individuals and groups of varying size had been coming to
observe the work in progress. In 1937 the Rockefeller Foundation of New
York urged Moses Coady, now at the apex of his power and fame, to tell the
"Antigonish story," weaving history and his philosophy of education into a
compelling and hopeful narrative. Shortly after the 1937 Rural and Industrial Conference, Dr. Coady saw Zita O'Hearn on the street in Antigonish

and asked if she would come to work for him. He told her that the Rockefeller people had given him a grant to write a book on "our stuff" and he needed a research secretary. Kay Thompson was too busy. Agreeing, Zita O'Hearn began, entering the intimidating world of A.B. MacDonald, Sister Marie Michael and Sister Anselm, George Boyle and A.S. MacIntyre. In the fall of 1937, Coady had a heavy schedule of short courses and speaking engagements and made little headway on the text.

Early in 1938, Rockefeller suggested that Coady find a quiet retreat at Beaufort, halfway between Charleston and Savannah, free from nagging distractions. After speaking in Boston on February 20 and 21, Coady was to travel to South Carolina for the rest of the winter with Zita O'Hearn, who would play scribe to the writer. In late January 1938, Coady wrote Miss Edna Hower of Hamden, Connecticut: "I am supposed to be working on a book on Adult Education and will remain there till the last of May. Things are going well at the moment."[59] Only a day earlier, Coady had written to his good friend, Father James Boyle of Havre Boucher: "I may tell you confidentially that I have a chance to go to S. Carolina. The Rockefeller people are giving me this chance to work up a book on our Adult Education program and I feel that I should take it."[60] However, according to O'Hearn, Coady was "no more anxious to get down to work than he had been at home. He missed his supporting audiences and his health was failing. I did not realize how much until, on our way in April, he had to enter a hospital in Boston."[61]

In the fall of 1938, with no manuscript in hand, Coady's loyal supporters and co-workers had to pitch in by listening, talking, taking notes, making suggestions. Zita O'Hearn and the others worked past Christmas and into the winter of 1939. Ida Gallant helped Coady with economic analyses. In and out of the hospital, Coady would send for Zita to come up, listen and take notes. Sometimes two or three would assemble in his room. And so it was written, classified and divided. On one weekend in May, the faithful scribes worked through the weekend because Coady was to take the manuscript to New York on Monday. Zita remembers the day.

> In the office after early Mass, then home for a quick lunch, then back to work. The sisters were there, and Kay, and Peter Nearing. Dr. Coady was feeling miserable and the tension was getting to him. At one point we had a visitor. The Old Rector. Dr. H.P. MacPherson wandered in to cheer us up. He made a few humorous remarks while Dr. Coady, peering over his glasses, told him curtly we were busy and had not time for chatter. After a few more sallies, the Old Rector left in good humor, having been just about verbally thrown out.[62]

Early Monday morning arrived, and last minute changes were made. After lunch, A.B. drove Coady out to the airport. A few days later, Coady was in hospital in New York, conferring with Harper's editors from his bed.

Despite extremely poor health during this period, Moses Coady and his friends had fashioned a text that would eventually be translated into many of the world's great languages. Coady had prepared for this project by inviting many friends and co-operative intellectuals and activists to offer their observations and thoughts on different dimensions of the Movement. He had needed accurate information about the occupational structure of the Maritimes, data on economic history, insights about how adults learned and precise statistics on the progress of the co-operative movement. He had wanted to get it right.

The writing of the systematic treatise had not really been Coady's cup of tea. One can imagine Zita O'Hearn sitting in front of the old Underwood typewriter while Coady paced the floor of the Golden Eagle Tavern (where they stayed) in the Beaufort, South Carolina, resort, trying to coax Coady into print. His spirits had perked up a little with the arrival of a letter from the Holy See approving of Extension's work. As Zita recalled, "Here at last was the answer for the doubters, the pharisees, and the sincerely concerned friends who could not help wondering if perhaps the men of X were not going too far with the realm of 'dirty economics', straying from the paths of mind and spirit."[63]

Coady's book project had allowed the Movement activists to pause and assess their philosophy and action. Coady had written his cousin, Father Tompkins, to help him determine when the radical idea that adults could learn had begun to take hold in Western liberal democracies. Father Tompkins' response revealed his intellectual acumen and relentless search for deeper understanding of adult learning. Tompkins pinpointed a momentous occasion: a conference called by Mr. Keppel of the Carnegie Corporation, which had been held in New York in June 1924. There, Keppel had asked those gathered what "America was thinking on the subject of learning for adults" and what they thought of the British book *The Way Out*. "We did not even seem to know how to pronounce the word 'adult'," Tompkins exclaimed, "in this connection. And we certainly knew little scientifically in regard to the ability of adults to imbibe knowledge at various ages." Keppel informed the group that Thorndike, the famous psychologist, had begun to investigate the subject. Tompkins told Coady that he had watched carefully and, in 1928, the text *Adult Learning* appeared. Focusing on chapter 13, "Practical Applications," Tompkins had discovered that

> there was nothing new in it. We had believed the very same things and had been acting upon them. Here is the point: I had been telling the fishermen the same story from January 1923 onwards but the answer came back–we have no schooling, pity we are so old. It is too late now etc. etc. I opposed to these escape mechanisms the scientific study of Thorndike and floored them. If somebody tells me he made chocolates from coal tar and shows me that he did it is not much use for me to deny. After I got the Thorndike theory over, I heard no more excuses. The fellows backed down and realized we had been on the right track and the scientific study made by Thorndike settled the question. So you see this book *Adult Learning* was for us an important milestone on the way.

Tompkins informed Coady that his copy was "probably the first to come to N.S. and was hurled into action from the very beginning." Tompkins got his ideas about the "ability of men to learn largely from the results of the W.E.A. in England and from the People's School though I always had an obsession in that direction—the wish was father to the thought when I looked around STFX and saw the poor little way we were plodding along and the lack of trained men on the staff."[64] As a result of this correspondence, Coady worked Thorndike into his published text.

Two documents written by prominent Movement activist-intellectuals Ida Gallant and A.S. MacIntyre for Coady offer a glimpse into the kinds of internal debates and critical reflections that occurred behind closed doors. For historians of the Antigonish Movement, these documents allow rare insight into movement debates. Gallant prepared a pamphlet on "Study Clubs" in the fall of 1937, in which she meditated on what factors made a good study club. She was convinced that a "good leader is the first guarantee of success. Yet, clubs are successful sometimes when none of the members have any outstanding qualities of leadership and this situation is found in groups whose members are especially eager to learn." In the latter case, the "chief requirement" was for simple pamphlets, clearly written and containing plans for study. MacIsaac's ubiquitous pamphlet on credit unions worked well because of its question and answer methods. Those who used Alanne's pamphlet, "Fundamentals of Consumer Co-operation," with its short chapters, questions and well-arranged references to other sources of information told Extension again and again that it was "easy to learn from." Gallant acknowledged that they needed curriculum specialists to prepare lesson material to "set groups on the way to efficient study at the beginning."

Gallant admitted to Coady that Extension did not have enough readable books and pamphlets available for the common people. "If we only could place an order with a writer as we do with the carpenter who is to build a house, and have him deliver what we want—economics in plain language according to the requirements of the man who has little time, patience or left-over energy after a hard day's work to puzzle over big words and difficult expressions!" Gallant vociferated.

> We come upon this criticism constantly. The readers tell us that the Bulletin is not written for the average man. It is no answer to say, 'Let the people learn to read difficult things.' The sight of many books that remain unread while people are asking for something to read on the very subjects which they contain must convince everybody who has anything to do with the matter that we need more literature that is easy to study.

Coady may well have smiled knowingly as his mind drifted back to the days when he and MacDonald had farmers reading a five-hundred-page text in the earliest study clubs.

The Movement struggled constantly with the question of motivation. Gallant admitted that there was "no difficulty in getting people to work hard when there is an immediate objective to be reached. When a group studies the credit union there is no lack of interest. Here is something tangible and near, not remote and abstract." Gallant then wondered how people could be trained "to reach out for everything that is in their way to an ideal community." This worried question indicated that, particularly in the towns, the Movement had often failed to

> reach the people who most need to be in study clubs. The public meetings where clubs are organized are attended only by certain classes of people and many of those who should be there are not there because they move in groups in accordance with their economic status. We notice this very clearly in the women's work. I do not refer to those who would never learn anything anyway but to those who have the ability and initiative, but who being in the very poor class do not have associations with the groups we find at the meetings through organization plans work. How reach these [*sic*]?

Although the Antigonish Movement appeared to be reaching only the elite strata within the producer classes, Gallant confided to Coady that it seemed

> impossible to find another medium of expression for the thinking that the average person may do about economic and social problems. If a man thinks at all about these things and if he cannot contribute the result of his thinking in a friendly gathering of the people with whom he works and talks, then he will very likely remain unexpressed. It is a question of salvaging mental talent wherever we may.

However, more careful, systematic preparation of study material would add to the success of the program.

A.S. MacIntyre had extensive experience in planning and acting in the face of power. His reflections[65] offer one of the very few insider critiques of Movement practice. MacIntyre began by detailing things that worked and things that didn't. He then followed these remarks with comments on weaknesses within the Movement and twelve points for consideration. Many of his initial comments are not surprising: indifferent leaders, irregular attendance at meetings, poorly arranged weekly programs, dictatorial or argumentative group leaders, failure to attend Associated Study Club meetings, wasted time on local gossip—all well-known blocks to adult learning. While thoroughly convinced of the "effectiveness of the individual study group and the associated monthly rallies," MacIntyre felt the study groups needed "personal attention and supervision of some responsible person in the community" to function properly. Then MacIntyre put his finger on a serious problem. "In the early stages of the movement," he told Coady, "the Extension Field Workers were able to give nearly all their time to the promotion of study clubs, monthly rallies, debates, public-speaking contests, etc. and in addition to this the Extension Department carried on considerable research in the preparation of certain economic objectives for which the study club members worked." But the Movement had developed "so rapidly and so enormously" that fieldworkers shifted their attention to educating the directorates of various co-operatives. Because the directors had been the original leaders of the study clubs, they were no longer able to lead the study groups due to their new responsibilities. MacIntyre identified this vacuum and the lack of finances to "employ more field workers to concentrate on the preliminary work in the field" as a most serious problem. MacIntyre doubted that the study clubs would flourish as they had in the past. The stretched fieldworkers could merely touch the high spots of the vast territories they had to cover. "We have accomplished wonders with the limited resources at our disposal. But if we are to grow, the whole organization must be enlarged. True we can carry on in a limited way with our present field, but we should not try to expand as some sections of our work are bound to suffer for lack of personal supervision." These strong words were far from the myth of the "modern miracle" and out of harmony with Coady's utopian aspirations for the new economic order.

MacIntyre's points for consideration raised many fascinating issues. He wondered if many persons prominent in the Movement had been justified in their wholesale criticism of politicians and if the frequent criticism of corporations, including banks and other financial institutions, was sound. In fact, MacIntyre thought that the Movement may have emphasized criticism at the expense of affirmative achievement. The most serious theme MacIntyre offered Coady for consideration was whether the successes of the Movement had been overemphasized. MacIntyre observed that Extension had overruled Movement supporters who disapproved of the publicity that Dover had received during the last few years. "It will be said, I know, that most of this publicity comes from outsiders, over whom the members of the movement have no control. Can those associated with the Movement escape responsibility?" He wondered out loud if a "thorough appraisal of the economic results of the Movement" could be undertaken with a view to ascertaining how much better off economically certain communities were than before the Movement began. To illustrate, MacIntyre pointed to Louisdale, the object of considerable publicity with regards to the transformative effects of co-operation. The Council of Public Instruction had only recently been asked to make a special grant for assistance to the Louisdale school. MacIntyre noted that the school section owed teachers' salaries, up to the end of last year, in the amount of $1,017, and that they had around $800 in other liabilities. They may have considerable money in their credit union, but MacIntyre wondered: Had they simply "taken money out of one pocket and put it another? Or ... set up a balance in their Credit Union by failing to pay their debts?" These were hard questions, destined to puncture myths. MacIntyre even wondered if the profits and surpluses of the co-operative stores were genuine. He wanted to know if the profits or bonuses they paid to their members were granted only after all debts had been paid, and proper amounts allowed for whatever charges were usual in such a business.

A.S. MacIntyre concluded his points for consideration with several serious questions. He asked if any assistance should be given to the co-operative movement by governments that was not given to private business. He wanted to know, in comparison to the co-operative movement in other countries, if the Movement in the Maritimes had to rely to a greater extent on government assistance. He asked if the main support of the Movement ought to come from within, that is, from the profits made by co-operative stores. He asked if the growth of the Movement was being "unduly forced," and he wanted to know what the experience or opinion of other countries was in this regard. His final two questions cut to the heart of Movement tensions and puzzlement: What, in fact, was the "ultimate goal" of the Movement? Was it "intended that the movement shall be political as well as social and economic in scope, and if so, what political philosophy does the movement hold? On the economic side, how far does the movement propose to go? Is it the aim to eliminate entirely private gain?"[66] Coady would spend a lifetime grappling with the latter two questions.

Coady had much thinking to do as he crafted *Masters of Their Own Destiny*. In his original text (which was considerably pared down by the publishers), Coady chose to skirt the really difficult issues raised by both Gallant and MacIntyre in favour of presenting the Movement in as glowing a light as possible. However, his philosophy and historical understanding is clearly articulated and the original text has a grittier, more realistic feel than the published version. This text was borne out of terrible pain and inner turmoil. Somehow the volume made it to publication, by Harper and Row, in late 1939. It would be greeted with accolades and appreciative reviews in the religious and co-operative press, and it is still read to this day.

CHAPTER 6

Conceptual Architectonics

I

n Western societies we want to free the text from its personal and historical contexts and have it speak universal truths about the human
condition. However, early twenty-first-century intellectual history no
longer permits this interpretative move. Texts are now embedded firmly in
multiple contexts, and writings are probed for contradictions and
cover-ups. We no longer assume that an author was fully aware of what he
or she was doing in crafting a text. Texts never represent the "truth" in an
objective sense. They are constructed with multiple aims in mind, and historians, like novelists, cannot escape telling a particular kind of story, trying to
make sense of their data and affirming (or negating) specific values and
norms. More is manifested on textual playing fields than meets the eye.

Masters of Their Own Destiny[1] (MOTD) was published at the apex of the
Antigonish Movement's history. This deceptively simple text, much
beloved by adult educators around the world, was, however, a significantly
reduced version of the original. Its publisher, Harper and Row, had cut the
chapters that dealt in considerable detail with Maritime history and com-
pressed many other sections. The publishers were not interested in the
stark reality of what the Maritime reformers were really up against. Rather,
they wanted to produce a text that would be inspirational, a source of hope
for those who had suffered through ten years of the Depression. They
re-stylized the text of the book for non-Canadian audiences, and this had
two consequences. First, the story of the Antigonish Movement was simpli-
fied and romanticized. Second, all mention of conflict inside the Church
and opposition to the Movement was deleted.

Moses Coady's MOTD cannot, therefore, be read as a fully accurate historical account of the Antigonish Movement. Coady did not tell the reader
all that he knew, or even all that he wanted to tell. His editors cut him down
to size. His intended audiences constrained him. His own purposes kept
him in check. Coady's sense of his public role in the international
co-operative movement restrained his public statements, setting up a fascinating dialectic of private/public and foreground/background. In his
personal correspondence, Coady loosened up and wrote more candidly
and, once on philosophical ground, he wrote freely.

Masters of Their Own Destiny, then, is a public representation of Coady's philosophy of adult education for co-operative action. It was written when the Movement was still in its utopic phase, when Coady thought the Movement was strong enough to withstand the opposition (in government, Church, and business sectors) then trying to undermine it. The fact that the Movement had caught the eye of the world, throwing numerous accolades its way, put pressure on Coady to write an inspirational-romantic text, but even in the published version, realism occasionally bursts through. Coady touched on the "dark early days" of the Movement's beginnings and dampened, a little, overexuberant claims about the "revolution at Dover." Coady's certainty that the co-operative movement was the solution to the problem of economic and political dependency created a tension in his person and writings. Like the personality that swings from exhilaration to despair, Coady was pulled to see the co-operative movement as creating opportunities for development in the most estimable social laboratory of the Maritimes, and also to face the overwhelming reality of endless problems in sustaining a social movement. Coady's heart attack in the same year as the publication of MOTD could serve as a metaphor of this unbearable tension. The tension exploded in his body, almost knocking this rugged man out of the action forever.

Coady had been preaching the co-operative gospel in Canada and the United States for a decade prior to crafting *Masters of Their Own Destiny.* His oral presentations are echoed, honed and distilled for the "common man." Certain ideas and phrases are recognizably culled from his speeches and reports. Twenty years earlier, Coady had discovered the secret of economic and social transformation in adult education, after which he would continue to write and refine his message until his battered old body finally gave out in July 1959. After his retirement from Extension in 1952, Moses Coady tried to write his final opus, a kind of autobiographical reflection on his life and the future of democracy. It remained incomplete and unpublished, with chapter notes and outlines, scribblings and jottings left in the keep of his secretary for over forty years. MOTD is not Coady's last word, but a careful reading of the original manuscript (and appropriate contrastive analysis with the published version) captures the core of Coady's philosophy of adult education. Reading Coady's speeches, reports and, particularly, his voluminous correspondence fills out a remarkable corpus of work on co-operative theory.

The context in which in any person lives and moves is never unmediated by culture and perception. We can put several markers in place to guide us in our reading of MOTD; we have seen Coady in action, heard his voice, obtained a feel for his sensibility and discovered some of the tendencies of his thought. Coady was deeply embedded in the pre-industrial, communitarian world of rural farm life. His fate was tied closely to that of his extensive clan. His core idea of self-reliance was rooted in his personal and communal experience in the Margaree Valley in the late nineteenth and early twentieth centuries. He seemed to take up the fate and struggles of the primary producers, from whence he began, into his own body and soul. Although trained in the Academy, Coady avoided its language, speaking instead with the accent of the "primary producers" of the land. He understood them. Coady could not help privileging the "rural" over the "urban," the "community" over the "individual." Nor did he move easily in the brutal world of industrial politics and trade unionism. He never seemed entirely comfortable in the urban-industrial environment, even though he spoke often enough in union halls. It is not surprising, in this light, that Coady chose to begin his account of the Antigonish Movement with an historical record of the economic plight of his people and the failure of the educational system to prepare them to understand and control their own world.

Coady is a Christian thinker, yet when one reads MOTD, it is clear that the theological underpinnings of this text are in the background. One has to read them back in from later theological reflections. His formal theological education inculcated Thomist principles. Like the "Common Doctor," St. Thomas, Coady was certain that the worlds of nature and society were knowable through reason, that a blueprint for the right ordering of the human world existed and that it was discoverable through "scientific" thinking. Coady used the words *formula*, *blueprint* and *science* over and over. The scientific way of doing things is set against ignorant ways of thinking and acting in the world. We can see how Coady's Thomism fuses Christian ideas with key elements from the Enlightenment tradition. A reasonable, scientific understanding of society, then, reveals the regulative principles for ordering the economic, political and social worlds. The "natural law" tradition of Catholicism allowed Coady to link "co-operation" and "religion." Coady believed, simply, that there was a way of regulating human existence that conformed to God's purposes for humankind.

This world-view, fusing Christianity and the Enlightenment, however, opened up Coady to potential problems that have troubled early twenty-first-century men and women. If the human world is scientifically knowable, then those who know the laws (or claim they do) are positioned to legislate on behalf of others. Here we see a tension point in Coady's thought and practice. He believed the "learner is all important in the educative process," (Introduction, p.3) yet also believed that he could apprehend scientifically where this educative process ought to lead his learners. Coady's rendering of Thomism gives education the pivotal role in the emancipatory process. Right education and ideas hold the potential to clear away the dark clouds of ignorance and beam reason's light upon the regulative principles that ought to govern economic and social life. This knowledge of God's laws provides the basis for right action. Coady was committed to finding the "one best way." Stated thus, Coady's thinking seems static, but he also wove developmentalist notions into his world-view. Called into being by God, the world contained potentialities within itself. His dominant metaphors—potential, release of energy, development—indicate Coady's ontological conviction that the purpose of creation is to unfold its potential. In the human worlds, wrong ordering (sin) can block the developmental potential of nature and humankind. The educational process is mandated within this world-view in order to enable human beings to reach their full potential as thinking and acting subjects.

As a Roman Catholic Christian thinker and social reformer of the early to mid-twentieth century, Coady thought and acted within certain ideological constraints and papal traditions. Coady was a young lad when *Rerum Novarum* (RN) was published in 1891, and Extension was barely underway when *Quadregismo Anno* (QA) was declared forty years later. These encyclicals made it easier for the Movement intellectuals to respond to the economic plight of their people, and they used these documents politically and strategically. MOTD in no way applied encyclical teachings to social issues in a formalistic manner. Leo XIII's "cry of protest" against the harsh exploitation of the European working classes was welcomed by Coady and Tompkins, but Pope Leo left reformers in the lurch when it came to offering concrete solutions. RN encouraged clergy and laity to become more involved in social issues; it permitted the state to intervene on workers' behalf; it relied, however, on offering moral counsel to the rich and powerful. If they didn't listen, or were simply impervious, Leo XIII counselled the Church to acquiesce. Leo seemed to think that "social justice" depended on the "change of heart by those who held economic and political power."[2]

Coady never accepted this position. On November 3, 1937, Coady wrote Chris J. Tompkins, who was active in the Alberta Knights of Columbus, that "vested interest people, even Catholics … were impervious to any constructive doctrine." In the decades following MOTD, Coady would argue that the people's movement needed to match force with force to counter the vested interests' continued domination of working people. Coady rejected outright the idea that having a clear-cut social philosophy was sufficient. Writing to Percy Robert of Westmount, Quebec, on September 16, 1943, Coady declared:

> The big vested interests which are growing more monstrous all the time are not going to give up their hold by any appeal from religious quarters. To think they would would be to lack realism. Society will be reformed when there are institutions adequate to do the work owned and operated by the people. It will require the application of ruthless political, economic, and social forces to do the job. Above all, the people must have instruments that will give them new economic power and a greater share of the wealth.

Unfortunately for many Catholics, their institutions are intimately tied up with vested interests. Many Catholics, it seems to me, resort to abstract pronouncements as an escape mechanism from the odium involved in the practical work of reforming economic society. If Catholics came out foursquare for the masses of the people, the Church might lose some of its upper economic brackets, but this would be preferable to the possibility of the greater loss of the masses of the people.[3]

Leo XIII pitied the poor; Coady chose to organize them. Leo wanted to instruct the people from the top down; Coady wanted to start from the bottom up. By nature and tradition, Roman Catholics seldom begin from below.

Coady did agree with Leo that "co-operation rather than conflict" should be the basis of the social order.[4] This shibboleth is pretty easy to agree with, but hidden behind this cliché is Leo's rarefied ideal of harmony: he feared disorder and disturbance and socialism so much that he could not bring himself to advocate for "strong and united movements of workers."[5] Coady parted company with Leo here. Coady's ultimate goal may well have been some kind of harmonious social order, but Coady took his stand with the primary producers of the Maritimes and the world against the exploiting classes. The Antigonish Movement was a class-based movement that challenged vested class interests. The Catholic ethos of his time, particularly the anti-socialist and anti-communist sentiments, pressed Coady to downplay the Movement's class basis and politics. So, where appropriate, he did. Simply put, he had to keep the hierarchy reasonably happy. His Bishop, Morrison, abhorred the idea of a distinct Catholic political formation.

Quadregismo Anno bears the marks of the world depression of 1929. Published in 1931, this second of the great social encyclicals was discussed in the Antigonish diocesan meetings of the early 1930s. The priests thrashed around the document's key idea—the proposal for a corporative or vocational ordering of society—to see if they understood what Pius XI was driving at and if it made sense in the Maritimes. In the forty years since RN had been published, more wealth had become concentrated in the hands of the few, leading to a concentration of economic and political power. The number of poor people had increased vastly in the Americas and in the Far East. Unemployment was widespread. Thus, Pius XI pushed beyond Leo XIII's moralizing injunctions to look at the "basic causes of injustice and poverty."[6] Recognizing that the state was, in fact, largely controlled by the wealthy corporations and that the market was neither free nor open, Pius supported unions as the means by which workers could "protect themselves against oppression."[7] But, like Leo, Pius wanted to avoid "opposition or confrontation between the whole class of workers and employers as a whole."[8] If society could be organized according to "vocational spheres" cutting across both employers and employees, then the social order could be maintained. All Catholic thinkers, because of their fundamental belief in the Church as the "organic unity of believers," feel threatened at some deep, mysterious level by sunders in the "social body."

While Coady was no different in this regard, the corporatist tendency of Pius XI that allied itself so easily with Italian Fascism did not appeal to Coady and most of the intellectuals around him. The Antigonish Movement restricted the "vocational group" as ordering principle to the primary producers and industrial working class. They did not consciously create any organizations, other than the Church, that cut across employer-employee relationships. Coady's commitment to the co-operative movement was in no way corporatist. He offered little consolation to those Catholics who flirted with fascism. Coady was fashioning an indigenous philosophy of action for Maritimers.

Coady, a modern Moses in the eyes of many, can be placed within the prophetic tradition of Christianity. "The prophetic themes from Judaism," says David Deschler, "are primarily in the Torah, Amos, Hosea, Jeremiah, Isaiah, Jonah, and the Psalms. The message is a proclamation of liberation from bondage and slavery, castigation of the establishment for oppressing the poor, and warnings about genocide and nationalism."[9] Maritimers were afflicted, lashed by ruthless taskmasters in coal pits, on the docks and in the marketplace. God had heard their cry, and sent Moses Michael Coady to "deliver them out of the land of the Egyptians, and to bring them up out of that land to a good and broad land, a land flowing with milk and honey."[10] One could press this analogy too far, but the prophetic narrative (moving from bondage to a new land) served as a grand narrative for Coady. When linked with the idea of "perfection in another sphere," the utopian dimension in Coady's thought is revealed. He is confident that human beings have the capacity to fashion in the transient world a "simulacrum of the transcendental."[11] The "kingdom of God" can present itself in historical forms of economic and social organization. All the constituent elements of MOTD make sense within this frame.

These two markers, Coady as the voice of the suffering primary producers and Coady as a prophetic Catholic Christian social thinker, set useful parameters for our close reading of MOTD. Within these parameters, we can try to make sense of Coady's philosophy of the co-operative revolution.

II

Every text presupposes an audience. In Coady's opening "Introductory" remarks, the reader appeared to be the conservative Church hierarchy and educational critics. Coady stated that the adult education movement sponsored by St. Francis Xavier University had been accurately described as "education for the masses." Coady then immediately tried to justify this claim, which obviously privileged some and not others as the object of educational attention, by claiming that an educational program, to be successful, must be "shaped to fit the needs of a specific group, with common interests, a common background, and like capabilities." Rejecting derogatory uses of the term *the masses,* Coady insisted that the term, as he was using it, was based "fundamentally on vocational interests." It included those on a farm, in a mine or a factory or in service occupations who "derive their daily sustenance" from "jobs," rather than "professions," "positions" or "business enterprises" (Introduction, p.1). The 1931 census, according to Coady, indicated that 84 percent of the population of the Maritimes fell into his category of "the masses."

The clerical reader, however, would easily link "masses" with "class strife." The rhetoric of the masses was an integral part of the socialist movement. Coady was aware that he could not be seen to fall into that camp; he was also aware that the social encyclicals RN and QA privileged social harmony and order over rebellion and militancy. Coady argued that it was a "serious mistake to conclude ... that the St. Francis Xavier program is therefore promoting or encouraging class strife." Indeed, Coady appreciated the contribution made by those who were not a part of "the masses." Every sort of talent must be rewarded in any attempt to "reconstruct the social order." However, the message was addressed to the masses for three reasons: first, the Movement had to select a "homogeneous group"; second, the "group selected is largely consistent with an effective educational program"; and third, the masses stood "most in need of whatever cultural or economic benefits it may have to offer" (ibid., p.2). Coady downplayed his even more basic belief: that "the masses" were an exploited and oppressed class that needed liberation from the "vested interests" (code for "class oppressors" in the Coady vocabulary).

Coady seemed to recognize that his latter argument was slightly disingenuous. He quickly noted that the Movement did not "expect to proceed without opposition. Its experience has demonstrated that opposition tends to increase when its purely educational efforts are followed by programs of economic action, and to grow in intensity in the measure that such action is blessed with success" (ibid., pp.2-3). Much opposition, Coady suggested, arises from a "real conflict of economic interests." In the following sentence, Coady tangled himself up, suggesting that many interpret the Movement as a "challenge to their economic, social, or political interests" because they both fail to understand the Movement's principles and distrust the intentions of the proponents of social reconstruction. The insinuation here is that, if the principles of the Movement were understood, the opposition would cease. Further, Coady recognized that many persons sincerely opposed the Movement's aims and its means for their attainment.

Coady concluded his opening with a rhetorical flourish. "To its opponents ... whatever be the reason for their opposition, the Antigonish Movement flings no challenge. It dedicates itself, not to the extermination of opposition, but to the realization of a Christian, democratic social order." Inevitable opposition will be met, Coady says, with a "determination born of the unfailing confidence that its program is in complete conformity with the basic ideals of a Christian, democratic society" (ibid., p.3). Coady's use of the adjectives "unfailing" and "complete" in the latter comment brooked no philosophical opposition or dialogue and hardly provided much encouragement for his opponents to sit around the kitchen table for a chat about democracy. This section on "opposition" was cut from the published text.

Coady next set the stage for the following two chapters of MOTD, "The Maritime Setting" (TMS) and "Formal Education" (FE), neither of which were included in the edited text. The Antigonish Movement was founded on the "pedagogical principle that the learner is all-important in the educative process. The educator should take him where he finds him and work through his background, interests, and capabilities" (ibid.). For Coady this meant thoroughly embedding the "learner" in historical context. The "learner" could not be turned into a generic, disembodied, decultured being who learns according to the universal principles of individualist psychology. "Since our group is the masses of the Maritime provinces," Coady told his reader, "it behooves us to investigate the Maritime economic and social background so as to understand the people for whom our educational program is designed" (ibid., p.4).

III

We have already seen how Coady constructed Maritime history in our Chapter 3, "Fields of Lost Opportunity." The natural world of the Maritimes was a land blessed of God, a land of plenitude, but the Maritimes as a great social laboratory had to be imagined as such. Coady's imagination was at its richest when it cascaded over eastern Canada, challenging his audiences not to underestimate her assets. His own Margaree clan must have occasionally tired of trying to sort out which of Coady's latest development schemes (poultry, mink farming, and so on) was actually viable. Above all, Coady valued its people. They were its greatest assets. Co-worker Ida Gallant said,

> It was from his unshakeable faith in the worth and dignity of the common man that his followers drew inspiration and courage. If he wept at the sight of the road of life, strewn white with the bones of lost opportunities, he nevertheless foresaw a future in which the people, through intelligent individual and group action would repossess the earth.[12]

Coady's genuine compassion for ordinary people earned him the right, it seems, to lay on the "rawhide lash."[13] Coady upbraided the people for their "failure to remedy their adverse situation, yet we have faith in their willingness and ability to rise to the crisis, if they are given encouragement and training.... If we did not believe that the people of eastern Canada had brains and ambition, we would be starting on a wild goose chase" (TMS, p.6). Gallant said that if he "sometimes scowled at them and shook his fist in their faces and pointed out their failings, it was because he was in a hurry to arouse them to action."[14]

Coady laid the "rawhide lash" on Maritimers who blamed everyone or everything else but themselves for their plight, especially those who used Confederation as a "convenient alibi" for not finding innovative solutions to their economic problems. Nova Scotians were not leaving Confederation; they had to "make the best of it" (ibid., p.15). Coady even thought that Maritime pessimism often obscured the fact that many people actually had relatively high standards of living. Prince Edward Island, Coady thought, was "probably the most solvent state in Canada. Its people, on the whole, have had a satisfying life. Many farming and fishing sections of New Brunswick and Prince Edward Island have also enjoyed standards of living comparable to the best on the North American Continent" (ibid., pp.15-16). Coady concluded that if a reasonable percentage of Maritimers had achieved a reasonable standard of living, others could do the same. He also believed that, even with all the difficulties in the coal fields and steel mills, the rate of wages and annual incomes of the coal miners, if certain coal fields were excluded, "compare favorably with those in other lands" (ibid., p.16). This argument was strengthened, he maintained, by the fact that the fishing industry and farming were "not disadvantageously affected by Confederation" (ibid.). Yet these latter two sectors evidenced the "same unscientific and unprofitable exploitation that is so characteristic of Maritime primary producers in general." Eastern Canada practically had a monopoly on lobsters; yet the "history of the handling of lobsters in eastern Canada is the old story of primary producers getting only a fraction of the worth of their product" (ibid.).

Coady argued provocatively that the "people are responsible for much of their misery" (ibid., p.17). On the political front, one might have expected that the people of eastern Canada, knowing well about "Confederation disabilities," would have brought "effective political pressure ... to bear on the question of our disabilities." But they hadn't. "It would seem to be a logical conclusion that the strong arm that could implement the findings of the Royal Commissions and in general secure for them a redress of their grievances would have been a Maritime political party" (ibid.). Such a party might have held the "balance of power in the Canadian parliament and long ago secured what we are continuously asking for as our right" (ibid., p.18). However, Coady counselled Maritimers to look beneath the political machinations of Confederation to the economic foundation. "Confederation did not destroy our wooden ships; science did. The iron ship with its steam engine replaced the old wooden ship with its sails, and gradually a great deal of that which had made Nova Scotia prosperous, disappeared" (ibid.). Moreover, the self-sufficient economy of eastern Canadians endured "well on to the end of the nineteenth century," gradually being displaced by the "money economy"(ibid.).[31] The people did not create an adequate "marketing program" and ended up, in the ensuing crisis, having "recourse to the merchants who supplied them with goods on credit" (ibid., p.19).

Coady blamed this credit system for rural depopulation, quickly adding that the infamous out-migration of the Maritimes was "not merely a local phenomenon" (ibid.). Many rural sections of North America, from the Ottawa Valley to the New England states of Maine, New Hampshire and Vermont, sustained continuous depopulation up until the crash of 1929. In Coady's estimation, people had not left only for economic reasons. Many rural communities were dull and drab without any kind of "satisfying social life" (ibid.). The consequences of out-migration were dramatic. Communities were left without adequate manpower; the migration of youth deadened communities; those who were left felt paralyzed. Coady cited statistics indicating that nearly one-third of Maritime farmers were over sixty years of age. Was it to be "wondered at that the problems confronting farmers and primary producers in general ... could not be met by a people who had lost so much of its manpower" (ibid., p.20)? Coady's message of resettlement and repopulation resounded throughout the meeting halls of the Maritimes to little avail.

Coady knew well, however, that, even if Maritimers could right the wrongs of Confederation and become more technically efficient, they still would not achieve great prosperity. He believed that conditions in Canada since 1929 had proved conclusively that "finance capitalism" could not distribute its wealth for the "good and abundant life." Coady argued that the farmers and fishermen are "victims of a system which has impoverished people in all parts of the world. Something more than technological efficiency in production is required" (ibid.). Coady did not merely argue that the Nova Scotia economy must modernize itself. All the scientific production, processing and marketing in the world could not put "purchasing power in the hands of the millions of unemployed who should be the consumers of these goods" (ibid.). Anticipating his critics, Coady confronted them with the collapse of banks, steel and automobile industries. They were highly efficient enterprises, yet they collapsed, slumping down to a small fraction of normal output. "Evidently," Coady averred, "there is need of social architecture as well as technological efficiency" (ibid., p.21).

Anger always seemed to be simmering close to the textual surface of Coady's writing. Coady asked how the primary producers of eastern Canada could have imagined that they had a right to expect prosperity: The powerful capitalist interests had long recognized the value of organization; the primary producers, in contrast, had not seen the significance of it. They had the "hardest job" and the "poorest tools" with which to carry out their work. Primary producers, Coady argued, were never asked for their opinion as to the appropriate price for an automobile, but they were the ones who would say, "What price will you give me for my fish? What will you pay for my farm produce?" (ibid.).

The class of primary producers never left Coady's consciousness. What could one expect, he surmised, from such a neglected class? They were not self-organized, they were poorly educated, their industry underwent very little scientific research. Not only was research for the fishery and farm inadequate, but the information it did produce was not fully utilized. More than brawn was required to "cope with the complex life that grew up with scientific advancement" (ibid., p.22). Coady echoed Marx's famous aphorism in *The 18th Brumaire*, that human beings make history, but not under conditions of their own choosing. The primary producers had the innate capacity to be masters of their own destiny. However, their cultural-educational formation left them unable to assume this role and the "social architecture" of their lives tipped the scales towards the vested interests.

IV

Coady is one of our foremost philosophers of adult education. In the chapter "Formal Education," excised from the published text, he set out to discover how the formal educational system had contributed to the underdevelopment of the Maritimes. Within Coady's own Aristotelian-Thomist conceptual architecture, we know that education was given tremendous power. Indeed, it was the human instrument that set the enlightenment process in motion, opening up the possibility of transforming the social architecture of people's lives. Coady framed his narrative by reminding us that his ancestors had "dared the dangers of the expansive Atlantic and braved the perils of the vast new world" because they were "inspired by a spirit of freedom and an idea of liberty" (FE, p.1). They were preoccupied with religious and political liberty and cast aside economic considerations, often accepting the "poorer sections of the country for settlement." Coady thought that their obsession with political liberty had "rendered them oblivious to the fact that economic considerations would eventually play such a determining role. They little realized that political freedom can be rapidly nullified unless founded on economic independence" (ibid.).

Although Coady's forebears had brought little material wealth with them to the new country, they had brought a deep "love for learning." They imagined, Coady said, that "education would redress their wrongs and unlock the treasures of the new found world" (ibid., p.2). His ancestors worked hard to establish institutions of learning, from common schools to higher education. However, despite yeoman-like service, the "multiplicity of institutions of higher learning" (ibid., p.3). were too small, parochial and poorly equipped to "do the work usually expected from a real university" (ibid.). The Carnegie survey of the educational status of the Maritimes, Coady reminded us, revealed that the universities were appallingly indifferent to the "general educational problems of the provinces" (ibid.). Only in 1926 did the universities take some responsibility for the training of teachers. And we know that Coady played an important role in organizing the teachers of the Maritime provinces to acquire professional status in the 1920s.

Notwithstanding these efforts, Coady argued, and even though the Maritimes had the educational trappings of a "progressive civilization, the results in general have not been satisfactory" (ibid., p.4). The reason lay partly in the way education is "both cause and effect." Economically depressed peoples have poor educational facilities. Those living in marginal areas or who are engaged in low-wage occupations seldom have adequate educational opportunities. "Scientific knowledge and adult education would enable them to improve the social and economic order among them." Thus, education clearly causes "social improvements and in turn is improved by social conditions" (ibid., pp.4-5). Left to themselves, impoverished and exploited primary producers would remain entrapped in economic marginality and cultural ignorance.

Coady's harshest criticism was reserved for the consciously constructed functions of the formal educational system within an unbalanced society. From the vantage point of the Maritime elite, the education system worked. Its favoured "sons" were skimmed from the system, and fed into schools of law, medicine, theology and teaching. Coady did not think that the schools had "adequately prepared people" for the lives they would lead; nor had they "given them the scientific and technical knowledge required for vocational needs" (ibid., p.5). Unlike some critics, Coady did not want to turn schools into narrow "scientific and technical institutions" (ibid.). He thought that a "race of people with technical skills and scientific knowledge" might still be unable to solve the main problems. The crux of this matter (still unsolved, even exacerbated, at the beginning of the twenty-first century) is simply that society itself must be able to provide employment for its educated labour.

Coady's educational thinking was fed from several streams. He had been educated formally in early twentieth-century pedagogy and learned most of the secrets of adult education through experimentation. Coady believed that all human beings are endowed with a certain fund of energy. The educator could not add any energy to the individual, but he or she could take on the task of "releasing the human energy available" (ibid., p.8). For Coady, right ideas were the "effective mode" of releasing mental resources, catalyzing the "human dynamo." Native capacity could be made to work "more smoothly and in more directions; it could not be intrinsically strengthened.... When all human energy is thus made available and harnessed, the work is done as nearly perfectly as possible. To release and direct this energy is the task of education" (ibid.). Coady clearly saw parallels between the natural world as a field of underutilized energy and the human one with its vast "latent power and unused energy," (ibid., p.9) but he did not stop there. He appears to have believed that "great-points" in civilization, such as Greece in the age of Pericles, Rome in the time of Augustus, or Ireland in the days of "saints and scholars," were the achievements of outpourings of human energy into constructive fields of activity. "Properly inspired" and "adequately motivated," human beings could achieve mighty things (ibid.).

The releasing of this "switch of human energy," however, was not easily accomplished: a proper "co-ordination of ideas is required" to "create an attitude or state of mind in the learner before they will release the dynamic forces of action" (ibid.). Coady used an awkward phrase, the "attitudinizing of the human mind," to capture something rather complex. The right ideas could not simply be poured into the learner's skull. Educators had to awaken in slumbering learners the belief that they could make a better world. Coady believed that some attitudes energized learners; other "colorless pattern[s] of attitudes" were "responsible for our general backwardness" (ibid.). Ideas, then, addressed the learner as a situated, embodied whole person. If they didn't touch the heart and emotions of learners, the energy potential latent within the person could not be released.

Within Coady's world-view, the "attitudinizing of the human mind" had to lead learners to engage their own worlds. He thought that the "traditional mental structure" (ibid., p.10) of Maritimers predisposed them to see "education" as flight from the "drudgery of labor and ordinary life." His forefathers may well have come to the new world of Nova Scotia to escape the domination of the upper class, but ironically, they ended up in a new class society as "relatively uneducated and illiterate masses who possessed little or nothing" (ibid.). They then instilled in the children of the generations that followed the "dangerous idea that through education they could escape the drudgery and hardship of life to which they were born." They taught their children to identify success with money. "Rarely," Coady argued, "was education regarded as a preparation for future service to the community" (ibid., p.11).

Certainly Coady was committed to the liberal ideal that each person should have equal opportunity to realize their capacities and be provided with opportunities for a complete and happy life. "Such aims may be realized, however, not by escaping early environment and entering the service of capitalism, but by exploring, exploiting, and serving the native environment and rendering life therein more abundant" (ibid.). This latter ideal fuelled Coady's many letters of advice and encouragement to the various youthful members of his clan. Leo Coady, his nephew, received numerous letters of advice on how he and his young friends could make a fine life for themselves in the Margaree Valley.

The out-migration of the Maritimes removed its "bolder and more daring souls," (ibid.), luring them into the urban areas where they could find a "steady job" and a "regular pay envelope." Coady deeply lamented the plucking of promising youth from their own communities and the placing of them in "spheres of activity far removed from their native milieu…. The whole concept of education as a preparation for teaching, business, nursing, book-keeping, secretarial work, civil service, banking, and the rest of the while collared occupations, is to be blamed" (ibid., p.12). Few high school graduates took up fishing, farming or coal mining. High school and university education turned people away from their origins. Coady had a strong streak of moralism in his personality, and he excoriated Nova Scotia's "patriotic sons and daughters" to show "some noble idealism" (ibid.). Coady found it strange that altruistic youth would die on Europe's battlefields, yet were seemingly unwilling to "return to the fishing, farming and mining communities of these provinces for the primary purpose of helping our own people to solve the problems that beset them" (ibid.). Coady's anger was so aroused, it seems, because the children of the primary producers were forced to commit class treason.

The philosophy of the Antigonish Movement, Coady argued, was itself designed to

> enable the forgotten common people to educate themselves to the point where they can so manipulate the forces of society that they are their own masters—free men not serfs. When this objective is attained, men and women may still leave their communities to serve society according to their respective capacities. But they will not leave for economic reasons or to escape the conditions of the masses. They will find no firmer security elsewhere (ibid., p.14).

Here we have arrived at the heart of Coady's philosophy of adult education. A sound philosophy of education must link a "cultured and accomplished people" with the locating of "opportunities of life in the immediate environment" (ibid.). To develop a great Maritime people, educated Maritimers had to "remain at home and fight their way to the good life" (ibid.), but Coady knew this required an attitudinal revolution: the creation of the "possibility-hunting mind" (ibid., p.15). Essentially, Maritimers had to believe that opportunities were as "good in the Maritime Provinces as they are anywhere else, or at least in most places" (ibid., p.14). Coady believed that the unstable conditions of the late 1930s aided his cause. Economic possibilities were not so good elsewhere, and this compelled young adults to turn inward and appraise the economic opportunities in their own backyards. The questions Coady had asked one of his first adult education study circles in the mid-1920s remained pertinent: "What should people do to get life in this community? What should they think about and study to enable them to get it?"

Coady shared progressive sentiments with regard to the use of the "project method" to "foster a social spirit and develop the techniques of group action" (ibid., p.20) in the school system. One can easily anticipate his argument: "If co-operation and the socialization of additional public utilities are to be a genuine part of our future economic lives, the duty of the school to furnish the proper orientation in this regard becomes all the more imperative" (ibid.). Echoing Dewey, Coady believed that the school should be a "miniature society," with students pursuing their studies in a co-operative manner. Students would learn "civics" by forming a simulated municipal council. This "mode of action" prepared "future citizens for intelligent participation in government, in a manner scarcely possible through individual learning" (ibid.).

Coady didn't believe that children would be the ones who would change the world. Adults had to be building the kind of co-operative world that would provide the guiding aims for the school system itself. The transformation of the attitudinal outlook of Maritimers had to take precedence. Coady needed to find a motivational starting point that would link the right ideas with people's life situation. Throughout his life, Coady was preoccupied with finding the right techniques to "mobilize the people to study" ("The Economic Approach in the Adult Education Program," p.1). He was adamant around finding appropriate methods, and never stopped experimenting. By the mid- to late 1930s, many Canadian and American adult educators, as well as the illustrious Scandinavians, had reached consensus that the study circle was the most "adequate means of conducting a program of intensive mass education" (ibid.).

In surveying eight years of study club organization in the Maritimes, Coady still believed it was the "right instrument for the job that lies at hand" (ibid.). However, adult educators did not agree on the question of where to begin. Some adult educators, such as E.A. Ned Corbett and the University of Alberta circle, carried a culturally oriented program into the rural towns and villages. Coady scorned those educators who would "offer the masses caviar before they had learned to like olives and even before they had acquired the wherewithal to purchase them" (ibid.). Though this latter comment is a little ornery and does not adequately valorize non-economically oriented initiatives that were occurring throughout Canada, it does reveal Coady's firmly held axiom that "cultural or political development" was not the starting point for St.FX's adult education program. Coady knew this was a controversial assertion (bread before Brahms) and provided arguments in its defence. Indeed, Coady and Tompkins did not always seem to agree about where one should start. By the late 1930s, Tompkins was not restricting his work to the economic, but was launching co-operative housing initiatives and promoting libraries.

Coady believed that education should enable "a man [*sic*] to realize his possibilities" (ibid.). Here Coady had effectively translated Aristotelian notions into a simple assertion. The "full life" was the "gradual realization of human potentialities." God had created within all beings the seeds of its possibilities. The *telos*, or end purpose, of both natural and human beings was the unfolding of its purpose as God had decreed. The perfection of created beings would only be fully achieved in the end time. Human beings, Coady acknowledged, were created with a "whole gamut of human possibilities—physical, economic, institutional, cultural and spiritual" (ibid., p.2). They could never exhaust their inherent potential in any of these spheres, nor was it adequate for a person to develop potentiality selectively. "It is not sufficient," Coady declared, "that an individual enjoy a perfect physique and at the same time suffer from an undeveloped intellect or an inadequate income" (ibid.). The principle of symmetry applied. Coady's ideal was of the balanced, or harmonious person. "A three legged stool that has one leg shorter than the others is of little value and less beauty. An unbalanced man is no more desirable." Thus, for Coady, the "true function" (ibid.) of education was to enable persons to attain symmetry of development. Coady had most certainly absorbed the classical Greek humanist ideal of the perfected being into his own educational philosophy.

Coady considered it "good pedagogy and good psychology" to begin with the "economic phase." Like Abraham Maslow, who invented his famous "hierarchy of needs," Moses Coady thought that spiritual and cultural development was higher in the developmental chain, that one had to move through the "economic" to reach the higher plateaus. Coady thought that some critics would brand Antigonish Movement "education in economics as propaganda" (ibid., p.3). Coady countered this by asserting that such an accusation "might itself be propaganda for the status quo" (ibid.). A teacher, he said, who refused to

> criticize conditions as they exist invites suspicion. He looks dangerously like a paid agent of the vested interests. He would not think of calling instruction in algebra or arithmetic propaganda. But he does not hesitate to place that name upon our efforts in the economic and social fields. If, however, it is propaganda to point out the eternally right and basic relations of man to man in society, then I am a propagandist (ibid.).

The rhetorical aggression of this language scarcely disguises Coady's dogmatism. Coady conflated the truth-claims of natural science with those of the human, but these worlds are not homologous. The dogmatist always claims that his views are "eternally right." Even Church social teachings through the ages indicate clearly that Christian teachings are compatible with many different forms of economic and social order. The Antigonish intellectuals, for instance, did not ever seriously consider creating either Catholic unions (unlike their Quebec colleagues) or a Christian Democratic Party (like their European counterparts). Coady elevated his interpretation of right relations for humans into an eternal principle. Once there, with the principles dwelling in the transcendental light, dialogue about pedagogy and economics, or spirituality and pedagogy, became unnecessary. Coady had transformed one option–isolating the "economy" from "polity" and finding "co-operative" solutions–into the essential option for Christians.

Coady believed it was "good pedagogy" to begin with the economic phase, because needs determine interests, and persons learn best when their interest is keen. He thought it inconceivable that anyone would deny the "urgent economic needs of the masses" or "suggest that they are disinterested [*sic*] in the goods and services which they cannot obtain" (ibid.). The question of who has the right to determine what another human being "needs" is very controversial in adult education theory. The concept itself is both normative and descriptive, and therein lies part of the problem. Coady might have been correct in his judgement of what "the masses" needed, but he still thought that he kenw what they "needed." To be sure, one can converse, do research, scour educational texts or reflect on other's initiatives for clues, but one can never know, objectively, what people need. People need many things, all at the same time. Coady sought to ground his pedagogy in rational analysis, but the real test lay in the results of his experiment in leading the "people into the field of adult education by the economic route." (ibid.). Coady believed that the masses' interests lay in the economic realm. After beginning there, he could lead them into other fields. The masses, as Coady knew them, would not study for their own sake. That was simply "too much to ask ... in the beginning" (ibid.). Like Dewey, Coady held strongly to the notion that problems occurring in everyday life were the appropriate pedagogical starting points. In Coady's view, the suffering and exploited masses' main "problem" was how to get their collective hands on the throttle of economic destiny.

One can see how Coady's vision of the co-operative revolution (he thinks he knows the solution) shapes his pedagogical thinking. He is confident that co-operation is the way out of economic exploitation for Maritimers. His plan required that he funnel the primary producers' energy in economic directions, so it is not surprising that Coady was compelled to motivate learners through the economic way. If they were going to be drawn into the Movement for the long haul, they would have to be hooked and kept on line. Coady's bait was the quick results, "easily appreciated and readily enjoyed," (ibid.) that adult learners would see while travelling the economic road. Adult learners who were not accustomed to study, so Coady assumed, would experience a "sense of accomplishment that spurs them on to renewed and persistent effort." The ensuing pleasure at finding that "thinking pays in dollars and cents" (ibid., p.4) would spur them on to new fields.

Coady was certain that he knew how the mass-man works. He would only desire to explore the rich cultural heritage of civilization once his economic needs have been met. "That is the kind of being he is," Coady insisted, "and we as educators are blind when we fail to understand his nature and to lead him in the way he can be led and be made greater. If we are to make an idealist of him we must first satisfy his realism" (ibid.). In his nine years of work, mainly in the economic field, Coady found "sufficient evidence" for his "formula that visualizes culture through lobster factories and other agencies that minister to the material wants of the people" (ibid.). Tompkins, on the other hand, never thought in this kind of cause-effect chain. Through libraries, people had access to cultural riches; they didn't need lobster factories first.

Coady saw a close relationship between class and culture. He thought that cultured people were generally possessed of wealth. They could purchase cultural capital and had the leisure time to attend galleries, libraries, concert halls, and to travel near and far. They had better health, clean workplaces and lovely homes. The masses, in contrast, scraped by on low wages. They couldn't afford to buy books. Having a radio or a musical instruments was a luxury. They couldn't travel. In recent years, however, they had had time. Their salvation lay there. Coady imagined that the "wise use of that leisure time" would "permit them to explore the economic fields which will yield a harvest of material and, in time, cultural and spiritual fruits" (ibid., p.5). Coady capped off this line of reasoning with the interesting argument that economic activities could in themselves be seen as cultural. If culture were growth, then, as people realized their potential through the economic, they were, in fact, attaining culture. This circular form of argument wouldn't convince the sceptic.

Coady's final argument in defence of beginning with the material and concrete as a means of arriving at the spiritual and cultural rested on assumptions about the development of human thought. Coady claimed that his "procedure" was "in harmony with the development of human thought itself" (ibid., p.6). This is a big claim. Coady rejected Platonic idealism. Instead, he turned to Aristotle, who argued that there is "nothing in the human mind ... that is not derived through the material senses from the material world." Following Aristotle, Coady perceived the human intellect to be the active agent that receives "stuff" from the senses. Then, by a "process of abstraction, refining and patterning," the intellect "builds up the ideas that enable the mind to carry on its abstract reasoning" (ibid., p.7).

Arguing by analogy, Coady maintained that one should, therefore, "expect that the creation of the good and artistic society will be achieved in the same way" (ibid.). The adult learning process recapitulates the mind's traversal from lower to complex levels of thought. Adult learners interact with economic and physical forces. They control and manipulate them for their own purposes. This mastery of the material forces of their lives clears the way, Coady argued, for human development in other, higher cultural spheres. This is an intriguing argument because it is similar to Marxian theory. Coady privileges the "economic," giving it almost an ontic primacy. However, it can be argued, contrary to Coady, that human learning does not proceed in phases, or steps, from lower to higher. Rather, human beings learn simultaneously along a double axis. Learning in interaction with nature, Coady's primary material realm, can be distinguished from learning in interaction with others. Human beings are capable of speech and action. They are also capable of using power to dominate and exploit others. Coady's ontology of learning did not adequately distinguish the two axes of human learning (Habermas labels them the "instrumental" and "practical" learning realms). Thus, the ontic primacy of the "economic" may be questioned philosophically.

Coady was writing MOTD at a time when the "common man" was celebrated, even deified, in the Western world. Intellectuals like Ortega y Gasset wrote of their "revolt"; socialist realists turned them into massive icons; journalists discerned their emergent power in the West and stirrings in the East; educators such as the University of Chicago's Robert Hutchins and Moses Coady honoured their new-found capacity to absorb the cultural riches of the world, its languages and literature.

> If we look upon Latin and Greek as synonymous with the culture of the ancients, it may be possible to place even this at the disposal of the people. The art, literature, and philosophy of the ancients was theirs. All that the mind of man has excogitated in the intervening years belongs to them. But greatest of all, what still lies hidden within themselves is theirs, theirs to enjoy and to pass on (ibid., p.8).

Coady shared Hutchins' vision of the "great possibilities of the common man." The job of all educators was to "give the mass-man a chance to appreciate his rich heritage and to express himself." But, in order to erect his new Pantheon, he had first to "build his lobster-factories" (ibid.). Few educators, including Hutchins, connected lobsters and Pantheons. Coady believed, unshakeably, that once the exploited primary producers ceased "to worry about bread," they could "begin to enjoy Brahms" (ibid., p.9). Once the economic question was settled, they would be free to "devote their time and energies to the more enjoyable cultural pursuits." Adult education's first mandate was to release energy and channel it towards economic mastery and self-reliance. Only then would human energy be able to flow back to the person and community. Coady imagined that a "people, raised to new levels" would produce "their poets, painters, and musicians to give expression to the new and yet eternal truths that beat within their breasts. As in nature, so in man, the lofty mountain peaks shall rise not from the level plains but from the foothills" (ibid.).

For Coady, the primacy of the "economic" was an ambivalently masculinist framework. The discourse of the "mass-man" not only tended to homogenize variation and difference (ethnic, religious, community, personal), but it also presupposed male economic activity as the norm. The primary producer and industrial worker was male. Certainly women were engaged in some waged labour and contributed to the household economic management of fishery and farm, but early twentieth-century Maritime women were located primarily in the lifeworld where they managed scarce household resources, tended to too many children and generally held the hard-pressed communities together. They fit into Coady's axial category, the "economic," mainly as goods managers and not as producers. Coady's construction of the mass-man assumed the classic sexual division of labour: men "produce" and run the "public" sphere, women "reproduce" the lifeworld and manage private matters.

Women did not fit neatly into Coady's "economic" category, but there was some seepage. The craft movement pursued by the female leaders of the movement encouraged women to create "cottage industries" within their households to sell their crafts. Both credit unions and consumer co-operatives appealed to women's role as household managers. Women would, however, face great difficulties achieving real power within the co-op movement itself.[15]

V

Coady was one of the international co-operative movement's foremost philosophers of co-operation. Although he never stopped refining his thinking, MOTD set out his philosophical justification of co-operation as the solution for the persistent problems of Maritime poverty and exploitation. Coady came to the conclusion that the capitalist system severed the masses from the "control of the instruments of production and distribution" (CSB, p.1). Trade unionists, whom he sometimes mocked as "glib and final in their conviction about what is wrong with the world," had rejected taking a "hand in the management of their economic affairs" (TMS, p.3). Coady didn't care much for profit-sharing schemes either because they "could never be called effective ownership in the real sense of the term" (CSB, p.1). The primary producers had once been independent owners but were now propertyless farm labourers, share-croppers and tenants. If, however, the people had co-operated, they could have

> piped down to themselves some of the wealth that flowed so generously in other directions. Had they done this in the past they might now have institutions earning dividends for them while they work or lay or sleep. Then the masses would cease to be masses in our present sense and would become real citizens participating in the fruits of all our democratic social institutions (ibid., p.3).

Coady distinguished "economic co-operation" from social democratic distributionism. It was not a means of sharing wealth acquired by others. Rather, it was a "method of doing business whereby its members can relay back to themselves the new wealth that each creates in proportion as he creates it" (ibid.). It was production for use and not profit. Coady was convinced that economic co-operation would resolve the paradox of "an almost infinite capacity to produce" combined with "a definite inability to distribute because so many must profit by the process" (ibid., p.4). Coady interpreted the economic problem of the Great Depression as, essentially, the absence of purchasing power. "To break the present economic deadlock," Coady claimed, "we need to lower the cost of goods and raise wages." (ibid., p.5). He thought this position was in line with that of "reputable economists and business men all over North America.... Through consumers' co-operatives, credit societies and socialized industry, which is co-operation in its compulsory form, the prices of goods and services are lowered to their actual cost. Through marketing co-operatives, labor unions, and social security, the income to the masses is increased" (ibid.). Few social democrats would argue with this viewpoint.

Coady preferred the co-operative solution to capitalism's crisis because it harmonized with his primary metaphysical beliefs. Coady, the Catholic thinker, did not desire the violent rupturing of the economic processes. He sought an "evolutionary, constitutional way" out of the crisis. "We take things as they are and work through the old into the new so that while we build, there is no cessation of the normal functions of society" (ibid.). This may have been a hard message for some Maritimers to swallow, given their continuing experience of the disruptions and vagaries of the international capitalist economy. Coady did not think that co-operative organizations should aim for a "complete co-operative democracy" (ibid.). In 1939, co-operative enterprise played only a small part in the North American economy. Coady thought that "our own people" could gain a "measure of economic independence" by controlling a small percentage (10 to 15 percent) of the country's business (ibid., p.6).

Coady believed that learning to effectively manipulate economic forces would catalyze people to take control of the "other forces that should operate in a democratic society." Once their intellectual powers had been awakened through instrumental learning processes, these dynamized intellects would turn towards civic affairs, Coady's "other forces." This argument is fundamental to an understanding of Coady's view of democratic politics. He consistently argued that the masses had to be prepared for political action through their experience with "economic democracy." Once prepared, they could engage in two other "general types of social action which logically follow it" (ibid., p.7). The first was intelligent political action. Coady argued that the masses learn a realistic attitude towards politics through functioning in the economy. Essentially, Coady thought that the "propertyless citizen" could not be expected to take that "responsibility in political affairs that is characteristic of those who own and direct our present economic institutions" (ibid., p.8), for power lay in economic control. The alienation of the masses from the instrumental regulation of societal processes led to their separation from government. (This argument is similar to that of the early Marx in his famous *Economic and Philosophic Manuscripts* of 1844.) From this alienated state of mind, Coady proffered, "arise the evils of the present political system" (ibid.). In the capitalist form of economic and political organization, human beings give their power over to the system. Their own creations, wealth and governance, end up as their dominators.

Coady's criticism of contemporary party politics is plain Marxism (class power equals political power). Businessmen usually select the candidates for political office, and these candidates tend to "represent the interests that put them in power." They feel little obligation to the people. Coady was also disturbed by the masses taking their citizenship so lightly that they scarcely raised their voice at the evident corruption in Maritime politics. They didn't protest against reckless political spending; they didn't really know what the vital issues were; they had to be cajoled to vote; they were silent about the "iniquitous patronage system" (ibid.). "All these evils," Coady claimed, "are inherent in the present political system because the masses of the people in a modern democracy have no immediate vested interests" (ibid., p.9). Civic affairs in many of the cities of Canada and the United States remained in the "hands of the anti-social political machine" (ibid.). Yet, despite this powerful analysis of the degradation of civic affairs, the Antigonish Movement never consciously educated its people for collective action in civil society.

A second open avenue for the masses lay in the socialization of certain industries. Like the democratic socialists of the 1930s and 1940s, Coady advocated "common ownership" of industries that could not be "safely left in the hands of individuals" (ibid., p.10). He approved of the route Canada had already travelled in socializing highways, schools, the postal service and railways. Coady dismissed the cry of "socialism" by private business at the "mere mention of state ownership" (ibid.). The railways had little trouble, Coady said, passing their failures off onto the Canadian taxpayer. And the inability of private industries to take care of their workers in times of stress made for a powerful argument for "some form of socialism in our day" (ibid., p.11). Coady was uncertain as to how much socialization should be carried out. Catholic radicalism was very suspicious of state interference in civil society and economy. However, his commitment to the revitalization of rural life and to equitable resource distribution compelled him to embrace the "complete socialization of electric power" (ibid.). Private concerns provided power to the profitable urban centres. "Under compete public ownership, if the country were properly zoned, the densely populated urban areas could balance the sparsely settled rural districts and all could get power at much reduced rates" (ibid.).

The central challenge of both co-operation and democratic socialist reform movements was to regulate the capitalist marketplace in the interest of meeting the full range of human needs. Left unchecked, the capitalist market's sensors were not attuned to the developmental needs of human beings and nature. Coady's writings, speeches and letters reveal that he was deeply troubled by and perplexed with this problem of regulating the market. In the original version of MOTD, Coady grappled with this problem. For a start, Coady didn't think that private enterprise was going to disappear overnight. "Some check, however, must be placed on business; it must be disciplined by itself or by some outside force" (ibid., p.12). Interestingly, Coady thought that the realm of instrumental learning might include "double loop" mechanisms, enabling business to learn from its mistakes. Competition was expected to do that, but competition was "dead and economic dictatorship" had "taken its place" (ibid.). However, one could argue that the self-disciplinary learning processes of business are governed by the principle of efficient production. The learning sensors would not sniff out other needs or interests.

Coady thought co-operation could be the "outside force" that might challenge "many of the disguised and carefully concealed malpractices that have been introduced into business as a consequence of economic dictatorship" (ibid.). Two competing principles would be operative in the economic sphere. Coady advocated that the co-operative movement function as the "eye of the enlightened masses who have been regenerated through education and co-operative action" (ibid.). For example, Coady imagined that when the co-ops established "just prices," conventional capitalist enterprises would be pressured to watch their own. When the Swedish co-operative Luma lowered its price of electric light bulbs from 33 cents to 21 cents, repercussions were felt around the world. Any significant influence on the hegemonic economy comes from the emergent alternative economy, and not from civil society. This appeared to be an axiomatic principle of influence for the Antigonish intellectuals.

Coady made a poignant case for co-operativism against corporatism. He never made his case for co-operation against trade unionism. In fact, Coady believed that establishing co-operatives would increase the effectiveness of trade unions, placing them in a better position to bargain with industry's captains. By "entering business on their own accord," the masses would be safeguarded from the "ill effects of the vocational group idea." Coady thought that contracts between labor and industry, if too rigidly applied, "would entrench the vested interests and perpetuate the status quo and a caste system in society" (ibid., p.13). Coady justified Extension's choice of approach to organizing the fishermen. They could have organized the fishermen into a union or a corporatist syndicate and the operators, or packers, into another syndicate. They could then have brought them together to "discuss wages, conditions of labor, and other topics pertaining to the industry" (ibid., p.14). Instead, the lobster fishermen were encouraged to process their catch on their own initiative, thereby illustrating that the industry did not need private packers and that the fishermen could conduct their own business. Coady did not think that corporatism could break the stranglehold the vested interests had over key sectors of the Maritime economy. He was also realistic enough to know that the co-operatives (at least in 1939) could not take over industries requiring large outlays of capital.

The three types of social action—economic co-operation, intelligent political activity and the socialization of particular industries—led "logically to the control of the cultural and spiritual agencies now used by powerful individuals and groups to determine the kind of society we live in" (ibid.). Coady thought that radio and the press, the key agencies of publicity within civil society, could be constrained by an expanding co-operative business. As co-operative power increased, Coady surmised, the people could create for themselves "instruments that will permit them to voice their own case and cause" (ibid.).

Coady was willing to trust the democratic, experimental and communicative process of social transformation. He believed deeply that the co-operative way was in harmony with the "natural evolution of society," which had place for the "unforeseen repercussions of invention and discovery." It left to the "aggregate intelligence of all the people the decision on what steps they shall take in the light of future developments." The "co-operative formula" enabled people to proceed with "evident, feasible things" with the assurance that, if "enough of the eternally right things" were done, "presto, all the problems of the people" would be solved (ibid., p.15). Coady thought that the easy applicability of the co-operative formula enabled all the people, including the "poor and those of low-grade intelligence," to contribute to the reconstruction of society. United in strength, each person could add their little blow of the hammer to the other in "building the new social structure" (ibid.). As the "common people" became masters of their own economic affairs through co-operatives, they inoculated "themselves against violent revolution because no people rise against themselves, and dictatorships from the right or left meet with their strong resistance" (ibid., p.16).

Coady feared that the confused and confounded masses of the West were prime objects for the "communist dictatorial" option. He was particularly troubled that so many panaceas offered to the people were abstract plans that the people could not carry out. "If the people cannot do the things advocated," Coady announced, "then some sort of dictator must do them if they are to be done at all" (ibid.). Coady also maintained that the "quick, virile, red and bloody way of revolution" (a fascinating alignment of masculinist adjectives), while intriguing, appeared to the proletariat to be the "easy way to solve the social problem." But the "revolutionary method" was unscientific because it applied brute force precisely where intelligence was needed. "We need to be as exact in social architecture as we are in building material structures" (ibid., p.17), Coady declared. "While in the building of society, we cannot hope to attain mathematical precision, yet it is a delicate task, one in which the temporal and eternal destiny of man is at stake and loose thinking and imperfect calculation are out of the question" (ibid., p.18). Coady thought that the zealous minority of Canadians who were promoting the "inevitable revolution" were founding their position on a social contradiction: could the same person who smashed society build it up again? Only by "intelligent individual and group action" could the "masses repossess the earth. The democratic formula, of which economic co-operation is a vital part, was adequate. It took the appeal out of the Marxian call to arms and said instead: 'Workers of the world, arise! You need not be proletarians'" (ibid., p.19).

The Antigonish dreamers envisioned that the co-operative movement would outbest the communists and gradually undermine the vested interests of capitalism. They would be wrong on both counts in the global context. At century's beginning, the international co-op movement, despite its strengths, has not yet succeeded in forcing global capitalism to attune to the majority of people's needs and interests. Coady would not be out of job today.

VI

As priest and Christian believer, Moses Coady had to justify his choice of the "co-operative formula" within his religious world-view. He had to satisfy himself that his chosen way to alleviate the economic and political crisis, first in the Maritimes, then radiating out to encompass the world, was harmonious with Christian social teachings. He also had to ensure that the co-operative movement was not perceived to be sectarian. Coady began his discussion in "Co-operation and Religion" (CR) by noting that the Rochdale pioneers "heartily endorsed and vigorously defended" (CR, p.1) the neutrality principle. Coady agreed, arguing that unity against the "common foe" (ibid., p.2) was found through the "common denominator of right reason which is the norm according to which every activity of society should be directed." However, Coady insisted that "co-operation needs religion and religion needs co-operation" (ibid.). Both charity and justice had their foundation in religion, and were necessary to prevent bigotry. Opponents of co-operation, Coady argued, used the "propaganda of religious bigotry" (ibid., p.3) to "divide and rule" the co-operative movement. Behind these words was the Antigonish Movement's experience of being accused by Protestant communities of using the Movement as a wedge for the papacy. True to his Thomist roots, Coady maintained that one could no more speak of "Quaker Chemistry" as of "Buddhist or Catholic" co-operation. Truth was non-denominational, open to all, and co-operation was a "body of natural truths acquired by the light of reason" (ibid.). Even people without religion could apply co-operative principles and obtain good results. The danger, for Coady, lay in co-operation's very goodness. People might want to turn it into a new religion. For progressive Catholic thinkers, co-operation as a new religion simply provided us with another version of the "totalitarian economy" (ibid.).

In Coady's conceptual universe, "religion" (one assumes he usually meant Western Christianity) was the animating spirit of the co-operative movement. Coady worried constantly throughout the Extension years that the co-operative movement was going to be outdistanced by the communists because they had more zeal and dedication to their cause than the Christians. In 1939, he chose the myth of Sisyphus to portray the precarious nature of the co-op movement. "We are still rolling the huge stone up the steep hill. If at any point in the ascent we take off the pressure it will go crashing to the bottom" (ibid., p.4) A little success in retailing or manufacturing would not provide the spirit necessary to roll the stone up the hill. Workers had to be "refreshed from the well springs of the altar. It is the spiritual concept of life that gives zest to the struggle" (ibid.) Thus, for Coady, religion was not an opiate; it provided the energy and stimulation for men and women in the co-operative movement to press onward to "loftier and more noble, more soul-satisfying heights" (ibid.). "The great accomplishment of the new age will be to restore the spiritual by using the material as it ought to be used, a means to a higher end" (ibid., p.5). This is a powerful, controversial and demanding argument. The adult educator has the challenging task of intervening in an unfavourable environment to set in motion the enlightenment process. Once in motion, the spiritual challenge shifts to the people themselves. They must remain in the spirit, charging the co-operative movement with energy and dynamism. If the movement grows lethargic, stagnant or corrupt, the people have, once again, exercised a great default.

Religion, Coady said, also needs co-operation. Like the Church's embracing of Aristotle, contemporary religious people ought to embrace co-operation because it is the truth. "The religiously minded man will use all the good things of God's creation to further the cause of humanity and to ensure the salvation of souls" (ibid.). Imbued with charity, honesty and courage, this religiously minded man would dare to confront a hard, relentless and cruel system that "sins against nearly every ethical principle" (ibid.). Truly religious, he would recognize what is "fundamentally good and recognition ought to mean immediate adoption" (ibid.). He would contribute to tightening the "restraining bonds on capitalism," enabling it to re-learn the forgotten virtues of justice and charity. In biblical language, Coady's "poor" would confound the "wise." If enlightened, the meek might inherit the earth.

Coady thought that in his day the economic question had particular religious significance. In fact, he thought it the "great modern religious question" (ibid., p.6). If not solved, freedom, culture and religion might be "seriously endangered" (ibid.). For Coady, economic considerations were intimately connected with spiritual activities. Coady believed, as Jesus taught, that "by their fruits you shall know them." Religion was, in essence, not about correct beliefs; it was about personal and social practice. Spirituality resided primarily in the interaction between people. "The economic question," Coady claimed, "is a religious question ... because the relationships of man to man are involved, the relation of employer and employee, of consumer, producer, and distributor, of individuals and the state. It is more than a question of supply and demand, more than a matter of food, clothing, and shelter" (ibid.). Drawing on an old theological principle, the "proximate occasion of sin," Coady interpreted this as meaning that persons could not be considered "seriously solicitous" about their spiritual welfare while they remained in this "occasion." If people were living in slums, poverty and misery, they would not be inclined towards spiritual matters. He believed that co-operation rendered the proximate danger of economic misery or suffering remote, making the world "safe for sanctity" (ibid., p.7).

This line of analysis reveals an important sub-text. Coady was disturbed that the Church had lost the masses. He thought that the masses

> had hoped, reasonably, that in the faith they would be delivered from degrading bondage. They did not seek, nor were they promised a paradise on earth by their religious leaders; but they did expect that the road to their heavenly paradise would not

be made humanly impossible to pass, beset with dangers and difficulties beyond the endurance of unaided mortal man (ibid., p.8).

In the lecture "Tackling the World Problem," delivered to the Sisters of Martha on February 3, 1952, Coady informed his audience that the Church had

> lost the masses in the 19th century because too many people in the Church and State were secretly, and in many cases openly, in favor of the feudalistic and aristocratic status quo.... Not finding a sympathetic consideration of their social and economic plight from those who should have been their friends, the workers of the 19th century left the Church and threw in their lot with those who fought against "feudalistic and aristocratic privilege, against monarchical absolutism and against all forms of political tyranny and state interference with the liberty of the individual."[16]

The Church turned away from the democratic revolution; the "great scandal of the 20th century is that we have not won them back." Coady thought that the Church was still losing the workers because they had "made peace with our old enemies, the economic liberals, the millionaire capitalists, and appear to have an alliance with them that is not good for the spiritual health of the world." The angry prophet from the Margaree Valley carried much heaviness of soul. By abdicating social responsibility, Coady's beloved Church had created a great vacuum in human history. "As a consequence, we are getting social tornadoes—revolution and wars.... The real answer is to fill up these empty spaces in the social lives of our people" (ibid.).

Coady inhabited the world of the 1930s, which, unlike our own time of chaos and unruliness, supported a belief in the possibility of social reconstruction in the interests of that decade's myth, the "common man." Coady's often florid language—the world transformed into a place where the "weeds of greed and injustice no longer choke the flowers of virtue" (CR, p.8)—may strike us as naïve, but this was the dream. Coady knew that few flowers bloomed in unhealthy environments. Coady rejected moral reform as "first requisite for that housecleaning job" (ibid., p.9). Like contemporary liberation theologians and activists, situated primarily in the Third World, Coady had a firm grasp of the socially structured nature of sin. He knew that structures inhabited people, shaping their bodies, morals and minds.

The challenge for Christians on the edge of World War II lay with creating this powerful "economic force," founded in religious idealism, to curb the anti-social forces. Christians couldn't look heavenward for assistance. They had their reason and could learn, slowly and painfully, to manipulate natural and social forces. Virtuous ideals would be reinforced by virtuous practices.

Although religion dictated as a "fundamental principle that social justice should obtain in the world," justice alone was "not enough to ensure a smoothly running world" (ibid., p.11). Charity had to ensure that justice was merciful, and co-operation, in Coady's view, reinforced the "idea of charity in a new and powerful way" (ibid.). Religion would prove itself when it showed "that it pays to pour out one's self for one's neighbour … that the Divine Banker may be taken at His word when He promises to pay 100% of any loan of love" (ibid.). Coady constantly reached for the right metaphor; this one is a little troubling because it suggests that Coady's perception had been pervaded by the commercial ethos to the point wherein God could be imagined as a "Divine Banker."

Coady's imagination had an apocalyptic side. As an organic intellectual of the primary producers, Coady saw the world's "little people" as lost sheep in a Darwinian world where only the fittest survive. In a system ruled by "jungle ethics," the common people were in "peril of salvation" (ibid., p.12). It was nigh impossible for them to be useful citizens. "In droves they seek safety in our cities but are led to the slaughter instead. Or they cower alone in the shelter of their rural ruins and slowly are becoming degenerate to the point where nothing can be done for them except to transport them to a state farm" (ibid.). The old form of charity, lending a helping hand from time to time, was insufficient. The only appropriate form of charity was through "co-operation, the embodiment of charity in economics" (ibid.). Charity had to be manifested in structures capable of giving "needy brothers" a "chance to live and to contribute to the general good and the greater glory of God, where man, with his marvelous power to recuperate, will find the strength to rise, straighten himself up, throw back his noble head, and gaze into the sun" (ibid., p.13).

Coady drew strength and inspiration from the famous New Testament passage in which the Great Judge metes out to humanity its reward and retribution.

> Then shall the King say to them that shall be on his right hand: Come, ye blessed of my Father, possess you the kingdom prepared for you from the foundation of the world. For I was hungry, and you gave me to eat; I was thirsty, and you gave me to drink; I was a stranger, and you took me in: naked, and you covered me: sick, and you visited me: I was in prison, and you came to me (Matthew 25: 34-37).

Coady's Church had taught him that corporal works of mercy were an "integral part of a religious life" (ibid.). But the irrepressible Coady pressed beyond the exercise of holy personal offices. Corporal works of mercy had to be transformed, reaching

> far out into the wastes of mankind to aid through organizations those whom they cannot contact personally. They will feed the hungry, give drink to the thirsty, and clothe the naked by establishing co-operatives whereby the poor may obtain their daily material needs in full and adequate amounts. They will harbor the harborless, visit the sick, bury the dead, and ransom the captives by the establishment of those free, democratic, just, and charitable co-operative organizations which will permit men to help themselves and their unfortunate neighbors to move forward under the power of newly released group energies and give expression to the innate charity of man which finds its natural outlet in an organic, interdependent society (ibid., p.13).

VII

In the final section of his original manuscript, "The Future," (TF) Coady asserted that the adult education movement involved the "creation of economic institutions co-operatively owned" (TF, p.1) He immediately informed his reader that this involved "opposition, active opposition from the vested interests, passive resistance from the masses" (ibid.). However, reform movements, such as the movement for political democracy, always faced opposition from those in power. The "vested interests" (read "monopoly capitalists") had "merely displaced invested lords and nobles. We, the people, have the ball and chain removed from one foot only. And the dictators laugh while we hobble along in an unequal race, handicapped by their friends who live in our own camp—our own dictators, our men of money. And if we lag, democracy gets the blame" (ibid.). Anticipating his critics, Coady said that it could be "doubted that the so-called ignorant masses are capable of rising to the economic, moral, and intellectual level necessary for the effectual operation of their economic and political machinery. But that is our dream" (ibid., p.2). How was it possible, Coady wondered, to "grant the privilege of political democracy and at the same time withhold the opportunities for economic democracy on which it should be founded"? (ibid.). This would, indeed, Coady continued, be a "contradiction between our fundamental philosophy and our application of it" (ibid.). Coady seemed to think that his co-operative revolution, for this is surely what he was committed to, did not lay too heavy a burden on the common people. They didn't have to theorize too much to run practical affairs, nor did they need despair of failures that had "marked the road of economic group action" (ibid.). Coady argued that conducting a co-operative business required intelligence, and it was not unnatural that there would be some inefficiency in the beginning. "Being a co-operator implies learning, the learning of new techniques; and no one can learn a new technique without suffering a period of temporary inefficiency" (ibid., p.3). People had to unlearn old habits and relearn new ones. This took time, but Coady took heart from British and Scandinavian progress in adapting a more scientific system of production and distribution.

> If these common people, economically handicapped, and in the face of great opposition, have accomplished so much, what might have happened if the people of North America, blessed as they have been with education for many generations, had received a helping hand from the institutions of society that are supposed to exist for the enlightenment of all? (ibid., p.5).

Even the story of capitalism itself could be read favourably. Men [*sic*] of capacity, ambition, industry and ruthlessness had emerged from the masses to command "great economic ventures" (ibid., p.6). Coady did not doubt that the necessary leadership for the co-operative movement would emerge from the masses. "Stripped of their ruthlessness and equipped with a greater measure of justice and charity, they will provide the necessary executive ability for new and greater economic enterprises, while the masses of men, likewise equipped, will support them with intelligence and good will" (ibid.). Coady was preoccupied, not to say obsessed, with the question of leadership for the people's organizations. Extension organized short leadership-training courses throughout the Movement's study club phase. After World War II broke out, the study club as a mass movement ended, and the Extension leadership concentrated on training managers and leaders for the co-operative organizations.

For Moses M. Coady, the Christian visionary, all of the attention to the prosaic detail of running co-operatives was only the beginning. He had no desire to

> create a nation of mere shopkeepers, whose thoughts run only to groceries and dividends. We want our men [sic] to look into the sun and into the depths of the sea. We want them to explore the hearts of flowers and the hearts of fellow men. We want them to live, to love, to play and pray with all their being. We want them to be men, whole men, eager to explore all the avenues of life and to attain perfection in all their faculties. We want for them the capacity to enjoy all that a generous God and creative men have placed at their disposal. We desire above all that they will discover and develop their own capacities for creation. It is good to appreciate; it is godlike to create. Life for them shall not be in terms of merchandizing but in terms of all that is good and beautiful, be it economic, political, social, cultural, or spiritual. They are the heirs of all the ages and of all the riches yet concealed. All the findings of science and philosophy are theirs. All the creations of art and literature are for them. If they are wise they will create the instruments to obtain them. They will usher in the new day by attending to the blessings of the old. They will use what they have to secure what they have not (ibid., p.10).

This is one of the most rhapsodic, and famous, passages from Coady, who longed for the cathedral world of the spiritual and the cultural. Ironically, Coady could take his masses there only after they had spent time in the dog-house worlds of ledgers and lobsters, stores and wholesales, prices and taxes. The road to the promised land, shimmering afar on the horizon, could only provide mere hints of what it meant to discover that all of "art and literature" was for them, the disinherited peoples of the earth.

CHAPTER 7

The World Might Break Your Heart (1939-1945)

I

The outbreak of World War II in September 1939 marked a turning point in the history of the Antigonish Movement. The grassroots momentum, unleashed in the early mobilizing phase, was vitiated as dynamic young men and women, the spearhead of co-operative action in the local communities, departed overseas or into war-time industries. The war severely ruptured emerging community leadership structures. The Movement intellectuals believed that the co-ops had to "modernize and consolidate" if they were to create liberated space within the monopolistic capitalist society.

One of the main ways the intellectuals thought they could consolidate the Movement was through creating federated structures. In 1934, the leaders had created the Nova Scotia Credit Union League (NSCUL) to serve the legal, educational and expanding credit needs of its constituents. In 1939, they created the Nova Scotia Co-operative Educational Council (NSCEC), comprising the St. Francis Xavier Extension Department, the Credit Union League, the United Maritime Fishermen (UMF), the United Mine Workers (UMW) and the Co-operative Wholesale. The leaders of these organizations joined together to "consider the question of mobilizing the leadership and finances of these organizations and to plan a unified program of adult education."[1] The idea was to form local councils made up from the various co-ops. The local councils would then federate into district councils, which would feed representatives to the provincial council.

The objective of St.FX Extension had always been to "help people to the point where they could help themselves. When an organization became strong enough to carry on its own work, in both its financial and educational phase, it is expected to do so."[2] This policy was, of course, related partly to Extension's perennial shortage of funds and staff. Coady spent enormous energy searching for part-time fieldworkers. The federal Department of Fisheries provided financial assistance for fieldwork among the fishing communities in the Maritimes, excepting work in and around Lunenburg, the base of the deep-sea fishery. Lunenburg was off-limits for the Antigonish Movement because of the political manoeuvring of prominent federal Liberals such as William Duff. This annoyed Coady to no end. In early January 1940, he confided to MacIntyre that they had a "crack at Bill Duff and the salt fish merchants" who were "fighting Michaud on the salt fish board program."[3]

The danger for the Antigonish Movement leaders lay precisely in the convergence of two historical patterns. The momentum of the early phase was undermined by the mobilization of Canadian society for war, as energy was channelled away from social reform into winning the war for democracy. Study clubs were still organized throughout the war years, but on a smaller scale. In response to increasing complexity and internal differentiation, the leaders of the Movement added another layer of organization. The focus shifted from mobilizing the common people at the grassroots, where they had been able to act directly in creating the first, simple co-op organizations and self-help projects, to promoting organizational development and training elite managers and community leaders. Moreover, Movement leaders had to contend with the changing economic and political contexts within which they were building their people's society. Capitalists were now regaining its strength and began to fret about the gains the co-operative movement was making in Canada.

The Movement leaders did not believe they had any choice other than to consolidate their gains, expand where they could and wage political battles on national, provincial and local fronts on behalf of co-operatives. And there were plenty of battles, large and small. Coady was preoccupied with two on the national front: the restructuring of the fisheries and the taxation of co-operatives. It must have been disconcerting for Movement leaders to realize that the common people were not supporting either the credit union movement or the Co-operative Educational Council as they thought they should. Movement intellectuals continued to speak of the co-ops as democratic people's organizations, but it was becoming more difficult to ensure that all those who should be at the decision-making table were present.

II

There appeared to be dark days ahead for the St. Francis Xavier Extension Department. The Department had unleashed forces and developments in eastern Nova Scotia and elsewhere that were now becoming exceedingly difficult to control and manage. Even Coady's continuous presentation of an assured public face could not mask the difficulties confronting the Movement. For one thing, the Movement depended on Coady's inspirational leadership, yet his health was poor. No one really knew how long he could continue his work. A.B. MacDonald's words to George Keen—"We are all greatly worried about his condition, but we are hoping that he may eventually improve"–were rather typical of his friends' concerns.[4]

Like a fir tree felled by a big axe, Moses Coady suffered a severe heart attack in 1939. Perhaps this event could have been anticipated. Coady had spent a month or so in a Boston hospital in April 1938 and had remained ill through the late spring while he was in Antigonish. He spent most of 1939, from June until late November, in a New York hospital. One of his frequent visitors, Dr. Benson Y. Landis, reported that Coady had told him: "They've found four things wrong with me, and every one of them is bad. But they couldn't find anything very bad, so I'm going back to my work." The New York doctors told Coady, then aged fifty-seven, that he would probably never be able to go around making speeches again.[5] He confided to Jean Brown that the "principal trouble is heart. I had a series of operations and developed a bad heart condition. I will never be able to do the rough stuff of other years, but I have a chance to live and to carry on in a milder way."[6] In February 1940, his health was improving, and he made a few speeches. By April, his heart was bothering him again. Although he returned to a New York hospital for three weeks in April 1941, he seemed to be in pretty good cheer by the end of that year. Able to make an occasional hour-long speech, he was finding a "new lease on life." He informed Mary Arnold that he had spoken at short courses for the fishermen at Sydney and a course at Bras d'Or. He had also spoken to the high school kids in New Waterford for an hour a day for three days. "I was able to go on twice a day and I felt as strong as I ever did."[7] By January 3, 1942, Coady could write to Robert Lester of the Carnegie Corporation, that "we are all well and happy. My own health is particularly good. I stopped smoking six days ago and while I find it hard, I can notice that my health is better. I am sticking it out in any case. I go with the boys for the next three weeks on short courses." Coady didn't tell Lester that he was now beginning a "carless career behind the purring engines of these great cars."[8] On January 5, with his old boyish exuberance returning, Coady told Marion Gilroy that he was "getting dangerously dynamic."[9] Miraculously, Coady, who turned sixty in 1942, would have ten more vigorous years until he was struck down by gallstones and yet another heart attack.

All of this time in American hospitals set Coady back financially. While in hospital in New York, Coady wrote to Senator W.H. Dennis of Halifax:

> I want to say next that I am getting over my big line of operations and am doing nicely. I have been up for the past five days and am able to sit up and walk around. It will cost me approximately another $1200–to get out of here, depending upon how much the doctors may charge me. I have already paid the hospital and nurses $1900. I am trusting that you will be able to advance me this money. I have no one else to look to big enough to help me out of this difficulty.[10]

Coady had a stoical outlook on life. He received what God presented to him with equanimity, be it serious illness, world war or bitter conflict in some sector of the co-op movement. He was faithful to his path. During his prolonged illness, he remained more committed than ever to the gospel of co-operation as the solution to humankind's problems. On May 7, 1940, he wrote to journalist Evelyn Tufts: "If we can keep things going, we will yet do great things here." This little phrase reveals that Coady was not certain how it would go for Extension, but if they held the fort, they might yet be positioned to build the co-operative kingdom. Coady could also swing in the opposite direction. Only four days after writing to Tufts, Coady wrote Peter Nearing that the "troubled condition of things in Europe hangs like a black cloud over the world and takes the good out of all of us. However, we shall have to face it. It looks like the coming doom."[11]

St.FX also had few financial and human resources at its disposal. The bleak 1930s had pushed the university deeper into debt, making it more hesitant about funding Extension. In the late 1930s, Coady and others, such as Tompkins, had tried to raise "big money" from wealthy supporters of the Movement, but nothing significant seems to have come from these initiatives. During the war years, Coady tried constantly to negotiate with the federal Department of Fisheries for the continuation of their grant, as there was no guarantee from year to year. Coady was forced to play politics and do what he could with the resources he had.

His fisheries fieldworkers also suffered from the lack of adequate funding. Father Ben Saindon, who worked in New Brunswick under the Rev. J.L. Chiasson's supervision and the imprimatur of the Bishop of New Brunswick, told Coady that he was "somewhat stunned at your grant being cut and the very idea of giving up the work in a real active manner makes my heart sick."[12] A year later, Saindon confided to Coady that he hoped that "it will not be late before orders to proceed with the work come out. There has always been a certain amount of uncertainty of my position and also almost yearly about the grant."[13]

St.FX had never had an adequate number of fieldworkers to organize new study clubs and tend to the endless needs of the fledgling co-operative organizations in the rural farm areas, fishing communities and industrial towns. During the war, Coady had still fewer good people to choose from, and the Department of Fisheries was reluctant to support women fieldworkers. Yet the war years revealed the inherent weakness of Extension fieldwork: it was always simply too ad hoc in nature and erratic in delivery. Many of his fieldworkers, and specialists from the Nova Scotia Departments of Agriculture and Marketing, were wise organizers; Coady used the resources he had astutely. But Father Charles Forest's correspondence with Coady reveals both brilliance and fatigue. His community of Larry's River was responding fairly well, but he was doing all the work of bookkeeping and maintaining the momentum. Other reports often disclosed concern over low wages, terrible travelling conditions and just plain weariness. These impressive efforts of talented people were never adequate to the task of building the new co-operative social order. Coady responded to the obvious difficulty of maintaining vibrant study clubs in all the Maritime fishing communities by offering short courses in as many communities as they could manage.

III

The reports of the Nova Scotia Credit Union League from 1938 to 1945 reveal the difficulty the Movement was having during the war in sustaining the common people's interest in the co-operative revolution. The tireless A.B. MacDonald served as the League's managing director from its inception in 1934. In 1938, MacDonald addressed hundreds of credit union meetings, appeared before the House of Commons Committee on Banking and Commerce and challenged credit union offices in the Maritimes to "take the lead in promoting education in neighboring communities."[14] This man knew the scene. What he noticed disturbed him. Only a very small percentage of the provincial membership was taking an active part in the work of credit unions. A.B. thought that "members look upon their union as an organization for which they can secure money when they are hard-pressed; but they are not alive to the social significance of credit union work. They know very little about either the operating principles of the union or the principles by which it strives to promote social justice."[15]

It was also deplorable, MacDonald acknowledged, that the job of electing directors and committee members and of formulating policies was "left to a comparatively small group." He urged the League members to find the ways and means whereby a larger percentage of its members could take an "active, intelligent part in every phase of credit union work. How much we shall contribute to the justice and control of a more Christian society will depend upon the extent to which each individual credit unionist takes part." The credit unions also needed to spend more money and pay more attention to the "educational side of credit union work."[16] Many credit union study clubs had translated learning into the creation of people's banks. By 1938 some of the 131 credit unions in the province (14 in Halifax) were having difficulty gaining member interest in credit union ethos and practices. This problem continued into the war. At their 1941 meeting, St. Patrick's Parish Credit Union proposed this resolution:

> Whereas it is being felt in many quarters that credit unions and co-operative in general have not been living up to their earlier educational promise, and have been lacking both in machinery and zeal in the promotion of co-operative thought and the building of character, therefore be it resolved that the Credit Union League take such steps as it deems necessary to have this deficit remedied.[17]

A troubling rift was forming between a small, active minority of credit union leaders and a majority of passive members.

At the 1942 annual meeting, which Coady managed to attend, MacDonald noted that in the early days of credit union development, many part-time paid Extension workers spent a considerable amount of time aiding in their organization. "War demands are such that socially-minded, enthusiastic citizens haven't the time to devote to credit union work that they had in pre-war days." Only eight credit unions had been formed in the previous year (bringing the total to 208). However, Extension had been able to employ Lloyd Matheson in the late 1930s to work part time at reviving dormant unions. MacDonald also didn't think that the supervisory committees were working well. The way was left open for carelessness and inefficient work on the part of treasurers. He left his harshest words of criticism for an anti-democratic tendency in the credit union movement. As the League was now constituted, only the larger credit unions were strong enough financially to send delegates to the conventions. Over 50 percent of the smaller credit unions were unrepresented and without a voice in the control of the affairs of the League.

Since 1930, the Extension Department had helped to foster the co-operative movement as a "school of the countryside" for the masses. According to Alex Laidlaw,

> thousands can now conduct meetings, record minutes, keep accounts, discuss a balance sheet, and in other ways take an active part in business for the first time in their lives. One can imagine the amount of practical education, in terms of study, reading, meetings, and accounting, that has gone, for example, into the credit union movement in the Maritimes, through which the people have successfully handled loans amounting to thirteen million dollars.[18]

No doubt Laidlaw was right, but this was not the whole story. The pedagogical methods of Extension had done some fine work, but they had not produced miracles. In fact, the Movement seemed to have reached an impasse of sorts. MacDonald told the League delegates that many credit union members were still using

> banks, financial corporations, store credit and installment buying. Such sources are used by credit union members even if there are ample funds in their own organization to meet every requirement. It would seem, therefore, that credit unions should redouble their educational efforts for the purpose of informing and enlightening their members on how to make use of the moneys available through their own society (Nova Scotia Credit Union League, Annual Report, 1938).

The Extension Department did its own survey of puzzling behaviour on the part of credit union members in Antigonish County in the early 1940s. They discovered that people evidently needed credit but were not making use of their credit unions. They learned that some members didn't borrow from the credit union because they didn't want their neighbours to act as co-makers of the loan. They wanted their loan to be kept private. They feared being shamed. And the old Depression "dime and nickel" mentality of the early days still prevailed. Many thought that credit unions were okay when they only had nickels, dimes and quarters to deposit. Credit unions were the bank's "poor relative," to be utilized only in times of economic depression. The survey concluded that,

> on the whole, the people of Antigonish County seem to be unaware of the possibilities of credit unions. The development of credit unions organized in the County has been very slow. As a result, the credit unions are still too small to give a maximum service to their members. Since the service of a credit union is limited by the amount of its capital, the present, basic problem of credit union development in the County is to increase the savings of a credit union member.[19]

The eradication of outdated attitudes towards credit in Nova Scotia would demand more pedagogical time and attention than the St.FX Extension Department had to give. Bright spots, such as Cheticamp, persisted, but development was uneven, with an obvious decline in many of the rural communities. L.P. MacDonald, inspector of Credit Unions for Nova Scotia, reported that, as of September 1944, rural credit unions were not in as good a shape as those in the urban or industrial areas. Inverness credit unions, for instance, lacked leadership and those requiring loans were not using the credit union. The rural credit unions in Cape Breton and Victoria counties were declining both in membership and in loans and savings. In contrast, Sydney Mines had "new blood pumped in and is coming along in great strides."[20]

The war forced St.FX Extension to reorganize its mode of operation. The "era of specialization" had arrived, bringing in its wake both solutions and new problems. The co-operators created a special organization for credit union organization, the Nova Scotia Co-operative Educational Council, to attend to education pertaining to credit unions. The federal Department of Fisheries' grant was determining the educational activities among fishermen in the Maritimes; the NSCUL was created to "plan a unified program of adult education" in the local communities. The co-ordination of adult education activities and the supplying of teachers for various meetings had become rather complex. The Council director's report for 1943 acknowledged that war conditions had "greatly cut down" the amount of fieldwork that could be done. It was also "very difficult to organize study clubs in rural areas because of the large number of people who have left to enter the armed forces or to work in war industries." And steady employment in the towns, with three shifts operating, made study club organization "more difficult than ever." But the director, no doubt reflecting Movement leadership thinking, declared that they were not

> satisfied that the local co-operatives and co-operative members understand as yet the way they can and must function as living and vital units of the provincial organization. To ensure the proper functioning of the Council every last small co-operative in Nova Scotia must be a vital cell of the central body. One of the most urgent duties of our

workers is to convince the directors of the local societies that they are the local councils, and that the Provincial Council will never function as it should until each community has an active council. The university, with its small staff, and the Council, with only one paid employee so far, cannot go into each community.

The intellectual masterminds of the Council were now confronted by a new pedagogical challenge. They had to "mobilize this local leadership, as was done in the early days of Extension work." This was the "first and most pressing problem. The second task was to obtain the financial support of each co-operative society in the province."[21]

No doubt creating a co-operative council made philosophical and strategic sense in the midst of the global conflagration then occurring, but Coady and the Movement's leaders were spreading themselves very thin. Ironically, their visions of the co-operative blueprint were either not understood completely at the grassroots level or were simply not shared. The choice of creating federated and differentiated structures appears to have been the intellectual's choice and not necessarily that of the people. In fact, one detects a persistent tension in the Antigonish Movement between a local, static, community-oriented economic practice and the intellectual's dream of "bigger is better." One cannot help feeling that, without malice of intent, Coady was harnessing the beloved masses to his vision of the "good and abundant life."

IV

It had only been a decade since Moses Coady had first travelled around the fishing communities of the Maritimes to organize the United Maritime Fishermen. As director of Extension, Coady was responsible for overseeing an increasingly complex range of activities. He had good lieutenants and many effective community leaders to assist him. To be sure, a few priests continually tried to subvert Coady's work. Anti-co-operative priests attacked the Co-operative Commonwealth Federation (CCF) in the late 1930s. They used flimsy excuses to blast the co-operative movement, such as the failure to close the co-operative store (in Dalhousie, New Brunswick) on All Saints' Day, which had caused resentment from Protestants in the community. Coady feared that "some priests" took "advantage of those difficulties to mess things up."[22] They battled with their perceived co-operative enemies over the control of the St. Joseph's Hospital board in Glace Bay.

Father John Quinan of Halifax was one of Coady's most persistent clerical critics. He accused him of manipulating Protestant opinion against the Catholics on the fascism issue at a Rural and Industrial Conference in the late 1930s. Quinan also accused Coady of interfering with the selection of teachers at Terrance Bay. Angered, Coady told Quinan that he found it "strange that you should go over my head and take this matter to my ecclesiastical superiors when it could so easily have been settled out of court."[23] Quinan continued to needle away, however, and attacked Coady in an August sermon for transforming Christianity into economics. Coady was quick to rebut.

> In the August 11th issue of the Halifax Herald there is a report of a sermon you gave at the dedication of a church in the vicinity of Digy in which you are quoted as condemning some college professors for claiming that what is needed today is "to transform Christianity into economics". The foundation for your statement, I suppose, is the account of the interview between Dr. Kagawa and myself which was released by the Co-op League of the US some months ago. The writer of that document had no foundation for attributing any such statement to me. The simple truth is that I never said such a thing. The merest tyro in theology would never make such a mistake. What I was talking about, as I fancy anybody could easily divine, was that Christianity should be put into economic, social and political life.[24]

One didn't mess with Moses M. Coady and emerge unscathed.

Some priests participated in local co-op affairs half-heartedly or with limited understanding. However, many priests were behind Coady's brand of co-operative revolution, some (particularly the Acadian priests in the fishing communities) with almost revolutionary fervour. This social network, only dreamed of in the inaugural days of Extension, was in place by the outbreak of World War II. This network enabled Coady to travel around a lot to preach his big-picture gospel. He could also relax a little, knowing well that the Movement was not in his hands alone.

From the late 1920s onward Coady had taken special responsibility for developments in the Nova Scotia fishery. The fishermen, particularly along the Guysborough shore, were the most exploited and destitute of all primary producers. On March 13, 1939, Coady wrote Michaud that "these people of the Guysborough Shore have been so long subjugated to miserable conditions that an appeal from them is not so likely to demand attention."[25] Coady thought that the redemption of the fishery was key to Maritime economic and social development. If the fishery went under, or somehow returned to pre-1930 conditions, then his co-operative dream would become a nightmare.

During the war years, Coady poured considerable energy into maintaining the Fisheries grant. Fortunately, the Minister of Fisheries, the Hon. J.L. Michaud, was basically an Extension and UMF supporter. Despite this support (others in government circles were not so favourably disposed), the grant was still cut in half in 1940-41 and 1941-42 (to $19,500). The original grant of close to $37,000 was resumed in 1942-43 and 1944-45. These monies enabled Coady to keep fieldworkers, pay for twenty fishermen to attend yearly short courses and cover the attendant administrative costs. Directors with less stamina than Coady would have been driven crazy with this incessant juggling.

Coady expressed what he wanted to accomplish in the fishery during the war in a candid letter to Michaud on May 6, 1940. He had just been notified that all "educational workers" would receive no further remuneration. Stunned, Coady told Michaud that

> we are all convinced that a continuation of this program is more necessary than ever. We have started many things and have had encouraging success. To suspend operations now would be to expose the whole movement to the possibility of failure. It will take several years more of assiduous work to bring these fishermen to the point where they will be able to carry on under their own power and pay for their education.... Furthermore, the strenuous time in which we are living makes it important that the fishermen be whipped into line to work as hard as they can during these war years so that they may not be a burden to the country during the slump that in all probability will come in the post war years. These would seem to be the propitious years for the fishermen. They can come to their feet if they work hard and long enough and along the right lines.[26]

Coady thought that it was possible to "hold the fort" through these tough times, but as he confided to his friend Michael Gillis, he didn't really know what was "going to happen in connection with our work in the fisheries.... Everything is off for the time being."[27]

By the late 1930s the UMF had made some headway in establishing itself as the central marketing agency for Maritime fishermen. The early success of the small and relatively uncomplicated fishery co-ops had resulted from reduced price spreads rather than increased productivity. Member fishermen could play an important role in their simple operations, even though they were inefficient from an economic point of view. However, the UMF was still having problems with convincing all the local co-operators to actually market their catch through the central agency and in organizing efficient markets for the fishermen. The fishermen themselves were quite individualistic; some were even rascals, willing to steal and deal their fish for a price. Educating some of these boys was a tough job. The federal government, despite persistent cries from Canso, refused to erect bait freezers and a cold storage plant. They also refused to set a minimum price for fresh fish. The latter two issues, placed as resolutions at the 1938 annual meeting of the UMF, would be central planks in the UMF's presentation, "A Reconstruction Program for the Fishery," to the federal government in April 1944. By the mid-1940s, Coady sensed that the relatively high prices fishermen were getting for their products (the UMF did $1,441,075.63 worth of business in 1943-44, an increase of 70 percent over the previous year) obscured the structural weaknesses of the co-op fishery vis-à-vis the technologically sophisticated capitalist fishing industry.

The UMF had certainly received a substantial boost to its marketing initiatives when three key players were appointed to the Department of Agriculture. Waldo Walsh, a larger-than-life, hard-driving agriculturist, had been appointed director of marketing in the mid-1930s. Following him, the intellectually refined R.J. MacSween took the position of marketing representative (with special reference to fisheries) and Brian Meagher (a Canso militant activist) was added to the staff as assistant marketing representative for Cape Breton, Antigonish, Guysborough and Pictou counties. Digby, Yarmouth, and Shelburne were also to receive special attention. In late 1941, Coady wrote to his friend Col. A.L. Barry, supervisor of Fisheries for New Brunswick, that he had received "encouraging news about southern Nova Scotia and New Brunswick" from MacSween.[28] They were tying up the smelt markets. Barry thought this coup would "create a tremendous effect on the market."[29] On December 11, 1941, a jubilant Barry told Coady that "things are going 'blazing guns' with the smelt groups in south west Nova Scotia. Brian Meagher is staying right with the latter and [Alonzo] St. Pierre is organizing small lots into car shipments on the east coast of New Brunswick. It should turn out to be a big year for the UMF."[30]

This good news showed Coady that the "boys" could still do their "stuff." It also tempered the bad news Coady received in late winter of 1941 that the Fisheries grant had been cut in half. The Rev. J. Hill, one of Coady's stalwart New Brunswick "point men" from St. Thomas College, received the news resignedly. "With all emphasis being placed on war production and activities, the curtailment of support for efforts along other lines, no matter how important, is to be expected. However, we shall carry on the work here as best we can."[31]

Chiasson was not so phlegmatic. "I wish to point out," he apprised Coady in no uncertain terms, "that it is almost impossible to discontinue such work at the stage we are arrived at present." The feisty Chiasson went on to show that in Gloucester County alone they had nineteen fishermen's co-operative groups. Of these, fourteen had membership in a District Cooperative Federation known as the Gloucester Cooperative Fisheries. These different groups looked after the marketing of live and canned lobsters, smelts and other lines of fish. Chiasson noted that these groups needed a lot of "supervision and organization" to permit them to "get along in their production and marketing." Left to themselves at this stage, they would surely fail. They also had twenty-two credit unions in Gloucester County; these unions were "doing great work" for the fishermen, providing them with credit for fishing gear and supplies. As well, they had two co-operative stores. "This goes to show that the demands for help, etc. from these different groups are very pressing and I feel that they cannot be left to themselves, for fear that the work we have done would be in danger of being seriously weakened."[32] This importunate letter evidently impressed Coady and influenced his immediate petitioning of Michaud for continued support.

Coady had to endure a politically stormy December in 1941. Nova Scotia had held its provincial election in late October 1941. The Liberal

Minister of Mines and Labour, L.D. Currie, had been defeated in Cape Breton Centre, his long-held riding. Angry and incensed, Currie had sought a scapegoat. He found it in A.S. MacIntyre and St.FX Extension. Currie had seen MacIntyre standing outside the poll at Steele's Hill, Passchendale, Glace Bay, on October 28. Inquiring as to what MacIntyre was doing, one of Currie's section workers told Currie that MacIntyre was talking against him. Currie wrote to the Rev. H.P. MacPherson, the "Old Rector" of St. Francis, complaining bitterly that "a large number of those who were leaders in the St.FX Movement in Glace Bay voted against me and some voted and worked against me because they said to me that the principles of the St.FX Extension Movement and the policies of the CCF party were one and the same. I have undeniable evidence of that fact." Clarifying his position, Currie said that he wasn't accusing St.FX of colluding against him. However, he claimed that if others had his experience of sitting down "night after night in my office, in the homes and standing upon the street, with leaders and members of the Credit Unions in Glace Bay, they will find out that what I said is absolutely correct. I spent a great deal of time endeavoring to explain that the St.FX Extension Movement is diametrically opposed to the socialistic aspects of the CCF platform." While he regarded Dr. Coady as "one of the great Nova Scotians of this generation," Currie informed MacPherson that "it should be born in mind that the Credit Union Movement of itself is not a part of the fundamental basic principles of the Co-operative Movement, and there is confusion as to that."[33] Currie was the confused one. The Glace Bay miners perceived correctly that the CCF's principles were basically in harmony with Extension's purposes, and credit unions were an integral part of Coady's co-operative philosophy.

For the dour MacIntyre, who had been through hundreds of battles with unfriendly politicians and ruthless coal bosses, this dispute was small potatoes. MacIntyre told Coady that, prior to recent times, he and Currie had been good friends. Still, he figured that Currie had been holding a grudge against him ever since MacIntyre had worked to get Father M.A. MacAdam of St. Anne's Presbytery in Glace Bay, leader of the anti-socialists, off the board at St. Joseph's Hospital in the late 1930s. In fact, Father MacAdam had written St.FX's president, Dr. D.J. MacDonald, on November 27, 1941.

> You can quite readily understand how easy it is for the common people to associate College Co-operation and its activities with the CCF movement, and how readily the CCF will take advantage of this. As a result the CCF is profiting and the College is the loser, and when the College is the loser our religion must necessarily suffer.[34]

There was no love lost between MacAdam and the former United Mine Workers labour leader. MacIntyre disregarded Currie's claim that he had been working actively against him. He had been at the poll for only about fifteen minutes. He told Coady that he had not canvassed any families or interested "himself in the election in any way whatsoever."[35] Kay Thompson and Ida Gallant corroborated MacIntyre's contentions.

In the early 1940s the federal Liberals were becoming increasingly apprehensive about the gains the CCF party was evidently making in different parts of the country, particularly in British Columbia, Ontario and industrial Cape Breton. Currie got in touch with Michaud. He knew full well that Michaud held the purse strings and could bring political pressure to bear on Coady. On December 12, Coady informed Michaud that the charges against MacIntyre were "absolutely false." Then he reiterated Extension's policy of neutrality in politics.

> All our workers have been advised to this effect. They can vote as they please but they are not allowed to take part in any political activity. Not only this, but for the past ten years I have continuously in my speeches among the miners and steel workers of Cape Breton pointed out that our movement is educational and economic. Moreover I have stressed the fallacy of putting too much emphasis on political action. This, I have said, is too easy to be effective. No political party can do the job that is to be done in Canada unless the people themselves are lifted to new intelligence and new economic efficiency. Political action to the organized workers looks like a quick remedy but there is nothing quick about it.

Coady was being perfectly consistent with his "economics first" position, but he was unwilling to be pushed in the direction Currie and a "few clergymen" wanted; namely, his denouncing of the CCF. "Whatever I may think about the CCF and its program, this would be disastrous. It is a political party and if we openly attack it we are then in politics." His logic was impeccable. Coady pointed out to Michaud that, if they were playing politics, there should be evidence in other counties where they were even stronger than in Glace Bay.

> Malcolm Patterson, the Liberal member in a Cape Breton constituency went in on the majorities he got in the fishing communities where our program is very strong. The same is true in Richmond and Guysboro Counties where both Liberal candidates were weak men. Antigonish and Inverness Counties, where our movement is particularly strong, gave sweeping victories for the Liberals.

Coady then confided to Michaud that, with the "exception of once in my life, twenty years ago, I have always voted Liberal. Many other members of the St.FX staff are Liberals. This is a private matter and nobody here ever takes any open part in politics."[36]

In a candid letter to the Rev. John T. McGee, Coady articulated his views on the CCF.

> I should say that in my opinion there is nothing in the CCF program that would bar a Catholic from joining it. It is a social democratic party—a federation of many groups—socialists, labor groups, farm groups, and seamen, etc. That is why it is called a federation…. Its general tendency is toward the socialist side, but there is nothing in the manifesto up to the present that would be objectionable on moral or religious grounds. Personally, I am not too impressed with the idea that the solution of social and economic problems is going to come by the easy, political way. There is no ques-

tion that we need some socialization, but we do not need and should not have complete socialization. The inconsistency of the program of such a group such as the CCF is that in one breath they say that they are going to reform society by using the political instrument. They cannot use the political instrument if they have not got it. This is the lack of logic in the situation. My thesis is that we ought to first develop the people educationally and economically so that they can wield the political forces in society.

Coady then added that even Bishop Morrison, "answering a question posed to him by the priests of Cape Breton on the standing of the CCF, did not object to them. His answer, two or three years ago, was practically the GO sign to the Catholics of this part of the world."[37] (In the 1950s Coady would confess to his nephew Leo Coady, a CCF supporter, that he was thoroughly fed up with old-line parties and maybe it was time to support the CCF.)

In mid-December, Michaud lectured Coady in tones redolent of the infamous Canadian Liberal Party arrogance. "It seems that when my estimates come up in the House," he informed Coady icily, "there will be a debate on the whole question and I will be accused of favouring the aggrandisement of the CCF Party at public expense." Next, he told Coady that he had "similar complaints from British Columbia when, two or three years ago, we sent some [St.FX] propagandists in that direction. It was represented to me that they spent their time with the CCF organization and preached their gospel." Then Michaud warned Coady that he could not "but feel some misgivings for the success of your work if it becomes, in the public mind, associated with any political party and particularly the CCF. In my opinion, the CCF Party will never have any chance of success in Canada, except in some radical labour centres and among the radicals of the Prairie Provinces." (Three years later, Michaud would be proved wrong with the election of Tommy Douglas's CCF party in Saskatchewan in October 1944.) Coady must have flinched a little at the lecture. "It would be well to have it understood among your propagandists and field workers," Michaud instructed Coady, "that they are to free themselves from any political alliance and refrain from propounding their political views under the cover of your Movement. They should confine themselves to the preaching of economical doctrines and refrain from political action."[38]

Two days later, Coady reinforced his original argument with Michaud. Currie was continuing with his line that the rank-and-file miners were CCF members.

> I have already pointed out to you that there is nothing we can do about this. In fact, doing anything directly about it would bring us immediately into politics.... It has always been my belief that whether it be in education, economics, or politics, the right program should be progressive enough to meet the legitimate demands of all the people. In other words, it should be radical enough to be progressive, yet sufficiently conservative to be sound. I fail to see where anybody can successfully maintain that this is not the characteristic of our whole movement. It is economical-educational and we will not be sidetracked into politics.

Coady then reminded Michaud that the Nova Scotian Department of Agriculture was promoting a program "founded on the same philosophy as ours," and it was the "most popular Department in the province."[39]

A week later Michaud replied to Coady's letter of the 18th, underscoring his belief that "no encouragement should be given to those associated with your work to leave the public under any impression that they are sympathetic to the CCF party or to any political Party."[40] Coady adhered to the Rochdale principle of neutrality in politics. Explaining the co-op movement's relationship to organized politics to the Rev. R.H. Thatcher of Eganville, Ontario, Coady outlined his views.

> Our attitude, however, does not mean that we are not interested in politics or that political action is of no account. We feel, however, that there is danger in giving the people an idea that the solution of our social problems is political. It looks easy in the beginning. It is an escape mechanism for everyone. It is easy to brand the politician as the villain in the picture. To say that society cannot be regenerated by political action alone is not to deny the value of politicians and political action. This is especially true of democratic societies where the people are supposed to rule, where in fact we are supposed to have representative and responsible government. If the people are going to rule effectively politically, then they must be prepared and conditioned by education and economic and social action to make them competent to carry out their political functions.[41]

This is a clear statement of Coady's perspective on political action. Coady adamantly refused to be sidetracked from his "economic co-operation and education" project just because the CCF, or any other party, supported co-operation. Coady and the Extension Department may not have engaged in "party politics," but they attempted to influence state policy by creating deliberative spaces in civil society (conferences, forums and so on) where ordinary people could debate issues pertaining to their welfare. And, in the Catholic fashion of the day, they worked the backrooms, willing to use the Catholics in high office to help them get what they wanted.

In mid-January Coady received another missile from Michaud that revealed how closely politics was tied to the purse strings. Representations had been made to Michaud indicating that the control of the canning of lobster in Gloucester County was being passed over to a private company—the Gulf Fish and Trading Company—through the activities of the Rev. J.L. Chiasson. Michaud had also heard that the firm of Burnham and Morrill in Portland, Maine, was "getting quite a control on processed fish of all kinds in the districts where Cooperatives are in existence. These people know their business and try to establish themselves where they have a chance to make easy money. They get all the work done by the cooperators and derive the benefits." Michaud told Coady that he had written Chiasson a stiff letter. "Unless the members of the individual Cooperative Societies which have been organized through the efforts of your Movement are willing to fully cooperate and deal through their central Agency, the United

Maritime Fishermen Association, I do not feel very much enthusiastic about spending more money to better their situation."[42]

Michaud informed Chiasson that he was riled that a private company was being seen as the "recognized agent" for the sale of the co-operatives' fish. He could not

> look upon favourably to the hold which this company is taking on the Cooperatives organized at public expense. After all, if they must fall from Charybde to Scylla, it is useless to strive to educate the fishermen. It would have been just as well to leave them in the clutches of the existing companies which have exploited them heretofore.

Michaud could not understand why the "Fishermen's Cooperatives persist in their refusal to negotiate through the Central Agency of the United Maritime Fishermen." He could hardly believe his ears that the Gulf Fish and Trading Company had the monopoly on lobster packing in the Shippegan region. He thought that if the fishermen's co-operatives "had taken the trouble, they should have easily been able to establish a lobster canning factory just as well as the private company which did not do it in the interest of the fishermen." Then came the kick:

> It is hard for me to justify the expenditure of $50,000 per annum for the education of fishermen if the latter do not feel like following the counsels that are being given to them, and I am not altogether certain that next year it will be possible to continue the existing propaganda at public expense. I thought it wise to impart to you these few considerations in order that you might understand my worries and troubles.[43]

These were serious accusations. Answered inadequately, Michaud might have ceased to support Extension's work among the fishermen, or at least further curtailed finances (the grant had already been cut in half for 1941-42). However, the clear-minded and mentally tough Chiasson responded to Michaud on January 23: The co-operatives in Gloucester County were small with limited resources. They lacked modern equipment. Consequently, during the preceding year, they had had difficulty and sustained losses during the lobster season. Fearing loss, last spring they had decided to sell their lobster fresh to Gulf Fish and Trading Company Ltd of Newcastle, New Brunswick. Gulf Fish had an active staff and large trucks able to transport the fish to the American markets. The main problem for them, Chiasson admitted, lay with the Central Office of the UMF. In the past it had lacked initiative in organizing the central marketing of the fish of New Brunswick. The co-operatives had been forced to sell locally with all the risks that entailed. Only this year had the UMF opened up an office in the north of New Brunswick on the Miramichi River with Alonzo St. Pierre in charge. Already, smelts from the co-ops on the Miramichi, Neguac, Portage River and those around Shippegan had been sold by the Central. Now that precedent had been set, Chiasson maintained that the "commercial activities of the co-operatives cannot help but increase." He foresaw the sale of other lines of fish, such as cod, through the Central. In the past, it appears, the local co-ops had been stymied because the Central lacked connections with markets for cod and oysters. Chiasson thought the prospects for the future were promising now that the office in northern New Brunswick had been established. He emphasized that "it requires considerable time, as you know, to free the fishermen from the old individualism and ancient prejudices, and it is, at times, quite discouraging for those who have at heart the economic rehabilitation of the people, to see that the fruits of the educational campaign are slow to appear." Finally, he thought it would be most unfortunate "to discontinue the mouvement [sic] at the point we are at present. Without undue optimism, I believe that with the organization that we have at present, the organized groups of fishermen will show very encouraging results from now on."[44]

For his part, Dr. Coady interviewed Chiasson at Moncton on January 24. Coady essentially agreed with Michaud's stricture regarding the co-ops use of private marketers.

> Father Chiasson agrees with me that the day should be speeded when the fishermen would be able to deal entirely through their own central organization. He claims things are shaping up in that direction about as fast as could be expected.... As far as I can find out, there is no disposition on Father Chiasson's part to favor the above-named interests (Gulf Trading and Burnham and Morrell). I heartily concur with your views in connection with the development of the UMF and I promise you that I shall see to it that all our workers carry out your wishes in this regard.

In concluding, Coady thought that "things look pretty promising and if you can keep the pressure on for a few years we will have the fishermen in a position to carry on when this terrible war nightmare we are going through passes away."[45] While in Bathurst, New Brunswick, for the funeral of the late Bishop, Michaud met Chiasson and they had a long conversation: "He reassured me on the progress of the work of the fishermen of the North Shore, and I feel satisfied that before long the fishermen will come into their own. Note is being made of the successful courses at Wellington, P.E.I., and at Canso."[46]

At the annual meeting of the UMF in 1943, a Reconstruction Committee had been appointed to formulate a "reconstructionist" program for the fishery. Its members were Moses Coady, Antigonish; the Rev. J.L. Chiasson, Shippegan; the Rev. Charles Forest, Larry's River; Alonzo St. Pierre, Chatham; Leo Roberts, Ballantyne's Cove; Louis Pothier, Wedgeport; and J.H. MacKichan, Halifax. Coady was appointed chair. Coady, Alonzo St. Pierre, president of the UMF, and J.H. MacKichan, general manager of the UMF, presented the brief to the Minister of Fisheries and his deputies at Ottawa on April 17 and 18. By the mid-1940s the UMF had evolved beyond a mere "educational and protective" organization to one whose role included representing the in-shore fishermen on matters related to "fishery policy and legislation." The research committee consulted every local unit of the association. The resulting brief, "A Reconstruction Program for the Maritime Fisheries," was crisply conceived and tautly written. It reflected both the continuing struggle in the fishing communities and their leaders' efforts to influence fishing policy in Ottawa.

The brief vigorously defended the in-shore fishery. Marshalling statistics, the UMF declared that it was perfectly obvious that, from the "standpoint of the number of people involved, and of volume and diversity of population the in-shore fishery is of surpassing importance to those Provinces, and that upon the success of this branch of the industry depends in overwhelming measure the welfare of the fishermen." Every clause in the document (there were ten) then followed logically from this central axiom: the well-being of the in-shore fishermen and their communities had to be guaranteed in a rapidly changing and perversely competitive world.

The "success and welfare" of the fishermen, for the UMF activists, depended upon several enabling conditions. The UMF wanted to maintain fish prices on parity with other commodities. The persistent problem of great discrepancy between the price the fishermen received and general commodity levels had dogged the path of the in-shore fishermen for decades. Above anything else, Coady and the UMF leadership feared that, unless prices were stabilized, the fishermen could be thrown back into the "hopeless conditions which prevailed in the pre-war years." They wanted a floor under fish prices, and thought, reasonably enough, that Prime Minister King's initiative in that direction for farm commodities boded well for their proposal.

They were wrong. The Department of Fisheries was decidedly unsympathetic. The new Minister of Fisheries, the Hon. Ernest Bertrand, informed the UMF that this idea was not feasible. The Department seemed to think it was impossible to achieve uniformity of grading. Harold Connolly, one of two representatives from Nova Scotia present at the Ottawa hearing, thought the idea was "very dangerous, all shot through with error." Surprised and disappointed with the "very evident attitude of the Department," MacKichan retorted that the "fishermen will positively refuse to submit to a repetition of the starvation prices handed to them in the '30s and it surely was not beyond the capacity of the Department's personnel to work out a basis of floor prices."

Another persistent issue for the impoverished and poorly equipped in-shore fishermen of Nova Scotia and New Brunswick was that of ensuring a uniformly high quality product. The peculiar local conditions of the Maritimes, with its coastline of some 2,000 miles and a limited number of freezing and cold storage facilities, handicapped the fishermen in "their production operations because of lack of fresh bait and baiting facilities." This problem underlined the vulnerability of the co-operative movement in the mid-1940s. The UMF, and the co-operative movement in general, lacked the capital resources to build their own modern freezing and cold storage plants. Opposed to private control of cold storage plants, the UMF insisted that it was the "function of the state to provide these facilities for the people and to operate them under a board or commission as a state-owned public utility." In the past, the UMF argued, cold storage plants controlled by private enterprise had proved unsatisfactory. "Accordingly we urge that the government formulate a freezer and cold storage policy for the fishery under which a chain of freezers will be established and operated as a public utility."

This clause provoked a lengthy discussion, but the federal Department of Fisheries seemed prepared to go a long way in support of the UMF's proposal. For his part, Coady used the discussion of "freezers for the people" to outline his dream of the model fishing community. Country Harbour, he imagined, could be the site of a model fish industry where a scientifically planned community with modern schools, electric power and paved highways leading to the railway could be built. With one of the finest harbours in the world in close proximity to the best fishing grounds, the success of the venture would be assured. It would also serve as an inspiration and example to other fishing communities.[47] Upon questioning, Coady claimed that he was, in fact, in favour of "large type plants owned by the groups."

Nothing agitated the fishermen's soul more than the trawler. The UMF was "unalterably opposed to the general operation of otter trawlers or draggers." Trawlers and draggers were designed for ground fish (cod, haddock, rose fish and flounders). However, with 87 percent of the fishermen "engaged in a diversified form of fishing which includes in addition to cod and haddock the production of lobsters, mackerel, herring and a score of other varieties not producible by trawlers this instrument is utterly impractical." The UMF did not question its efficiency, but the widespread use of the trawler would cause in-shore fishermen to lose that portion of their income not derived from cod or haddock. "Clearly the use of trawlers is inimical to the interests of the in-shore fishermen, and on behalf of its members this association must continue its opposition to them."

A wide-ranging discussion followed. Mr. Connolly thought that the UMF had used language that left room for the development and protection of the in-shore fishermen. MacKichan reaffirmed that the matter of the trawler had to be studied and solved from the "humanitarian viewpoint of the fishermen." St. Pierre raised Department hackles when he argued that trawlers destroyed fishing grounds. Dr. Stewart Bates, author of the influential *The Canadian Atlantic Fishery* (1944), who would be appointed Deputy Minister of Fisheries after the war, thought Alonzo St. Pierre was off-base; Dr. D.L. Cooper from Halifax agreed generally with Bates, but claimed that "in some cases the use of trawlers will deplete certain types of fish, but not cod." All participants in this policy deliberation did agree, however, that there was a decided trend towards the production of fresh fish. That was a given. Therefore, it seemed necessary to lengthen the fishing season at places such as Louisburg, Canso and Country Harbour. And lengthening the fishing season required that the fishermen use "long liners" and modernize their equipment.

Coady's bottom-line on these weighty issues seemed to be that the fishermen were not opposed to a "gradual change-over to more modern methods of production as long as markets are not disturbed." He hammered this point home by arguing that "big business" was not introducing new technological changes because, if they did so, their profits would become obsolete. Coady also thought that "certain co-operative areas could own and control draggers as well as small craft." It is not clear if this view on co-operatives and draggers was shared by either St. Pierre or MacKichan. Perhaps Coady was arguing that the threat of the technology could be overcome if it were controlled by co-operative organizations. The notes of the conference provide little detail. But, clearly, by the mid-1940s, Coady believed that the defence of the in-shore, rural, fishermen's way of life required the embracing of scientific production as well as scientific approaches to marketing, credit, education and consumer goods. Coady may well have seen the handwriting on the co-operator's wall. The federal government, and its academic supporters, were giving more freedom to trawlers; long-liners were being developed; processing and packaging of fish was shifting from the traditional salting to filleting and freezing. If the co-operative movement in the fishery did not keep up with these developments, Coady's "emancipatory project" would be thwarted.

On April 27, 1944, Coady reported on the Ottawa meeting to Chiasson. Coady thought that the "Ottawa affair" had been

> very quiet…. They seemed adverse to putting on a floor price to the fisheries but I think we changed them somewhat. They were not anxious about creating cold storages as public utilities, while not giving up our advocacy of these things as public utilities, we were agreed that in some places they might be privately owned either by co-operative groups or companies. Nothing, however, was decided.

Coady informed Chiasson that he sensed that Ottawa wanted to equip the fisheries with "better boats, either long liners, or larger boats for in-shore work." He thought they should "study the situation."[48]

In the fall of 1941 Moses Coady had assessed the UMF's situation and declared to Sister Mary Hugh that "on the whole we are getting along marvelously." Success stories had been pouring in from the Magdalens, Cheticamp, southern Nova Scotia and Dover. Experiments in cultivating land on the Dover coast had been underway. Coady had thought that the combination would "mark a new era in the life of this eastern country."[49] However, the rather chilly reception from Ottawa these years later in April

1944 was a little menacing, signalling, perhaps, a waning of the Department of Fisheries' support for the preservation of the in-shore fishery as a way of life. Nothing in Coady's nature and outlook would allow him to imagine that the fight was over until the last co-operator was left standing on the economic and political battlefield. Coady was "fighting Irish," descended from battlers like Mogue Doyle. Barriers existed to be transcended. Coady handled adversity by seeing possibilities where others didn't and by calling for more dedication and sacrifice from the common people and their leaders. The danger in this almost superhuman dedication to re-make the world was that, in the end, the world might break your heart.

In the mid-1940s the fight for a co-operative fishery was still very much alive. Coady had a dynamic contingent of six full-time and twenty-eight part-time fieldworkers (including two women, Tat Sears in Nova Scotia and Theresa Hache in New Brunswick) running short courses, organizing study clubs, forums, broadcasts, conferences and regional and general meetings. All told, they held 1,023 meetings (with 42,778 in attendance), and 1,090 smaller meetings for members and directors of the co-ops in 1943-44. Coady was convinced that the Movement among the fishermen "has been and is making great progress. We are fast coming to the point where every fishing community in eastern Canada will have a credit union." He was excited by the fact that one credit union (as of October 1943) had $125,000 in funds. Coady thought that, "on the whole, the idea is growing that they are on the road to the improvement of their economic and social conditions. The outstanding success made by some of the better organizations of the fishermen is gradually arousing the interest of those who were not at first interested in this educational program." Communities such as Cheticamp were having their best returns ever. Good feeling among the fishermen was evident. "It will probably take another five years," Coady thought, "to get them to the point where they will be unmistakably able to carry on without any fear of failure."[50]

In the spring of 1945 Coady surveyed the accomplishments of the co-operative movement in the fishing communities. The UMF had managed to start ten new locals in 1944-45. They were doing $1,243,928.34 worth of business, 50 percent of which was in lobsters. Fifty-three UMF locals were operating nine lobster factories, canning fish in three centres, and handling pickled, dried and boneless fish in eleven centres, mackerel in five and fresh fish in three. Fishing centres now had fifteen co-op stores, with a membership of 1,804, and were doing a total business of $477,734.00. Fifty-two credit unions had been established in the fishing districts with a total membership of 5,165 (the three largest were in W. Pubnico, Cheticamp and St. Bernard). Coady was particularly happy with the one- to two-day short courses that Extension had organized in eleven

centres, with an attendance of 532. To help train the bookkeepers to run
the growing business of fishery co-operatives in the Maritimes, St.FX ran a
short business course of four weeks duration in February 1945. Twenty-five
students learned how to keep books (taught by the chief auditor of Maritime Co-operative Services) and listened to special lectures on math,
English, co-operative philosophy, banking, economics and public speaking. Emphasizing the positive, Coady noted in his report for 1945 that the
Island Fishermen's Co-op, located on Shippegan Island, was "one of the
largest and best equipped co-operatives in the Maritime provinces." In
only four years of operation they had built a quick-freezing plant, a cannery
for the purpose of canning different kinds of fish, as well as two other plants
for processing herring and cod. They were doing around $200,000 worth
of business.[51] However, the Island Fishermen's Co-op was having serious
problems with the UMF central office. The UMF owed them $30,000.
Chiasson confided to Coady that this made it "extremely difficult for them
to operate, as they have not the money to pay neither for the fish nor for
wages."[52]

Moses Coady, more beleaguered than he would admit publicly, drew
the following "unmistakable conclusions" about the future of the Maritime
fishery. He believed that they had discovered "undreamed of ability among
fisherfolk." This had been one of the "greatest revelations of our extension
program." Coady was also more convinced than ever that the welfare of
the fishermen (and all other producers) would not be "secured by activity
in one field alone." The fishermen had to learn how to "manipulate many
vital forces if they are to enjoy the good and abundant life." They had to
develop the "triple structure": Local groups needed to manage a financial
structure to carry on their community activities. They would then be part of
a regional wholesale built on a sound financial basis. With the second tier in
place, they would then market their fish through the UMF, itself built on a
solid Maritime basis. Coady thought that some communities had "already
gone far in the establishing of this triple structure. All the communities are
gradually getting into it but it will take years to perfect it."

The more troubles the co-op movement faced, the more Coady went
back to his architect's table. All the trials and tribulations and upheavals of
war-time drove him to search for the right formula for changing circumstances. His thinking crystallized around the core idea of total, or
integrated, co-operative development—a formidable message from a
co-operative movement now threatening enough to induce serious opposition from the "vested interests."

Coady, however, knew that there was still much work to be done among
the many thousands of fishermen who had yet to be "organized for enlightenment." He fervently hoped that they would see the "fishing industry as
their calling" and acquire the "scientific knowledge" appropriate to their

vocation. Coady knew of no other way of solving the fishery crisis except through "group study and cooperative activities." The only force Coady could apply to challenge the momentum the vested interests were gathering in the fishery was the "force of ideas."[53] Coady was concerned that the fishery crisis in Atlantic Canada be resolved in a "way that the benefits derived from it will be reflected in the lives of as many people as possible. This means that the dominant note in the development of the fisheries of the Maritime Provinces should be the human values as against the financial aspects of the industry."

Coady persisted in confronting the power of big business with human values. He also thought that the fishermen could use the "war prosperity to consolidate their position and initiate themselves into a new way of carrying on the business of their lives." This steeling up would put them in a position to "weather the hard days that may lie ahead." Coady deeply feared that the post-war world would plunge the fishery back into another depression. Addressing critics' judgements that the "educational revolution" among the fishermen was too dilatory, Coady countered by insisting that

> continued effort in education and organization will infallibly produce the desired results in a reasonable time. In fact, we believe that the work that is going on among our fishermen is one of the bright spots in our Maritime economy. These rejuvenated fishing communities will be able to take care of their present population; and when peacetime conditions return they will absorb many of our returned men and others who want to go into the fishing industry. There is no better presage of future development than the sound local community; but the local community cannot be built except through the people who make their livelihood in it.[54]

Coady's commitment was clear enough. However, he was receiving signals from Ottawa that something was "brewing that does not augur well for the future." Ottawa was looking for a new Minister of Fisheries, and Coady had heard rumours that Morrow, manager of Lunenburg Sea Food Products, was being talked about as a possible successor to Michaud.

IV

The war forced Extension to consider what educational programs were appropriate and possible in such straitened circumstances. The Nova Scotia Co-operative Education Council's goal was to link all co-operators and continually educate its members. This was, however, becoming an intricate task. The Maritime co-operative movement was not unified; it had a multiplicity of organizations criss-crossed by a variety of sometimes conflicting perspectives and interests. Nonetheless, the Council pressed on in the early 1940s with the usual hectic fieldwork in order to sustain the Movement.

The essential pedagogical strategy of the Council's intellectuals was to shift from mass mobilization to educating a leadership cadre. The Council also began to extend their pedagogical forms to include radio and film. Coady was particularly pleased with the "Labour School of the Air" on station CJFX in Antigonish, directed by the Rev. Joe A. MacDonald, professor of economics at St.FX. Launched in 1942-43, the Labour School targeted co-operative movement activists in the coal towns and in Sydney. Council fieldworkers managed to organize 108 listening groups around the broadcast themes. Here, St.FX was simply following the great initiatives of the Canadian Association for Adult Education in using radio to mobilize Canadians to consider the emergent post-war world in its Farm Radio and Citizens' Forums.

The Council transformed the role of the study club as the Movement became more complex and diversified. Now the study club began to be used as an instrument for the purpose of studying specific topics. For example, in 1940 the Council had several groups studying co-op insurance. In 1941 study clubs focused on the study of co-op medicine. Other clubs (at Reserve Mines, New Waterford, and Florence) studied the possibilities of co-op burial services.

The Council supported the struggle for a regional library system with enthusiastic support from the community. They also organized conferences for managers, bringing them together from all parts of the province to study their merchandising and marketing problems. The Antigonish Movement was having considerable trouble integrating women fully into its program. Photographs of the era are disconcerting to contemporary viewers. Men in suits dominated all facets of co-op leadership, with the exception of a woman sprinkled here or there who had managed to get into a leadership position. In 1943, the Council tried to infuse energy into the women's program. Sister Marie Michael from St.FX spent two months in the industrial area of Cape Breton organizing study clubs on consumer education, co-op principles and credit unions, handicrafts, nutrition and gardening, as well as several general conferences for women in Sydney.

The Council was busy, but war conditions had greatly reduced the amount of fieldwork that could be done and the number of study clubs that could be organized. For his part, Moses Coady was participating, when he could, in the short courses, keeping up a steady stream of correspondence with friend and foe alike, building morale through the rousing, optimistic speeches on his usual co-op circuit, fighting the big battles out beyond the local communities and writing about co-operation within the context of global war. Coady did not appear to be as worried about the decline of the study club movement as did A.B. MacDonald. At his retirement banquet on August 24, 1944, MacDonald had warned those gathered that "only through study clubs could people become aware of things to do and receive the motivation, since the people could not be expected to strive after the things they did not know about."[55] Despite MacDonald's admonition, the momentum of the early to late 1930s was never regained.

World War II tested the limited of Coady's abiding faith in the world as a "field of opportunities." His Christian imagination had to filter through the carnage on the European battlefields. Coady believed that those left at home had to mobilize themselves for "clear thinking and purposeful action."[56] People had to stay at home and fight their way to the good life. There was no "time for frivolity and sensual pleasures."[57] The war provided an opportunity to re-examine economic and social structures. Coady imagined that the "present struggle" might be a prelude to a "new order of peace." The Augustinian "City of God" could rise out of the rubble and death of warfare. God moves in fathomless ways, and Coady thought that the strife of global warfare was throwing people together and breaking down cultural barriers. Perhaps the "foundation for the solidarity of the human race" was "being established without our knowing it."

Coady also thought that the world's democracies were growing "soft and decadent." In an important speech, "Youth and the New World," delivered on May 21, 1944, Coady fretted that the youth in the democracies needed "some explosive and dynamic idea to take the place of the motivation of war. This is the great problem confronting us."[58] Four years earlier, Coady had discussed this matter with Dr. Claude Brown, president of the Catholic Army Huts in London, Ontario.

> This war is a battle between democracy and dictatorship. We all know that democracy needs some shot in the arm to make it work better. We trust that it will not go down this time, but unless we can do something about our own inefficiency, it will not long endure in the world. What is really needed is some technique whereby we can continuously enlighten free people, during the period of active life so that they can do effectively all the things that society requires of them without being driven to it by any kind of dictatorship. In other words, we believe that the force of ideas which comes through education will make us efficient enough to meet the challenge of dictatorship.[59]

Coady longed for a radical learning society; he sought to achieve it only through developing the masses' "social intelligence" so that they could apply the blueprint worked out by the expert social architects.[60] Indeed, sometimes Coady became a little excessive in preaching on his theme of "high destiny" for the Maritimes. In one speech, Coady stated that the "so-called common people, by virtue of their numbers, have a messianic role to play in this drama of progress. They will kill us with their ignorance or save us by their enlightenment."[61]

During the war, Moses Coady began a lifelong correspondence with his brother Joe's son, Leo Coady. Leo had turned eighteen in 1941, and Coady tried to nurture in Leo those qualities he believed were required for a revitalized democracy. Leo was chosen as Moses Coady's protégé for the Margaree Valley. He had great expectations for Leo and the other

Margaree youth and lavished advice on them year after year. "My advice to all of you boys," he counselled Leo, "is that you be good and sensible. I do not mean old-fashioned or dour, but full of enthusiasm that comes from a vision of great things to be done. The world can be tremendously interesting to a man who has the vision and moral fibre to discipline himself in preparation for a great career." Coady advised Leo that a great career awaited a "man born on a farm who will, after receiving a thorough education, come back to the farm and then after he has succeeded or while he is succeeding, will take a hand in the public affairs of the country."[62] Several years later, in August 1945, Coady was not pleased with how Leo and the boys were doing.

> I am hoping that you are beginning to think and plan. A man who does not plan is just dumb. If you read and study and think you can work a great career for yourself. Nobody can do it for you. All the successful men in the world are men who had ideas and the moral fiber to carry them out. I hope you will get going. The next twenty-five years are our good years—the good years of any man. If you miss them you miss life.

Coady informed Leo that he was sending them a book on Builder's Estimates that contained everything worth knowing about building, from turning ground to electricity. Coady told them to get studying it.

> If you fellows cannot make a spectacular go of things you are not worthy descendants of the pioneers who grubbed the alders, cleared the fields, and made the country habitable. The man who is always on the fence, undecided as to what he is going to do, is not worth the powder that will blow him to the other place. Indecision never releases any energy. No man can dedicate himself to any worthwhile job and succeed unless he gets off the fence and decides once and for all on a program that he is going to make a success of.[63]

Coady was applying the lash to Leo and it must have stung. This letter reveals a rather unpleasant side of Coady's character; the tone is a little bullying and moralistic. Still, Coady was treating Leo in a manner similar to how he treated his beloved masses who could kill or save depending on their degree of enlightenment. The City of God could not manifest itself out of the ashes and carrion of World War II without immense dedication and sacrifice from God's ordinary people.

Several new themes appeared in Coady's thinking during World War II. In the early 1940s, the international co-operative movement leadership believed that within co-operativism lay the germ of future peace. At the dedication of the Eastern Co-operative Wholesale in Brooklyn, New York, in the spring of 1943, J. Peter Warbasse, the renowned author of *Cooperative Democracy* and many other works, invited the assembled to "pledge our hearts, our brains, our energies, to the building of a world in which men may live as brothers, in peace, amid plenty." Present along with co-operators from China, Poland and many other countries, Coady hoped that the "stress of the times" would incline millions to a "message that squares with eternal truths, to goals that can be reached without climbing over the dead bodies of others."[64]

Coady's two new themes arose directly out of this utopian ardour. First, an integrated co-operative movement, buttressed by the creation of people-owned manufacturing plants, could be organized in zones. He argued that the "movement had started with the poverty-stricken Maritime provinces as a zone. To complete the job it would be necessary to take the rest of Canada in zones—Quebec, Ontario, the prairie provinces, the Pacific Coast areas, each with its different problems."[65] Once Canada had a "national people's consumer co-operative movement," Coady outlined, Canada could "then federate with co-operators in the US and other parts of the world and lay the foundation for universal mutual self-help and fellowship."[66] His second theme flowed from the first. In early 1942, Coady wrote several important letters in which he indicated his concern for South America. He told Robert Lester of the Carnegie Corporation that

> for years I have been thinking what an opportunity we have to help out the South Americans. They have a lot of submerged groups of people and much illiteracy. It would seem to me that our adult education technique would be just the thing for everything south of the Rio Grande. These people are officially Catholic and that might make it easier for us to talk to them. It seems to me that the US and Canada should be definitely interested in bringing these people along the road of education and democracy. In another five years our adult education program will be so well established here in eastern Canada that there will be no question any longer of its permanency.[67]

Coady was simply irrepressible. The next day, he wrote Dr. Alex Johnston in Ottawa that it was "too bad we are not a little younger to enjoy the golden age that may be dawning."[68]

Moses Michael Coady reflected much, in numerous letters and speeches, on the meaning of World War II for the future of democracy and the co-operative movement. However, Coady offered no reflections on either the controversial anti-Semitic actions of his Pope, Pius XII (the former Eugenio Pacelli), or the fate of the Jews in the Holocaust. By the spring of 1943, the Nazi death camps were working overtime. From all over Europe, Jews by the hundreds of thousands were being shipped in crowded cattle cars to Auschwitz, Sobidor, Treblinka and other German murder chambers. In the Warsaw ghetto alone, well over a million Polish Jews had been murdered. Although the pogrom against the Jewish people had begun on the infamous Kristallnacht, it was not until the end of 1942 that the nature of the Nazi's "final solution" had been disclosed to the Allied governments. From 1938 until 1943, Jewish organizations and the Canadian National Committee on Refugees and Victims of Political Persecution had worked tirelessly to promote a pro-refugee movement that would force changes in what appeared to many Canadians as an openly anti-Semitic government policy. One of Coady's fellow adult educators, Watson

Thomson, had spoken on April 25, 1943, on the CBC's "Our Special Speaker" program on the "Jews in Europe." Thomson feared that the vision of a "forward-moving world with a place for all, regardless of race, or creed, or of a world where there is neither Jew nor Greek, bond nor free, but only the deepening harmony of a great human brotherhood"[69] had been cast aside.

John Cornwell's recent book *Hitler's Pope: The Secret History of Pius XII*[70] chillingly documents how Pacelli, who became Pope in 1939, failed to challenge Hitler directly and was guilty of anti-Semitic attitudes and practices. Pacelli accepted the stereotypical identification of Jew with Bolshevik. He undermined Catholic resistance to Hitler in the early 1930s with his ill-fated manoeuvrings to save the Church by getting Hitler to agree to spare Catholic churches and schools in exchange for disbanding the Catholic Center Party. He lived in an ethereal spiritual realm far above the fishing villages of Nova Scotia, and, it seems, the Jewish ghettos of Warsaw.

Why was Coady silent throughout the war years on the fate of European Jews and Canadian immigration policy? The only published fragment in reference to Jews is found in his notes for his "Unwritten Book." Addressing the matter of resistance to the transition to a new co-operative order, Coady comments: "Thus, Christ was punished, persecuted and killed by the Jews in the name of their traditions. In other words, the tradition is the law, the man-made structure of society was cited against the enduring, absolute and eternal moral law which our Lord had tried to promulgate in the world." Coady's identification of Jews as Christ-killers, a deeply rooted tradition within Roman Catholicism, may have had something to do with his silence. As well, Coady hated communism and was inclined to reduce all human problems and evil to the people's lack of ownership of production and distribution. However, economic explanations fail to account for either the murder of Jews or the identification of millions of people with totalitarian regimes.

Coady needed to be a man of resolute hopefulness, committed to a God who was prodding the world towards the new time, because the enemies of co-operation were gaining strength towards the war's end. At the beginning of 1944, the co-operative movement in Nova Scotia and elsewhere was abuzz with nervous energy. At regional co-operative conferences and celebrations, the co-op leadership positioned itself for the upcoming tax battle. MacDonald went to the Co-operative Union of Canada to orchestrate the movement against taxing the co-operatives. Alex Laidlaw, a Port Hood native and veteran educator, took over from MacDonald as Coady's assistant. The leaders displaced the old Co-operative Educational Council with the new Co-operative Union, and put A.S. MacIntyre at the helm. Coady's speeches in late 1944 conveyed alarm at the "ever greater concentration of industry and big business through the organization of cartels."

Co-operative employees were assuredly in the "front line of the New Order in Canada." It was up to them to "help establish the new order."[71]

In the meantime, it was up to the co-op leadership to ensure that "private industry" did not win the tax debate by organizing the presentation of briefs for the Canada Royal Commission on the Taxation of Co-operatives (later named the MacDougall Commission). *The Financial Post* of October 28, 1944, published a cartoon showing "Policeman" Dominion Government helping himself freely to fruit at the stand of private industry while the neighbourhood co-op store was not touched. The caption read, "Why does he always pick on my store?"[72] This slice of propaganda nicely captured business sentiments and infuriated the co-operators.

Maritime co-operators opened their newspaper, *The Maritime Co-operator*, on March 15, 1945, to a full-page spread under the banner headline, "Maritime Co-ops present eleven briefs." Journalist George Boyle covered the hearings in Moncton (March 1) and in Halifax (March 5) and described what he saw. At the centre of the stage was seated the chair, the Hon. Errol MacDougall, dignified, good humoured, with a glint of sternness; on his left, G.A. Elliot, slender, eager of face, a brilliant economist, and J.J. Vaughn, a typical elderly executive; on his right, B.N. Arnason, strong-faced and rangy, whose voice of fine timbre would be frequently heard asking evocative questions, and J.M. Nadeau, black-haired and large of frame. The Maritime co-operative movement had brought in all of its big guns for the occasion. They were questioned by E.T. Parker, chief counsel for the Commission, whose kindly face concealed an "inquisitive disposition." W.B. Francis was counsel for the co-ops.

The Halifax session opened in the Court House, and R.J. MacSween was first to be called to the stand and questioned on bookkeeping practices. MacIntyre then summarized the growth and aims of the Movement in his brief for the Nova Scotia Co-op Union. Howard MacKichan, manager of the UMF, appeared for the fishery co-ops, and J.D. Nelson MacDonald presented the brief for the Nova Scotia Credit Union League. The president of the British Canadian Co-operative, Neily MacDonald, a miner for fifty years, and Joe Laben, a coal-miner from Reserve Mines, testified as to how the co-op movement had eased some of the anguish of theirs and their fellow workers' lives. Both Charles Forest of Larry's River and Reid Sangster, Extension fieldworker, told of the value of co-ops in typical fishing communities.

Anti-co-op interests were also present, stirring up trouble and confusion as usual. Donald McInnis, King's Council, presented a brief for the Halifax Board of Trade. McInnis argued that some co-op organizations were merely masquerading as co-ops. The Annapolis Valley Fruit Co-op, he insisted, was "now developing under the present set-up into big business with the hopes of its directors for dictatorial control over both members and those who prefer to operate independently, utilizing their favorable tax position to attain this end." Representing the Apple Society, George Nowlan, King's Council, snorted that this brief was built on "thin air." The independent dairies also presented a brief. They contended that they, like others in Canada, might be forced out of business by their untaxed competitors.

Moses Coady presented the St.FX Extension Department's brief, "The Social Significance of the Co-operative Movement," in the concluding session in Halifax. This thirty-page text (later published as a pamphlet), his first major writing effort following *Masters of Their Own Destiny*, bore witness to the "social and human values at stake in this investigation." Coady was not preoccupied with the technical matters associated with taxation. For him, "something of much greater and deeper significance is being decided. In truth, this is a stage in the struggle between the profit-motive system and the cooperative way of life." Coady thought that the Commission would have to decide if the "cooperative method of business is to receive full recognition before the law and if it is to be permitted to operate untrammeled in carrying out the program which it has designed for the uplifting of the great masses of the people."

This document is full of emotion and passion. Its intellectual interest lies primarily in the themes Coady underscored at a moment of crisis for the Canadian co-operative movement. First, Coady argued that St.FX, endeavouring to "bring new life to all the people in whatever callings they were found," had discovered that "abject poverty" prevented the realization of the good and abundant life. Second, Coady stressed that co-operation could only be an "effective instrument of social and economic betterment" if the "various phases of the movement [were] built together on an integrated pattern." Third, Coady extended the liberal notion of the "right of free association" to the right of ordinary people to "form mutual self-help associations in the economic field." This was (and is) a powerful argument: "True democracy no longer exists," Coady asserted, when the state or economy blocked the self-organization of the people. Denying the common people the right to form a business enterprise through "co-operative techniques" denied the first principles of liberal democracy. To those who argued that co-operation put some out of business, Coady replied that, "even if it does put some Canadians out of business, [it] puts other Canadians in their place. This is in harmony with our fundamental democratic principles. We believe in the greatest good to the greatest number." Fourth, Coady anticipated his opponents' accusation that co-operation was a subversive ideology by insisting that co-operation worked within the "framework of the present system of finance capitalism.... The only public business is state-owned business, and co-operation is definitely not state-owned. It is collectivist to be sure, but so is every modern large business from the simplest joint stock company to a great corporation." Definitely troubled by the threat of totalitarianism from the left or right, Coady thought that the "double program of individual private ownership and group private ownership" met the totalitarian threat. Co-operation could serve as a "buffer between the individual and the omnipotent state. It is the last great democratic obstacle in the way of complete statism."

The latter possibility simply horrified Coady, the radical Catholic thinker. For Coady, co-operation was the essence of democracy. He informed the Commission that if democracy was "participation by the people in all the vital and important social processes," then it followed that co-operation aimed "to realize this democracy by placing the country and economic forces in the hands of our own people. If there is any virtue, therefore, in our democratic ideals and principles, it must be agreed that co-operations promote the common good." This was the real test of a democratic movement. Unless the people could "own and operate the economic institutions that lie close to them and which are vital to their very subsistence, then democracy will be impossible." Coady's notion of democracy was excruciatingly exacting. Finally, pulling out all the stops, Coady concluded that co-operation permitted both "charity and the practice of mercy, for the performance of which the Divine Master promised eternal life." Indeed, co-operatives were the "channels through which Christianity can operate in the world." Through co-operation, co-operative nations could "make the world a family. There is here the germ of world peace. Until this foundation is laid for peace, there is not much hope for the future."

CHAPTER 8

Living in Dangerous Times (1945-1952)

I

"**N**ever has the face of the globe and human life been so dramatically transformed as in the era which began under the mushroom clouds of Hiroshima and Nagasaki."[1] The post-war era following the defeat of Nazi Germany did not bring the longed-for peace. The world was now divided into warring camps, with the United States championing "freedom" and "democracy" and the Soviet Union, "communism" and "equality." This confrontation was labelled "cold," capturing the ideological nature of the conflict between these two competing "Western" economic and value systems. Each country influenced other, less powerful nations, while other nations bobbed cagily between non-alignment and wary commitment. To make matters even more complex, the Chinese communist revolution swept tens of millions of non-Westerners out of the capitalist orbit without placing them securely in the Soviet camp. In the colonial worlds, from Africa to India to the Caribbean, insurgent intellectuals mobilized the masses to toss off the shackles of foreign domination. In the decade following World War II, the world seemed extraordinarily unstable, uncertain and dangerous.

For Catholic thinkers close to the Vatican, the world was "filled with ruins and nothing thus far ha[d] been constructed which gives hope of a new and more human civilization."[2] The growing power of the international communist alliance chilled the "Christian West" to the bone. Many Christians thought that democracy was weak; militant and dedicated communists could easily sway the miserable masses in their direction. Indeed, Moses Michael Coady thought that "dark clouds" were hanging over the world. The fate of civilization was in the balance. This "big-picture" man faced the greatest challenge of his career. He had to show that the co-operative movement was "the solution" to the problems that had flared out on the global horizon. To do so, Monsignor Coady had to fight his way through Christian gloom and world escapism, his own terrible fears, the growing power of large corporations and mounting evidence that the average co-op member was not willing to pour sufficient energy into everyday co-op activities. He faced overwhelming odds, but the old warrior gathered his prodigious strength for his final battle. Coady needed his ancestral strength and a faith that could move mountains.

At the end of World War II the co-operative movement in the Maritimes and the rest of Canada was strong and successful enough to permit Moses Coady to imagine that, if properly directed, human energy could surmount any problem. Movement leaders trotted out statistics indicating that the Maritimes had 431 credit unions with assets of $8 million ($25 million in loans); 200 co-op stores with a business of $10 million; 1 fishery wholesale (the UMF); 71 houses built co-operatively with 170 still under construction; and many farmer groups and producer co-ops doing a business that totalled several million.[3] Coady wryly observed that "social betterment" was "so easy to perceive, but difficult to reduce to statistics."[4]

The Maritime co-op movement was complex, diversified and bustling, but distress flowed through Coady's thought in the decade after the war. Even when the Movement was celebrating (at testimonials or marking co-operative anniversaries), an uneasiness prevailed. The craziness of the post-war world drove co-operative leaders into almost manic-depressive modes of perception. Their utopian desire for the co-operative kingdom pulled them towards a naïvely optimistic outlook on the power of co-operation to change the world. Their intimate knowledge of the failings of the co-operative movement pushed them towards hopeless pessimism. Realism was difficult to achieve.

This bi-polarity was epitomized in Coady. At times he told his post-war audiences that the "evils of power" would vanish when individuals merged with the "organic whole" of the co-operative.[5] Coady thought that co-operation would never exploit the people; that would have been an essential contradiction. At other times, Coady descended into an extremely bleak world-outlook as darkness closed in around his heart. While in that darkness, Moses Coady, Christian believer, found some solace. He confided to Sister Josepha that, after reading about St. Catherine of Alexandria who was thrown into a dirty prison before being put to death on a spiked wheel, "I had the idea that, after all, this life is only just a period of waiting in the prison for the final day of our martyrdom, which is death. We don't look upon death as martyrdom, but it is, and we should be grateful for the chance of being martyrs."[6]

Maritime and Canadian co-operators also faced new economic and political circumstances in their own country. Coady had often remarked that the war had been good for co-operative business. This was certainly true in the fishery. Coady had also feared that, with the war's end, another depression could easily set the Movement back on its heels. In the late war years, he had had inklings that the restructured Canadian economy and state, the "vested interests," was creating a hostile environment for the co-operative movement in the regional economy of the Maritimes, throwing structural roadblocks in the face of Maritime economic development.

These structural changes in the larger Canadian economy were not particularly conducive to the growth of the co-operative movement.

On January 1, 1944, the Royal Commission on Provincial Development and Rehabilitation (the Dawson Commission) reported that, while federal war spending had enabled central Canada to greatly increase its industrial facilities, contracts awarded to Nova Scotia "served only to create serious problems of labour adjustment arising from the attraction to wartime jobs of farm and fishery labour."[7] The Antigonish intellectuals and activists were struggling to both defend and modernize the "self-reliant, subsistence-oriented rural economy prevalent throughout much the region in the 1930s."[8] The war drained off surplus labour from the fishing and farming communities, adding to the co-operative movement's woes. Labour could not simply be dumped back into rural primary industries, yet without a sufficient labour force, neither the fledgling co-operative organizations nor private enterprise could flourish. Coady poured enormous energy into developing schemes that would both modernize industry and keep the people in the rural areas of Nova Scotia. However, the secular trend was slowly undermining Coady's goal of keeping people in their rural vocations.

The actual number of Maritime farms had decreased dramatically since 1911. In 1941, agricultural labour comprised 26 percent of the total labour force of the Maritimes; by 1961, two years after Coady's death, it was down to 5.6 percent. In addition, Nova Scotia actually had a smaller percentage of commercial farms to total farms (when compared to central and western Canada), with production barely increasing between 1945 and 1963. As various commissions pondered agriculture's future in Coady's later years—the Gordon Commission (1957), the Special Senate Commission on Land Use in Canada (1957) and the Royal Commission on Rural Credit (1957)—they insisted that greater availability of long-term credit was crucial to any continued process of farm consolidation and expansion. R.D. Howland, an influential economist who had Ottawa's ear, considered that the high percentage of Maritime small wood-lot owners undermined efficient, large-scale development in the forestry. Commissioners, from Jones (1934) to Gordon (1957), worried about the disproportionate number of people engaged in marginal activities such as seasonal logging. And "post-war developments in both logging and fishing—occasioned principally by the demands of pulp and paper mills and larger fishing vessels—had altered and lengthened work seasons, making it increasingly difficult for individuals to combine logging in winter with small-scale farming or small-boat fishing in the summer."[9]

Moses Coady and the co-operative movement faced serious learning challenges. The post-war Canadian economy was racing relentlessly towards efficiency, rationalization, large-scale production units and the displacement of primary sector workers into the burgeoning urban industries.

The economic modernizers were not concerned about maintaining rural ways of life. In the fishery, for example, National Sea Products Ltd. (NatSea), was chartered in 1945 as an amalgamation of eighteen companies and their subsidiaries. Large companies such as NatSea were able to exploit the favourable federal grant structure for phasing out in-shore schooners and replacing them with long-liners and other craft 55' and over in length. By the end of the 1950s, one hundred long-liners would be built by government subsidies, and the number of Canadian trawlers in the Atlantic fishery would rise to thirty-seven. These companies bargained hard, and were able to defeat strong efforts to unionize fishery wage-workers. Nonetheless, even with significant capital expansion in fish-processing, packaging and cold-storage and increase in output, the fishery "continued to be dominated, in terms of numbers if not value of catch, by inshore fishermen."[10]

These trends, left unchallenged, could easily undermine the co-operative movement and the Antigonish goal of a revitalized country-side. The self-reliant, subsistence way of life would be seriously eroded. Migration to urban centres would continue unhindered. Many would also be pulled into the dynamic manufacturing centres of central Canada or New England. Coady, however, thought that the co-operative movement could integrate modernization processes with the rural way of life. By doing so, the movement could solve endemic problems such as uncompetitive and uneconomically small agricultural production units and the persis-tence of a relatively impoverished rural, non-farm population. As if this weren't daunting enough, Coady and the Movement intellectuals had to face the dispiriting consequences of federal state policies that did not ensure the "expansion of investment in regional manufacturing indus-tries."[11] The Liberals, under MacKenzie King, re-elected in 1945, were "growth-oriented, continentalist, business-minded."[12] The Maritimes did not fit comfortably into this scheme; namely, that Canada would play the role of "staples hinterland for American investment.[13]

II

On April 5, 1945, Coady addressed the Annapolis Valley Farmers' Asso-ciation. During the course of this speech he commented on the formation of National Sea Products Ltd., which, for Coady, signified "a most exten-sive development both within the fishing industry and in other directions as well."[14] Coady's premonition would be borne out in the decade follow-ing the war. The co-operative warrior must have bristled when he read Stewart Bates' 1944 report on *The Canadian Atlantic Sea Fishery.* Bates, fed-eral Deputy Minister of Fisheries from 1947 to 1954, epitomized the new breed of Ottawa bureaucrat. Bates was a Harvard-educated economist who thought he knew what the fishery needed. The Atlantic fishery was "under-capitalized, inefficient, and lacking in technology that could raise productivity."[15] He adopted the prevalent romanticized stereotypes about the "rural fishermen" and lamented the "absence of organizations among either the fishers or the exporters."[16] He seemed to have little real commitment (or interest in) a co-operative fishery. He believed that the Atlantic fishery had to abandon its schooner-based, in-shore orientation to salt fish and begin to produce frozen fish for the glittering North American supermarkets. Miriam Wright captures Bates' vision.

> A centralized, industrialized, highly technical frozen fish industry seemed to promise a path towards higher productivity, higher efficiency, and higher returns to labour and owners. An educated, "forward-thinking" workforce, from fishers to plant workers to company owners, who had shed the shackles of "traditionalism", suggested a prosperous future from the entire Atlantic region.[17]

No one had fought as hard as Coady for a prosperous and educated fishery over the prior decade and half. Now, however, the federal Ministry of Fisheries (and its expert minions) was no longer as sympathetic to St. Francis Xavier's initiatives among the fishermen as it had been under Michaud's regime. But Moses Coady was not yet ready to give up on the movement to save the in-shore fishery. By the end of 1947, Coady felt confident enough to assert that the movement was "now big and complicated, but it is promising."[18] Statistics until September 1946 indicate that the credit unions, while not booming, were holding their own. Forty-nine credit unions were operating in the fishing centres. They had 5,270 members with total assets of $406,700. Coady was pleased that a new organization, the Northumberland Co-operative Fisheries, had emerged in 1946. Other organizations on this New Brunswick shore were "progressing satisfactorily, with the turnover of consumer and marketing co-operatives now over $100,000." Coady saw reasons for hope along the eastern shore. Perennially troubled Canso was marketing live lobsters; Tor Bay Canning Company was doing $150,000 worth of business; a new co-op at Port Bickerton was handling 1.2 million pounds of fish; Grand Etang and Cheticamp fishermen were operating five co-op stores and two fish plants, with a turnover of about $400,000; a new co-op had been established at Westport (near Yarmouth-Digby), which had returned about $67,000 to its members.[19] Yet Coady sensed that the fishermen had to keep pressing. They could only achieve the "good life" if they became "more scientifically minded ... ready and anxious to receive and put into action the findings of the various government departments on the possibilities of the fishing industry."[20]

In 1938-39 fishermen and plant workers had responded to declining real incomes and wage cuts by going on strike in Halifax, Lunenburg and Lockeport. They had had marginal success. Only plant workers had received recognition as a legitimate union. The Nova Scotia government had deemed fishermen "co-adventurers" with processors and vessel-owners. They were, therefore, ineligible to organize unions. In 1946 and 1947, the Canadian Fishermen and Fish Handlers' Union (CFFU) entered into a long and bitter strike. Branded as "communist" by the government for its association with the communist-led Canadian Seaman's Union (CSU), the CFFU did not succeed in gaining union status for the fishermen.[21] Coady was not in favour of the strike. He believed that unions deflected the in-shore fishermen from the more fundamental goal of owning their own industries. In his report for 1946-47, Coady quoted approvingly from a letter from Leo Roberts, regional director of the United Maritime Fishermen from Ballantyne's Cove. The UMF was

> not communist-led, and these other fishermen could have followed the same ideal and perhaps now owned their schooners outright had they been taught co-operation. The plant has been paid for out of savings over and above the going price.... The people don't go on strike against themselves. As far as we're concerned, the absentee capitalist and the communist agitators should be put in the same boat—and set adrift.

These were harsh words. In late February 1949, Coady reflected on the struggle to unionize the fishery in a letter to the Rev. Michael O'Reilly, Bishop of St. George's, Newfoundland.

> Those parts of the province, where we were prevented from establishing the UMF have since gone over to the Seaman's Union. This [union] is plenty red, as you know. There may be a need for unionizing certain groups of fishermen but that alone is not enough to build free men. Our program of co-operative activity on both the producer and consumer ends is proving its worth and will ultimately free the fishermen. What is more, it permits the fishermen to tie up with farmers and city consumers, and helps the economic development of all the people.[22]

Coady and Roberts also had to face the unpleasant truth that, with the balance of power having clearly swung towards the companies, these hungry entities could "pursue strategies based on cheap wages, outmoded and inefficient technology, and poor working conditions without the fear of worker militancy or the compulsion to seek to maintain productivity and profit levels through other means."[23]

Coady identified several urgent problems confronting the post-war fishery in his report for 1946-47. First, faced with falling prices, market difficulties and the inflationary-deflationary problems of the time, fishermen would need information and solid organization to deal with the difficult days ahead. Second, Coady thought that "our major problem is to find out how, through proper mechanization and application of modern technology to the industry, the men in these communities can participate in the off-shore catch of ground fish. The problem is, in other words, how the total industry can be made to function in the lives of as many people as possible." Coady did not think it was a good idea to draw "too sharp a distinction between in-shore and off-shore fishermen. It might be better to consider them integral parts of the total industry." This was, indeed, a big problem, because the bottom line for those committed to rationalizing production is efficiency and profitability and not preservation of livelihood and community. Coady captured this sentiment beautifully in a poignant letter to Jerome Morris: "The signs the last few years in the Department of Fisheries, both provincial and federal, would indicate that there is a strong leaning towards big companies. The emphasis seems to be taken off the human side of it." Coady also believed that the "new Nova Scotia Department of Fisheries, under the Hon. Harold Connolly and his top man, Dr. Cooper, is definitely anti-co-operative and pro-big companies."[24] Third, Coady thought it time to end, once and for all, the "dead hand of feudalism from the fishery of eastern Canada. There are plenty of potential leaders among the fishermen if they are properly organized. They are capable of great things if we only put faith in them."[25]

Coady knew the co-operative fishery was in difficulty. Like other non-co-operative sectors, it was having trouble producing a consistently high quality product. The co-op members couldn't always guarantee continuity of supply. They lacked adequate cold storage and holding space. All too often, despite heroic efforts by Extension fieldworkers, the local co-ops were poorly organized and managed. Some of the co-ops had corrupt managers. Coady's strategy in these dangerous times was to push hard for continued expansion in all marketing and purchasing phases of the co-op program. He wanted "modern facilities for the fishing industry owned by the fishermen." He wanted the credit unions to expand to provide increased savings and credit facilities (Nova Scotia, through its affiliation with the American-based Credit Union National Association [CUNA], now provided credit union insurance). He wanted more attention paid to land use and specialized farming for fishermen, with special emphasis on nutritional value. (In the late 1940s, Coady became obsessed with health and organic food and other dietary matters. He began to preach that poor physical fitness and depleted energy were primary sources of Maritime lethargy. A whiff of the old eugenics movement lingered around some of Coady's speeches on health and the movement for a better world.) He wanted a co-op housing program for the fishing communities. He also called for a special study on the extension of all forms of medical and hospital services to rural areas. Nothing less than a "continuous and intensive program of adult learning using all the available facilities and approved techniques" would suffice. Coady was now becoming, like the Tompkins of old, a voice crying in the wilderness.

Coady completed his Fishery Report for 1946-47 in the early spring. In the following months, the state of the fishery was rather grim. In July 1947, vessels and trawlers were all tied up, and the situation at Canso was still anguished (Coady thought that the Strait of Canso was the number one problem for the eastern Canadian fishery). The credit union of this historic fishing community and inspirational locus of the Antigonish project had failed and its co-op store had done poorly. They still couldn't fish continuously because they didn't have adequate cold storage facilities. During the fall and winter of 1947, Movement intellectuals worked furiously to rectify the situation. In a long, candid letter to his cousin, Father Jimmy, written on January 17, 1948, an ebullient Coady claimed he had just spent his happiest week ever. "The people at Canso and other places on the coast were saying things and beginning to do things for which we patiently awaited during twenty years."

At an important meeting of co-operators in Canso, key leaders in the Movement (Alex MacIsaac, Father Forest, Howard MacKichan of the UMF, and Coady himself) had lambasted the Canso fishermen. Coady often spoke of administering the hypodermic needle when flagging co-operators needed motivating. These Movement leaders had brought their medical kits. MacIsaac told them that they either didn't understand the co-operative movement, or, if they did, they were pretty poor stuff. Ed Power, one of Canso's leading activists, told a little group at breakfast that he "knew the damn Scotsmen would betray us." On the following day, after speeches by MacKichan and Forest, who reminded them of their past successes, MacIsaac blasted them again. "It was generally admitted that among all the animals the dog was the one that could be kicked and booted and battered by his master and when everything was over, would look up trustingly in the face of the master. 'The dog has got nothing on you,' Alex said." Coady watched Power roaring with laughter. They seemed able to swallow this unpleasant medicine and understood the game.

Coady was convinced that "at long last the Canso fellows can fish continuously and make something out of their work. They will be able to build the complete unit in a few years and nobody can stop them." Coady was riding a cresting wave of emotion. He was utterly confident that the fishermen of Nova Scotia's rocky shores could convert the wealth of the blue sea into "life for a growing population on this eastern shore." With the door on the "Canso affair" about to close, Coady opined to Tompkins that there were no other real problems. "The fishermen are successful in every other part of the Maritimes—they need more science, more knowledge, more honesty, etc. but they are all on the right line, and will have a perpetual crescendo of new life. This Guysborough-Richmond shore has baffled everybody in the past, but the solution is in sight. The historic hour for Canso and environs is here." Canso had initiated the

> whole fish fight—they first brought the credit union to Nova Scotia and they, on account of their geographical position, would yet be a great center. We all like the people of Canso. They have some of the great souls of this province—Ed Power, Walter

McNeary, John Chafe, etc. It's reward for a lifetime of struggle to see the poor fellows coming to the point where their efforts are unmistakably successful.[26]

This fervid letter is remarkable. Coady was deeply in love with the Atlantic fishery, a very fickle lover. And Moses Coady had other problems he did not mention to old Father Jimmy, who was beginning to lose his razor sharp mind to Alzheimer's disease.

Coady's relationship with the Acadian fishing communities was rather vexatious. The tension between the Acadian and Anglo-Celtic wings of the Movement has seldom been acknowledged in historical scholarship; we glimpsed it in the early phase of Coady's career as a UMF organizer. Publicly, Coady constantly emphasized the way the Movement was breaking down prejudices and promoting harmony in a religiously and ethnically segmented society such as Nova Scotia. But prejudices run deep and people aren't easily educated to tolerance. The Acadians had been "ethnically cleansed" from Nova Scotia (and removed from the best agricultural lands) in the dreadful year of their expulsion in 1755. St.FX University had been removed from an Acadian community in the mid-nineteenth century and placed in the centre of Highland Scottish culture in Antigonish. The Acadians spoke French and were of different ethnic origin from the Scots, Irish and English who settled in Nova Scotia. And resources for the Acadian and Anglo-Celtic fishing communities were always scarce.

On January 23, 1947, Coady wrote to Father J.M. Hill, Bishop of Victoria, B.C., that A.J. Boudreau, formerly of Cheticamp, lately of St. Anne de Pocatiere, now manager of Quebec United Fishermen, was planning to do away with the UMF and substitute the Atlantic United Fishermen in its place. Coady told Hill that he was "personally scared of the leadership. I feel also that their record for honesty and efficiency leaves a bit to be desired." Coady's alternative was to "go on as we are for ten years at least so as to establish here in the Maritimes a co-operative philosophy in the minds of the people, so that it will come as second nature to them."[27] Coady intensely disliked those Acadians, such as Boudreau, whom he believed were trying to undermine a united co-operative movement. In fact, Coady had tried unsuccessfully to have Boudreau fired from his position as "ag rep" in the late 1930s. He told Michael Gillis, in a letter written on January 17, 1948, that he was going to Moncton for a meeting where he would see Chiasson to "talk over this French question which is causing us some concern, but which likely will be settled amicably, or fairly so, in the near future. They are all skunks, but the world can't seem to get along without a little smell."[28] This smell would stay around for some time. Indeed, Coady perceived the "language situation" in New Brunswick as a "smouldering danger" that the priests could easily exploit unless mollified.[29]

In fact, the tension between some Acadian communities and St.FX Extension Department was so severe that French-speaking communities refused to have an English-speaking person address any of their meetings from 1948 until the early 1950s. In a confidential letter to M.J. MacKinnon, who had just replaced the very ill Coady as director of Extension, Coady gave an account of their troubles with the Acadians.

> In the past five years New Brunswick, on account of the appearance of the nationalistic spirit, asked none of the top Extension men to speak in any of the French-speaking communities. In the first years they took our doctrines with great rejoicing. I think the record will show that New Brunswick has suffered on account of the change in attitude. This is using co-operation and education for narrow purposes that defeat the whole program. In a very delicate way you will have to get back to the point where the top STFX men [*sic*] will be able to speak at strategic times and places.[30]

Only several days earlier, on March 3, Coady had written to Stewart Bates about his desire to continue the grant and revealed his own racist bias. After praising some of his fieldworkers, which included several francophones (Denis Aucoin from Grand Etang, Anselm Cormier, now chief worker in New Brunswick, and the veteran Percy Pellerin of Larry's River), Coady commented: "You will notice that they are not Anglo-Saxon, but I can assure you that they have picked up wisdom from this work which I think justifies my saying that they have been Caledonized. In their wisdom and strategy they are close seconds to the representatives of your own smart Scottish race."[31] Coady, this great lover of humanity, could not quite escape his own ethnic blinders. He had many close Acadian associates (such as Chiasson) and supporters, but, nonetheless, many Acadians perceived that Extension was privileging the English and favouring the Scottish and Irish fishermen. The top male leaders at Extension (Coady, Laidlaw, MacIntyre, J.D. Nelson MacDonald) were all Scottish or Irish. Of the women (Ida Gallant, Sister Anselm, Sr. Marie Michael, Kay Thompson, Zita O'Hearn), only Ida had an Acadian background. No matter how respectful the Celts were of the Acadians, they were still basically running the show from the centre of Highland Scottish culture and power.

At the beginning of 1948 Moses Coady still exuded confidence and strength. The Canso coast seemed to be "on the march" and the men had "tasted economic blood and are new wild men that will fight in the future."[32] Feeling his oats, Coady informed Gillis that he felt like saying, "Let the big boys come on; we have the beginning of the solution of the toughest of our fish problems; the solution of the Canso problem would enable us to take on the world." His health, for the moment, was awfully good. "I feel like Churchill, 'We will fight them on the sands,' etc."[33] A trip to the Digby-Yarmouth part of Nova Scotia impressed him deeply. Coady told several of his relatives that the "French people ... seemed to be on a much higher plane of living than the people here. Laidlaw and Roddy MacMullin who went down to West Pubnico one day, counted from one point in East and West Pubnico 246 beautiful, well-painted homes." Coady also went down the Digby Neck, originally settled by United Empire Loyalist stock, and thought there was a "beautiful development going on in that country. The manager at Brooklyn ... told us that their business for the year would reach half a million. They have their own grain elevator and grind their own wheat. They have just opened two new branch co-operative stores in other parts of the rural area."[34] Coady's up-beat frame of mind enabled him to see through the numerous difficulties of the Movement towards the permanent establishment of a co-operative beachhead in a hostile land.

This mood continued until the late fall of 1950. He apprised Father Adolphus Gillis of his health. Although Coady had gallstones, the new heart specialist in Halifax, Dr. Laufer, had given him a good report. Once again on a diet, Coady, who loved good food, lost twelve pounds. He joked with Father Adolphus Gillis that he was "getting good looking again and am feeling fine." Coady thought that "on the whole, things are wonderful. The UMF convention was a great affair. The Canso coast down to Halifax is developing in a splendid way. P.E.I. is doing well as far as I know." Coady was very impressed with Father Mike MacKinnon's work with the labour people in Cape Breton and a new fieldworker, Eugene Gorman. There was sad news, too, as the Movement had just buried Catherine "Tat" Sears, whom Coady described as a "great soul." Coady was headed to the Margaree for Christmas with a plum basket full of Island potatoes and cheese, a gift from Duncan Campbell. Trouble was, he advised Adolphus Gillis rather wistfully, "I am not permitted to eat cheese or potatoes any more."[35]

Coady's effusive mood, however, would not hold for long. Coady revealed his fundamental attitude towards hardship to his old buddy, Michael Gillis. All we can do in life, Coady explained, is

> apply with persistent and unfaltering effort the right democratic formula. It matters not how slow it is or how great the difficulties in the way, that will ultimately win. There is nothing worth copying from the Communists, but their persistent zeal should make us ashamed of ourselves. We Christian Democrats—and the clergy are included in this—are impatient, ready to skip intermediaries and contradict nature, prone to defeatism at the difficulties which are part of the human drama. My answer is: let us nose our ship in the wind and sail it to the bitter end. We will win in proportion to our faith.[36]

Coady needed this sort of spiritual resolve to face what was ahead. In the winter of 1951, Coady's effervescent mood seemed to evaporate. His old friend of the fishing wars, Col. A.L. Barry, whom Coady thought was a "brilliant fellow, a wonderful speaker, dedicated to the cause of the people and absolutely fearless,"[37] had been passed over for the position of Deputy Minister of the federal Fisheries. Coady was also very disturbed that the UMF had not given Barry a position. Coady confided to R.J. MacSween, the director of marketing for Nova Scotia, that Emile Blanchard, president of the UMF, and Alonzo St.Pierre were operating behind the scenes. Coady couldn't "get it out of [his] head that we have probably been sold down the river." Coady then told MacSween that the solution to the "French question" was a strong consumer wholesale and retail movement in vocational goods and in farm, fish and forest products. Coady thought that the English-speaking priests, instead of acting like a

> bunch of babies, all the time moaning about French domination, would have in this technique an honorable, honest way of solving this vexing question. There is nothing underhand or crooked about my suggestions. I am really saving the poor French fishermen of New Brunswick from their own crooked leaders who, for political or other motives are feeding them the wrong philosophy. This is only saving the poor people from themselves so to speak.[38]

These intemperate comments issue from Coady's shadowy social engineering impulses. The main trouble, as Coady now saw it, was not so much with the co-operative blueprint, but rather with a seemingly resistant grain in the "crooked timber" of humanity. Coady told Constance Sutherland of Victoria, B.C., that the "biggest obstacle" in the UMF's way was the "lack of education, ambition and moral fibre in many of the fishermen themselves."[39]

On January 23, 1952, just a mere two weeks before his heart attack, Coady had recovered a little of his buoyant spirit. He informed Mary Arnold, who had pioneered co-operative housing with Father Jimmy in the late 1930s, that the "story of the progress of the fishermen from Margaree to the lower end of Cheticamp is one of the most scintillating things in our history." Port Bickerton and White Head had emerged from feudalism. "This is our greatest story and one that has significance for the undeveloped parts of the earth–I would say the key for the Colombo Plan or Point Four." Only four years earlier, Coady had imagined that the Canso problem had been solved. However, he now told Ms. Arnold that "the Canso situation is still bad. We are hoping against hope that we will be able to hold on there. We need a big unit of operation to demonstrate our program. Big fish companies are now operating out of Louisburg and new ones are coming in to Canso and Petit de Gras. This may interfere with us to some extent."[40]

On February 6, 1952, Moses Coady, the sixty-nine year old Extension director and prophet of the co-operative revolution, was struck down again with a heart attack and gallstone troubles. Coady's secretary explained his situation to Mrs. B.F. Coady, resident in West Newton, Massachusetts.

> He took a serious heart attack on February 6–had mass in the morning, took breakfast, and shortly afterwards took a severe pain while in his own room. He phoned one of the other priests, who came immediately and summoned a doctor as well as the Sister Infirmarian and the Rector. The doctor arrived in a few minutes and his first reaction was that he could do nothing for Dr. Coady. However, he gave an injection and set up the oxygen apparatus. After some time, Dr. Coady revived; but his heart-beat was

very erratic and the doctor would not move him until the following day when he took him to the hospital. He is still in the hospital and is considerably improved, but his heart is not back yet to normal rhythm. Until it is, he will have to remain in hospital....
Another thing, they claim that unless his heart does return to normal rhythm, there will be another crisis. Dr. Coady knows this and is resigned to whatever may happen.[41]

This latest assault on his body did not appear to dampen his spirit. On February 21 Coady dictated a letter to Francis Coady exclaiming that "our movement was making the most tremendous strides—out of all proportion to what we might legitimately expect."[42]

However, Coady must have been feeling slightly miserable as he penned several lengthy commentaries on the state of the Maritime fishery. In 1952 Coady wrote candidly, without the usual hyperbole, to the new director, Father M.J. MacKinnon, offering him counsel on how to proceed with the treacherous fishery. He encouraged him to review the whole program and consult with the leaders (in Halifax, MacKichan, Sam Campbell, MacSween and Walsh; in New Brunswick, St. Pierre, Sam Cormier, Bishop Camille LeBlanc and Archbishop Robichaud). He emphasized that the

inefficiency of our people in the Maritimes to run co-operatives, especially co-op stores, is due to lack of education and experience, and in some cases to a lack of moral fibre. It should be emphasized, also, that if our people are to be freed from the domination of monopolistic conspiracies that are even now gaining control, we must work fast and sincerely at the job of extricating them.

Sensing that the fishery was sliding out of the Movement's grasp, Coady urged MacKinnon to teach the people not to proceed so slowly. "We have to teach the people that in order to get ready for the big bite, say a fleet of trucks that will convey our fish to the American markets, or a big fish plant or any big central processing and manufacturing plant, we cannot always be gradual." They had started small, successfully, and now they had to "grow big." However, there weren't many grains of sand left in their hourglass. Coady thought that the situation in the lobster fishery was terrifying.

Here is an industry where the fishermen have complete control on the production end, yet we see growing before our very eyes the Connolly-Melanson and other monopolies—we see slipping away from the people the very business that I, from the very beginning, held out to them as the means of their delivery. In my books this multi-million lobster business would free the common people forever from the shackles of their serfdom. But we are not doing it. In fact, we are reverting to a new serfdom.

The optimistic glow of 1948 had vanished; Coady was rueful of the tragedy now occurring.

In his final "Report of Fisheries Work for 1952-3,"[43] penned a year after his heart attack, Coady stated that Extension had aimed to "bring greater economic independence to the fishermen of this region, to make it possible for them to share in the improved conditions of the past number of years, and to build a better social order in the sector of our country that lives by the fishing industry." In twenty-five years, Coady imagined everyone

would experience "progress ... beyond our fondest expectations." But the
Movement fieldworkers had to adapt their program in accordance with the
trends of the times, for the most "important trend" affecting the organization of fishermen in the Maritimes was the "change to larger units of
operation." Thus, fishermen had to "do away with the local cannery and to
centralize lobster canning at a few strategic points with modern plant
equipment." Fieldworkers, Coady insisted, now had to convince the organized fishermen of the Maritimes to centralize. Coady was also pleased that
some of the fishing co-ops—Port Bickerton, for example—were using larger
and heavier boats. "A few years ago it would have been quite unthinkable
for inshore fishermen to own and operate boats of this kind; but today there
is a definite change in attitude and more of them are undertaking to finance
and operate equipment of this kind."

Coady positively assessed the educational program among the fishermen. Although the study club movement had declined in the fishing
communities over the last decade, Coady was heartened that some interest
in study clubs had been re-awakened. However, despite improvement in
attitude towards education in somewhat discouraged areas such as Richmond County, the old verve and energy really had dissipated. Sixteen
short courses had been conducted in 1952-53 and a four-week training and
leadership course had been held in Antigonish. In February 1953, the
UMF and St.FX had jointly sponsored a fishermen's week to discuss the
wider problems of the fishing industry. All the old themes were on the
table—lobster marketing, problems of inspection and grading, marine
insurance, forms of security for fishermen, conservation, the relative merits
of draggers and long-liners and the financial structure of the UMF.

Three years after the completion of Coady's report on the fishery, the situation seemed disheartening. An anonymous critical report entitled
"Fisheries Fieldworker"[44] observed that, by 1956, the leadership courses
had been discontinued and the study club movement had disintegrated. As
the different co-ops had built their own staffs, the educational focus had
been lost. No plan of organized education among the people now existed.
The field staff had turned to business without "training or aptitude." Co-ops
now had members who did not own and directors who did not direct. By
May 1957, a committee appointed to present a brief on fishery co-ops at a
meeting of the Maritime Planning Committee observed that it was "quite
evident that our co-operatives have not kept pace with other competitors."
In New Brunswick, Lameque was the "only co-operative actively engaged
in production and processing of ground fish." In Nova Scotia, only
Cheticamp and Port Bickerton were well established in this field. The Isle
Madame Co-operative and White Head had a limited volume. In Prince
Edward Island, there was very little to boast about.[45] The situation was
indeed dispiriting.

Coady believed ordinary people could do great things.

In 1949, St. Francis Xavier University honoured Roy Bergengren and A.S. MacIntyre with honorary degrees for their immense contributions to the co-operative movement.

Coady at the height of his fame as preacher of the
co-operative revolution.

Coady believed he had discovered God's blueprint for
the people's economy.

III

Intellectually, the post-war years were remarkably vital for Moses Michael Coady, the man who liked to cast himself simply as "little Mosie from the Margaree." After the war, with the exception of the usual bouts of flu and lumbago, Coady had enough strength to travel widely in the Maritimes, Canada and the United States (with one stressful trip to Rome). He was in endless demand as a speaker on the co-op circuit and he wasn't prone to sitting at home knitting. He didn't have the stamina of old, but then he had probably been given enough for two. He had, moreover, many problems with which to wrestle. He had to determine precisely what role the St.FX Extension Department would play in an increasingly muddled and diversified co-op movement. He had to figure out how to confront the threat of communism in a dangerous world. He had to discover how the co-op movement, clearly under siege, fit into the changing world of global politics and national economies. He had to attend to the minute and often irritating problems of his own clan. Coady was one of the co-op movement's leading captains, and he would stay with the ship until the very end.

In the post-war world, co-operative movement intellectuals had enough evidence of the way in which co-ops could renew community life to believe that, with more dedication and strategic thinking, they could complete the task of building sound "social and economic houses." These houses would be able to withstand both the "bitter cold winds of a competitive world" and the heat generated by the "squeeze of the exploiters and the general inclemencies of the modern environment." Coady desired the co-operative movement to be so permanently fixed in the world that he imagined that those who built "sound co-operatives" could "feel that if they should come back 5000 or 10,000 years from now they would still find their co-operatives in a flourishing condition."[46] This wild dream of a permanent millennial order inhabited Coady's religious outlook on time and space, yet on its underside lay deep anxiety that the world would actually turn out to be chaotic, unpredictable and exploitative of God's little people of the earth.

Coady's general speeches in the late 1940s and 1950s indicate that he was rather disconsolate about the Movement's future. Coady's role in the North American co-op movement placed extreme pressure on him. He was the magnanimous leader who had to cheer everyone else; to praise constantly the co-op movement's accomplishments; to squeeze every last ounce of hopefulness out of the Movement's successes; and to cling fast to his belief that no problem in the world was insurmountable if human energy was properly directed or controlled. This latter belief was a hard taskmaster, placing excruciating demands on his spirit and generating much of Coady's distress. When people inevitably failed to be "properly

directed," Coady could only resort to imprecating the people for their failure. Coady's longing for an indestructible economic order placed
unbearable burdens on God's poor, sinful earth-dwelling creatures.

On December 19, 1946, Coady wrote to several young men of the
Margaree (Mose Campbell, Leo and James Coady) informing them that
the Extension Department had undertaken the "difficult task of mobilizing
the people of Eastern Nova Scotia in continuous adult learning, with the
hope that they will find for themselves new life in these provinces." He told
the young men that he was certain that the Maritimes could offer a "satisfying, beautiful and even high standard of life. We know the formula by
which that can be done." However, the

> great difficulty in doing it is to get people to see it. It is quite impossible, as you will
> readily understand, to get all the people to realize the possibilities of such a program.
> We never expected such a reaction. Tens of thousands of our people are still primitive.
> They are not primitive by nature–they are descended from great races, but they have
> fallen from their high estate. For the time being it is impossible to get their attention in
> the way necessary for the vigorous prosecution of a program of progress.

Coady thought that it should be possible to get "enough bright young men
in each community to champion the cause."[47]

Coady often penned piquant little pieces for a column entitled "Anvil" in
The Maritime Co-operator. In the February 25, 1948, issue, Coady
announced: "We have put before the people a double-barreled program of
adult education and economic co-operation as a formula for social progress. We have told them that this formula will lead them on the road to
progress. It is not the total program, but it does condition the people to the
point where they can put over a total program." Coady was thankful for
what had already been accomplished, but he wondered why it was that
"such a simple and promising plan is not adopted and carried out with
vigor by everybody in these provinces. The answer is that the people have
no faith. They don't believe. Their leaders are not convinced. Many of
those toying around with the co-operative movement are waiting to see
which way the wind is blowing."

The world was resisting the imposition of co-operation and was behav-
ing irrationally, unwilling to succumb to Coady's blueprint. Coady seemed
to believe that some of the fishermen were betraying the co-operative
movement. He recommended to M.J. MacKinnon that he, as director of
Extension, discretely question the "morality of our fishermen, their honesty," on conference agendas. The morality question required "devastating
logic that will puncture the hide of the most obtuse–something in the
nature of blockbusting is necessary. The people have to be told that dishonesty, lack of morality, is the great obstacle to their progress." He accused
the fishermen of ignorance, lack of intelligence, carelessness, irresponsibil-
ity, greed, love of special privilege and downright cussedness and

dishonesty. The angry prophet had turned his wrath on his people, just like Jeremiah and Isaiah of olden times. Coady was plainly distraught, reaching for something to shake the people out of their lassitude and into vigorous action.

> We, the children of light, who believe in free will and the dignity of the human person and the importance of the immortal soul, act as if we believed everything was run by materialistic laws of economics, and that we were all in the grip of smart acting businessmen, financiers and industrialists, and there was nothing we could do about it. It will take some jet propelled bombs to smash these false beliefs out of the minds of our people.

Concluding on a dark note, he confessed to MacKinnon that, "judging by the present outlook, more difficult things than these, not yet even thought of, will be a reality in the not too distant future"[48] Perhaps, as he intimated in a letter to Mose Campbell and Leo Coady, one of these "more difficult things" was the "darkening of the understanding of our people, especially of our Irish and Scottish people.... As far as I know our people," he told the young men, "they are as anxious to make a dollar as anybody else. But when it comes to figuring out plans to do that, they have some kind of queer complex that makes them resist every suggestion, makes them suspicious that the suggestor [sic] is trying to put something over."[49] Coady had the co-operative blueprint in hand; the formula for convincing enough people to accept it was sliding from his grasp.

Faced with the possible deterioration of the "Antigonish Project," Coady dug deep. The more threatened he felt, the more his fertile mind dreamed up schemes for maintaining the Movement. He called on everyone, particularly its leaders, to commit more of their time and energy. On February 1, 1951, he again shared his imaginings in a letter to fellow agrarianist Michael Gillis. He dreamed of decentralized housing movements for industrial Cape Breton where people could live on from five to twenty acres in the "midst of life and beauty." He could see new, flourishing parishes from Grand Narrows to Boularderie. Fishing communities, such as White Head and Port Felix, could be built up with 500 families settling on good plots of land. A continuous rural settlement program could be carried out. A community such as Judique could hold 350 or 400 families, all "living in economic security and in an environment calculated to inspire the best that's in man. Make the whole of Inverness County, in a word, a real rural garden." Coady thought that a big consumer co-op on the Miramichi River in New Brunswick would help solve the conflicts between different ethnic groups.

Coady insisted that

> our program of giving food, shelter and clothing, and gradually all the other things necessary for the good and abundant life, is the road to the heart of man. Psychologically, this is the answer to the world problem. Whoever does this will win the alle-

giance of the human race. There is no institution capable of making a greater contribution to this than the Catholic Church, and especially is this true of the Bishops and the secular clergy.

Yet, the realization of this project required a

great deal of motivation to cause them [the common people] to syphon their money in this direction rather than fritter it away on so many useless and pernicious activities. The co-operative movement, therefore, fits into the larger, cosmic philosophy in a way the most optimistic of us never thought of before. Instead of bemoaning the sad condition of the world today we should probably rejoice that finally the world is getting bad enough to be reformed. This is our finest hour, to translate Churchill's beautiful words from a British boat into a real pean of thanksgiving for us Christians.... When we meet red communism with real red Christian blood, then we will get the dazzling pure white world that we have so long sighed for.

Coady concluded this startling letter to Gillis by stating that what was wrong with the Christian world, including "holy Nova Scotia and Antigonish," was that

we don't believe in anything. To be just on the side of the thing if it costs us no sacrifice, is not good enough. Unfortunately that's what we are. We are first and foremost on the side of money and comfort.... We, you and I, sons of the poorer classes, change our minds when we get into even such a holy calling as the priesthood. How did we ever get it into our heads that we should have the nice things in life, even if the poor people can't have them? I am all for the nice things for you and me, but I swear we should fight that the common people should have them also. The world, the Christian world, from the Pope to the last poor priest in Patagonia has not done this. That's why we are losing the working classes, that's why we are being engulfed by this unspeakable, hideous thing called communism. If we all went into overalls, so to speak, for fifty or a hundred years, and came out four square for the common man in the way our Lord taught in his parable on the good samaritan, there would be no need of bombing armies today.[50]

Late in 1951, Coady returned from a hectic co-operative tour of the United Kingdom and Western Europe. He also attended an international conference of laymen and laywomen in Rome, but missed most of the International Co-operative Alliance meeting because of illness. On November 13, 1951, he wrote Mrs. Constance Sutherland about his trip.

Things are very bad over there. France and England were never so near financial collapse—poverty everywhere and imminent danger of war and revolution. This is dangerous, but probably a very interesting and important era in human history. Out of all this turmoil will probably come a better world—if we can survive the materialism and downright atheism of the ethically and culturally illiterate barbarians who are rising to power all over the world. Perhaps that is the price we have to pay for the sins of the western world with its injustice, its monopolistic capitalism. It is terrible to think that in a scientific age like this we shall probably have to go through the horrible bloodbath that lies ahead to bring justice and brotherhood into this longsuffering world. We have achieved such miraculous things in science and technology that it is sad to meditate on our unscientific stupidity when it comes to the realm of the social and economic.

A little sadly, Coady added that he had received an invitation two weeks ago from UNESCO to go to Thailand to work as an educational expert. "It is too bad to be getting old."[51]

Coady's thinking had taken a decidedly apocalyptic turn. He told Michael Gillis on January 31, 1951, that he had had a

> great talk with John Angus Rankin the other night. He was in the dumps, as a good many of them around here are. I made the suggestion to him and MacCormack that we get together a small number of our leading men who will meet as occasion offers from time to time. Among them would be at least these fellows: Fathers Dan M, Michael MacSween, Joe A., MacCormack, Rankin, the two Roberts boys, yourself, Laidlaw, Alex MacIsaac, Teddy, Steve Dolhanty, Allan Mac, Fathers Hogan, Frank MacIsaac and probably J. Gillis of SW Margaree and J.H. MacEachern, St. Peter's. My idea would be that I would notify the fellows of a given area that some of the boys were to meet, say in Sydney, at a given time. Only the central fellows would know the whole gang. In this way we would avoid jealousies. This is only to resurrect the technique of a former day before we started Extension. The number is rather formidable but I can't see how we could possibly not take the fellows mentioned above.

No women and no Acadians were included in Coady's conspiratorial elite. He had hoped that the forming of this co-operative vanguard would "keep up morale and build the fellows who are going to lead in the future; it will, and this is very important, create a very strong, although possibly a silent, pressure group that will keep all our top leaders on the right track, so speak." This vanguard, meeting in "these little private seances," would determine what ideas "should prevail at say St. Joseph's Society, clergy meetings, rural and industrial conferences."[52] In the heady, post-World War I days of battling the conservative church hierarchy, Father Tompkins had spearheaded a conspiratorial elite of priests to shape the Church's social agenda. A weary and sick Coady, though, was unable to pull this group together. This letter to his mentor Gillis reveals Coady's desperation. This great proponent of democracy—of, by and for the people—was even willing, in his darkest hour, to manipulate both the people and some of their leaders in order to control their destinies.

IV

In 1922, Lewis Mumford, a thinker Coady appreciated, wrote a book entitled *The Story of Utopias*. While Mumford found the "authoritarian discipline" and "dictatorial tendencies" of man utopias distasteful, he noted that utopians addressed the "reservoir of potentialities" to which no society was "fully awake."[53] These latter phrases beautifully captured Coady's co-operative utopianism. He was constantly scanning the horizon for signs of potentiality. During World War II, he had sensed that the "Antigonish Project" was relevant to the teeming masses of the Third World, particularly in South America. In the post-war world, with his reputation spreading far and wide, Coady had the opportunity to test his ideas in the international arena.

At the end of the war, the United States had the "world's only thriving industrial economy." To promote "economic recovery, full employment, free trade, and economic stability," Britain and the United States had designed a "set of international institutions" such as the United Nations Relief and Rehabilitation Administration (UNRRA), the General Agreement on Tariffs and Trade (GATT), the Breton Woods institutions, along with the Marshall Plan to revive Europe.[54]

In early June 1946, Coady had travelled to Washington as papal envoy to purchase food. He bought $150,000 worth of wheat, which was to be consigned to Pope Pius XII to be used as he saw fit. The money had been collected in the Catholic dioceses of Canada. The apostolic delegate at Ottawa had given St. Francis Xavier the honour of doing this for the Vatican. The money ($37,000 collected in the Maritimes) was deposited in an Antigonish bank to Monsignor Coady's credit. While in Washington, he met with UNRRA officials. Coady's imagination must have been stirred by the increased possibility of preaching the co-operative gospel to underdeveloped nations. Indeed, a magazine article, "The Good Life in Antigonish," observed that the name "Antigonish" had been bandied about at a recent Caribbean Social Action congress held in the Dominican Republic. "People in all countries seemed to have lost the sense of control of their economic destiny."[55] Antigonish intellectuals such as A.S. MacIntyre thought that the West was "doomed to suffer the consequences of its indifference" unless the "common people of all countries" saw the necessity of "establishing a sane social and economic system of society based on Christian principles and social justice for all."[56] Coady perceived that the St. Francis Xavier Extension Department was a "series of SOS calls to the people of all the world to investigate possibilities and change these potentialities into actualities."[57] Like jack-in-the-boxes, possibilities seemed to be popping up everywhere.

Moses Coady's massive arms now sought to embrace the whole world. The Co-operative Extension Service people in Philadelphia had honoured Coady as the outstanding co-operator of the year in 1948. His acceptance speech, "Loyalty to Democracy," warned the gathered that "it is well known that those who rule economically rule politically and every other way. History teaches, therefore, that the people will lose their power to rule if they lose economic ownership." Coady told his American friends that he thought that the dominant note of the economy of eastern Canada would be co-operative. Co-operation was "founded on such a solid philosophical basis that there is no danger of making any mistake in working towards it. As a matter of fact, if the whole world could be set up on a co-operative basis, we would immediately eliminate from it this annoying characteristic of unreasonable change and instability. The world would come back to equilibrium." Coady believed the "human heart desires the everlasting, the eternal. We like to feel that we are setting up things that will last forever after we are gone. Economic co-operation has all the elements of perpetuity or immortality." Pondering the fate of human civilization, Coady offered his co-operative audience a choice. "We can be a permanent crescendo of life and civilization, and as eternal as the everlasting hills if we build our economic and social structures on the eternal verities of truth and justice. That is what economic co-operation can do for us." A new tonality appeared in Coady's speeches, erupting from his unconscious. Coady was now dreaming of immortality, imagining that the co-operative movement could defeat death and impermanence and pushing his own desire for such into the international arena.

Coady saw incredible potential for the co-operative movement throughout a world "ripe for revolution." Armed with a blueprint blessed in heaven, Coady thought co-operation could move mountains.[58] His imagination seemed truly on the side of the impossible. Coady was obsessed with the idea that the acute problems of the world could be wrestled to the ground through the release of human energy hinged to an animating idea. The world was poised on the brink of disaster. People had to break free from their inertia. There was a "vacuum in the minds of the masses," and "sooner or later the tornadoes of revolution will blow in there." Somehow a way had to be found to "pump life back into these lives. That is the only answer to revolution and instability."[59]

There was no stopping the single-minded Moses Coady as he travelled the co-operative and adult education circuits. Elected president of the Canadian Association for Adult Education (CAAE) in 1949, he called the Canadian adult education community to consider a "national educational movement for the real progress of democracy. We must mobilize the common people everywhere in this country and give them practical aims. Adult learning is the guarantee of our democracy."[60] One can only gasp at his audacity, particularly when it was evident that the CAAE had succumbed to the Cold War ethos, moving away from the reform-orientation of the early 1940s. In fact, leading social reform-minded adult educators had been expunged from the adult education scene for alleged communist sympathies. Watson Thomson had been fired by Tommy Douglas in Saskatchewan in 1946, Drummond Wren of the Workers Education Association had been squeezed out of his role by warring communists and social democrats in 1948, and the legendary founder of the documentary, and first director of the National Film Board and friend of adult educators, John Grierson, had been asked to appear before the Kellock-Taschereau Commission of investigation into subversive activities in Canada in 1946. Even the moderate Ned Corbett, director of the CAAE, had come under fire in 1946 from right-wing businessmen who couldn't stomach the idea of Citizen's Forums where people openly discussed a range of ideas. There is no evidence that Coady was deeply concerned with what was happening to his colleagues in the Canadian adult education movement. What evidence there is simply suggests that Coady was shocked at the conservatism manifest in the CAAE in the early 1950s.

In late February 1949, Coady went to Washington, D.C., to outline his program to U.S. state department officials. He met with Wilfred Maldenbaum, chief of the state department division of International and Functional Intelligence, and one of several officials engaged in a preliminary study of "point four" of President Truman's inaugural speech. Truman had proposed that representatives of "backward countries" receive the benefits of American scientific advances and industrial progress. Moses Michael Coady was now playing with fire, entering into an alliance with rabid anti-communists. Not surprisingly, Coady adopted anti-communist rhetoric in an attempt to persuade state department officials to accept the co-operative blueprint. He told the officials that the non-denominational Antigonish Movement had struck a major blow to communism in the Maritime provinces, and that the Movement had spread to Haiti, Jamaica and Australia, and parts of Maine, Ohio, Kentucky, Michigan and North Carolina.[61] *The Ottawa Citizen* reported that, if Coady had his way, "Canadian experience will be heeded in the development of backward areas of the world promised by Truman."[62]

Coady used the same anti-communist line in his appeal to Stewart Bates, Deputy Minister of Fisheries, for continued support for Extension work among the fishermen.

> We are demonstrating here in this perfect social laboratory of the Maritime provinces how people of different racial origins, languages and religious beliefs can get along harmoniously together. We are showing in a democratic way how they can improve their economic and social status in the world. Canada, in addition to making its fundamental contribution to fight communism in other parts of the world, could do nothing better than give this demonstration at home.[63]

Coady was offering the Antigonish project to the leaders of the free world as an antidote to that "hideous thing" called communism. He was also skating on thin ice, pushing the Antigonish Movement on the world without solid evidence of its transforming effects. In fact, from the harsh retrospective of history, the Antigonish Movement had really run out of steam and energy by the late 1940s.

In March 1949, Coady was back in the United States for meetings in Boston and Washington. He met with a newly formed group known as the International Friends of the Antigonish Movement, with headquarters at 30 E. 22nd Street, New York. They wanted to raise $935,000 to train fieldworkers and others in St. Francis Xavier methods in order to launch a counteroffensive to militant communism in parts of the United States, the West Indies, South America and other depressed areas. Coady's old friend, Benson Y. Landis, was secretary of the New York branch of the Friends of the Antigonish Movement. At the invitation of Willard Thorp, assistant secretary in charge of Economic Affairs in Washington, Coady, Dr. H.J. Somers, vice-president of St. Francis Xavier, and Wallace Campbell, co-director of the Washington office of the Co-operative League of the USA, met with seven members of the staff of the state department responsible for the development of the president's program. The press reported Coady as saying that the Antigonish program embodied the "formula which can save many areas of the world from the depressed state which faced the Maritimes twenty years ago." Communism could be uprooted by "increasing the standard of living and the morale of the people through a positive program of democratic action."[64] Coady knew he was "engaged in a pretty big, tough proposition, but it is coming. I was before the State Department last week in Washington telling them that we had the formula for the rehabilitation of the depressed areas of the earth. We really have this and they probably recognize it."[65] A utopian co-operator such as Roy Bergengren believed that St. Francis Xavier had found the "golden key which has unlocked unsuspected human capital for self improvement." The Antigonish Movement had "set a light–a blazing light, fed from the fires of freedom, to show us all the way to that finer democracy which will, by its service, banish communism."[66] In the end, nothing much came of Coady's gallant attempts to influence his detested "vested interests" in a co-operative direction.

In June 1949, the Cold War warrior, flying the white banner of freedom, held numerous meetings in Saskatchewan (a public meeting in Hotel Saskatchewan in Regina, an official opening of the Regina Co-operative School, attendance at Farmer-Labour-Teacher Institute at the Qu'Appelle Valley Centre). He was hugely applauded at the public meeting in Regina for his clarion call to "stabilize this world against revolution and other ugly things…. If we don't, we shall have instability and perhaps social tornadoes as long as there are unfulfilled legitimate desires for better living."[67] From Saskatchewan, Coady travelled to the United States to attend the summer conference of co-operative personnel at Lake Geneva, Wisconsin, from July 12-15. In late August, Dr. Coady appeared before the United Nations (U.N.). The world was now focused on this fearless, rough man who had risen from obscurity to speak at a U.N. podium. His speech, "Organizing Rural People for the proper use and conservation of Natural Resources," was one of his most sagacious.

It is not certain exactly when Moses Coady became preoccupied with conservation. From his childhood days in the lovely Margaree Valley, Coady had loved the natural world. He knew its intricacies and appreciated its delights. He enjoyed the simple joys of berry picking with his staff and friends and horseback riding up through the wooded hills around his old homestead. In the late 1940s, Coady began to sound alarm bells about the way human beings were sinning against nature. He believed that thoughtless agricultural practices were poisoning the Annapolis Valley. He observed longstanding, careless practices in the fishery. He didn't think that people were eating properly and began pushing organic methods of farming and co-operative medical practices. Coady began to link physical fitness with the very future of Western civilization. When the Movement's spirit started to wane, he blamed the people's absence of energy for their reluctance to put the co-operative blueprint into practice.

In his important speech to the U.N., Coady pressed beyond the conventional wisdom of the day. It also revealed the way Coady's view of the "man-universe relationship" did not break radically with the classic model of man as subject and nature as object. Like most other Christian thinkers, Coady was radically anthropocentric in perception, unable to valorize all creatures' right to exist for their own sake. Coady called for a "proper appraisal" of humankind's relation to the universe, but the non-human other was still a "resource object" for humankind.

> It is in the very nature of things that the earth and the fullness thereof is for Man. Natural resources, therefore, fulfil their purpose when they minister to human life on earth. This is their manifest destiny, so to speak. Proper use and not abuse is, therefore, the rational and hence, scientific way of exploring and developing Nature. This should immediately dictate to us the wisdom of, first, consuming at the rate of "holding out" in those things such as minerals, that are exhausted with use and cannot be replaced, and second, replenishing wherever possible the materials that are destroyed by use. This is the positive side of the picture and lays the foundation for the proper use and conservation of the resources of the earth.

Coady still thought of "nature" as subservient to "Man," as an object to be used and exploited. At the beginning of our own century, with nature almost irreparably degraded, feminists and ecologists are crying out for a revolution of human sensibility: human beings must learn to relate to the natural world as subject to subject. Coady might have come round to this position, and his linking of ownership and caring is worth considering.

Coady believed that humankind had sinned grievously against nature, and listed three reasons for this to those assembled. First, humankind was simply ignorant of the "fundamental sciences of biology, chemistry and physics." The desertification of many parts of the world revealed humankind's stupidity. Second, Coady linked the masses' lack of ownership with their uncaring attitude towards nature. "Tenancy, share-cropping, the emergence of a rural proletariat, and the landlordism that is still so widespread, have all tended to make the masses of the world's people feel that they have no stake in the world. The good earth was not theirs and why should they care?" Third, and finally, Coady identified the "false motives" of those who "explored and developed" nature, driven by the profit-motive and greed. "No scientific development of natural resources is possible," Coady proclaimed, poignantly for our time, "under the dynamics of such a motive; greed will drive out reason." Unless restrained, power-mad individuals would "cut down every last tree in the world, dig out all the precious metal of the earth, and destroy all the fish in the sea, to add to the glory of their passing day." Moving on to familiar conceptual ground, Coady urged the assembled to

> find a formula by which the undeveloped masses of the world's people, who have heretofore never had any interest, ownership or control of the good things of the earth, may be capable of the task. The problem, in a word, is to find a programme that will bring the undeveloped people of the earth up the road to progress to the point where they can own and control the earth—their earth—and become "masters of their own destiny."

Coady offered a "double-barrelled programme" of "spiritual enlivenment and mental enlightenment" for the "right use and conservation of natural resources." There was the requisite formula, carved out of the perplexities of life and revealing Coady's simple idealism. The self-assured prophet told the U.N. delegates that one could only tackle the "education of the people" by regions or zones. He thought that given zones had common economic, social and political problems. This supplied a "natural unit for education purposes. The zone should be large enough to be significant, and small enough to be manageable. Education action on a national scale comes from a federation of zones. Federation of national movements gives us a programme on an international scale."

Coady constructed the bridge between carrying on economic activities in simple economic organizations and care for the natural world. When rural people had a complete unit for handling and processing all of their commodities for the markets of the world, they were forced to learn the "scientific use of raw materials and their conservation. This is for the simple reason that they have their money invested in their own materials. These plants will be useless to them if they run out of raw materials." Coady was straining to find a way to break with capitalist logic. Capitalist industrialism severed the integrity of ownership and a caring sensibility; the co-operative organizational form could transform adult's perspective on the natural world. Rural people would realize the "absolute necessity of a wide scientific knowledge of land, plants, animals, and the processes by which they are made available to the consumers of the world." It was impossible, Coady insisted, to

> long conserve our fisheries, forest or lands, if the great bulk of the human race have only an indirect interest in doing so. On the other hand, it is almost certain that the sense of responsibility that comes from ownership, and the ability to use the products of the earth for the elevation of the great masses of the people will make them jealous guardians of Mother Earth. We are finding in Eastern Canada, especially with the fishermen, that as the people take over the co-operative development of the fisheries, there is no need for a great police force to prevent poaching and other undesirable practices of the former days.

If the people were given a chance "to call the earth their own, everything else will take care of itself." Coady had a blinding faith that co-operative forms of economic organization could replace the instrumental view of nature as resources awaiting exploitation. Only when the earth's common people experienced the "joy of living" would they become "jealous of their natural resources, their earth; they will have vested interest in Mother Earth and will fight to defend it."

Coady concluded his speech rhapsodically.

> In a really friendly world, built up by such activity on the part of the people, they will come to the conclusion that, after all, the resources of any part of the earth are in a sense the resources of all the people. True, the people of a given nation will own and control the products within their own territories, but let us hope that the day can truly come when a Swiss can say with real truth that he is proud of his diamonds in South Africa, his oil and rubber in the East Indies, his cotton in the U.S., and his fruit in the tropical countries. We hope further that the time will come when all people will look upon these things as their own, because they really are the products of their earth, which under an enlightened programme of education and economic development will really some day become One World.

One senses that Coady was looking beyond existent colonial relationships of exploitation in the Third World, but this unfortunate passage reveals a deep-seated Western ethnocentrism and naivety. All of the commodities Coady mentioned were products of colonial exploitation, resulting from the violent subjugation of the peoples in South Africa and other lands. Coady appears to have assumed that he could hinge the Antigonish blueprint to the "foreign policy" of the United States as the means to create his one world. However, the United States' geo-political purpose in the post-war world was to ensure that the world remained safe for the exertion of their corporate and political power.

Coady's dream of the common people owning the earth was a fantastical utopia, with no realistic chance of fulfilment in Canada or the far corners of the earth. Coady's bloodless co-operative revolution relied on organization, enlightenment and education. He clung to the force of ideas in a world where power proceeded mainly from the barrels of guns. Indeed, Coady's nemeses, communist revolutionaries such as Mao Zedong, understood that violent political action was the way to blast apart feudal orders and clear the path for the masses to gain a stake in the world.

In the early 1950s, Coady seemed to be desperately searching for ways to stop the Antigonish Movement from sliding. He had little interest in becoming a prophet of decline. One idea that he had mulled over for many years still appeared to have life. To give lie to the old idea that "people can't save their souls in the cities," Coady recommended taking people out of "attics of slum areas in the cities and putting them on plots of ground." He imagined this would "off-set the monotonous dehumanizing effects of modern industrial towns." He also wanted to discourage "rural boys and girls from going to college for the next thirty years." Others could go to college, but

> let us build up our human stock on the farms, in the fishing villages and in the towns, and in fifty years we will have a great human bank that will enable us to build a great civilization. Sending our rural boys and girls to college now is certainly routing them away from our Maritime communities and defeating our whole effort. Those boys and girls who are unmistakably marked by God for certain vocations should go to College, of course, but we should try to impress the other philosophy on our people and show them that the second way is perhaps the best way to serve God in our time.[68]

Coady is plainly distressed at the Movement's failure to usher in the new, permanent co-operative order. The Movement's educational processes have neither succeeded in rooting out pessimistic cultural attitudes nor precipitated a sufficiently profound transformation of Maritime economic and social life. Sensing this, Coady made a rather reckless suggestion. He imagined that rural kids could be kept on the farms, free from the corrupting influences of the city and the university. Confined to the farm for thirty years, they could then reproduce a race fit to build a great civilization. This was not Moses Coady at his best.

Criticizing his own profession, the clergy, Coady told Fathers Gillis, D.F. Roberts, D.E. MacDonald and Frank MacIsaac that priests ought not be "dictator, a big stick man, the manager, board of directors, supervisory committee, auditor, and everything else of every co-operative." The priest's role was primarily to "lend his moral support, to help in all co-operative activities, through laymen, in organizing and educating the people." It wasn't a good idea for priests to attend conferences as delegates of the people. "Everything should come by free resolution from the people themselves. If he is a good educator and a good psychologist he can help nature and speed up the development of the people. The people cannot be built up unless they are permitted to function and come under their own steam." He also believed that priests were not focused adequately on essentials. He wanted to come away from an upcoming clergy conference with a clear agenda for the next thirty years.

> We will not try to do many things and thus fritter away our time and energies and money on activities that, however good they may be, can afford to wait or that will come, naturally, in any case when the main things are done. My whole thought is that schools, churches, social institutions, without people, have no meaning.

Coady wanted his friends to consider these things

> so that in this diocese we may have a growing body of men who will give us a great civilization. We must believe with a terrible belief.... If we were communists, we would be probably putting out our last dollar and every ounce of energy in propagating that ideology. How is it that we can't work up a holy enthusiasm and fanaticism for the only one true ideology? Solve that one.[69]

CHAPTER 9

Land of Moab (1952-1959)

I

Moses Michael Coady retired from the directorship of St. Francis Xavier University Extension Department in February 1952, just five months before his seventieth birthday. Though his body was wracked by pain and scarred from many an operation, Coady still glowed incandescently from the flame that had lighted his soul in the 1920s. In the last years of his life, Coady wrote countless letters to family and friends, gave speeches, participated in some backroom strategizing and compiled notes and chapters for his final book. He had not stopped dreaming, but this crusader had to set his suitcase aside. Shadowed by melancholy and despondency, he entered into a more pensive mood as he tried to sum up his life accomplishments.

Shortly after his retirement announcement, the accolades praising Monsignor Coady's deeds poured in to St. Francis Xavier University. These congratulations must have buoyed his spirits as educators, political scientists, co-operative thinkers and activists, Church leaders, and all manner of accomplished persons recalled how Coady had touched and influenced their lives. Stanley Hamilton of the Rural Life Association of Indiana took Coady back fourteen years to the great Rural and Industrial Conference of 1938: "It was on that visit that we became acquainted with Fr. Ligutti, Dorothy Day, Fr. Tompkins and many others. You not only showed us democracy at work with the grassroots or little people doing the work but you let us in on the techniques." Old co-operative comrade Benson Y. Landis of the National Council of the Churches of Christ told Coady that he appreciated the "spiritual quality that you have shown—your genuine friendliness and sympathetic insights, your spreading confidence and plain good humour, your exemplification of all that religion high and true means in human life." Morris Mitchell of the Putney Graduate School of Teacher Education confessed that for years he had "looked northward to Nova Scotia when I have most wanted to feel a sense of light in the darkness of our over-shadowed times. In driving once from Antigonish I looked back and saw with singular clarity the beautiful Aurora Borealis. That light seemed a symbol of the spirit of your leadership of the Antigonish Movement." Long-time co-operative philosopher James Warbasse believed that Coady "exemplified the soul of indomitable youth; and your spirit, uncompromised by time, goes on, spreading itself wider and wider from every spot wherever you touched the lives of men." The names of many of the movers and shakers of the international co-operative movement are recorded touchingly in a hand-bound book lodged permanently in the archives. Mary Arnold, Roy Bergengren, E.R. Bowen, J. Henry Carpenter, King Gordon and many more sang the praises of this co-operative warrior.[1]

Coady reflected playfully on his moment in the sun and on his physical condition in a letter to his brother Joe's daughter, Teresa, on March 7, 1952, while in St. Martha's Hospital.

> My resignation from the Extension Department has called forth a lot of eulogies which, of course, a man of my modesty and stability does not notice at all. One has to survey the passing scene, however. I wanted to consult the doctors there [in Halifax] about my gallstones, which were the immediate cause, I think, of my attack. I knew for three years that I had nine gallstones.... They put me on a very rigid diet for four weeks and I knocked off over twenty pounds. I am getting good looking again–but I am feeling really wonderfully well. The only thing wrong with me is that the rhythm of my heart is destroyed. I had this before but got back on the rails.

Coady thought that nothing could stop Extension now. It was going in a

> tremendous way. I told the Bishop one day when I was very sick that I was surely going to die before long because I could sincerely say like St. Simeon what he said when the Blessed Virgin presented the Child Jesus in the temple. Realizing by Divine intuition that this was the Messiah, he burst out into the canticle: "Now Thou dost dismiss thy servant, O Lord, according to thy word in peace: because my eyes have seen thy salvation, which thou has prepared before the face of all peoples: a light of revelation to the Gentiles and a glory for thy people Israel."

Having retired, Coady thought he was "going to enjoy life now, free from the top things, which for the last years I was not doing very well in any case, and having an opportunity of doing the things that I like and perhaps, if the health lasts, have a new phase of my career at this business."[2]

On the same day, Coady made fun of himself in a letter to Mrs. Mary Coady. A "fellow never knows how popular he is until he is about to die–but I have been used to this so long that my hat fits the same as usual." However, he was "glad of one thing, that this year the Extension has come to the point where there is not much possibility of its ever failing."[3] Coady may have resided in the land of Moab, but he thought his Joshua, the taciturn Father M.J. MacKinnon, had the puissance to lead the co-operative band into the promised land. However, MacKinnon, while respected by his fellow-priests for his judicious judgements, would not be able to sustain Extension's relationship with the fisheries through the 1950s, nor revive its sagging fortunes.

Coady was affected by the demise of Father Jimmy, whose candle was flickering in the winds of dementia. On May 22, 1952, Coady reported that Tompkins "is not very much worse than he was for five years but he has no continuity of thought. He knows his friends temporarily. He has, as you know, hardening of the arteries of the brain, and is not capable of carrying on a conversation or doing any reading. He is gradually getting smaller."[4] Coady was not given to sentimental outpourings, but it pained him deeply to see this man who had once had a razor-sharp mind reduced to a little bundle of bones. Coady figured that Tompkins had simply burned himself out in the late 1940s—he "read too much, talked too much, was agitated too much."[5] Though Tompkins' end was rather sad, Coady knew that this would "never obscure the brilliance of his performance. He will be remembered as he was, an outstanding pioneer whose achievements speak for themselves."[6] Tompkins spent his last days in St. Martha's Hospital. He died in 1953, the centenary year of the Extension Department that he had urged into existence.

In mid-summer of 1952, Coady was experiencing yet another time of well-being. He wrote Sister Frances Dolores, who had worked so brilliantly with Tompkins in Reserve Mines in the late 1940s, that he was "feeling wonderfully well. As a matter of fact, yesterday was the best day in a dozen years. I read the manuscript till 11:30 last night and felt like a fighting cock. I guess it's the strawberries and salmon." Typically, once Coady felt a little better, off he went to a meeting. "I am going to Halifax for a Fishermen's Loan Board meeting a week from today.... We are witnessing real revolutions happen before our very eyes."[7] Coady continued to be enraptured with Extension's success into mid-August. We are "almost sure of final success," he proclaimed to E.R. Bowen of the Co-operative League of the USA.[8] However, early in September, the Canadian co-operative movement learned that one of their own revolutionaries, A.B. MacDonald, was dying of lung cancer. "I am going to Ottawa on Thursday to see A.B. who is dying with cancer of the lung. He has only a few weeks to live. I am also going to Ottawa for September 28 to speak at a College there."[9] Coady's response to MacDonald's impending death almost seemed matter-of-fact. Everyone had to die one day; life flowed ever onward; what mattered was the working out of divine purpose in the eternal scheme of things. Still, movements need leaders and when they lose a great one, the movement suffers.

No one could match A.B. MacDonald's commitment to the building of a people's economy in Canada and everywhere else. He had begun working for the Co-operative Union of Canada (CUC) in the early 1940s, and the fire that burned in the youthful visionary organizer had remained undiminished throughout the decade. Like other co-operators across Canada, MacDonald had wanted to gain control over the insurance business. By the end of the war, co-operative insurance companies had been formed in Ontario and Saskatchewan. A.B. had assisted the Saskatchewan co-operative life insurance company in gaining a charter in 1947. He was excited about building a national fire and casualty company. At the 1949

Congress of the CUC, a committee consisting of MacDonald and several others was appointed to investigate the future of a national co-operative insurance program. This committee faced the vexing problem of decline in the unity within the Canadian Movement.

By maintaining a frenzied schedule of meetings across the country during the winter of 1949-1950, MacDonald had kept the dream of a fire and casualty company alive. The Union's leaders had believed that the Movement could only flourish if it had access to its own capital. They had sought to build an integrated system that could be entirely self-financing with the resources to develop new co-operative ventures. They had known the co-op movement lacked capital and that the co-op housing sector needed funds. Sadly, to realize this dream of a people's economy, the CUC needed more resources that it had. It also needed much stronger and vital provincial organizations. The Saskatchewan union had been the most successful, producing educational literature, films and other activities. Other provincial organizations had insufficient funds, inconsistent leadership and often indifferent support from many of the commercial co-operatives. The base had been simply too weak, and the CUC could not prosper.

In September 1952, A.B. MacDonald died of cancer. On his death bed, he had been awarded an honorary doctorate; he ought to have received a "Doctorate of Organizing." His funeral in Heatherton, Nova Scotia, was a luminous occasion, attended by hundreds of religious and community activists and co-operators. In his eulogy, published in *The Casket* on September 18, 1952, Moses Coady proclaimed:

> As a brilliant Scot who had come up the hard way, from a tough Nova Scotia farm, many of the old line professions of law, engineering, medicine, and business, might naturally be expected to beckon him on to build an economic empire for himself. But he threw this all over for the more arduous, uncertain and what our elders likely thought foolish field of trying to build an economic empire of little people in Canada, and all over the world. He never got big money for himself, it is true, but in a short life time, he won a name among the hundreds of millions of people who are members of the vast empire of co-operative societies.

Another old friend, the Rev. J.A. Murphy from Prince Edward Island, lauded MacDonald's "magnetic personality" and unrivalled ability to teach.

> His many audiences, small and large, will long remember his apt illustrations, his enthusiasm and his constructive line of action to make the world a better place in which to live. He could break up a hostile camp and make them his friends. I worked with him during the lean 1930s and always found him the genial AB, the loyal friend, the big-hearted man who gave his best to help his fellow man to help themselves.

One by one, the big-hearted dreamers, the first generation of male Movement activists, were exiting from the battlefield. Three months before MacDonald's death, on June 9, 1952, the co-operative movement had lost A.S. MacIntyre. MacIntyre had spent his entire life fighting the vested interests and labouring for the common people until his life force simply drained out. Like the other big men, MacIntyre had worked feverishly in the post-World War II era to create a unified co-operative movement. In 1946, he told a group of social workers in Nova Scotia that "we are surrounded by rivalries and contending factions, and the great danger is that these differences will hinder our social progress and that our energies will be dissipated in petty squabbles. We need some unifying force, and co-operation supplies that force." He poured energy into establishing a co-operative medical plan for Nova Scotia, and worked with the Newfoundland Department of Fisheries and Co-operatives for a time in 1949.

In 1949, St. Francis Xavier University honoured A.S. MacIntyre by granting an honorary master of arts degree to this unschooled man. The university, which was also honouring H.H. Hannam, Stephen J. MacKinnon and Roy Bergengren, celebrated MacIntyre's

> fine spirit of sincerity, loyalty and love of justice which characterized him as a trade unionist while vice-president of the UMWA. In the various positions of trust which he has filled, whether president of the Nova Scotia Credit Union League, field worker for the Extension Department, or managing director of the Nova Scotia Co-operative Union, Mr. MacIntyre has striven continuously to uphold the Xaverian motto "Whatsover things are true."

On the day of his funeral, MacIntyre was to have spoken at the annual conference of the Nova Scotia co-operative store managers. Many of the Maritimes' great co-operators were in attendance at the funeral–W.H. MacEwan of Maritime Co-operative Services, R.J. MacSween of the Nova Scotia Department of Agriculture, J.H. MacKichan, general manager of the United Maritime Fishermen (UMF), and S.J. MacKinnon, who had attended the first People's School in 1921. His active pallbearers were mainly men from his beloved Reserve Mines. Some of his priest comrades, such as M.J. MacKinnon, Dr. Dan MacCormack, Bishop John R. MacDonald and Moses Coady, were also there. If they had listened closely, they might have heard his words of six years before echoing in St. Ninian's Cathedral: "Yes, you are your brother's keeper, for you can have neither security nor lasting happiness here unless you walk hand in hand with him along the road of universal brotherhood."

The bodies of these great men may simply have worn out in the service of building the people's economy. MacIntyre had gone into the pits at a very early age and he suffered the consequences of coal dust, poor food and poverty. Tompkins simply agitated too much. MacDonald never stopped organizing and constantly smoked. Coady's body also bore the marks of his feverish activity. His early heavy drinking, smoking and love of rich food did little to sustain his health.

Coady had decided, it seems, to use whatever healthy moments he had left to serve the co-op movement in some way or another. In November

1952, Coady believed he was well enough to travel to Chicago for the congress of the Co-op League. On his way, he made three speeches in Halifax and three more in London, Ontario. However, he then became ill with a gallstone attack and ended up in St. Michael's Hospital in Toronto. The doctors couldn't operate, and once again Coady had to seek money to pay hospital expenses. The Bishop of London gave Coady $200 to defray costs.[10] At the end of the poignant and excruciating year of 1952, Coady was once again back in Antigonish nursing his wounds.

II

Coady's retirement from the directorship of the St. Francis Xavier University Extension Department freed him from the persistent, nagging troubles of negotiating Extension's place in the constellation of the diversifying co-op movement. Coady spent a good deal of his time writing letters. In these letters Coady could strip off some of his ecclesiastical garments, and step momentarily out of his role as the famous director. He could let his hair down and relax a little. He could enjoy the everyday delights of food, gossip, the weather, the progress of clan members. He could get involved in heated family disputes over land. Yet Coady was actually a busybody and fusspot, and he could never quite free himself from the priestly uncle role. Like a country pharmacist, he dispensed his advice tablets to all around. This man seemed to have a blueprint for everything, from the best type of underwear to use (Stanfield's woollens), the kind of stockings (nylons) smart young women should wear and the proper method of defeating athlete's foot (boil the socks).

Coady's preoccupation with how others comported themselves was in accord with his own fastidiousness about dress. Coady's hats had to be immaculately blocked and his shoes spit-and-polish clean. Coady liked fine physical specimens, strong character and moral seriousness. He derided men who were effeminate. In an unpublished reflection on leadership, Coady ruminated that

> many men destroy their leadership through vanity. This is the sissy, this is the man who gives too much attention to his person. His hair is overdone; he exudes the odour of perfumes and ointments; he is too prim and set. He is the man who does his face with noxzema before he goes to bed and even resorts to powder and rouge. His idea of beauty is that of the pretty standardized women. He would be better advised to have a careless unstudied cleanliness and order in his dress and personality. Nobody likes a male sissy, not even a woman. A leader is a man's man.[11]

He valued proper speech, and instructed his clan members on proper pronunciation. There was more than a modicum of old-fashioned, rigid, masculinist, Victorian quality to this complicated man.

Coady fussed continuously over his health and diet. He became an animated advocate of organic food and the healthy diet. He hoped that

The favourite clergymen of militant atheists and calmer agnostics.

Coady fought for the co-operative movement through enormous
pain and sickness.

The Antigonish Movement caught the imagination of people throughout the world.

Coady laid to rest by a steelworker, a miner, two farmers and two fishermen.

members of his extended family would not become "cornflake Coadys," and was relieved to learn that his family were eating breakfasts of good, substantial oatmeal porridge. A bit of a hypochondriac, Coady's post-retirement letters are a sad tale of a body that was grinding to a halt. Like an old, but much beloved, car that gradually falls apart, Coady's body seemed to be wearing out one piece at a time. In 1938 Coady had had his first major coronary attack, after which he wasn't particularly well. In February 1952, he had another huge heart attack, which effectively finished his directorship. Coady's enjoyment of his retirement activities would be constantly punctuated by extremely painful breakdowns of his weary body.

Shortly after his heart attack in February 1952, Coady had troubles with his gall bladder. He was confined to bed for three weeks.[12] By May he was suffering from gallstones, and feeling rather miserable. By December, he had been struck down again by another gallstone attack. In May 1953, Coady suffered another heart attack and was in an Amherst hospital for seventeen days. In late October, Coady was operated on in New York. "I had kidney trouble coming on for many years,"[13] he confided to Chris Tompkins and his wife. Shortly after his operation, Coady suffered from congestion on his lungs. He informed friends that the "doctor visited me and fixed me up with penicillin, and I am up today—for no other reason than to tire myself out so that I can sleep in the night and avoid the awful sciatica pain and the pain in my right kidney that I am suffering since I came home." Coady informed them that he was getting "ready for the big event that will come sooner or later. I have confidence, however, that I am going to live this thing out and carry on for a while yet."[14] He was right.

Still, his physical troubles persisted. In October 1954, Coady was in New York to see his doctors and also in Boston for a visit with his eye specialist.[15] A month later, his long-suffering niece Teresa heard yet another tale of his health woes. "Last Sunday I took the chills again, likely from the new anti-biotic I was taking along with other pills. I called up Dr. Grace in New York yesterday and told him about it. He advised me to cut out everything for awhile. My hemorrhages are cleared up and I guess I'll be all right."[16] He was not "all right" for long. Coady wrote his troubled protégé Leo Coady from the Halifax Infirmary on January 13, 1955, that he was "going to be operated on the first of the week. They say I will come through with it but if I don't, I die happy in the thought that my blueprinting is being realized much more surely than I ever had any right to expect."[17] Toward the year's end, Coady was suffering from shortness of breath. He had travelled to the United States for Bergengren's funeral on November 14, but the trip was so difficult for him that he came back from Montreal by train, collapsing after saying mass.[18] In early December, Coady summed up his health to Ursula Tompkins.

I have had it rough from a physical point of view during the last two and half years. I have had several serious surgical operations and have a slow malignancy which, thank God, they say will not kill quickly. I am retired now for nearly four years and I live here in my old quarters, making the occasional speech and doing some writing. I am nearly 74 years old but if my strength keeps up, I will be able to do a lot of things before I die…. However, I have no regrets. I had my day and I had a go at a good many things, which, thank God, have turned out to be more successful than I had any right to expect. I am proud of what I did in organizing the teachers, bringing a new kind of philosophy to the rural communities by the school in Margaree and later by the organization of the fishermen and the adult education movement which ultimately will prove to be of even greater significance than we have dreamed about.[19]

At the end of December, Coady revealed that illness had also attacked his rectum. "I had a severe pain in my lower rectum where I was operated on and it looked serious…. In the last three days I got clear of this pain and there is good hope that I will be all right again."[20] Coady never lost hope that he could bounce back and stay around for a little time yet.

In 1956, his old physical troubles persisted and a few new ones were added. He wrote Mrs. John MacKinnon on March 6, 1956, from the hospital where he had been confined for six days. His body may have been giving out, but not his gallows humour.

I was suffering from shortness of breath, as I told you in a former letter, and the doctor found long ago that it was due to anemia. My blood was only 60% normal. He took me in here and I have already had four blood transfusions–Scotch blood at that. I have another coming up tomorrow. You may be sure that I will be growing more and more circumspect about my financial dealings in the future with all this Scotch blood in me.[21]

In April, Coady enjoyed an interlude from his pain. He told Joe Morris that he

felt exceptionally well after I came back here–said Mass every day and did not feel too much the old weakness and shortness of breath. With the coming of spring I think I will snap out of the whole thing. I feel a great ambition to go to work…. I felt the cold weather somewhat but suffered no ill effects–in fact, the experience gave me a new pep and life. Then our long conversations on social philosophy were a great inspiration to me.[22]

Coady managed to squeeze some pleasure in between his bouts of physical suffering. He had been up to Moncton, and along the way, on the other side of Pugwash,

we stopped and enjoyed your lunch. The coffee was wonderful–the smoked oysters, biscuits and date cake, too…. I have been feeling better since I came back. I guess my trip with you people, although I did perhaps too much moaning about my ills, did me a world of good. I was up bright and early every morning to say Mass without feeling any weakness and I am getting better every day.[23]

Coady was not feeling very well in the summer of 1956. He was having "severe pain in his back–kidney region or gall bladder" and wanted to get to "some warmer part of the North American continent during the coming winter."[24] However, his choice of San Antonio, Texas, was ill-fated. He arrived in Boston after Christmas, where he went to New York for six hours to see Dr. Grace, and after which he flew to San Antonio. Although he had a nice room there in a home for the aged, the climate did not suit him and he had more health troubles. He called Dr. Grace, and then flew back to Brooklyn where he was given a cystoscopic the day after he arrived. After more surgery, he remained in Brooklyn for three weeks. He then flew back to Halifax, trying to reach home, but he collapsed near Truro. He was taken back to Halifax, where he stayed for one week, and then to Antigonish, where he stayed in his room for six weeks. He did not say Mass for three months.

However, by the end of March 1957, Coady had perked up. He was saying Mass and gave a speech over the radio as honorary chair of the new Eastern Co-operative Services (ECS). Coady was absolutely convinced that establishing the ECS was the "biggest forward step we ever took in Eastern Nova Scotia."[25]

Coady struggled along until May 1958, contending with bouts of flu, an irregular heart beat and problems with his eyes (a cataract). In fact, one photograph of the day captures him at the podium, with a patch over one eye on his thin face, addressing a co-operative rally in Wisconsin. Coady had managed to travel to Madison, Wisconsin, to speak at the Credit Union National Association meeting on May 8, 1958. Coady shared the story of what then happened to him with Sara MacEachern on June 2, 1958. "In the middle of my speech to more than a thousand people, my heart gave way and I collapsed and was carried out on a stretcher. Fortunately, my speech has been mimeographed and they passed around a thousand copies of it. I got across some good sections of it but I am afraid I was halting and laboring in the doing of it." Coady was taken to a nearby military hospital, anointed, and then taken to St. Mary's Hospital, where he was revived by oxygen.

> This all happened on Saturday morning, beginning at 9:00 a.m. I was out on Sunday morning and back to my hotel. I remained for the next few days to attend a conference of the CUNA staff at a beautiful hotel at a lake sixty miles from Madison. The doctors warned me to go home in stages. I stayed, as a consequence, two days in Boston. Christena met me at the station and I saw both of them together several times. Christena is doing awfully well and I guess Katherine is too.

But Coady was home for only three days when another old trouble, prostatic, struck him in "what looked like to be a very serious way." He went back to Halifax for ten more days in the Infirmary.[26]

Coady knew that he was nearing the end of his earthly sojourn. On June 3, he informed Sister Edna Marie that he had talked to her dying father about how one prepared for death. Coady, the Christian priest, found solace in the belief that we in our old age and our sickness will not only get forgiveness for our sins but we also will be helped in our physical infirmities. Through the anointing of the human body by the oils of Extreme Unction our souls are purified and made fit for immediate entry to the Beatific Vision and in many cases we are cured of our illness and recover. This is the Faith that lifts man from the low status of animality to something a little less than the angels.[27]

Coady remained rather unwell throughout the summer and managed to give only a few speeches. By November 1958, he was receiving many blood transfusions. His misery was alleviated a little by visits with Leo, Mary Ellen, Teresa and others. Coady told Carmel Coady that he had asked her mother to send him two roast chickens and a piece of nice pork. "I had a yearning for these things which I used to enjoy so much in the old days at your mother's and Mary Ellen's. Your mother went through all kinds of trouble to cook them for me that Sunday morning before the folks left."[28]

Coady's immune system was now wearing thin. In 1959, he seemed to have continual influenza, and the medics were rushing him to and from the hospital. After one transfusion, he told Teresa that he had perked up, and was "already hard at work on my book, sleeves rolled up and loins girded and a glint in the eye. If I can live until Christmas, I should have it pretty well under way."[29] In May 1959, for the first time in his long life, his stomach gave out. He was nauseated, unable to eat, and his heart was enlarging. He had only three months to live and would not see another Christmas.

III

During his post-retirement days, Moses Coady was deeply entangled in the life of his Margaree clan. He was constantly dispensing advice about matters of property, working his way through the intricacies of his family's dynamics without hurting too many tender feelings. No relationship illustrates the depth of his attachment to his clan more than the one he shared with Leo Coady. Coady loved Leo like the son he never had. He had begun encouraging the young Leo to make something of his life in the mid-1940s. As Leo grew to manhood, married Mary and produced ten children (four sets of twins), the burdens on Leo to gain property, manage a prosperous farm and raise his family were very weighty. As well, Uncle Coady had chosen Leo as his stand-in for the Margaree Valley, which placed grave responsibility on him, and left his uncle open to considerable anguish.

Moses Coady wanted Leo to succeed financially, to make a go of it in the rural countryside. He wanted Leo to comport himself responsibly and raise his children as pious Catholics. He also wanted Leo to raise the white flag of the co-operative movement. From his late teens, Leo had received numerous bits of advice and lists of must-read books from his uncle. This advice continued into Leo's twenties and thirties. On October 18, 1955, Coady urged Leo to wear woollen underwear; his father, Whistling Mick, had, and so should he. He then encouraged Leo to "have a book to carry around in your pocket to take down statistics and startling things that you hear from speeches or read as you go through life. You could have a large book which you transfer, under appropriate headings all this data."[30] Leo's book would no doubt assist the self-improvement process. On September 14, 1956, Coady offered Leo a "little bit of general wisdom." He wanted Leo to avoid conflict with personalities in his public utterances.

> If you think about it seriously, you can always find a way to put across your idea without incriminating anybody. There is no need of naming anybody for whatever unsatisfactory situation you're condemning. The remedy, the scheme, the doctrine, the subject of your conversation should be far enough in the abstract so as not to incriminate anybody. A man can get away with some slashing for a little while but in the long run the man who uses incriminations and specifically names his opponent loses his prestige and his ability to influence the people with whom he comes in conflict. This is the best wisdom I know.[31]

This was sound advice, based on hard lessons learned by a rough Irish farm boy from the sticks who had had plenty of enemies of his own as he fought his way onto the world stage.

Coady was very much at home, priest that he was, in telling Leo and his wife how to raise pious and moral children. Coady told Mary that each child should have statuettes of their patron saints in their rooms and a grotto of the Little Flower. Coady also thought that the children should have tasks assigned to them (much like modern parents do, though usually with little success). Coady and the intellectual leaders of the Antigonish Movement had fought for decades to create an enlightened rural civilization. One can easily see this passion in Coady's instructions to Leo and his wife.

> This question of the beautification of the home and facilities for culture will lift the rising generation out of the awful quagmire of enjoying rough dances in dirty halls where they have to drink rum and moonshine to get them into the mood to enjoy themselves…. Cars and cabins are the great danger spots for our modern civilization. It is going to be some problem to save young girls, and boys, too, from moral contamination in the world that lies immediately ahead of us.[32]

Coady couldn't endure the thought of Leo and Mary's children being lured into the seductive world of cars, cabins and rock and roll.

No one understands fully what compels men and women to turn to alcohol to deal with life's burdens, but both Moses and Leo Coady did so. The correspondence between Moses and Leo opens a fascinating window on Coady's attitude towards alcohol. He never quite openly confesses to Leo that he had drowned his own sorrows in alcohol, but this is implicit in his denunciations. On January 13, 1955, while in the Halifax Infirmary, Coady reminded Leo that he had a "unique opportunity … of building for yourself a great career…. In my concept you should be a businessman—not a landlord but a man who has the ability and the character of helping settle the community where you live with your own boys and other worthwhile people brought in from other places." The only way Leo could be successful at managing cattle, credit and money was to remain sober. Coady believed that both he and Leo had come from a

> breed of people that lack judgment if we drink. We can't do it and be rational. Consequently, your first great resolution is not to drink. This calls for character. You should attend all the farmers meetings, county, provincial, etc. but when the conferences are over and the jolly vacation starts you should be strong enough not to start drinking when others do.

Coady didn't think that Leo could possibly command respect in people's minds if they saw him half-drunken.[33]

As it turned out, Leo wasn't strong enough to resist the demon. In 1957, Leo was drinking, squandering his money and breaking up cars, racing them over old dirt roads. The news of Leo's actions, Coady told Teresa, was the "worst blow that I ever received in my life." Distressed, he confessed that Leo "just hasn't got what it takes." He continued: "I have had lots of glory out of the Extension but I have to witness lots of failures—such as the Margaree Credit Union and stores and many other sad failures all over the Maritimes but nothing like this ever came across my path before. I take it all in the spirit which I suppose the Lord intends it for me." Coady added that he didn't

> look upon these failures of Leo as anything extraordinarily unexpected. He comes by it naturally. He doesn't get this from the MacKinnon side of the house either. It's the pure Coady-Tompkins-MacDaniel failing. He is just a carbon copy of my brother Thompson. Poor Thompson wasn't bad but just simply did not have a sense of responsibility that he should have had.

Coady told Teresa that he had sacrificed for Leo to "elicit from him a noble response of the best manhood that was in him. It turned out that he didn't see it that way." He wanted her to realize that it was harder for him than for other members of the family because "his success has a lot to do with the ultimate success of my movement."[34]

Coady's own identity was now intimately bound up with the Movement. The Antigonish was his movement, and Leo's apparent lack of success as a co-operative leader reflected badly on him. Two weeks later, on June 19, 1957, Coady wrote Teresa, who was then living in New Hampshire, underscoring his belief that "Leo and his future is a very significant part of my dream of building a new society in this part of the world. He could be the finest demonstration in the Maritimes of the philosophy that we have been dedicated to all the years. Nothing stands between him and spectacular success except drink and foolish squandering of time and money." Apparently Teresa, Leo's sister, thought her prominent uncle had been spying on Leo, since Coady had travelled down to the Margaree two weeks earlier. In no uncertain terms, Coady informed Teresa that he had actually been down there to rescue an agriculture representative who had left his wife and seven children for his stenographer and taken up drinking and carousing. Coady didn't think that Leo was

> yet an alcoholic in the extreme sense but there are some people who by nature are more or less alcoholic and they have to be a thousand times more careful. My father, Dr. Jimmy Tompkins, Dr. Coady, Jim the Tanner, etc. could drink liquor and get away with it. It didn't rob them of their judgment. But that is not true of the rest of us. We inherited a highly wrought nature that does not need alcohol to stimulate us.[35]

Coady desperately wanted his own family to succeed and set an example for the rest of eastern Nova Scotia. Coady got over his disappointment with Leo and continued to support him over the next few years, but he never did stop advising him. In October, 1957, Coady continued his lecture on the devastating effects of alcohol. Coady was alarmed that Leo had been travelling with a well-known heavy drinker to farm meetings in Inverness County. "I felt yesterday like saying at the meeting that the people especially in Inverness County have lots of money saved up. They could finance this whole thing themselves if they wanted to. They put it in the bank during the last few decades. Their bank was the Inverness Liquor store and the other stores of Inverness County." Coady thought that excessive drinking was the "curse of the country. Until we do something on straightening our people up on this score I'm afraid that nothing much can happen except the gradual disappearance of the Scotch and Irish at least from the rural communities—farming and fishing." Coady's moral strictures were once again confronted by the crooked timber of humanity. Coady assured Leo that he wasn't

> writing this because I think you were drinking yesterday or were going to drink on the way home. I, with all my soul, hope and pray that you will decide once and for all to avoid the men and the places who might be instruments of your destruction, I remember you every day in my Mass, that you may have the grace to see the glorious opportunities that are yours.[36]

Coady urged Leo to get into beef or dairy cows and to go into vegetables. In order to succeed at this, he would need an irrigation system, and Coady instructed him on how he could use the river. Coady thought that the new ECS would send trucks down to the farm to take his stuff away. Coady's main purpose in writing Leo was to impress upon him the "necessity of getting down to a program of careful financing for the next five years. I mean that you should not spend a dollar, you or Mary, on anything that is not absolutely necessary." Coady's self-interest was creeping into his advice, however.

> I pointed out in Joe's letter that the success of my program will depend upon getting the people to accept the production program and developing new energy in their work. The Dutch are doing it but our big problem is to get the Scotch and the Irish to wake up. No family can make a living on seven cows, two pigs and eight sheep and fifteen hens, it matters not how prices are or how good times are, this will not give them their fair share of the national income…. They have been in the past blaming rural life and the government and other institutions. The real cause is in themselves.[37]

Coady had argued along these lines in his celebrated chapter in *Masters of Their Own Destiny* on the "great default of the people."

Coady's personal ailments made him a little grumpy and excessively agitated. In the late winter and spring of 1959, Coady became entangled in Leo and Mary's plan to buy Donald MacDonell's property and inherit his father's, Joe Coady's, big house. Joe Coady had, apparently, promised to leave Leo the big house and build a smaller one for himself. However, Joe was reneging on his early promise, and, according to Coady, "continuously rubbing it in to Leo, telling him that he has him over the barrel." Coady surmised that Joe's recalcitrance could have a bad effect on Leo. If Leo stayed there, he confided to the Rev. D.F. Roberts, parish priest in South West Margaree, "he will always be a boy. Joe might easily live twenty years more and Leo in the meantime will not be able to plan or act for himself or bring up his children as he wants without having this eternal domination of Joe for everything he does. This will ruin Leo's character." Coady thought the whole matter had to be handled delicately.

> Joe might retaliate by willing the whole property to Kevin or one of Leo's boys. That would tie up the place forever. If Joe comes to talk to you, I would suggest that you talk straight to him. Give him no quarter and tell him that after all these years there is no other possible solution. Everything will work out in the end and the Mick Coady property will come back and be what it was intended to be. This is all a sad business for me. It is sadder for Joe's loyal girls who are away. It will kill Katie.[38]

On April 25, 1959, Coady wrote Teresa and Carmel that Joe was still refusing "to give Leo any property and also refuses to sell the property (which he offered to do just last week)." Coady was pretty disgusted with the whole business. He told Teresa and Carmel not to "give any more money to Joe. He has more than is good for him now. Mary Ellen made the fatal mistake of willing her property to Joe and the kids as far as I can tell. Giving property or money to children is the scientific way of sending them to hell. They will be drunkards before they are twenty." The disgruntled Coady thought Mary Ellen had been stupid for not consulting him.

> Leo and Mary, Katie and Mary Ellen discussed this matter all last week and took it up with Joe last night. Leo was in good cheer today and is accepting this challenge like a man. I think he will come out of it all right and perhaps it's the best thing that ever happened. I wouldn't worry about these things too much if I were you—Leo will ultimately get all the property.[39]

On the same day, Coady had written to Francis Coady, telling him that he himself had deeded the Campbell forest to Joe after his father died. "I gave him considerable money over the years. There must be something gone wrong with his brain. I am not trying to get you involved, but if you can do anything it would be a great service to God and religion."[40]

Coady was particularly upset that Mary Ellen had willed her property at the Forks to Joe "two or three years ago and that she put some money in insurance for the kids. Why Mary Ellen would do a thing like that is beyond me. Joe has everything now." Coady allowed that Mary Ellen was now old and forgetful, but Coady told the Rev. Roberts that he was dropping a note to Leo's sisters "telling them that I am through with everything as things stand now." He didn't think it was of any use talking to Joe, either.

> I wrote Francis a secret and confidential letter a few days ago suggesting that he get Mary Ellen to deed her property to Leo but Francis, as usual, is timid and thinks that he might talk to Joe. If all of us talking to Joe could make no impression Francis hasn't much chance. I am writing Francis telling him to say nothing and do nothing if he cannot get Mary Ellen to deed her property to Leo.[41]

Coady was, it seems, totally exasperated with his clan members. He wrote Katie and Mary Coady that he was "so disgusted that I have grave doubts about the wisdom of any of you any more. For God's sake don't make any more mistakes. Take a little counsel and advice from people who have had experience in such things."[42]

The Rev. Roberts wrote a tender letter to the "tough, old codger" (as Coady characterized himself late in his life).

> You are, I am afraid, worrying too much about this matter. It is easy for me to understand. But your health is not good enough to let it weigh too heavily upon you. It is going to come out alright and perhaps will be the best thing in the world for Leo and his wife and family too. It will be hard on Katie but she will bear it with Christian fortitude. We want to have you around for a while yet. So take it easy. When it gets warmer come down and spend of couple of nights with me…. I have a lot to learn from you yet.[43]

Coady was feeling miserable as his blood count was very low. Then things took a turn for the better in the family. The deal to buy the MacDonnell farm had gone through. Leo had had no difficulty at all in getting a $13,000 loan from the Farm Loan Board. Elated, Coady wrote Carmel.

> Leo looked fine and was in great cheer. He told me that his mother and father and Father Roberts were in equally good cheer. In fact, Joe was happy himself and very co-operative. Leo agreed with his father to not only give him an acre of land and the lumber to build a house but also that he would help him get the lumber out of the woods and to the mill.

Leo also got the old tractor; he would paint the house white, the roof green and the barn red ochre. Moses Coady was very proud of his protégé. "When this deal goes through, it will be a very great event because our farm probably is the best one on the island of Cape Breton and, with a proper program of development as the children grow up, they can make a lot of money and have a real life."[44]

Coady was happy that Leo would not have to take a job in the co-operative.

> I was trying to solve the biggest problem in this country, which was rural life. For me to take the largest farmer in Margaree and switch him over to some co-operative job, say manager of the Margaree Forks store, would be for me to contradict myself. It was always my avowed purpose, clearly expressed, that a civilization is built by the devel-

opment of neighbourhoods. I held out to Leo from the very beginning that that was his job when he grew up—to build the neighbourhood first by settling his own boys who would take to that sort of thing, and bring in worthwhile people to fill up the vacant places in the community. These vacant places meant something vastly different from the little farms of a hundred acres. I was thinking in terms—as we all must today—of four to six hundred acres or so. Now, one word about my position on co-operatives. I built the co-operatives not to give jobs to our people but to give the people who stayed on the land a chance to get their fair share of the national income. The principal thing was not the co-operative; the principal thing was the life that came out of it for those who belonged to the working classes and for the primary producing classes, such as farmers, fishermen and lumbermen. This is my apologia in the matter.[45]

On June 23, a happier old codger wrote to Ida Delaney that his doctor had told him that his "days were numbered and that I had not too long to sojourn on this planet. I will be taking off pretty soon, by the way they are talking."[46] Now he could fly away content that his beloved Leo would do well after all.

IV

One can imagine the battle-scarred old veteran of the bloodless co-operative revolution gazing out of the window of his hospital room out across the rolling hills surrounding Antigonish, dreaming of what lay in store for the world. Sick in body, Coady also seemed to carry the sorrows of the world and the co-operative movement deep within his soul. Though he was constantly in and out of hospital, Coady poured out a steady stream of retirement essays and speeches. Coady's writings are touched with heaviness, a repetitive return, running again and again over the same ground as if in search of something he never quite found. By the mid-1950s, Coady's mind was concerned only with the bare essentials. After decades of reducing complexity to propaganda for the community halls, years of searching for the catchy phrase, the zinger, the telling anecdote to motivate his beloved masses, Coady now handled his topics with a hammer, without lightness, elegance or sophistication. This restless soul wanted to get straight to the heart of things. He had neither the mind nor the commitment to explore the nuances of fascism or human capitulation to authoritarian leaders (unlike Hannah Arendt in *The Origins of Totalitarianism* or Albert Camus in *Between Heaven and Hell: Essays from the Resistance Newspaper 'Combat' 1944-47*). His style was declaratively prophetic in tone. In the end, he was like the drummer beating out a simple tune with only the odd variation. And in the end, it seems not enough people were listening to his music or willing to march in his parade.

The biographer can never truly know the interior landscape of his subject, but Coady's speeches from 1953 to 1959 reveal a soul under considerable duress. The root of Coady's distress lay primarily in the utterly unequal distribution of power between the owning and producer classes. The new financial dictators were creating integrated production and distribution systems (Coady called this "functionalism"), leaving the co-operative activists with precious little opportunity for ownership. He looked at the "present sad plight of the world" unfolding before his eyes. The world seemed dark and gloomy, with 75 percent of the world population of 2.4 billion on the verge of starvation. Economic competition appeared to be dead; economic dictatorship had taken its place. To Coady, the world had become the "happy hunting ground of the western imperialists." As he asserted in his speech "Organizing Our Thinking for Leadership" in February 1953, "helpless millions in the last few centuries have come under the domination of economic imperialists. In our day the fascist state, black, brown and red, threatens them with a new despotism. This last fear of dictatorship is the most subtle of all the cruelties ever inflicted on a long-suffering humanity." Coady feared that the world was entering a new "era of slavery" to "finance capitalism." These "new financial dictators," such as the two hundred corporations in the United States, owned "nearly half of the corporate wealth of that country and 2000 directors control them." The old feudalism he had fought so hard to defeat in the 1920s and 1930s had appeared in new clothing, with a vengeance.

Coady was clearly being pushed into a corner. Huge numbers of people had been swept under the Soviet Union's skirts in the non-capitalist world, Mao ruled in China, the colonial world was boiling in Africa, Indonesia, India and South America and the liberal democracies had turned into financial dictatorships. The world's masses were hungry and illiterate. This left very little space for the masses to assume ownership of their economic institutions. There didn't seem to be any clear path leading from the people's predicament to Coady's coveted co-operative ownership. Coady now pursued one of several intellectual options open to him. The blueprint for the co-operative reconstruction of society existed; leaders were needed to implement an

> adult education program that will enable the masses of the world's people to see these great truths. It will give them the ability in the first place to know their friends from their enemies. It will enable them to understand the cheap rationalization which the so-called great of the earth have indulged in since the beginning of the age of finance capitalism, now monopolistic capitalism.[47]

Coady never really deviated from his belief that the truth had to be brought to the masses by dedicated, authoritative leaders. Still, Coady seemed distraught that the "Antigonish Movement" project, despite enviable successes, had broken down in the application phase.

Coady tried to find the answer to this perplexing pedagogical question. In a remarkably candid speech, "Charting the Course for Maritime Provinces," delivered at the annual convention of the United Maritime Fishermen in Amherst, Nova Scotia, on February 17, 1954, Coady faced the bleak economic conditions of the Maritimes. Embarrassed and saddened, Coady called for some drastic action. Coady may have doubted the future of the steel and coal industries in the Maritimes; he had none about the fishing industry. Like his UMF colleagues, Coady denounced a fishery run by trawlers owned by large companies. The fishing industry was not about proper mechanization. It called for "fishermen living all along the coast near the fishing grounds. And since they have to be there anyway, reason would dictate that they should equip themselves to handle as much inshore and offshore ground fish as is compatible with modern science and technology."

Coady never stopped defending a humanizing economic system that sustained the people's lifeworld, but he knew that, notwithstanding all the efforts of Royal Commissions and co-operative action, the Maritimes still lagged behind the rest of Canada. Coady's own rugged upbringing, in which one had to depend on one's own resources to survive and flourish, had so shaped his outlook that he could not really stomach explanations that laid the blame on the "big bad wolves of Quebec and Ontario." The Maritimes needed cheap power and transportation and adequate credit facilities, and they had themselves mainly to blame for not getting them. (Even so, Coady never tired of lashing the "financial leaders in this country who, while talking private enterprise as the only legitimate business, have failed to supply credit facilities for the people.")

Coady then turned his guns on his own people. The Antigonish Movement was committed to organizing the "people for continuous learning." However, this was "precisely what thousands of the people don't want. They hate this talk about education and enlightenment as the remedy for their ills.... They don't understand that in the last analysis the solution of their problems and of the problems of the whole world, for that matter, is the improvement of the quality of human beings." The fishermen resisted continuous learning because it was very easy to enter their work culture. They lived mainly on "scraps of knowledge gathered from tradition and gossip, in blind imitation of [their] ancestors." Moreover,

> generations and perhaps centuries of poverty, illiteracy and ill-health as share-croppers of the sea, under dominant and dominating fish barons, have dulled the intelligence of the poor people, weakened their wills and almost destroyed ambition in them. As a consequence, they cannot see the connection between knowledge and the success of their lives. They prefer to trust to native ability—to horse sense, as they say. It is well named. Because of this thinking, 3/4 of the human race are on a level of living very little above that of the good old horse. I am afraid we shall have to admit that in the long history of our own Maritimes we have contributed a sizeable quota to this great army of misery.

Coady accused the fishermen of ungratefulness. Even though the organization of the UMF was followed by increased prices for lobsters, mackerel and many other varieties of fish, some fishermen still refused to come into the Movement. "Old line business met the competition and paid the price. Numbers of our fishermen were guilty of using the ungrateful excuse that they could get as much for their fish by remaining outside the UMF as they could by joining." How could the UMF possibly grow, Coady lamented,

> if thousands of our fishermen hold aloof with the stupid attitude of comparing prices? If this is the right way for the fishermen to do business, why are they hesitating? One moment's thought should convince these canny in-and-outers that if there were no co-operatives the prices would immediately snap back to where they were in the old days. It takes education and enlightenment to know and weigh these things.

Coady was plainly vexed that some co-operative business executives had turned sour.

> The enemy from without will naturally try his wiles on our business leaders, but the real enemy is the one from within. We know that in the credit unions, co-operative stores and producer co-operatives we have had leaders who have embezzled money, defrauded the people in some other ways and had secret agreements with old-line profit businessmen. By their betrayal they weakened the confidence of the people in the noble cause of co-operation. What is the answer to that? Education of course. If 80% of the fishermen of this country get the scientific knowledge, the proper under-standing of social techniques, and the fundamental co-operative philosophy that will make them deadly in earnest, then no co-operative business manager anywhere in this country would dare allow himself to be bribed by the enemy.

The old prophet wasn't pulling any punches. Still, the picture wasn't all dark. The Havre Boucher fishermen had given fifty-two free days in building their co-operative lobster factory. That was something to cheer about.

Next, Coady slammed the "sectionalism and provincialisms" of the fishermen: "The marketing of fish or farm products cannot be done in a scientific way if one section of the country or one province is pitted against the others." Coady's words then reflected his anguished struggles with Acadian separatists: "If we cannot rise above these differences, then we deserve to be the underlings that we have always been." Coady thought it would be a hard job to "overcome our individualisms, our prejudices and passions and in general to iron out the kinks from our crooked minds. But organization, ideas and a real philosophy of progress will do it."

Coady finished this extraordinary speech by affirming his belief that "love of material well-being, common decency and idealism should supply the fishermen, and indeed all groups, with the dynamics for carrying out such a program." His Lord had admonished the fishermen of old to "put out into the deep."[48] This admonition could be a

> command to our fishermen to launch out into that other sea of economic and social activities. The boats that sail this sea are not made of wood and steel. They are associations of people for voluntary group action and the nets that are to be let down for the draught are consumer and producer co-operatives. May we hope that for this type of fishing, too, you will secretly say in your hearts, "Lord, in thy word, we will let down the nets."

Even as the dream of realizing the co-operative kingdom on earth faded, Coady still presented it before a suffering humankind as an ideal worth striving towards.

In almost every speech given by Moses Michael Coady in the 1950s alarm bells are sounded. In his second important speech of the mid-to-late 1950s, delivered at Antigonish on September 30, 1958, Coady abruptly announced that "progress in many sections of the country is disappointingly slow." And yet again he turned to the theme of betrayal by those leaders of the fishermen who "secretly, and sometimes not so secretly, took sides with the vested interests against the fishermen." Coady informed his audience that the Movement had discovered an "instrument" in the credit union "through which the studying and thinking of the people could issue into positive action." Many people, upon embracing the credit union, found the way opened up to all types of group action. But the "philosophy of this great thrift agency" had not been taken seriously enough by all of the people. If it had, the significance of the credit union movement would have been "infinitely greater and undoubtedly would have served as a corrective of the more glaring weaknesses in the moral character of our people."

Coady's fading hopes were revived by the setting up of the new Eastern Co-operative Services. On October 17, 1956, Coady travelled a few miles down the road from Antigonish to Havre Boucher, the scene of early self-help initiatives. Coady was overjoyed as he proclaimed:

> Today we are witnessing a great new step in the creation of an organization that is the synthesis to a large extent of the total program that was envisioned 28 years ago. This proposed new step in the organization of the people of Eastern Nova Scotia is, without doubt, the biggest single step ever taken for the social and economic development of our people here in Eastern Nova Scotia.

He reminded his audience that, at the outset of Extension's project, it was impossible to begin with a "complete co-operative set-up that would include a complete set of facilities or agencies by which primary producers (fishermen, farmers, lumbermen) could produce, process and market in a scientific way the products which were basic to their mode of life." Coady insisted that a complete set-up of co-operative agencies was the solution to the so-called rural problem. The ECS blueprint promised nothing less than a "new era in the lives of the people." The beginnings of the Movement had contained the seeds of its later unfolding.

The wielding of the other economic, social and educational forces that would enable them to join with their fellows of other vocational groups to establish a real democracy necessarily had to be a later development. These operations, both among primary producers and consumers, involved difficult problems. All economic fields were already occupied by private profit enterprisers who would not willingly and easily give up their privileged position. The people, too, accustomed as they were to an old oidei of economic society, could not easily raise their sights to see the possibilities of a new order.

If the people were to raise their sights, Coady argued, then the leaders had to attend public meetings and demonstrate to the people that they were behind them in their activities. The task of experts was to enlighten the people. This called for

> attending a meeting once or twice a week. But even if it called for a meeting many nights a week for the next few decades or for such a time as it takes to bring our people to the point where they will automatically follow crescendo of progress, we wouldn't be asking our people to do more than the communist leaders all over the world are voluntarily doing for the cause they represent.

This latter challenge was a familiar refrain in Coady's writings of the 1950s. Coady imagined that ordinary people who were primarily occupied by the mundane activities of life, raising kids, attending barn dances, working, shopping and cooking and gabbing, could find the resources and will to act in a radical, single-minded fashion.

Coady admitted that it was exceedingly difficult to create co-operative facilities, organize the people for study and inspire leaders to take a hand in the work. Somehow, however, a dynamic had to "fire the imagination of both leaders and people and set them off to a new performance never before realized in our free society." For Coady, the dynamic lay in understanding that humankind was engaged in a gigantic fight against a "threat never before experienced in the history of man. We must, therefore, find a dynamic or a motivation for peace that will be as strong as what we experienced in warfare." Coady realized that this militant call would be resisted by those who shied away from "conflict with the great financial difficulties of our time, advocating prudence and the humility of the people." This was the "counsel of death. It is a superficial and despicable philosophy, especially for a Christian leader. On this philosophy the Apostles would have never tried to convert the world." Coady ranted on against those who were

> selling out the people, our own brothers, our own flesh and blood because we, too, love the flesh-pots and haven't got the stamina to oppose the monopolistic over-lords, landlords and warlords who are enslaving the world.... Quite plainly, we need a powerful and irresistible dynamic to brace us against this terrible weakness of the leaders of our world and the people who follow them.

Coady was trying to frighten his audience into action and supporting of the ECS. Monopolistic capitalism was the new feudalism; there was little room for anyone to start a business; the future of democracy was being undermined; and monopolistic commercialism through its chain stores created a "new functional society that, if carried to its legitimate conclusions, will drive our people from the farms of this country and put in their place huge production individuals and corporations that will largely take over the work of primary production." Coady's haunted imagination envisioned that the "last stronghold of an owning people will thus be destroyed and the complete proletarianization of Canada and North America is well under way." Coady believed that these truths should arouse the people, supplying them with a "potent dynamic" to press through the trouble and annoyance attached to the "Antigonish twin program of adult education and economic co-operation as a work of love."

Coady informed his audience that it was simply "impossible for primary producers to have orderly and scientific marketing without an organized consumer movement in the cities." Coady fretted much about the emergence of chain stores in Canadian life, giving considerable reflection to their challenge to the co-operative movement in his "unwritten book." Plainly worried, Coady saw the retail stores encroaching on the co-op movement's space, with monopoly capitalism creating an integrated system of near total control of production and distribution. This particular threat touched a very sensitive nerve in Coady's co-operative philosophy. Though not entirely consistent in his views, Coady was arguing incessantly in the late 1940s and 1950s that the producing and working classes as well as rural and urban dwellers would find their unifying ground in consumer co-operativism. Consumer co-operation was the "one type of co-operation that, above all others, enables the people to become masters of their own economic destiny."[49]

Coady was excited about the ECS because it represented a higher stage of evolution within the co-operative movement. Coady may have been sick and scarred in body, but his prophetic voice spoke passionately when he informed his audience that

> an adult education movement that will bring to the people the scientific knowledge and social technique for a proper evolution of our western society will contradict the superficial idea that the little places, and especially the rural communities, are passing off the scene, that, in a word, all people will be in big cities in the future. This is 19th century cheap popular thinking which drove people from the isolation and inconvenience of the rural and small villages to the big bright cities.

Coady defended the rural way of life until his last breath. The world, though, it seemed, had developed its own blueprint, casting Coady's aside. His dream of pioneering urban communities on the beautiful Bras d'Or Lakes or on the great Sydney harbour never materialized, dashing Coady's desire to create a "pilot plant for many parts of the world."

For Coady, the creation of the Eastern Co-operative Services in Antigonish was the

> synthesis of all our education and all our activity for the whole 29 years of our existence. Our credit unions, co-op stores, co-op fish plants and other farming and fisheries co-operatives, all were built for the day when the whole movement could be topped off by a comprehensive, central organization, such as ECS, to give our fishermen, farmers, townspeople and industrial workers the necessary facilities for conducting their economic affairs.[50]

Coady believed that he now had the right social architecture in place to effect a permanent co-operative society. To imagine that the people would not support it would be like "telling a man who has laboriously built a magnificent home for himself to walk out and let it go to rack and ruin."

In April 1952, Moses Coady had telegrammed Wilfred MacKinnon on the occasion of the opening of the new Sydney Credit Union building. He told him that if the "job of leading men to God is ever to be complete we in our day must create out of the more fragile and delicate social and economic institutions that will express our belief in justice. Your performance is a significant step in this social architecture." As God's appointed architect of the new social order, blueprint in hand, shirt sleeves rolled up, Coady saw the ECS as the capstone of his lifetime of architectural design.

> The beauty of the ECS program is that it serves not only the small land-holder who is capable of developing great wealth through the natural resources he has in the land, the forest and the sea, but it serves equally well the dairy and beef producers and all those who have large acreages. Neither should we forget that Eastern enjoys the unique position of being integrated with Labor and all organized consumers of the region. In this set up, the possibility of taking over integration ... can become an actuality.

The ECS, Coady argued, would defeat his bitter enemies—the "traitorous leaders" who sold the people down the river, the "smooth artists" who hoodwinked the people, and those foes who maintained that the Extension program was "not spiritual enough or not scientific enough."[51]

Coady would depart from the world certain that his dream of an integrated co-operative services had been put in place. Sadly, this would turn out to be an illusion. Operations would prove non-viable, and the ECS would officially shut down in 1965. Alex A. MacDonald would attribute "its failure to the lack of sufficient market demand in the region, lack of adequate capitalization, and lack of business, agricultural and management expertise, and finally the failure to anticipate these problems through feasibility study and analysis."[52]

Coady struggled to his last breath to find the appropriate social and economic forms to realize his "positive, democratic program." In the 1950s, he continued to rail, perhaps more stridently than before, against his own Church's failure to "bring back the masses of the laboring people who have left and are leaving the Church by espousing a realistic program that is calculated to off-set the tide of our day to monopolistic capitalism and its concomitant, the complete proletarianizing of the working classes and a great sector of the primary producers of the world." Coady had little time, and even less patience, for statements of Churchmen who endlessly reiterated principles outlined in *Rerum Novarum* and *Quadregismo Anno* and the teaching of economists and sociologists who dealt in abstract statements.

Nor did he have any time for "negative counsel": lists of what to avoid and what not to do.

Coady was a very impatient man. He thought that the only way to "bring back the lost sheep and attract the teeming millions of those who are outside the fold" was to formulate a program that "in the minds of the world's people, will be adequate to meet the challenge of revolutionary socialism." Coady believed that civilization had

> come to the point ... where it will take a most unmistakable declaration on the part of the representatives of our Christian civilization to undo the harm that our alliance with the vested interests in the past has brought upon the Church. Only a declaration that will be as revolutionary as Christianity was two thousand years ago will jolt nominal Christians out of their lethargy and attract the heretical, schismatic and pagan world. We are only temporizing and playing a clever game of opportunism if we are going to keep on indulging in the platitudes that have been characteristic of our statements in the past.

Nothing less, it seemed, than a monumental act of Christian will was going to deliver the world from the vested interests. Coady was certain that the "connection between the political and the economic is so intimate and so vital that if the working classes leave the control of business and finance in the hands of a dwindling powerful few, then they are implicitly giving up the idea of political democracy as well." The masses of the world were looking to their Christian leaders for a declaration that would "strike them as a call to action by men who not only believe what they teach but give the impression that they are convinced of its ultimate triumph. This will enable us to avoid the imputation that we are waverers, if not apologists of a status quo that has very little to commend it."[53]

Coady's call to the Christian church would go unheeded. No declarations were forthcoming as global Catholicism adjusted its message to the emergent consumer society and Cold War mind-set. Indeed, the sheer force of Coady's criticism of his Church belies his own faith in remnants of ancient Roman Catholic triumphalism (the Church should be the directing force for all of society). Like his controversial, anti-Semitic pope, Eugenio Pacelli, Coady believed that only the Catholic Church could counter the nihilistic forces at prey in the world. This ardent belief, however, rooted as it was in another historical time, could not be realized in the modern, pluralist, industrial world taking shape in the aftermath of World War II. The Catholic Church, though powerful, was merely one among many of the world's great religions. It was both utterly inappropriate and historically inconceivable for any religion, be it Islam, Buddhism, Hinduism or Christianity, to unify the world. The post-war world was marching irreverently towards a secular and rational kingdom.

The first half of the twentieth century was not a time of modesty. The men who dominated during this time dreamed big and had little compunction about imagining that they could remake the entire world in their image, no matter the cost, as exemplified in the actions of Lenin, Hitler and Stalin. Moses Michael Coady shared in this abstract ethos of a grand, sweeping reconstruction of the social order. He wanted to impose his vision of the "good and abundant life" on a pandemonious world, though he dreamed of a different world than the tyrants, of a bloodless revolution.

V

For forty years Coady's unfinished book had lain in his former secretary's little bungalow in Antigonish, stored in files and cardboard boxes hidden from the researcher's eye. Only a few people, probably Zita O'Hearn, Ellen Arsenault, Malcolm MacLellan, Alexander Laidlaw and several others, knew of its existence. This book presents the historian with problems. Dictated mainly from his sickbed, it consists of notes, outlines, fragments, chronologies, lists of categories, numerous aphorisms, references to speeches, restless repetitions. It presents a kind of puzzle for the biographer because some of the notes are autobiographical whereas others probe in and around Coady's favoured themes.

Coady felt considerable urgency to complete this written work. In the foreword to a fragment entitled "My Unwritten Book," dated January 12, 1955, Coady set forth his reasons for writing it. "As I now lie sick in the hospital, I am confronted with the sense of a large phase of unfinished business in my life. This unwritten book is part of it." Coady wanted to give his friends a "fuller idea of my thinking on this important question of democratic development of the world." This latter commitment is closely linked with the subject of one of Coady's key speeches of the late 1950s, "A Plea for Democracy," delivered in Kansas City with considerable media fanfare. Coady hadn't decided what the title of his unfinished work would be, but his January 1955 version was "Positive Democracy" or "The Positive Democratic Program." Many other titles appear scattered throughout the notes: "The Story of Antigonish"; "The Antigonish Way of adult education"; "The Antigonish Way of building a democratic world"; "Building the democratic world through adult education" and "In Search of Possibilities." Coady wanted to outline an "adequate positive, concrete, democratic formula by which the people can get for themselves the good and abundant life." Coady imagined that his formula would "bring to the people the benefits of science and technology in the development of the natural resources of the earth which the benign Creator gave them as their heritage."

Coady admitted that the ideas for this book were embryonically present in *Masters of Their Own Destiny*, and in his many pamphlets of the prior twenty-five years, but he thought that the "spectacular development" of the Movement called for "new thinking and new writing." Coady deemed it "natural and almost inevitable" that what was now occurring called for "new interpretation and appraisal." The post-World War II world posed a severe threat to Western Christian civilization and the future of liberal democracy. The co-operative movement, the container of Coady's desire for the new millennium, had to chart its redemptive pathway in an antipodean environment.

In his last days, Coady reflected on his life, some of which found expression in his text, "My Story," prepared for a CBC television interview in July 1957. In these fragments, leafed here and there throughout the compilation, Coady strained to find the spiritual sources of his monumental project. He found it in the natural world. As Coady had listened to the creaking of his beloved Margaree forest, they "seemed to be appealing to me to free them, as it were, to achieve their destiny." He imagined that he was the one who would emancipate nature through transforming it to serve humankind's interests. "The valley itself was beautiful. It showed me the role of wood and growing things in the lives of men. That was what the Creator gave man. This was the key: The Coming Age of Wood–Science and Technology today and the modern use of wood."

Coady believed that all of life coursed with energy and potentiality. Someone must, however, release this energy towards life-sustaining ends. "That gave me the idea," Coady explained, that "I was looking at something unrealized–it was unrealized in the whole world. It was the job of the human race to realize all their possibilities."

> Fundamental principles: in that we mobilize the people to release their energies on worthwhile activities. That is the secret of the greatness of individuals and of civilizations of the past. It is, above all, the cause of the better world that we hope for. It will come as fast as we can mobilize the people, all the people.

Coady was infected with the virus of passion for grand schemes. Just as the tree required the human to release its potential as a commodity, humans themselves required educators to be coaxed into activity.

Coady turned often to the mountains as his most beloved metaphor. Their beauty supplied the animus for his life. Their intimidating presence, walling the people off from the outside, enticed Coady even further to find "life beyond the mountains." As a youth, Coady tells us in one fragment, he dream-travelled, "likely due to the influence of the mountains of Margaree." Mountains also symbolized life's harshness. "We could see beyond the mountains–possibilities that meant life"; "You can't have a valley without mountains"; "You can't have a world without mountains of difficulties and problems and the challenge to great things, compensating things made possible by the difficulties, difficulties typical of life."

Like Arnold Toynbee, master of the sweeping historical survey, Coady thought that life was basically about challenges and responses. These mountains and valleys of the Margaree, Coady was certain, had "supplied an environment calculated to inspire and lift the soul–supplied a basis symbolic of life as I came to maturity…. I felt that something should be done about tackling the problems of life there and to extend that philosophy to the world." Life, for Coady, was a fight. Potentiality had to be wrestled out of the stuff of existence.

One cluster of aphorisms captures Coady's essential Aristotelian sensibility. "The nature of progress—Aristotelian sense—Progress is the bringing into being things that are good for man's advancement in the world, things that did not exist before, like the findings of science or a new technique for economic betterment." The first step was the "vision of things"; the second was "to find the technique by which we can flood the minds of the masses of the people with these visions." On March 2, 1959, Coady scribbled: "We need to wrestle with the impossible, with difficult things, to build character"; "Life is the realization of possibilities: that determines the nature of education. The natural resources and the environment must be developed…. If people study the possibilities of things in human society, the vision of these possibilities tend to become realities"; "If we translate possibilities into actualities then we have progress—the continuous utilization of human possibilities for good." Rather than actually constituting something new, Coady's notes feel more like well-worn gems that have survived the fierce tests of wind, rain and storm.

Coady was proud that he had emerged tough and strong, forged into shape by elemental forces of ancestry, social and environmental heritage. Indeed, Coady's masculinity, his sense of himself as a man, is a powerful undercurrent in his co-operative philosophy. Coady was proud that he had survived the fires of a "tough environment," fit only for a "man who was physically fit and dominated by radical ideas, by nature born to surmount difficulties and fight for new things." Coady figured that continuous struggle and poverty in the Maritimes had forced his people to be creative. Like true men, Coady and his ancestors "did not run away…. We stayed and fought and out of that fight came the conviction that we were going to get our difficulties and find life right here."

For Coady, transformative learning was possible because people were only as "good as their attitudes; therefore, the logic would be to strengthen the weak attitudes and then we are on the way to progress." The educator of ten thousand workshops and seminars and classes ran over his list of "weak attitudes" of Maritimers. Maritimers couldn't "see life at home—migration." They were "extreme individualists." The school curriculum socialized them poorly for life in their own place. A "co-operative attitude" had to be developed. The people seemed unable to "change their ways with the times. It is taking us about 100 years to get away from the sailing ships." The possibilities were infinite. Adult education was the "essential agency that will organize the people of the world" to establish economic democracy.

VI

Coady remained convinced that economic democracy was the golden key bequeathed by the divine architect to a suffering humanity. People had to "go into business for themselves." Economic group action was the "finest flower of private enterprise" and the "future solution of the world's difficulties." He continued to believe that the "whole story of the Antigonish Movement" could be a "guide for many parts of the world, especially for the underdeveloped parts." Coady retained his conviction that he could "securely establish forever the economic and educational phases of our Movement." If "real democracy" could be established in Atlantic Canada, it would "likely do it in all the earth."

Yet one of the more mysterious aspects of Coady's thought on "real democracy" is the absence of attention to its everyday workings in the network of people's co-operative organizations. Coady focused his considerable energy on blasting monopoly capitalism and prophesying the revenge of the "exploited and enraged peoples of the earth" who "will pay us back in a way we will not like." Coady believed that leaders with co-operative vision could engineer, with sufficient organization, education and will, co-operative forms of enterprise. Once formally established, these co-operative enterprises would put real democracy in place. However, from the war years to the late 1950s, co-operative organizations had exhibited decidedly non-democratic, elite-dominated tendencies. A.B. MacDonald had sounded alarm bells in the war years, as had A.S. MacIntyre. Coady knew, as well, that the fishing co-ops had not attracted wide enough support, that corrupt leaders were too much in evidence and that the fishers were resisting the blueprint offered them.

Coady's writings contain no reflection on the process and procedures of democracy. Coady's old associate, Alex Laidlaw, raised the pertinent issues seventeen years after Coady's death. Laidlaw argued that, in too many co-operatives, democratic control was "something to which only lip service is paid." Many co-op members simply thought that democracy meant "one member, one vote," but Laidlaw insisted that democracy was "something that permeates an institution and is made apparent in everyday operation." Laidlaw thought that "democracy in co-operatives is not seen or judged in any one way but fifty; that democratic control may be endangered as the co-operative system becomes large and complex; and that democracy is slipping in many co-operatives because it is assumed to be operating when in fact it is not."

Laidlaw considered the way the annual meeting, a vital learning space, could, in fact, be anti-democratic: astute leaders can easily manipulate a meeting taking place only once a year; only a small percentage of the members may attend; the social aspects can cloud debate on salient policies.

Tendencies that were evident in Coady's period were full blown by the mid-1970s.

> In many co-operatives, perhaps the great majority, it is now assumed that only a small percentage of the members are going to attend the annual meeting anyway, and indeed the members begin to assume that this is the normal way to conduct affairs.... The result is that, generally speaking, most co-ops are run with only a very small input from the membership.

Laidlaw worried (as Coady didn't in his published works) about size, but observed that bigness did not necessarily equate with ineffective participation. Some of the most undemocratic co-ops Laidlaw had ever seen were small ones, "usually run by one person or a small clique." Laidlaw thought that the large co-ops had to find innovative ways of ensuring widespread participation. Laidlaw insisted that, next to the membership itself, the board of directors had the "chief seat of control" in a co-op. Co-operators, he argued, could not claim that their organization was "democratic simply because it has a board of directors elected by the membership, for the whole mechanism of the board can operate either for or against the democratic participation of members."[54]

Laidlaw thought that the "democratic character of an organization is also marked by the flow of information and the educational programs provided for the members." He concluded that it was not too much to

> say that the degree of democratic control in any institution or organization can be gauged by the extent to which vital decisions come from the general body of people concerned. In a democratic society, people are not only free to make decisions but in actual practice do make them. In a democracy, policies and decisions flow from the people to the leaders, in a dictatorial society from the leaders to the people.

Perhaps Coady had been so utterly preoccupied with the bankruptcy of democratic leadership in the West and the hideous threat of communism that the interior workings of co-op organizations were of little import. Laidlaw assessed the state of affairs in the Canadian co-op movement and found that the "general tendency" was to

> leave important decisions to a very small circle, chiefly upper-level management and the board, and frequently not even all directors but only the executive committee of the board. A few decide and many accept and agree. The trouble is that members are not given an opportunity to exercise their powers of judgment and decision, and like muscles that are not exercised regularly, these powers become flabby and useless.

Laidlaw also thought that, in too many co-ops nowadays, members were not "consulted in advance but [were] presented with a plan, a policy or a decision to rubberstamp and approve."

The Antigonish Movement had stopped being a grassroots movement when World War II broke out. To effectively run the array of co-op organizations that had sprung up everywhere, Coady and other co-operative leaders had to shift their educational focus to training officers and directors

of co-op organizations. To sustain the co-op movement in a hostile economic and geo-political environment, Coady and other co-operative
leaders had to push the co-op movement from above to grow big, diversified, complex, integrated. Yet the flaws were evident, if one looked closely,
almost from the first day the new people's organizations popped up out of
the ground. Coady's millenarian obsessions and beleaguered outlook
blinkered his perceptions of anti-democratic tendencies in his Movement
that promised to establish "real democracy" on the earth.

Laidlaw put his finger on problems about which Coady remained silent.
With the emergence of large co-ops (such as the ECS) and federated structures of organization (such as the Nova Scotia Co-operative Educational
Council), co-operators had to manage complexity. Democracy was no longer, Laidlaw argued, a

> simple matter of a person expressing views and casting a vote but involves the compli-
> cated affairs of huge institutions, vast bureaucracies and bewildering technology. It is
> very doubtful that co-operators know how they are going to keep democratic control
> and at the same time have the leadership which modern business demands in order to
> compete and grow.

These are prescient remarks. Laidlaw thought that several other matters
were also becoming clear. First, it was getting harder and harder to remove
officers (mostly male) from elected positions. Second, managerial
personnel were tending to have more and more influence on policy matters
that rightfully belonged to membership deliberation. Third, most
large-scale co-operative systems were not developing decision-making procedures that reached down into the general membership. For Laidlaw, the
"attitude that decisions must be made at the top rather than at the bottom
endangers all traditions of democratic control which are the very life-blood
of co-operative organization."[55] The seeds of these undemocratic tendencies were, however, sown by the Movement's intellectuals and activists
who were planning for the people in an unruly environment rife with unpredictable contingencies.

Nowhere in Coady's last reflections on the "democratic development of
the world" does he consider democracy as a deliberative process requiring
pedagogical and methodological analysis and attention. Like his silence on
the suffering of Jews in the Holocaust and quiescence on the persecution of
adult education comrades for alleged communist leanings in the 1940s,
Coady's muteness in the face of another kind of threat, the internal democratic workings of the co-op itself, is baffling.

In fact, there is only one genuinely new idea that appears in the notes for
his unfinished book. Pondering the need for educational agencies to realize
this dream, Coady suggests to his "fellow Canadians that the growth of
democracy in Canada can be accelerated by the creation at strategic points,
of Popular Democratic Assemblies. These would be built after the fashion

of the central meeting place of the United Nations." He thought that, at a minimum, there should be one in Moncton for Atlantic Canada, and one each in Montreal, Toronto, Winnipeg, Edmonton, and Vancouver. "These would be buildings well equipped with television and broadcasting facilities where the people of our nation could come to discuss their economic and social affairs, where those who send them there, could listen and look on." Typically, Coady imagined that this "might well be the new institution that ... makes possible the establishment of the new democracy in the world."

VII
━━━━━

The Casket of July 30, 1959, recorded that "Monsignor Moses Michael Coady died at St. Martha's Hospital late Tuesday afternoon, July 28th, following a short illness of less than six weeks." Only one hour after he had been talking on the telephone, the Sisters of Martha discovered that he had passed away quietly after an early supper. The "big man from the little places," as John Fisher had depicted him at a St. Francis Xavier University alumni banquet two years earlier, had left his little piece of earth for his celestial home.

In the customs of his Church, Coady's body rested in Morrison Hall for several days before transferral to the University chapel for the office of the dead. From the time of his death late Tuesday afternoon until the Solemn Requiem Mass on Friday morning, faculty, co-op officials, credit union officers and various representatives from religious orders maintained a constant watch. The Most Reverend J.G. Berry, Archbishop of Halifax and Metropolitan of the Ecclesiastical Province of Nova Scotia and Prince Edward Island, celebrated the Pontifical Requiem Mass. More than a thousand mourners, including two hundred clergy (Bishops, Monsignori and priests from all over Nova Scotia as well as representatives from distant dioceses and religious orders) crowded into the cathedral. It was entirely fitting, too, that a steelworker, a miner, two farmers and two fishermen (Alex Duguay, Shippegan; Duncan Campbell, South Margaree; Charley Joe Gallant, New Waterford; Lawrence MacIsaac, Sydney; Lennie McPhee, Cape George; and Ed Power, Nova Scotia) were his pallbearers, carrying their fallen leader to his resting place in St. Ninian's Cemetery overlooking St.FX University. It was also entirely fitting that Father M.J. MacKinnon, who as a miner's child had dedicated himself to following Coady to the ends of the earth, eulogized Coady as the man who presented "to the people themselves a positive program of self-help and mutual aid which would bring them knowledge and justice."[56]

The last of the great triumvirate of J.J. Tompkins, A.B. MacDonald and Moses Coady had now passed into history. *The Casket* captured the event:

"His death marks the passing of the last of the great triumvirate of the St.FX Extension Department. His partner in the spread of the credit union movement, A.B. MacDonald, predeceased him in 1952 while his kinsman, teacher and inspiration, Dr. J.J. Tompkins, died the year following."[57] Underneath a reproduction of the magnificent Karsh photograph of Coady, a *Casket* editorialist remarked that his passing "casts a pall that falls on the wash house and the pit head; over farm and wood lot. The long shadow will fall even in darkened jungles and in the days ahead white-garbed missionaries and natives will join in prayer for one who fought without hatred; who loved without reservation." Acknowledging that some pictured him as "brash, wholly confident and perhaps even a little boastful," the editorialist commented that Coady had "dedicated his life to clearing the skies that man, his mundane problems solved, might look ever higher."[58]

Across the country, newspaper after newspaper echoed the sentiments of *The Casket* in announcing that a giant had passed away. *The Canso Guysboro County Advocate* of July 31, 1959, characterizing Coady as a "broad-shouldered, ruggedly handsome man with flashing smile," noted how the "powerful, gentle hand of Moses Michael Coady guided thousands of Maritime folk during the severe economic depression that was the protracted aftermath of the First World War." Obituary writers particularly loved Coady's "broad shoulders," which symbolized for them, perhaps, Coady's heroic strength to carry the little people forward to new possibilities. *The New York Herald Tribune* of July 29, 1959, described him as "huge" and "vigorous"; *The Montreal Star* of July 31, 1959, as "big, red of face, with the shoulders of a lumberjack. He was salty and unclerical of tongue ... the favorite clergyman of militant atheists and calmer agnostics." Others could not resist flowery, gift-card prose. *The Halifax Chronicle-Herald* of July 29, 1959, announced that: "Although he condemned with fiery oratory the many evils in the economic set-up, he never lost his child-like faith that, beneath it all, the world was as pure as the meadows of Nova Scotia's beautiful Margaree where he was born January 3, 1882." Von Pilis, journalist for the *Union Farmer*, published out of Saskatoon, exuded that

> love was the power motivating Dr. Coady—love of God and his fellow men. Here was a man who had the utter faith that can move mountains; who gave all he had and himself to help the poor; who was patient and kind, felt no envy, never was proud or insolent; did not claim his rights, could not be provoked, did not brood over injury; took no pleasure in wrongdoing...a man who sustained, believed, hoped and endured to the end.[59]

Coady would have quickly disputed this idealized portrait. In fact, *The Casket* reported that just two months before his death, Coady had observed: "I'm not too long for this world. I'm going to have a lot to answer for. I'm not too sure I made the best use of my early years. If I had a little more experience I think I could have accomplished more. My, my I'd like to have a chance to start all over…. I'm sure I could do a better job."[60] Coady's self-criticism may well have merit, but few could doubt that the latter part of his life was devoted to "aiding the common man."[61] *The Windsor Star* captured the heart of Coady's message.

> Monsignor Coady was a believer in practical Christianity. To him preaching was not enough, when in the midst of poverty and other social ills. Singly these fishermen were too weak to do much of anything to improve their lot. They were at the mercy of the fish processors and others with whom they had to deal. But, in combination, it was something different. That was the idea that launched the co-operatives, now doing a business in the Maritimes in the tens of millions annually.[62]

Do not work singly. Work in unison. Education in co-operation is the welding force. This is your hope.

The Maritime Co-operator featured several commentaries from those who had worked closely with Moses Michael Coady for many years. Ellen Arsenault, Coady's last secretary, recalled the way her home phone would ring at 7:10 in the morning: "'Have you a pencil handy? Would you take down this idea?' Then would follow ten minutes or so of dictation, without let-up, while one prayed desperately for the ability to get down every last word, and at the same time hoped that the paper would hold out. One did not interrupt once that flow of dictation started, not even to get more paper." Arsenault found that "always in that flood of language there would be a literary gem to be caught up and noted before it would disappear as a beautiful bubble, formed for the moment, is dissolved in the foaming fury of a stormy sea." Arsenault eschewed any notion that Coady was a task-master "who would phone his secretary so early in the morning." She also shared several touching anecdotes. Apparently Coady had something of a reputation for not being particularly fond of children. Arsenault recounted the story of a little girl who met Coady one day in the old Extension hall. Coady had reached into his pocket, taken out a pear and passed it over to her. Then, taking her by the hand, he had led her to the water-tap, all the while lecturing on the importance of washing fruit before eating it. For his faithful secretary, Monsignor Coady remained a "kind Father" who "loved his Extension family."[63]

Ida Gallant, who travelled the speaker's circuit with Coady, recalled the early days of "alarm clock" meetings that were guaranteed to wake people up from their complacency or lethargy. She remembers that the

> preliminaries were always fascinating. Usually during the drive to the meeting place Dr. Coady would deliver a few short speeches explaining to us how he proposed to put his hearers "in a state of scientific humility." This was what he called "laying on the rawhide lash." After he had laid on the lash he would "pour oil in the wounds" when he spoke hopefully of a program that would help them to a better life. He believed that ordinary people could do great things and he told them so. He called it a great tragedy on the scene of life that all that is recorded of any man is that he is born and he dies. The things that man could have achieved and did not achieve should be regretted by

society…. Education should enable a man to realize all the possibilities that lie within him.

For Gallant, Moses Michael Coady was a utopian dreamer.

> It was from his unshakeable faith in the worth and dignity of the common man that his followers drew inspiration and courage. If he wept at the sight of the road of life, strewn white with the bones of lost opportunities, he nevertheless foresaw a future in which the people, through intelligent individual and group action would repossess the earth. The better society which he foretold to his hearers would come about only through participation in economic group action by the humblest of his hearers, this was the broad base on which his brave new world would be built.

Gallant recollected how Coady would thunder out that "every single man must be permitted to hit his own little blow. With co-operators every little blow becomes a sledge hammer lick in building the new society." This, Delaney observed, was Coady's idea of "real democracy." When he autographed her copy of *Masters of Their Own Destiny*, he wrote, "In a democracy the people don't sit in the social bleachers. They all play the game."[64]

Moses Michael Coady, born in 1882 to humble parentage in a lovely little patch of the earth, the Margaree Valley, played hard in life's game. The Divine Architect had revealed the blueprint and rules for how this game should be played. With astonishing single-mindedness, Moses Coady set out to implement God's plan for the co-operative kingdom on earth. For a flickering historical moment, the formidable Coady seemed capable of engineering the new economic order in the feudalistic Maritimes, but it did not come to pass. The old order failed to leave, and the new one ended up waiting. Once more, the complexity and mystery of living in the world defeated utopian desires and aspirations, leaving us with less than we long for and more than we would have had without the struggle.

CHAPTER 10

Dreaming beyond the Mountain

I

From 1930 until his death, Moses Michael Coady was at the heart of an extraordinary awakening of primary producers, household workers and industrial workers in Nova Scotia and the Maritimes. This Movement sought to break the stranglehold of deep feudal economic and political structures and a suffering peoples' mind-set of "limited horizons and reduced expectations."[1] The Movement spread throughout the Maritimes and Atlantic Canada. Leaping over regional boundaries, it spread to other parts of Canada, New England and the mid-West of the United States. From there it reached into the Caribbean, Latin America and other parts of the world.

For an evanescent historical moment, the Antigonish Movement captured the imagination of the world. Journalists, liberal-minded religious leaders, papal authorities, eastern seaboard intellectuals, professors, theologians, social reformers, wild-eyed dreamers, co-operative leaders and innocent youth came from far and wide to witness the "miracle of Antigonish." Hard minds and doubting hearts were transformed by the co-operative miracle as tourists witnessed rustic lobster factories, credit unions and co-op stores springing up in communities with previously unremarkable histories. Antigonish, now a rural town like so many others, graced by malls and fast-food outlets, glowed with a radiant light in the 1930s and 1940s. This rural town was transformed into an imaginative space into which people projected their social fantasies. Many people of Christian persuasion, spiritually dislocated and bewildered by the scale and scope of change in the post-World War I era, desperately wanted Moses Michael Coady to be their modern Moses and fashion a non-violent alternative to fascism and communism. They wanted someone to lead them out of the Egypt of oppression into the promised land of co-operation.

Historical narrative slices events from the flow of life. Like the poet, the historian shapes raw material into stories capable of being told, grasped and remembered. One of the main tasks of the poet is to transform "grief into lamentation" and "lamentation into praise."[2] Like poets and ancient storytellers, Coady fabricated a mythic redemptive narrative for his audiences. Contemporary economic historians such as Julian Gwyn have convincingly disputed one piece of Coady's mythic history of Nova Scotia and the Maritimes. Gwyn outright denies the existence of any "Golden Age" for Nova Scotia. When Nova Scotia began to industrialize in the 1850s and 1860s, it was, in fact, "outpaced almost everywhere in the Atlantic world."[3] Nova Scotia could never have accumulated enough wealth to sustain its population. According to Gwyn, its "soft bituminous coal" should have stayed in the ground after reciprocity ended in 1866; this most surely would have saved much human misery and grief. Before 1871, very few Nova Scotians were in any kind of favoured position. Those who remained in Nova Scotia were an "enduring lot with a history unremarkable except to themselves and to those blessed with the insights of the Haliburtons of this world, who celebrate them."[4]

Moses Coady's redemptive narrative, while not based on the actual possibilities of the Nova Scotian ecoscape and economy, was designed to arouse the ordinary folk who had accepted limited horizons and reduced expectations as their lot. Coady taught the people through his constructed narrative of hope. Even though the common people of the earth had never, anywhere, exercised control over their destinies, Coady imagined that his people, humble Nova Scotians, could acquire the necessary know-why and the requisite know-how to manage the economy and polity. Clearly audacious, this image of uneducated, simple, unsophisticated primary producers (on farm and at sea) and industrial workers (in mine and mill) running their own economic affairs turned out, in the end, to be mainly a beautiful fairy tale. Coady's chosen vessel of economic redemption, the co-operative movement, never achieved the critical mass that might have, perhaps, allowed the manifestation of some of the things Coady's heart desired.

This is not to say that Coady's narrative did not have some pedagogical power; many people were awakened to take action in their communities, lives were changed, hope made a brief comeback. But the speck of truth in the grand narrative was spelled out by A.S. MacIntyre in the late 1930s when he told Coady that the Movement had accomplished "wonders with limited resources." Here the "limited resources" qualifies the "wonders" accomplished. The numbers of credit unions, lobster factories and dollars spent in the co-op stores were not so impressive when placed within the context of the larger economy and spending.

Many of the Depression observers of the Movement (such as those who travelled with the Co-operative League's tours) read great significance into a small slice of experience in a particularly hopeless and troubled time. They failed to see, or did not want to see, all that was before their eyes. These co-operative initiatives were possible primarily because of the peculiar vulnerability of capitalism in a backward, scarcely even modern, economy such as that of Nova Scotia in the early twentieth century. For a brief time, economic space was available for small-scale self-help ventures in tiny fishing communities and small farms. These economic initiatives could be carried off with sweat equity and unsophisticated technology. The credit unions did not threaten big banking interests and may have, ironically, even helped them. However, we cannot forget the thousands of ordinary men and women (now almost faded from our memory) who learned that they could grasp some of the reasons for their economic exploitation and political dependency and exercise some control over their life-situations.

Those who came to see the miracle in 1938 and left praising the awakening of previously illiterate and semi-literate fishers through the study club movement could not have anticipated that, just two years later, this study club movement would be effectively over, severely curtailed by the outbreak of World War II. Nor could they have looked down the historical road and imagined the way the modernist impulse to bigness and efficiency would gradually crush Coady's dream of a vital, predominantly co-operative in-shore fishery. At the dawn of this new millennium, Coady's dream of the permanent co-operative kingdom has proved to be an illusion.

Today, one can visit the little fishing villages of Nova Scotia, some of which provided the exuberant scenes for the great co-operative tours of the late 1930s, and scarcely tell which village was a model of economic self-help and social dynamism. There are still many signs of co-operative enterprise in Nova Scotia, but they chug along more or less like every other economic venture. They may contain more democratic potential than mainline ventures, but this potential seems well hidden. One can still see initiatives in Cape Breton that claim to be in the lineage of the "Antigonish Movement," but they are small in scale, with little impact on the economic and political systems.

Nova Scotia appears to be the land of excessive expectations and unfulfilled longings, but our era engenders contradictory responses. Coady called Maritimers to use the resources of the sea to create a people-centred economy; some of the great briny species of the 1930s and 1940s have all but disappeared. The state of our forests and environment suggests that Coady's call to conserve went largely unheeded. Still, his gospel of self-help and self-reliance has some contemporary resonances. While the old-style political dependencies are still evident, a new spirit of self-reliance is percolating in Atlantic Canada. If old Father Jimmy came back to Nova Scotia for a brief visit, he would perhaps be the first to sniff out the learning potential of the new information technology, currently enjoying a boom in Atlantic Canada, along with vital cultural industries such as film and television. If Coady were to visit, he would perhaps follow his brilliant cousin, crafting a palatable message for a new, post-industrial age.

Movement publicists were under constant pressure to present the movement in positive, up-beat language, images and stories. The account of the emancipation of Dover is legendary in Antigonish Movement folklore, making it difficult to untangle the "something added" from the "objective reality." In the case of craggy, little Dover, the brutal reality was that, besides fishing, there was little real potential for any kind of significant economic development.

The Antigonish Movement is often praised for its linking of adult education with economic emancipation. Indeed, historians writing about the Antigonish Movement soon discover that it has been romanticized, serving different ideological purposes for many people and institutions. The sense of purpose and power in Canadian adult educators, for instance, is inextricably bound to the emancipatory myth of Antigonish. A conference held at St. Francis Xavier University in the mid-1990s called for, without a trace of irony, the revitalization of the "Antigonish Movement." (What exactly was to be revitalized? The co-operative movement? The Nova Scotian economy?) Most attendees thought that the principles of the Movement were sound, that only wilful application was lacking. This nostalgic reading of the Movement ignores the historical fact that all that learning for co-operative action could not deeply anchor a co-operative fishery in the face of the huge power of fish companies such as NatSea, backed by federal government policy and power. This is, no doubt, a rather unpalatable message. However, sometimes history reveals that the traditions that were drawn upon to confront serious economic and social problems in particular times and places were inadequate to the challenge. There are almost endless lessons, small and large, to be learned from the Antigonish Movement. And one of the big ones is surely that the co-operative movement did not enable Maritimers and others to become masters of their economic destiny.

Coady believed in the co-operative revolution with a terrible fanaticism. He constantly placed its successes in the foreground, read more into events that he should have and failed to face its flaws, thus fuelling the myth of the modern miracle and pushing himself into very dangerous territory. He actually came to believe that he had, in the end, been chosen by God to teach the entire world his divine blueprint for the "good and abundant life." People who knew the Moses Coady who playfully characterized himself at times as "little Mosie from the Margaree" often remarked on the genial and humble nature of this big, rough farm lad from the Margaree. But anyone who reads the voluminous correspondence and attends carefully to the endless speeches and writings of Moses Coady cannot help being struck by the ungenial and unhumble nature of his vision of the world. Coady was, in a word, a formidably flawed prophet of the new economic order.

II

Coady was forty-six years old when he erupted like a volcano on the Nova Scotia scene to lead the St. Francis Xavier University Extension onto the world stage. Once erupted, this vesuvius of a man never stopped thinking or writing about world revolution. Donning the prophet mantle in the early 1930s, Coady crafted his message of redemption for Maritimers, who were yet again living through hard times. In meeting hall after meeting hall, Coady told his Depression audience that, although the Maritimes were fields of lost opportunity, there were still opportunities of which they could take advantage. Coady valued deeply the possibility-hunting mind, and no one worked harder to arouse Nova Scotians and Maritimers from their slumber. What was, Coady taught, did not have to be. This simple lesson, that things can be better, remains vital to this day. By 1934 enough activity was mushrooming in eastern Nova Scotia to seduce Coady into believing that Depression-style co-operation in a backward, sparsely populated and underdeveloped economy such as that of Nova Scotia contained a kind of magical potion for curing the world's ills.

It wasn't long before the modestly consequential accomplishments of the St. Francis Xavier Extension Department turned into something more—the "miracle of Antigonish." Extension's herculean efforts to defeat the giant of feudalist capitalism had spawned a significant array of co-operative institutions in Atlantic Canada and other parts of North America and the world. Coady was hailed as the heroic leader of the non-revolutionary alternative to the black beasts of fascism and communism.

However, for reasons that remain hidden from us, Moses Coady crossed over the line from running an innovative and imaginative Extension Department to imagining that the Antigonish Movement was the solution to most of the world's problems. By the early 1940s at the latest, Coady firmly believed that he had discovered the "blueprint," that he had the "democratic formula" in hand, despite the lack of sufficient solid evidence from his experience in the Maritime co-operative movement.

In fact, the Antigonish Movement had been gradually cut off from the grassroots at the outbreak of World War II. During the 1940s, desperate co-operative leaders tried to organize federated structures to maintain the co-operative movement's presence against an awakening and militant capitalism. Most of the educational attention during the war and its aftermath was focused on training elite managers for the co-operative institutions. Evidence from co-operative reports of the 1940s clearly indicate that the common people, so iconographically significant in the literature, were not participating very much in the life of their institutions, nor had the Movement penetrated beneath the elite strata of rural communities to reach those most in need. By the early 1950s, the co-operative movement's utopian energy had dissipated, its emancipatory potential was exhausted and its first-generation leaders were dead or dying. In his last days, Coady imagined that the Eastern Co-operative Services, formed in 1957 to unify co-operative services, was the architectural capstone of the movement, the guarantee of its permanence. By 1965 it had collapsed. The old, dying Coady ended up scarred in body and soul, angry at his own people for betraying the co-operative utopia, calling the Church and ordinary folk to impossible acts of dedication and effort and railing at the darkness of the world threatened by that hideous thing called communism.

No one can be certain how Coady came to imagine that he had a divine mission to liberate the peoples of the world. However, we can trace some of the streams that flowed into the making of Coady's millenarianism. Coady's theology was a kind of everyman's Thomism, pruned of subtlety and complexity and pounded out on the forge of daily problem solving. From Thomas, whose own thinking had been influenced by Aristotle, Coady adopted the idea that God had revealed his blueprint for knowing God through the sacred text and his blueprint for ordering the economic, social, cultural and political world. There was only one true, or best, way of knowing God and ordering the world. In other words, Coady saw himself as God's architect of the new economic and social order. The correct formula for organizing the economy, for example, existed in the divine mind. Through scientific knowledge, humankind could know the correct formula. The blueprint could be worked out by expert social architects and applied to the masses to develop their social intelligence. Like the great dreamers of the Enlightenment, Coady saw himself as a legislator of the truth.

This assumption is key to Coady's meaning perspective. Yet Coady's theological certainty that he could discover an economic order that had transcendental approval placed immense burdens on him. Once Coady believed that he had a divinely appointed mission to implement the one best way, the co-operative way, he was faced with a huge contradiction. He wanted the little people of the earth to be "masters of their own destiny," but Coady already knew, before they did, what their destiny ought to be. Certainly this terrible belief fired the volcanic Coady to superhuman efforts on behalf of the economic emancipation of the exploited primary producers, but it was Coady himself, and not God, who imagined that the common people had a messianic role to play in the drama of progress.

Coady's belief that divine reason had revealed the blueprint for the remaking of humankind converged with the prevalent, illusionary ethos of the early to mid-twentieth century redemptive dreams. The first half of the twentieth century was not a modest time. The men who dominated this strangely violent and abstract time had few qualms about attempting to remake the entire world in their image. Moses Coady shared in this commitment to a grand, sweeping reconstruction of the economic and social order. In an obscure backwater of North America, a priest named Moses Coady imagined that, without armies and politics, the co-operative movement could compete on the world scene with those great propagators of secular liberation, Lenin, Hitler and Stalin. For Coady's part, perhaps this utopian dream was a manifestation of the Roman Catholic Church's age-old dream of universal domination of all cultures and spaces. Coady was in the grip of a world outlook that posited its particular truth as the Truth for all humankind. Although he downplayed his Catholicism on public stages, once off, Coady could tell his Catholic colleagues that the Roman Church was humanity's hope in its fight against communism. Coady wanted a different world from that of the tyrants, but he still wanted his vision of the "good and abundant life" imposed on a pandemonious world, even if the instrument used was "adult education."

III

Throughout his tumultuous mature years, from his mid-forties to his late seventies, Moses Coady thundered against the "vested interests" that kept the common people enchained and preached a gospel very close to syndicalism. Syndicalism is a difficult term to define, but the main idea is that the organization of workers at the point of production collapses the need for a political party. Coady's granite idea, his fundamental legacy offered to the twenty-first century, was simply that, unless the primary producers and industrial working class controlled production, talk of democracy was futile. Ironically, Coady's economism (the economy is the privileged domain within human experience, and the cause of most social problems and much suffering) parallels that of many twentieth-century Marxists. Coady thought that co-operative ownership was the one and best way of accomplishing this transcendentally blessed project. Coady never deviated from this axiom and believed fervently that the co-operative organizational form, in and of itself, once put in place, guaranteed democracy for the little people. This idea has not stood the test of time, however. The co-operative organizational form easily co-exists within capitalist economic systems and may or may not be democratic in process and procedure. In this present turbulent period of globalization, scarcely a peep has been heard from the co-operatives about alternatives.

Coady did not follow his beloved Aristotle's classic reasoning that man's defining trait was "his being a political animal." For Aristotle, the "more we strip away Man's political characteristics the more animal he becomes. In other words, he is rejected from the human commonwealth."[5] Ironically, Coady's economism, with its privileging of the productive, rendered the political a secondary, even derivative, domain for human action. In *Masters of Their Own Destiny* and in many of his speeches, Moses Coady counselled the exploited primary producers and industrial workers to eschew political action until they had enough knowledge and skill, gradually acquired through their experience of running co-ops. The opportunity for political action never arrived.

Here, then, is another paradox in Coady's thought. He wanted the little people of the earth to be masters of their destiny, but he could not see that the domains of civil society and state governance, while obviously impacted by economic power, were relatively autonomous spheres. The Antigonish Movement educated for co-operative forms of action. It did not have an adequate theory of citizenship, of the way collective learning originates within civil society and influences policy making and formation once inside the gates of governance.

The absence of an adequate conceptualization of the political has also obscured the actual politics of the Movement itself. Catholic reformers such as Tompkins and Coady constantly worked the backrooms, using their network of Catholic senators and politicians or St. Francis Xavier University graduates to accomplish various things. Extension's relationship to Michaud, who was Minister of Fisheries for a significant period of time, exemplifies this latter mode of politicking. Their shared faith (and Coady's own links with the Liberal Party) fuelled the flow of funds into St. Francis Xavier to support fieldwork among the fishers. There was, of course, a price to be paid. When threatened by an emergent Co-operative Commonwealth Federation, Michaud attempted to constrain Extension's actions. Coady did not ally Extension with any political party, although he knew well that the social democratic CCF had many adherents in and around Cape Breton who did not see much contradiction between the co-op movement and social democracy. It is also certainly true that the Antigonish Movement, as an association within civil society, created deliberative space in its many fora, particularly the Rural and Industrial Conferences. Here men and women made numerous recommendations that were presented to state policy-makers. In fact, the learning processes within the movement began in civil society with the study clubs and flowed from there, crossing the line of civil society and economy with the start-up of the co-ops. The process of gaining favourable legislation for the credit unions in the early 1930s is an illuminating example of the Movement's own politics. Extension had to have appropriate legislation (legislated by the government) in order for credit unions (hybrid organizations that were partly in civil society and partly of the economy) to function. Nowhere in the published works of Moses Coady does he reflect on either the Movement's politics or on the need for an autonomous education for citizenship. Coady did not want Canadians to sit in the bleachers, watching decisions being made for them. The only really important domain for decision making, it seems, lay in the domain of production.

Coady's assumption that he had found the form for the common people to become masters of their own destiny carried some potentially murky impulses and anti-democratic tendencies. By the early 1950s, Coady was trying to present a brave public front in face of evidence that the co-operative movement was not fulfilling its divinely appointed mission. Coady's desperation was revealed by his advocating the forming of a vanguard of male conspirators to bolster the leaders of the future, to create a strong pressure group to keep other leaders on the right pathway and to determine what ideas should prevail at the various gatherings of Church life. This great proponent of democracy was willing, in a dark moment, to engineer both the people and their leaders to control their destiny. If the Truth pre-exists communally validated learning processes and procedures, then the leader (or educator) is pressed towards instrumental and anti-democratic practices.

In his 1987 text *Critical Social Science*, Brian Fay distinguishes between "educative" and "instrumental" modes of altering how people think and act. Instrumentalists assume that the "laws of social life have an independent power which can only be dealt with by ascertaining what these laws are and regulating actions accordingly."[6] Because Coady, following St. Thomas, believed that "objective science" reveals the laws governing social life, Coady's pedagogical action is oriented towards enabling learners to bring their practice into line with the revealed law. Coady wanted the common people, fishers, farmers, coal miners, to reflect upon their life situation and transform their self-understanding. He must necessarily become alarmed when the people's reflective learning processes move away from the revealed law, i.e. the co-operative blueprint or formula.

Coady was fundamentally a social engineer who thought he had been mandated to instrumentalize God's blueprint for a dark world. His social engineering impulse is interwoven with his genuine longing for a democratic, people's economy. Coady spoke often (as did his followers and supporters) of carrying a concrete plan to the people. This plan did not emerge out of the collective learning processes of the common people themselves, with the possible exception of the very early days of self-help initiatives; for a brief time, the people in the fledgling study clubs had determined their own agendas and created their own projects. Shortly thereafter, Coady and the Antigonish Movement intellectuals channelled the people's action in predetermined directions (into credit unions, and so on). If one simply accepts the co-operative plan as the most feasible one, given the historical circumstances, then Coady's actions seem reasonable enough. Yet one has to agree from the outset with Coady's blueprint for the people. Thus, the study club movement never quite escapes the shadows of instrumentalism: Were they the social architect's chosen vehicles to create sound co-operative organizations? Were they genuinely democratic learning spaces where men and women could deviate from their leader's program? Was Coady an authoritarian populist?

Dogmatists don't always make good democrats. In the mid-1950s, co-operative progress in many sections of the country was disappointingly slow. The world was unwilling to bend in the direction Coady had in mind for it. Now Coady tapped into the shadowy depths of hubris: he turned against the people who were not following his blueprint. In an astonishingly candid speech to the United Maritime Fishermen on February 17, 1954, Coady railed against the fishermen whose poverty, illiteracy and ill-health had dulled their intelligence, weakened their wills and almost destroyed ambition. An utterly dismayed and furious Coady lashed out at groups of individuals who still sniffed around from week to week for a few extra cents. Coady even came to believe that some co-operative executives had betrayed the Movement. In his dying days, Coady was haunted by images of the betrayal and moral weakness of the co-op movement's leaders, the common people, the Church and political leaders. He believed that the Western leaders had sold out the people and that only a return to a pristine revolutionary Christianity could counter the forces of darkness and oppression.

Once Moses Coady had assumed the prophet's mantle and became God's amanuensis, he trod a path that would inevitably lead him to dark places. Christians have always believed that this world is not humankind's true home; permanence lies in eternity. Like Prometheus, Coady tried to steal some of God's fire, the coveted blueprint (or golden key) of God's plan for the earthly realm of economics, culture and politics. This impulse to control a world perceived to be on the verge of engulfment by the evil of overlords, landlords and warlords is a distinctly modernist impulse. Modernists want a dominant meta-narrative; so did Coady. Modernists want a rational world governed by scientific knowing; so did Coady. Modernists are inclined to blueprints and one best way of thinking and acting; so was Coady. When utopian desire is coupled with modernism, a potent and dangerous mix results.

Utopian modernism proffers a redemptive politics in the world. A look at the barbarousness of the twentieth century reveals what a ghastly illusion was created by communism and fascism. Yet millions of people in the world were caught in the grip of fantastical ideologies, and appealing to economics helps little in understanding the reasons why. Coady tried to counter fascism and communism by offering an alternative, the co-operative blueprint, but he too was caught up in a simplistic redemptive narrative that failed to deliver what it promised. Coady had not discovered the golden key or the holy grail of economic organization. Even with his relentless insistence on democratic control of the economy, Coady failed to consider that the co-operative form could only be formally democratic (one person, one vote) or could be anti-democratic, or that the co-operative movement could easily be engulfed by big capital.

One can certainly admire Coady's formidable struggle to transfer more wealth into the hands of the exploited. At the beginning of the twenty-first century, however, Coady's world outlook and thought seems naïve and simplistic. He did not respect the limits of the human capacity to comprehend and transform the world. His idea of dividing the world into zones strikes the postmodern observer as just plain silly. His belief in the extraordinary power of adult education to transform the world was overwrought. Knowledge by itself is not power; power is the ability to act and obtain what you desire. Coady's famous metaphor of "masters of their own destiny" assumed that ordinary men and women could master complexity. The twentieth century bore contrary witness to this affirmation. *Masters of Their Own Destiny* is a thoroughly modernist vision; its desire is excessive and promethean in urge. The horrors and illusions of the past century warn us that our transformative visions ought to be self-limiting, modest and respectful of mystery. Aghast at the horrors of the twentieth-century utopian experiments and our evident inability to master complexity, a modest utopianism is in order. There are no predetermined blueprints; all we can really count on is our ability to reason together. No one knows what kind of society will emerge down the road.

What is left of the Coady legacy? The historical narrative as unfolded here provides the reader with much to analyze and on which to reflect. Rather than a celebration of Coady's life, and unlike the usual scholarship on Coady and the Antigonish Movement, this chapter offers some provocations. However, they are mere observations, made after years of attempting to breathe life into a person out of endless heaps of paper.

After reading most of what he wrote, in speech, report and letter, Coady's message that one cannot have democracy unless the people control the production processes pounds within my head. He put all of his conceptual eggs in this basket. Those of us who face our own century with uncertainty and anxiety about the future of work can thank Coady for identifying "production" as a central space for human development, but Coady's specific message, linking co-operatives with economic (and ultimately, democratic) control, is inadequate for our time. Our global marketplace is the least likely place for democratic processes and procedures to occur, even though we must struggle for people-centred work against all odds. Civil society is the privileged domain for democratic learning processes, and Coady's brilliant intuition that people ought to study before they act can help us here.

Coady's fundamental belief was that there are more possibilities for human (and natural) development than are usually imagined and that life consisted of the realization of these possibilities. His developmental, humanist vision is one that withstands the ravages of time. Perhaps, when all is said and done, Coady's life, at least from his late thirties until his death, embodies a central idea that we are in danger of losing but one that Coady never let his beloved Nova Scotians and Maritimers forget: *the world as it is, is not the way it has to be.*

We honour Moses Michael Coady for his willingness to dream and the will to bring it close to the ground, and we honour the common people for believing that their lives could be better. In the end, we are left standing in amazement at the sheer audacity of "little Mosie from the Margaree."

Endnotes

Chapter 1

1. *Halifax Chronicle*, December 5, 1927.
2. In later writings, Coady would tend to skirt over the extent of the conflict, and bitterness, in the fight for an Extension Department at St. Francis Xavier. Coady also downplays the extent of the resistance from Bishop Morrison and the "Old Rector" Hugh MacPherson.
3. No records exist about the itinerary of this trip. One has to extrapolate from existing knowledge about the nature and form of adult education in the late 1920s in eastern and western Canada.
4. "Report of The Royal Commission Investigating the Fisheries of the Maritime Provinces and the Magdalen Islands" (Ottawa, 1928), p.81.
5. National Archives of Canada (NAC) [RG 23, vol. 131, 729-8-2(1)].
6. Whitman to Found, March 4, 1930 (NAC), [RG 23, vol. 1332, 729-9-8-2(4)].
7. Found to Whitman, March 10, 1930 (NAC), [RG 23, vol. 1332, 729-9-8-2(4)].
8. "Memorandum on Fishermen's Cooperative Movement," Ottawa, August 28, 1928 (NAC), [RG 23, vol. 1331, 729-8-2 (1)].
9. Ibid.
10. This chapter also made use of: "The Origin and Development of the UMF;" a term paper written at St.FX, 1945 (NAC), [RG 23, vol. 1332, 729-8-2 (4)]; Alex Laidlaw, "The Organization of the UMF, A great Coady saga" (NAC), [MG 31B, vol. 17, 1].

Chapter 2

1. C.J. Tompkins to Coady, July 23, 1940. St. Francis Xavier University Archives. Extension Papers. Antigonish, Nova Scotia: Personal correspondence of Moses Coady.
2. Malcolm MacLellan, *Coady Remembered* (Antigonish: St. Francis Xavier University Press, 1985), pp.20-21.
3. Cited, ibid., p.20.
4. Moses Coady, "My Story," July 8, 1957. Coady wrote these words in preparation for an interview for CBC-TV in July 1957, two years before his death in 1959.
5. MacLellan, *Coady Remembered*, p.14.
6. Ibid., p.16.
7. Ibid., pp.16-17.
8. Moses Coady, "Formal Education," *Masters of Their Own Destiny*, original manuscript (unpublished). St. Francis Xavier University Archives. Extension Papers. Antigonish, Nova Scotia (MG 20/3/1).
9. MacLellan, *Coady Remembered*, p.32.
10. Coady to Leo Coady, April 25, 1958. St. Francis Xavier University Archives. Extension Papers. Personal correspondence.
11. MacLellan, *Coady Remembered*, pp.32-33.
12. Handbound book with congratulations on retirement. St. Francis Xavier University Archives. Extension Papers. Departmental Records [RG 30-2/1/4771].
13. Kay Thompson, "Moses from the Margaree," *Reader's Digest* (December 1978), p.80.
14. Coady to Teresa Coady, November 5, 1957. St. Francis Xavier University Archives. Extension Papers. Personal correspondence.

15. Tompkins to Coady, January 24, 1915. Father James Tompkins Papers. Beaton Institute, University College of Cape Breton.
16. Coady, "My Story," p.2.
17. Etienne Gilson, *The Spirit of Thomism* (New York: P.J. Kenedy and Sons, 1964), p.59.
18. Ibid., pp.31-32.
19. This quote miscited in MacLellan, *Coady Remembered*, p.36.
20. Coady to Grace, March 23, 1957. St. Francis Xavier University Archives. Extension Papers. Personal correspondence.
21. "The Unwritten Book," Ellen Arsenault Papers (EAP) [now deposited in St. Francis Xavier University Archives, Extension Papers].
22. Alex Laidlaw, "The Man from Margaree," typescript, NAC [MG 31B 32, vol. 17, file 1].
23. Cited in MacLellan, *Coady Remembered*, p.40.
24. MacLellan, *Coady Remembered*, pp.40, 41.
25. Ibid., p.41.
26. "The Place of the Sisters in the Blueprint of Social Reconstruction," Feb. 3, 1952. St. Francis Xavier University Archives. Expension Papers. Coady's writings.
27. Coady, "My Story," p.2.
28. "Early History of the Nova Scotia Teachers' Union," *The Teachers Bulletin*, June 1953, p.99.
29. Ibid.
30. Ibid., p.100.
31. Coady, "My Story."
32. "Early History," p.100.
33. Coady, "My Story."
34. *Teachers Bulletin*, March 1923.
35. Ibid., January 1923.
36. Tompkins to William S. Learned, December 24, 1922. Father James Tompkins Papers. Beaton Institute, University College of Cape Breton.
37. Tompkins to Learned, c. May 21, 1922. Father James Tompkins Papers. Beaton Institute, University College of Cape Breton.
38. Coady, "My Story."
39. *The People's School: its purpose, its history, what the professors, the students, and the public say about it.* Nova Scotia Department of Agriculture, 1922, p.17.
40. Coady, "My Story."
41. Ibid.
42. J.R. MacDonald to Coady, Feb. 12, 1938. St. Francis Xavier University Archives. Extension Papers. Departmental correspondence [MG 20/1/1366-68].
43. John Glasgow, "The Role of Educational and Rural Conferences in the Development of the Extension Department of St. F.X. University." Honours Essay, B.A., St Francis Xavier University, April 22, 1947, p.9.
44. Ibid., p.10.
45. Ibid., p.12.
46. J. Hugh MacDonald to Gillis, January 18, 1938. St. Francis Xavier University Archives. Extension Papers. Departmental correspondence.
47. Glasgow, p.14.
48. Bishop Morrison, Circular letter to Diocese of Antigonish priests, December 1925.

Chapter 3

1. J. Gwyn, *Excessive Expectations* (Montreal: McGill-Queens University Press, 1998).
2. Walter Brueggemann, *Hopeful Imagination: Prophetic Voices in Exile* (Philadelphia: Fortress Press, 1986).
3. Coady does not mention the Black settlers to Nova Scotia or make reference to the presence of the aboriginal people, the Mi'kmaq, in his accounts of settlement patterns.
4. James Bickerton, *Nova Scotia, Ottawa, and the Politics of Regional Development* (Toronto: University of Toronto Press, 1990), p.35.
5. Ibid., p.39.

6. Ibid.
7. Moses Coady, *Masters of Their Own Destiny*, original manuscript (unpublished). St. Francis Xavier Extension Papers. Coady's writings.
8. United Maritime Fishermen (UMF) brief to Royal Commission on Cooperatives, Halifax, March 6, 1945.
9. Urbain LeBlanc and Howard Teaf, "The Rehabilitation of a Nova Scotia Fishing Village," Haverford College, Pa., 1954 [RG 30-3/1/1346].
10. R.J. MacSween, "Problems of the Fishing Industry." August, 1939. St. Francis Xavier Library [HD89F11C.1].
11. UMF brief, 1945.
12. "Facts for Fishermen," St. Francis Xavier University, 1939. St. Francis Xavier Library [HD89F9C1].
13. Laidlaw, "Information and Extension Work in the Fisheries," nd . St. Francis Xavier University Archives. Extension Papers. Fisheries.
14. Bickerton, p.40.
15. Bickerton, p.42.
16. Coady, "The Maritime Setting," *Masters of Their Own Destiny*, p.9. [unpublished version].
17. Ibid.
18. Ibid., p.10.
19. Ibid.
20. Ibid.
21. Bickerton, p.54.
22. See David Frank, *J.B. MacLachlan: A Biography* (Toronto: James Lorimer & Company Ltd. Publishers) for full story.
23. Ibid.
24. Bickerton, p.55.
25. Coady, "The Catholic Social Action Program of the Extension Department of St. Francis Xavier University, Antigonish, Nova Scotia," presented at Conference of Canadian Bishops in Quebec City, 1934. St. Francis Xavier University Archives. Extension Papers. Coady's writings.
26. Ian MacKay, "The 1910s & the Stillborn Triumph of Progressive Reform." In E.R. Forbes & D.A. Muise, eds. *The Atlantic Provinces in Confederation* (Toronto: University of Toronto Press, 1993), p.196.
27. Civil society, as I am using it, refers to the social space that includes friendships, family, voluntary associations, and public spheres. It interacts with the economy and state systems, but operates primarily according to a logic of communicative interaction.
28. David Frank, "Class and Region, Resistance & Accommodation." In E.R. Forbes & D.A. Muise, eds. *The Atlantic Provinces in Confederation* (Toronto: University of Toronto Press, 1993), p.236.
29. Bickerton, p.51.
30. Coady, "The Catholic Social Action Program of the Extension Department of St. Francis Xavier University, Antigonish, Nova Scotia," presented at Conference of Canadian Bishops in Quebec City, 1934. St. Francis Xavier University Archives. Extension Papers. Coady's writings.
31. R.J. MacSween, "A History of Nova Scotia Co-operatives" (Department of Agriculture and Marketing, 1985), p.23ff.
32. Ibid., p.31.
33. Ibid., pp.30-31.

Chapter 4

1. Moses Coady, "A.B. MacDonald—An Appreciation," *The Casket*, September 18, 1952.
2. "The Antigonish Movement," *Blackfriars*, 1946.
3. Coady to Dr. Alex Johnston, January 21, 1935, Ellen Arsenault Papers.
4. Coady to Helen Dingman, January 24, 1938. St. Francis Xavier University Archives. Extension Papers. Personal correspondence of Moses Coady.

5. Ibid.
6. Coady, "My Story," typescript, p.4
7. LeBlanc to A.B. MacDonald, Dec. 5, 1932. St. Francis Xavier University Archives. A.B. MacDonald Papers.
8. *Extension Bulletin* 1 (1), Nov. 7, 1933.
9. Coady to S.O. Bland, Nov. 29, 1938. St. Francis Xavier University Archives. Extension Papers. Personal correspondence.
10. "Foreword," *How St.FX University Educates for Action* (New York: Co-operative League of the USA, 1935).
11. Ibid.
12. Coady, "The Catholic Social Action Program of the Extension Department of St. Francis Xavier University, Antigonish, Nova Scotia," presented at Conference of Canadian Bishops in Quebec City, 1934.
13. Letter, October 23, 1930. St. Francis Xaviers University Archives. Extension Papers. Scrapbooks.
14. Cited in Coady, "My Story," p.4.
15. "Some Fundamental Considerations," Scrapbooks, 1930.
16. Doc. "Study Clubs," Oct. 1930, Scrapbooks.
17. Letter, Nov. 27, 1930, Scrapbooks.
18. *The Casket*, February 16, 1933.
19. Coady to C.J. Tompkins, May 7, 1932. St. Francis Xavier University Archives Extension Papers. Personal correspondence.
20. Coady to James Coady, February 24, 1932. St. Francis Xavier University Archives Extension Papers. Personal correspondence.
21. Coady to A.C. Chisholm, March 28, 1932. St. Francis Xavier University Archives Extension Papers. Personal correspondence.
22. Coady to Francis Coady, April 1 and 20, 1932. St. Francis Xavier University Archives Extension Papers. Personal correspondence.
23. *Extension Bulletin* 1 (2), Nov. 21, 1933.
24. Ibid., 1 (11), April 4, 1934.
25. Ibid., 1 (2), Nov. 21, 1933.
26. Ibid., 1 (4), December 19, 1933.
27. Ibid., 1 (7), Feb. 7, 1934.
28. R.B. to J.J.T., September 18, 1931, Ellen Arsenault Papers.
29. Ibid.
30. R.B. to J.J.T., December 21, 1931, Ellen Arsenault Papers.
31. Ibid., March 15, 1932.
32. A.C. Gartland to J.J.T., May 10, 1932, Ellen Arsenault Papers.
33. R.B. to J.J.T., June 18, 1932, Ellen Arsenault Papers.
34. Ibid., December 21, 1932.
35. Ibid., Dec. 21, 1932.
36. Ida Gallant, *25c a Week: The Coady Credit Union's First Ten Years: 1933-1943* (St. Francis Xavier University Extension Publications, nd).
37. *Extension Bulletin*, Feb. 21, 1934.
38. Ibid., May 30, 1934.
39. Ibid., Jan. 18, 1935.
40. Ibid., March 21, 1934.
41. Ibid., 1935.
42. Ibid., October 25, 1935.
43. Ibid., Nov. 16, 1934.
44. Ibid., May 2, 1934.
45. Ibid., Nov. 30, 1934.
46. Ibid., May 2, 1934.
47. Ibid., May 30, 1934.
48. Ibid., May 2, 1934.
49. Ibid., April 18, 1934.

50. Ibid., Feb. 15, 1935.
51. "A letter from the president to officers and members of the UMF, June 14, 1932." St. Francis Xavier University Archives. Extension Papers. Fisheries [RG 30-3/1/3933].
52. RG 30-3/1/3272.
53. Ibid.
54. "Director's Report," Oct. 23, 1935. St. Francis Xavier University Archives. Extension Papers. Fisheries [RG30-3/1/3359].
55. A.B. MacDonald to the Rev. A.E. Armstrong, January 19, 1943. St. Francis Xavier University Archives. A.B. MacDonald Papers.
56. Hanlon to officers and members of the UMF, June 14, 1932. St. Francis Xavier University Archives. Fisheries [RG 30-3/1/3933].
57. RG 30-3/1/3359.
58. RG 30-3/1/3742.
59. RG 30-3/1/3897.
60. Resolutions at Charlottetown, October 17-18, 1934. St. Francis Xavier University Archives. Fisheries.
61. National Archives of Canada [23, vol. 1333, 729-8-2(12)].
62. "With Alex John Boudreau," *Cape Breton's Magazine* 32.
63. Hanlon to officers and members of the UMF, June 14, 1932. St. Francis Xavier University Archives. Fisheries [RG 30-3/1/4048].
64. RG 30-3/1/4039.
65. Chiasson to Grote Sterling, July 22, 1935 [NAC. Op.cit.].
66. National Archives of Canada [RG 23, vol. 1333: 729-8-2(12)].
67. National Archives of Canada [RG 23, vol. 1333, 729-8-2(12)].
68. Coady, "My Story," p.4.
69. "Only total co-operation can build real democracy," Kansas City, October 17, 1948, Ellen Arsenault Papers.
70. "We Learn by Doing," St. Francis Xavier University, 1939.
71. Ibid.
72. LeBlanc and Teaf, "The Rehabilitation," p.18.
73. Ibid., pp.26-27.
74. "With Alex John Boudreau, Cheticamp Island." *Cape Breton's Magazine* 32.

Chapter 5

1. Coady to MacKinnon, March 14, 1952 [MG 31, B32, vol.3].
2. Moses Coady, *Masters of Their Own Destiny* (New York: Harper and Row, 1939), p.43.
3. Ibid., p.44.
4. Ibid. p.52.
5. Ibid.
6. Ibid., p.55.
7. Ibid., p.57.
8. Ibid., p.59.
9. Ibid.
10. Scrapbooks, 1931, speech to New Glasgow Rotary Club, nd.
11. Scrapbooks, *Halifax Chronicle*, August 25, 1932.
12. Reprinted from *Rural America*.
13. Gregory MacDonald, "Can anything good...?", *G.K. Weekly*, July 12, 1933.
14. Michael Ryan, "Co-operative effort in Eastern Counties", *Halifax Herald*, January 12, 1934.
15. Coady, *Masters*, p.50.
16. Scrapbooks, "Group Action Plan being tried out by Province of Nova Scotia."
17. Scrapbooks, *Journal of Education*, p.162.
18. J. King Gordon, "A Maritime Miracle," *New Commonwealth* (May 1935).
19. Evelyn Tufts, "Hundreds of Nova Scotians throw off their shackles and are co-operating," *Halifax Herald*, August 1935 (in Scrapbooks).

20. Evelyn Tufts, "Thousands secure solid benefits in co-operative move," *Halifax Herald*, September 11, 1935.

21. W.J. Dunlop, "The Movement in Other Countries: Canada," *Journal of Adult Education* VIII (June 1936), p.302.

22. Scrapbook clippings, April 1936.

23. Scrapbooks, clipping fragment.

24. Bertram Fowler, "Ownership returns to Nova Scotia," *The Co-operative Consumer*, August 23, 1937.

25. Scrapbooks, *The Casket*, Aug. 22, 1935.

26. Coady to Brunner, November 22, 1938. St Francis Xavier University Archives. Extension Papers. Departmental correspondence.

27. Coady, *Masters*, p.50.

28. A.B. to Boudreau, August 5, 1937. St. Francis Xavier University Archives. A.B. MacDonald Papers [RG 30-2/2227].

29. Scrapbooks, 1937.

30. Coady to Tompkins, November 16, 1937. St Francis Xavier University Archives. Extension Papers. Departmental correspondence.

31. L. Pennacchio, "The Torrid Trinity: Toronto's Fascists, Italian priests and archbishops during the fascist era, 1929-1940," in Mark McGowan and Brian Clarke, eds., *Catholics at the 'Gathering Place': Historical essays on the Archdiocese of Toronto 1841-1991* (Toronto: Canadian Catholic Historical Association, 1993), p.233.

32. MacIntyre to Coady, April 10, 1937. St Francis Xavier University Archives. Extension Papers. Departmental correspondence.

33. "Millions of dollars turnover in Maritime Co-operaitve effort," *Halifax Herald,* 1938.

34. Coady to MacIntyre, February 1937. St Francis Xavier University Archives. Extension Papers. Departmental correspondence.

35. Scrapbooks, 1938, nd.

36. *The Catholic Herald*, October 14, 1938.

37. *The Farmer's Advocate*, January 13, 1938.

38. *Halifax Herald*, April 27, 1938.

39. Bertram Fowler, *The Lord Helps Those ... How the People of Nova Scotia are Solving Their Problems through Co-operation.* (N.Y.: Vanguard Press, 1938).

40. Ihid., p.3.

41. Ibid., p.21.

42. Ibid., p.61.

43. *Extension Bulletin*, October 1938.

44. Zita O'Hearn, *Extension Chronicle*, nd [c. 1988], Ellen Arsenault Papers.

45. Ibid.

46. *The Sydney-Post Record*, July 2, 1938.

47. *Halifax Herald*, July 15, 1938.

48. Coady to Tompkins, July 9, 1938. St Francis Xavier University Archives. Extension Papers. Departmental correspondence.

49. "The Future of the Antigonish Movement," in George Boyle, *Father Tompkins of Nova Scotia* (New York: P.J. Kenedy and Sons, 1953), p.229.

50. "Who's Who and what's what at the Rural and Industrial Conference, August 16-18, 1938, Scrapbooks.

51. Carpenter to Coady, September 28, 1938. St Francis Xavier University Archives. Extension Papers. Departmental correspondence.

52. Rev. L. Ligutti, president, National Catholic Rural Life Association. In "A Tour of Nova Scotia Co-operatives: Report of Conference Tours conducted under the auspices of the Co-operative League of the USA & the Extension Department of St. Francis Xavier." NY: Co-operative League of the USA, 1939.

53. "Who's Who and what's what at the Rural and Industrial Conference, August 16-18, 1938, Scrapbooks.

54. Co-operative League of the USA. "A tour of Nova Scotia Co-operatives: Report of Conference Tours Conducted under the Auspices of the Co-operative League of the USA and the Extension Department of St. Francis Xavier," 1939.
55. Ibid.
56. F.W. Ransom of Winnipeg, Manitoba.
57. Coady to Bland, Nov. 29, 1938. St. Francis Xavier University Archives. Extension Papers. Personal correspondence.
58. Coady to J.J. Harpell, Greenvale, PQ, Nov. 28, 1938. St. Francis Xavier University Archives. Extension Papers. Personal correspondence.
59. Coady to Hower, January 21, 1938. St. Francis Xavier University Archives. Extension Papers. Personal correspondence.
60. Coady to Boyle, January 20, 1938. St. Francis Xavier University Archives. Extension Papers. Personal correspondence.
61. Zita O'Hearn, *Extension Chronicle*, nd, Ellen Arsenault Papers.
62. Ibid.
63. Zita O'Hearn, "Educational Mouse-traps," in *The Christian Family and Our Mission*, nd, Scrapbooks.
64. Tompkins to Coady, January 26, 1939, Ellen Arsenault Papers.
65. Gallant and MacIntyre to Coady, January 26, 1938, Ellen Arsenault Papers.
66. Ibid.

Chapter 6

1. Quotations from *Masters of Their Own Destiny* by Moses Michael Coady are cited in the text with the abbreviations listed below:
   MOTD: *Masters of Their Own Destiny* (New York: Harper and Row, 1939).
   MOTD, orig.ms.: *Masters of Their Own Destiny*, original manuscript (unpublished).
   I: "Introduction," *Masters of Their Own Destiny*, original manuscript (unpublished).
   TMS: "The Maritime Setting," *Masters of Their Own Destiny*, original manuscript (unpublished).
   FE: "Formal Education," *Masters of Their Own Destiny*, original manuscript (unpublished).
   EAAEP: "The Economic Approach in the Adult Education Program," *Masters of Their Own Destiny* (New York: Harper and Row, 1939).
   CSB: "Co-operation in Our Social Blueprint," *Masters of Their Own Destiny*, original manuscript (unpublished).
   CR: "Co-operation and Religion," *Masters of Their Own Destiny* (New York: Harper and Row, 1939).
   TF: "The Future," *Masters of Their Own Destiny,* original manuscript (unpublished).
2. Donald Dorr, *Option for the Poor* (Mary Knoll, N.Y.: Orbis, 1983), p.20.
3. Coady to Roberts, September 16, 1943, Ellen Arsenault Papers.
4. Dorr, *Option*, p.17.
5. Ibid., p.24.
6. Ibid., p.58.
7. Ibid., p.62.
8. Ibid.
9. "Prophecy: Radical Adult Education and the Politics of Power," in P. Jarvis and N. Walters, eds., *Adult Education and Theological Interpretations* (Malabar: Krieger, 1993), p.274.
10. Exodus 3:7-9.
11. F. Manuel and F. Manuel, *Utopian Thought in the Western World* (Harvard University Press, 1979), p.17.
12. Ida Gallant, "Teacher par excellence," *The Maritime Co-operator*, August 15, 1959.
13. Ibid.
14. Ibid.
15. Ida Delaney, *By their Own Hands: A Fieldworker's Account of the Antigonish Movement.* (Hantsport: Lancelot Press, 1985); Rusty Neale, *Brotherhood Economics: Women and Co-operatives in Nova Scotia.* (Sydney: N.S.: UCCB Press, 1998).
16. Conrad Bonacina, *Crosscurrents*, autumn 1951.

Chapter 7

1. "Report of the Educational Director, Nova Scotia Co-operative Educational Council, September 1943." St. Francis Xavier University Archives. Extension Papers [RG 30-3/7/3444].
2. Ibid.
3. Coady to A.S. MacIntyre, January 29, 1940. St. Francis Xavier University Archives. Extension Papers. Departmental correspondence.
4. A.B. MacDonald to George Keen, Oct. 4, 1939 St. Francis Xavier University Archives. A.B. MacDonald Papers.
5. Landis, "He Taught through Co-ops," *The Maritime Co-operator*, Aug. 15, 1959.
6. Coady to Jean Brown, Feb. 10, 1940. St. Francis Xavier University Archives. Extension Papers. Personal correspondence.
7. Coady to Mary Arnold, Dec. 9, 1941. St. Francis Xavier University Archives. Extension Papers. Personal correspondence.
8. Coady to Minnie Coady, October 14, 1941. St. Francis Xavier University Archives. Extension Papers. Personal correspondence.
9. Coady to Marion Gilroy, January 5, 1942. St. Francis Xavier University Archives. Extension Papers. Personal correspondence.
10. Coady to W.H. Dennis, October 16, 1939. St. Francis Xavier University Archives. Extension Papers. Departmental correspondence.
11. Coady to Nearing, May 11, 1940. St. Francis Xavier University Archives. Extension Papers. Personal correspondence.
12. Saindon to Coady, April 18, 1941 [4171]. St. Francis Xavier University Archives. Extension Papers. Departmental correspondence.
13. Ibid., June 12, 1942 [4173]. St. Francis Xavier University Archives. Extension Papers. Departmentalal correspondence.
14. Nova Scotia Credit Union League (NSCUL), Annual Report, 1938. St. Francis Xavier University Archives. Extension Papers. Credit Unions [RG 30-3/4/920].
15. Ibid.
16. Ibid.
17. Minutes of the 8th Annual Convention of NSCUL, 1941 St. Francis Xavier University Archives. Extension Papers. Credit Unions [RG 30-3/4/144].
18. Alex Laidlaw, "Is it Adult Education?", *Food for Thought*, November 1945.
19. Lesson 2, Borrowing/Your Credit Union. St. Francis Xavier University Archives. Extension Papers. Credit Unions [RG 30-3/4/400].
20. "Director's Meeting" [NSCUL], April 19, 1945. St. Francis Xavier University Archives. Extension Papers. Credit Unions [RG 30-3/4/400].
21. "Report of the Educational Director, Nova Scotia Co-operative Council, September 1943." St. Francis Xavier University Archives. Extension Papers. Departmental reports.
22. Coady to Chiasson, November 29, 1941."St. Francis Xavier University Archives. Extension Papers. Personal correspondence.
23. Coady to Quinan, July 11, 1941."St. Francis Xavier University Archives. Extension Papers. Personal correspondence.
24. Ibid., August 22, 1941. St. Francis Xavier University Archives. Extension Papers. Personal correspondence.
25. Coady to Michaud, March 13, 1939. St. Francis Xavier University Archives. Extension Papers. Departmental correspondence [3/1/4088].
26. Ibid., May 6, 1940. St. Francis Xavier University Archives. Extension Papers. Departmental correspondence [3/1/4105].
27. Coady to Michael Gillis, April 6, 1940. St. Francis Xavier University Archives. Extension Papers. Personal correspondence.
28. Coady to Barry, Dec. 1, 1941. St. Francis Xavier University Archives. Extension Papers. Departmental correspondence.
29. Barry to Coady, Nov. 15, 1941. St. Francis Xavier University Archives. Extension Papers. Departmental correspondence.

30. Ibid., Dec. 11, 1941. St. Francis Xavier University Archives. Extension Papers. Departmental correspondence.

31. Hill to Coady, March 10, 1941. St. Francis Xavier University Archives. Extension Papers. Departmental correspondence.

32. Chiasson to Coady, May 2, 1941 St. Francis Xavier University Archives. Extension Papers. Departmental correspondence.

33. Currie to the Rev. H.P. MacPherson, Dec. 9, 1941. St. Francis Xavier University Archives. Extension Papers. Departmental correspondence [RG 30-2/7/27].

34. MacAdam to D.J. MacDonald, Nov. 27, 1941. St. Francis Xavier University Archives. Extension Papers. Departmental correspondence [20-2/1/22].

35. MacIntyre to Coady, Dec. 15, 1941. St. Francis Xavier University Archives. Extension Papers. Departmental correspondence [20/1/489].

36. Coady to Michaud, Dec. 12, 1941. St. Francis Xavier University Archives. Extension Papers. Departmental correspondence [RG 20-2/1/21].

37. Coady to McGee, April 30, 1943, Ellen Arsenault Papers.

38. Michaud to Coady, Dec. 16, 1941. St. Francis Xavier University Archives. Extension Papers. Departmental correspondence [RG 30-2/7/35].

39. Coady to Michaud, Dec. 18, 1941. St. Francis Xavier University Archives. Extension Papers. Departmental correspondence [RG 30-2/7/37].

40. Michaud to Coady, Dec. 24, 1941. St. Francis Xavier University Archives. Extension Papers. Departmental correspondence [RG 30-2/7/39].

41. Coady to Thatcher, March 17, 1942. St. Francis Xavier University Archives. Extension Papers. Personal correspondence.

42. Michaud to Coady, Jan. 12, 1942. St. Francis Xavier University Archives. Extension Papers. Departmental correspondence [RG 30-3/1/4114].

43. Michaud to Chiasson, Jan. 12, 1942. St. Francis Xavier University Archives. Extension Papers. Departmental correspondence [RG 30-3/1/4117].

44. Chiasson to Michaud, Jan. 23, 1942. St. Francis Xavier University Archives. Extension Papers. Departmental correspondence [RG 30-3/1/4121].

45. Coady to Michaud, Feb. 7, 1942. St. Francis Xavier University Archives. Extension Papers. Departmental correspondence [RG 30-3/1/4124].

46. Michaud to Coady, Feb. 9, 1942. St. Francis Xavier University Archives. Extension Papers. Departmental correspondence [RG 30-3/1/4125].

47. "Notes taken by J.H. MacKichan at Fishery Conference at Ottawa, April 17 and 18, 1944." St. Francis Xavier University Archives. Extension Papers. Fisheries [RG 30 3/1/4017].

48. Coady to Chiasson, April 27, 1944. St. Francis Xavier University Archives. Extension Papers. Departmental correspondence [3/1/3819].

49. Coady to Sr. Mary Hugh, October 24, 1941. St. Francis Xavier University Archives. Extension Papers. Personal correspondence.

50. "On the educational work among the fishermen April 1/43 to March 31, 1944" St. Francis Xavier University Archives. Extension Papers. Fisheries. [RG 30-3/1/2935].

51. "Report on educational program carried on among Maritime Fishermen by Extension Department of St.FX, for year ending March 31, 1945" St. Fr St. Francis Xavier University Archives. Extension Papers. Fisheries. [RG 30-3/1/2967].

52. Chiasson to Coady, August 7, 1944. St. Francis Xavier University Archives. Extension Papers. Departmental correspondence. [RG 30-3/1/2926].

53. Coady to Jean Brown, Feb. 10, 1940. St. Francis Xavier University Archives. Extension Papers. Personal correspondence.

54. "The Present Outlook" St. Francis Xavier University Archives. Extension Papers. Departmental reports.

55. *The Maritime Co-operator*, Sept. 1, 1944.

56. "A Call to Arms!", *The Maritime Co-operator*, Sept. 15, 1940.

57. Ibid.

58. "Youth and the New World," speech, May 21, 1944. St. Francis Xavier University Archives. Extension Papers. Coady's writings.

59. Coady to Brown, April 5, 1940. St. Francis Xavier University Archives. Extension Papers. Personal correspondence.
60. "Mainsprings of Action," *The Maritime Co-operator*, January 15, 1941.
61. "Can Achieve High Destiny in Maritimes," *Halifax Herald*, January 1, 1941.
62. Coady to Leo Coady, January 28, 1941. St. Francis Xavier University Archives. Extension Papers. Personal correspondence.
63. Ibid., August 22, 1945. St. Francis Xavier University Archives. Extension Papers. Personal correspondence.
64. Scrapbooks, 1943.
65. *The Pictou Advocate*, March 15, 1945.
66. Speech, United Farmers' Cooperative Co., Toronto, *Scrapbooks*, December, 1944.
67. Coady to Lester, Feb. 27, 1942. St. Francis Xavier University Archives. Extension Papers. Personal correspondence.
68. Coady to Johnston, Feb. 28, 1942. St. Francis Xavier University Archives. Extension Papers. Personal correspondence.
69. Watson Thomson, *I Accuse* (Winnipeg: Contemporary Publishers, 1943), p.15.
70. John Cornwell, *Hitler's Pope: The Secret History of Pius XII* (London: Viking, 1999).
71. Scrapbooks, speech at commemoration of Rochdale pioneers, Stellarton, N.S., June, 1944.
72. W.H. MacEwen, "Co-ops and the Income Tax," *The Maritime Co-operator*, November 15, 1944.

Chapter 8

1. E. Hobsbawm, *Age of Extremes* (London: Abacus, 1994), p.177.
2. Rev. Ildebrando Antoniutti, apostolic delegate to Canada and Newfoundland, May 3, 1946, speaking in Sydney, N.S. Scrapbooks.
3. *Xaverian Weekly*, Feb. 14, 1948.
4. Annual Report [1946] of Superintendent of Education, N.S.
5. See John Diggins, *The Promise of Pragmatism* (Chicago: The University of Chicago Press, 1991), for a valuable discussion of these themes.
6. Coady to Sr. Josepha, November 25, 1947. St. Francis Xavier University Archives. Extension Papers. Personal correspondence.
7. J. Bickerton, *Nova Scotia, Ottawa, and the Politics of Regional Development* (Toronto: University of Toronto Press, 1990), p.97.
8. Ibid.
9. Ibid., p.101.
10. Ibid., p.104.
11. Ibid., p.111.
12. Ibid., p.122.
13. Ibid.
14. Scrapbooks, 1945.
15. M. Wright, "Fishing in Modern Times: Stewart Bates and the Modernization of the Canadian Atlantic Fishery," in J. Candow et al., *How Deep is the Ocean?: Historical Essays on Canada's Atlantic Fishery* (Sydney, N.S.: UCCB Press, 1997), p.197.
16. Ibid.
17. Ibid., p.203.
18. "Educational program for the fishermen of the Maritime provinces ... during 1946-47 by Extension under grant from the Federal Government of Fisheries, Ottawa." St. Francis Xavier University Archives. Extension Papers. Fisheries [RG 30-2/1/2989].
19. Fishery Report for 1946-47. St. Francis Xavier University Archives. Extension Papers. Fisheries [RG 30-3/1/2947].
20. "Educational Program ... during 1946-47." St. Francis Xavier University Archives. Extension Papers. Fisheries [RG 30-3/1/2989].
21. Bickerton, *Nova Scotia*, p.103.
22. Coady to O'Reilly, February 25, 1949. St. Francis Xavier University Archives. Extension Papers. Departmental correspondence.

23. Bickerton, *Nova Scotia*, p.104.
24. Coady to Morris, June 24, 1946 [RG 30-3/1/4136], marked "confidential." St. Francis Xavier University Archives. Extension Papers. Departmental correspondence.
25. "Fishery Report," 1946-47.
26. Coady to Tompkins, January 17, 1948.
27. Coady to Hill, January 23, 1947. St. Francis Xavier University Archives. Extension Papers. Personal correspondence.
28. Coady to Gillis, January 17, 1948. St. Francis Xavier University Archives. Extension Papers. Personal correspondence.
29. Coady to Laidlaw, January 23, 1947. St. Francis Xavier University Archives. Extension Papers. Departmental correspondence.
30. Coady to MacKinnon, March 14, 1952. National Archives of Canada, [Laidlaw Papers, MG 31 B32, vol. 3, file 1].
31. Coady to Bates, March 3, 1952. St. Francis Xavier University Archives. Extension Papers. Personal correspondence.
32. Coady to Tompkins, January 17, 1948. St. Francis Xavier University Archives. Extension Papers. Personal correspondence.
33. Coady to Michael Gillis, January 17, 1948. St. Francis Xavier University Archives. Extension Papers. Personal correspondence.
34. Coady to Sr. Josepha et al., October 9, 1948. St. Francis Xavier University Archives. Extension Papers. Personal correspondence.
35. Coady to Michael Gillis, November 20, 1950. St. Francis Xavier University Archives. Extension Papers. Personal correspondence.
36. Ibid., Dec. 20, 1950. St. Francis Xavier University Archives. Extension Papers. Personal correspondence.
37. Coady to Fred Scott, Deputy Minister of Fisheries and Co-operatives, St. John, Newfoundland, May 11, 1950. St. Francis Xavier University Archives. Extension Papers. Personal correspondence.
38. Coady to MacSween, January 31, 1951. St. Francis Xavier University Archives. Extension Papers. Personal correspondence.
39. Coady to Mrs. C. Sutherland, November 13, 1951. St. Francis Xavier University Archives. Extension Papers. Personal correspondence.
40. Coady to Mary Arnold, January 23, 1952. St. Francis Xavier University Archives. Extension Papers. Personal correspondence.
41. Coady's secretary (Ellen Arsenault) to Mrs. B.F. Coady, February 18, 1952. St. Francis Xavier University Archives. Extension Papers. Personal correspondence.
42. Coady to Francis Coady, Feb. 21, 1952. St. Francis Xavier University Archives. Extension Papers. Personal correspondence.
43. "Report of Fisheries Work for 1952-3" St. Francis Xavier University Archives. Extension Papers. Fisheries [RG 30-3/1/3019].
44. "Fisheries Fieldworker" St. Francis Xavier University Archives. Extension Papers. Fisheries [RG 30-3/1/2842].
45. "'Summary'—Meeting of committee appointed to present brief on fisheries co-operatives at August meeting of Maritime Planning Committee, May 9, 1957." St. Francis Xavier University Archives. Extension Papers. Fisheries [RG 30-3/1/3165].
46. "People in Business," published by Minnesota Association of Co-operatives, St. Paul, Minnesota, 1946.
47. Coady to Mssrs. Mose Campbell, Leo Coady, James Coady, December 19, 1946. St. Francis Xavier University Archives. Extension Papers. Personal correspondence.
48. Coady to M.J. MacKinnon, March 14, 1952. St. Francis Xavier University Archives. Extension Papers. Personal correspondence.
49. Coady to Mose Campbell and Leo Coady, April 19, 1951. St. Francis Xavier University Archives. Extension Papers. Personal correspondence.
50. Coady to Michael Gillis, Feb. 1, 1951. St. Francis Xavier University Archives. Extension Papers. Personal correspondence.

51. Coady to Sutherland, November 13, 1951. St. Francis Xavier University Archives. Extension Papers. Personal correspondence.
52. Coady to Michael Gillis, January 31, 1951. St. Francis Xavier University Archives. Extension Papers. Personal correspondence.
53. Lewis Mumford, *The Story of Utopias* (New York: Viking, 1922; 1962), p.8.
54. The Commission on Global Governance, *Our Global Neighbourhood* (Oxford: Oxford University Press, 1995), p.18.
55. May 1947, Scrapbooks.
56. MacIntyre's report to the N.S. Co-op Union, July 4-5, 1947, Scrapbooks.
57. Speech, *The Xaverian*, February 21, 1949.
58. Speech, Ontario Credit Union League, May 1, 1948, Scrapbooks.
59. Speech, *The Toronto Daily Star*, February 11, 1949.
60. "Foster Adult Education Maritimes visitor urges," *The Globe*, February 12, 1949.
61. *Washington Post-Record*, February 26, 1949.
62. *The Ottawa Citizen*, March 2, 1949.
63. Coady to Bates, March 3, 1952. St. Francis Xavier University Archives. Extension Papers. Personal correspondence.
64. Clipping, "Urges World to apply Nova Scotia plan to undeveloped areas," Scrapbooks.
65. Coady to Mrs. J. Coady, March 10, 1949. St. Francis Xavier University Archives. Extension Papers. Personal correspondence.
66. Speech, St. Francis Xavier alumni banquet, April 1949, Scrapbooks.
67. Address, June 28, 1949, Scrapbooks.
68. Coady to Fathers Gillis et al., October 5, 1950. St. Francis Xavier University Archives. Extension Papers. Personal correspondence.
69. Ibid.

Chapter 9

1. Hardbound book with congratulations on retirement. St. Francis Xavier University Archives. Extension Papers [RG 30-2/1/4771].
2. Coady to Teresa, March 7, 1952. St. Francis Xavier University Archives. Extension Papers. Personal correspondence.
3. Coady to Mrs. Mary Coady, March 7, 1952. St. Francis Xavier University Archives. Extension Papers. Personal correspondence.
4. May 22, 1952. St. Francis Xavier University Archives. Extension Papers. Departmental correspondence [MG 20/1 /1785].
5. March 16, 1948. St. Francis Xavier University Archives. Extension Papers. Departmental correspondence [MG 20-1/2011].
6. Jan. 13, 1949. St. Francis Xavier University Archives. Extension Papers. Departmental correspondence [MG 20-1/2017].
7. Coady to Frances Dolores, July 7, 1952. St. Francis Xavier University Archives. Extension Papers. Personal correspondence.
8. Coady to E.R. Bowen, September 8, 1952. St. Francis Xavier University Archives. Extension Papers. Personal correspondence.
9. Ibid.
10. Coady to Minnie Coady, December 5, 1952. St. Francis Xavier University Archives. Extension Papers. Personal correspondence.
11. "The role of leadership in social problems." St. Francis Xavier University Archives. Extension Papers. Coady's writings.
12. Coady to Joseph Coady, March 1, 1952. St. Francis Xavier University Archives. Extension Papers. Personal correspondence.
14. Coady to Helen and Evelyn [?], November 18, 1953. St. Francis Xavier University Archives. Extension Papers. Personal correspondence.
15. Coady to Carmel Coady, September 17, 1954. St. Francis Xavier University Archives. Extension Papers. Personal correspondence.

16. Coady to Teresa Coady, November 19, 1954. St. Francis Xavier University Archives. Extension Papers. Personal correspondence.
17. Coady to Leo Coady, January 13, 1955. St. Francis Xavier University Archives. Extension Papers. Personal correspondence.
18. Coady to Helen MacDonald, November 25, 1955. St. Francis Xavier University Archives. Extension Papers. Personal correspondence.
19. Coady to Ursula Tompkins, December 9, 1955. St. Francis Xavier University Archives. Extension Papers. Personal correspondence
20. Coady to Teresa Coady, December 28, 1955. St. Francis Xavier University Archives. Extension Papers. Personal correspondence.
21. Coady to Mrs. John MacKinnon, March 6, 1956. St. Francis Xavier University Archives. Extension Papers. Personal correspondence.
22. Coady to Joe Morris, April 11, 1956. St. Francis Xavier University Archives. Extension Papers. Personal correspondence.
23. Ibid.
24. Coady to Nicholas James Tompkins, August 28, 1956. St. Francis Xavier University Archives. Extension Papers. Personal correspondence.
25. Coady to Dr. A.J.A. Campbell, April 8, 1957. St. Francis Xavier University Archives. Extension Papers. Personal correspondence.
26. Coady to Sara MacEachern, June 2, 1958. St. Francis Xavier University Archives. Extension Papers. Personal correspondence.
27. Coady to Sister Edna Marie, June 3, 1958. St. Francis Xavier University Archives. Extension Papers. Personal correspondence.
28. Coady to Carmel Coady, November 15, 1958. St. Francis Xavier University Archives. Extension Papers. Personal correspondence.
29. Coady to Teresa Coady, April 2, 1959. St. Francis Xavier University Archives. Extension Papers. Personal correspondence.
30. Coady to Leo Coady, October 18, 1955. St. Francis Xavier University Archives. Extension Papers. Personal correspondence.
31. Ibid., September 14, 1956.
32. Coady to Mrs. Leo Coady, November 7, 1955. St. Francis Xavier University Archives. Extension Papers. Personal correspondence.
33. Coady to Leo Coady, January 13, 1955. St. Francis Xavier University Archives. Extension Papers. Personal correspondence.
34. Coady to Teresa Coady, June 3, 1957. St. Francis Xavier University Archives. Extension Papers. Personal correspondence.
35. Ibid., June 19, 1957. St. Francis Xavier University Archives. Extension Papers. Personal correspondence.
36. Coady to Leo Coady, October 17, 1957. St. Francis Xavier University Archives. Extension Papers. Personal correspondence.
37. Ibid., January 15, 1958. St. Francis Xavier University Archives. Extension Papers. Personal correspondence.
38. Coady to the Rev. D.F. Roberts, April 3, 1959. St. Francis Xavier University Archives. Extension Papers. Personal correspondence.
39. Coady to Teresa and Carmel, April 25, 1959. St. Francis Xavier University Archives. Extension Papers. Personal correspondence.
40. Coady to Francis Coady, April 25, 1959. St. Francis Xavier University Archives. Extension Papers. Personal correspondence.
41. Coady to the Rev. D.F. Roberts, May 2, 1959. St. Francis Xavier University Archives. Extension Papers. Personal correspondence.
42. Coady to Katie and Mary Coady, May 4, 1959. St. Francis Xavier University Archives. Extension Papers. Personal correspondence.
43. D.F. Roberts to Coady, May 6, 1959. St. Francis Xavier University Archives. Extension Papers. Personal correspondence.
44. Coady to Carmel, May 27, 1959. St. Francis Xavier University Archives. Extension Papers. Personal correspondence.

45. Coady to Teresa, May 9, 1959. St. Francis Xavier University Archives. Extension Papers. Personal correspondence.
46. Coady to Ida Gallant, June 23, 1959. St. Francis Xavier University Archives. Extension Papers. Personal correspondence.
47. "The Trend towards big farms," *The Maritime Co-operator*, March 1, 1956.
48. Luke 4.
49. "Message to the Young Christian Workers of Australia," January 7, 1958. St. Francis Xavier University Archives. Extension Papers. Coady's writings.
50. "The Dynamics of Progress," October 17, 1956. St. Francis Xavier University Archives. Extension Papers. Coady's writings.
51. "The Role of the Extension Department and in regard to the UMF, the credit unions and ECS," September 30, 1958. St. Francis Xavier University Archives. Extension Papers. Coady's writings.
52. A.A. MacDonald, "The Antigonish Movement after the 1950s: Restructuring and the response to new constituencies," in *University and Community, The Antigonish Movement: Beyond 2001* (St. Francis Xavier University, 1995).
53. Coady to the Rev. F.J. Smyth, July 13, 1956. St. Francis Xavier University Archives. Extension Papers. Personal correspondence.
54. "Speaking of Co-ops," *The Maritime Co-operator*, October 1976.
55. *The Maritime Co-operator*, November 1976.
56. *Cape Breton Post*, August 1, 1959; *The Casket*, August 6, 1959.
57. *The Casket*, July 30, 1959.
58. "A Giant Passes," *The Casket*, July 30, 1959.
59. *Union Farmer*, August 1959.
60. *The Casket*, July 30, 1959.
61. *Journal-Pioneer*, Summerside, P.E.I., August 3, 1959.
62. *Windsor Star*, July 30, 1959.
63. *The Maritime Co-operator*, August 15, 1959.
64. Ida Gallant, "Teacher par excellence," *The Maritime Co-operator*, August 15, 1959.

Chapter 10

1. Julian Gwyn, *Excessive Expectations: Maritime Commerce and the Economic Development of Nova Scotia, 1740-1870* (Montreal: McGill-Queens, 1998), p.233.
2. Zygmunt Bauman, *In Search of Politics* (Stanford: Stanford University Press, 1999), p.164.
3. Gwyn, *Excessive Expectations*, p.226.
4. Ibid., p.233.
5. A. Margalit, *The Decent Society* (Cambridge: Harvard University Press, 1996), p.155.
6. Brian Fay, *Critical Social Science* (Cornell, N.Y.: Cornell University Press, 1987), p.92.

Index

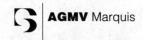

MEMBER OF THE SCABRINI GROUP
Quebec, Canada
2000